1–2 SAMUEL

In this commentary to 1–2 Samuel, Marvin A. Sweeney focuses on the qualities of leadership displayed by the major characters of the book. He reads 1–2 Samuel in relation to Machiavelli's *The Prince* and Sun Tzu's *The Art of War*, which provide a comparative evaluation of the qualities of leadership displayed by Eli, Samuel, Saul, David, Ish-Bosheth, Abner, Abshalom, Joab, and others. Additionally, Sweeney provides an analysis of the synchronic, literary structure of Samuel, as well as a new theory regarding its composition. He also re-evaluates the role of 2 Samuel 21–24 within the synchronic literary structure of the book, arguing that the so-called Succession Narrative in 2 Samuel 9–20 is a northern Israelite composition that stands as a component of the Jehu Dynastic History. Highlighting the geography and cities of the land of Israel, Sweeney's commentary enables readers to understand the role that the land of Israel plays in the narrative of the book of Samuel.

Marvin A. Sweeney is Professor of Hebrew Bible at the Claremont School of Theology, California. He is the author of some seventeen volumes in the fields of Hebrew Bible and Jewish Studies, such as *Jewish Mysticism* (2020); *The Pentateuch* (2017); *Reading the Hebrew Bible after the Shoah* (2008); *King Josiah of Judah* (2001); and commentaries on Kings (OTL, 2007); Isaiah 1–39 (FOTL, 1996); Isaiah 40–66 (FOTL, 2016); Jeremiah (Illuminations, 2 vols., in press); Ezekiel (ROT, 2013); the Twelve Prophets (BO, 2 vols., 2000); and Zephaniah (Hermeneia, 2003).

T0371258

NEW CAMBRIDGE BIBLE COMMENTARY

GENERAL EDITOR: Ben Witherington III

HEBREW BIBLE/OLD TESTAMENT EDITOR: Bill T. Arnold

The New Cambridge Bible Commentary (NCBC) aims to elucidate the Hebrew and Christian Scriptures for a wide range of intellectually curious individuals. While building on the work and reputation of the Cambridge Bible Commentary popular in the 1960s and 1970s, the NCBC takes advantage of many of the rewards provided by scholarly research over the last four decades. Volumes utilize recent gains in rhetorical criticism, social scientific study of the Scriptures, narrative criticism, and other developing disciplines to exploit the growing advances in biblical studies. Accessible jargon-free commentary, an annotated "Suggested Readings" list, and the entire *New Revised Standard Version, Updated Edition* (NRSVue) text under discussion are the hallmarks of all volumes in the series.

PUBLISHED VOLUMES IN THE SERIES

The Pastoral Epistles, Scot McKnight
The Book of Lamentations, Joshua Berman
Hosea, Joel, and Amos, Graham Hamborg
1 Peter, Ruth Anne Reese
Ephesians, David A. deSilva
Philippians, Michael F. Bird and Nijay K. Gupta
Acts, Craig S. Keener
The Gospel of Luke, Amy-Jill Levine and Ben Witherington III
Galatians, Craig S. Keener
Mark, Darrell Bock
Psalms, Walter Brueggemann and William H. Bellinger, Jr
Matthew, Craig A. Evans
Genesis, Bill T. Arnold
The Gospel of John, Jerome H. Neyrey
Exodus, Carol Meyers
1–2 Corinthians, Craig S. Keener
James and Jude, William F. Brosend II
Judges and Ruth, Victor H. Matthews
Revelation, Ben Witherington III

1–2 Samuel

Marvin A. Sweeney
Claremont School of Theology, California

CAMBRIDGE
UNIVERSITY PRESS

Shaftesbury Road, Cambridge CB2 8EA, United Kingdom

One Liberty Plaza, 20th Floor, New York, NY 10006, USA

477 Williamstown Road, Port Melbourne, VIC 3207, Australia

314–321, 3rd Floor, Plot 3, Splendor Forum, Jasola District Centre, New Delhi – 110025, India

103 Penang Road, #05–06/07, Visioncrest Commercial, Singapore 238467

Cambridge University Press is part of Cambridge University Press & Assessment, a department of the University of Cambridge.

We share the University's mission to contribute to society through the pursuit of education, learning and research at the highest international levels of excellence.

www.cambridge.org
Information on this title: www.cambridge.org/9781108472616

DOI: 10.1017/9781108560795

First published 2023

A catalogue record for this publication is available from the British Library.

Library of Congress Cataloging-in-Publication Data
NAMES: Sweeney, Marvin A. (Marvin Alan), 1953– author.
TITLE: 1–2 Samuel / Marvin A. Sweeney.
DESCRIPTION: Cambridge ; New York, NY : Cambridge University Press, 2023. | Series: New Cambridge Bible commentary | Includes bibliographical references and index.
IDENTIFIERS: LCCN 2023014151 (print) | LCCN 2023014152 (ebook) | ISBN 9781108472616 (hardback) | ISBN 9781108460040 (paperback) | ISBN 9781108560795 (epub)
SUBJECTS: LCSH: Bible. Samuel–Commentaries. | Leadership in the Bible. | Kings and rulers–Biblical teaching.
CLASSIFICATION: LCC BS1325.3 .S94 2023 (print) | LCC BS1325.3 (ebook) | DDC 222/.407–dc23/eng/20230425
LC record available at https://lccn.loc.gov/2023014151
LC ebook record available at https://lccn.loc.gov/2023014152

ISBN 978-1-108-47261-6 Hardback
ISBN 978-1-108-46004-0 Paperback

For
Soo
Song of Songs 2:1

Contents

Supplementary Sections

Preface

My interest in 1–2 Samuel goes back to my undergraduate years at the University of Illinois, Urbana-Champaign, 1971–1975, where I was a double major in Political Science, with concentrations in US Constitutional Law and International Relations, and Religious Studies, with concentrations in Hebrew Bible, Judaism and Jewish Thought, and Asian Religions. I am especially indebted to my undergraduate advisor in Religious Studies, Professor David L. Petersen, who did much to introduce me to the field of Hebrew Bible studies and who supervised my 1974 undergraduate thesis on the origins of Davidic Kingship, which enabled me to develop my interests in political science and Hebrew Bible studies. His ongoing friendship and mentorship have been special blessings throughout my career.

I would also like to acknowledge two other mentors who enabled me to develop my interests in Judean kingship and 1–2 Samuel. Professor Thomas W. Mann, my de facto advisor as a special, non-degree student at the Princeton Theological Seminary, taught a course on Religion and Politics in Ancient Israel in the Spring 1976 semester that greatly stimulated my interest in this area. Professor Antony F. Campbell SJ, z'l, taught a course on 1–2 Samuel while on leave at the Claremont School of Theology in the Spring 1977 semester that played a key role in deepening my knowledge of 1–2 Samuel and the Deuteronomistic History in the context of my Ph.D. studies. His ongoing friendship was another special blessing throughout the rest of his life during my tenure as a Professor at Claremont School of Theology. His memory is a blessing.

I am also grateful to Professor Bill T. Arnold, Hebrew Bible Editor for the New Cambridge Bible Commentary series, and Beatrice Rehl, Publisher, Religious Studies at Cambridge University Press, for their invitation to contribute the volume on Samuel to the series and their guidance in its production. I am honored to follow Professor Peter R. Ackroyd, z"l, author of the earlier Cambridge Bible Commentary on 1 and 2 Samuel, from whose work in Samuel, Isaiah, and other areas I have learned immensely throughout my career. I am indebted to copyeditor Robert Holden, who saved me from many mistakes. Any remaining are my own responsibility. I am grateful to my Research Associate, Mr. Hyunghee Kim, Ph.D. Student in Hebrew Bible at the Claremont School of Theology, for preparing the indices for this volume.

Although I am especially indebted to my mentors named here and to many others, I am also especially indebted to my lovely wife, Dr. Soo J. Kim Sweeney. She, too, is a Hebrew Bible scholar, and it is her love, support, and expertise that has seen me through major transitions in life, the writing of this commentary, and so much more. I therefore dedicate this volume to her with love.

A Word about the Names of G-d

In keeping with the practice of some circles in Judaism, this commentary uses YHWH, L-rd, and G-d as designations for G-d. Such practice is intended to acknowledge the holiness of the Divine.

The text of the NRSVue retains the full spelling of these terms in keeping with contractual requirements for use of the NRSVue.

Abbreviations

AB	Anchor Bible
ABD	*Anchor Bible Dictionary*, 6 vols. D. N. Freedman et al. (eds.). GardenCity: Doubleday, 1992
AIL	Ancient Israel and Its Literature
AnBib	Analecta biblica
ANEM	Ancient Near Eastern Monographs
ANEP	*The Ancient Near East in Pictures Relating to the Old Testament.* J. B. Pritchard (ed.). Princeton, 1969
ANET	*The Ancient Near Eastern Texts.* J. B. Pritchard (ed.). Princeton: Princeton University Press, 1969
BDB	F. Brown, S. R. Driver, and C. A. Briggs, *A Hebrew and English Lexicon of the Old Testament.* Oxford: Clarendon, 1907, 1974
BETL	Bibliotheca Ephemeridum Theologicarum Lovaniensium
BKAT	Biblischer Kommentar Altes Testament
BO	Berit Olam
BWANT	Beiträge zur Wissenschaft vom Alten und Neuen Testament
BZAW	Beihefte zur Zeitschrift für die Alttestamentliche Wissenschaft
CAT	Commentarire de l'Ancien Testament
CBC	Cambridge Bible Commentary
CBQ	*The Catholic Biblical Quarterly*
CBQMS	Catholic Biblical Quarterly Monograph Series
CH	Codex Hammurabi
ConBibOT	Coniectanea biblica: Old Testament Series
DDD²	*Dictionary of Deities and Demons in the Bible*, 2nd ed. K. van der Toorn et al. (eds.). Leiden: Brill, 1999
DJD	Discoveries in the Judean Desert

DtrH	Deuteronomistic History
EBR	*Encyclopedia of the Bible and Its Reception,* 20 vols. to date. H.-J. Klauck et al. (eds.). Berlin and New York: Walter De Gruyter, 2009–present
FAT	Forschungen zum Alten Testament
FOTL	Forms of the Old Testament Literature
FRLANT	Forschungen zur Religionen und Literatur des Alten und Neuen Testaments
HALOT	*Hebrew and Aramaic Lexicon of the Old Testament,* 5 vols. L. Koehler and W. Baumgartner (eds.). Leiden: Brill, 1994–1999
HCKAT	Handkommentar zum Alten Testament
HSM	Harvard Semitic Monographs
HUCA	*Hebrew Union College Annual*
IBT	Interpreting Biblical Texts
ICC	International Critical Commentary
JAOS	*Journal of the American Oriental Society*
JBL	*Journal of Biblical Literature*
JCS	*Journal of Cuneiform Studies*
JSOTSup	Journal for the Study of the Old Testament Supplement Series
KAT	Kommentar zum Alten Testament
LHBOTS	Library of Hebrew Bible and Old Testament Studies
LXX	Septuagint
MT	Masoretic text
NEAEHL	*New Encyclopaedia of Archaeological Excavations in the Holy Land,* 5 vols. E. Stern et al. (eds.). Jerusalem: Israel Exploration Society; Carta, 1993, 2008
NICOT	New International Commentary on the Old Testament
NJPS	New Jewish Publication Society version
NRSVue	New Revised Standard Version Updated Edition
OBO	Orbis Biblicus et Orientalis
OT Guides	Old Testament Guides
OTL	Old Testament Library
ResBibS	Resources for Biblical Study
ROT	Reading the Old Testament commentary series, Smyth and Helwys Press
SBL	Society of Biblical Literature

SBLDS	Society of Biblical Literature Dissertation Series
SBLMS	Society of Biblical Literature Monograph Series
SBT	Studies in Biblical Theology
SOTSMS	Society for Old Testament Study Monograph Series
TDOT	*Theological Dictionary of the Old Testament*, 17 vols. G. J. Botterweck et al. (eds.). Grand Rapids, MI: Eerdmans, 1974–2021
VT	Vetus Testamentum
WBC	Word Biblical Commentary
WMANT	Wissenschaftliche Monographien zum Alten und Neuen Testament
ZAW	*Zeitschrift für die alttestamentliche Wissenschaft*
ZBK/AT	Zürcher Bibelkommentar Altes Testament

1 Introduction

CANONICAL ROLE

The Book of Samuel is the third book in the Former Prophets (Hebrew *Nĕbî'îm Ri'šōnîm*) of the Tanak, the Jewish form of the Bible, following Joshua and Judges and preceding Kings. According to the Babylonian Talmud, Baba Batra 14b–15a, it is written by the prophet Samuel. The Former Prophets recount the history of Israel from the time of Joshua and the conquest of the land of Canaan in the Book of Joshua; the period of the Judges in the Book of Judges; the formation of the Israelite monarchy in Samuel; and the period of the Kings of Israel and Judah from the time of David through the Babylonian Exile in Kings, when King Jehoiachin of Judah was released from confinement by King Evil Merodach (Amel Marduk), the son of Nebuchadnezzar, of Babylon. The aim of the Former Prophets is to explain how YHWH granted the land of Canaan to Israel, but Israel was ultimately exiled from the land due to its alleged failure to observe the commandments of YHWH.[1] The Latter Prophets likewise envision a return to the land of Israel and the restoration of the Jerusalem Temple.

First–Second Samuel are the fourth and fifth books of the Historical Books of the Christian Old Testament, following Joshua, Judges, and Ruth,

---

[1] For discussion of the Former Prophets, often identified diachronically as the Deuteronomistic History in contemporary scholarship, see Marvin A. Sweeney, *King Josiah of Judah: The Lost Messiah of Israel* (Oxford and New York: Oxford University Press, 2001), esp. 3–177; see also Richard D. Nelson, *The Historical Books* (IBT; Nashville: Abingdon, 1998); Antony F. Campbell, SJ, *The Historical Books: An Introduction* (Louisville and London: Westminster John Knox, 2004); Antony F. Campbell and Mark A. O'Brien, *Unfolding the Deuteronomistic History: Origins, Upgrades, Present Text* (Minneapolis, MN: Fortress, 2000); and Thomas Römer, *The So-Called Deuteronomistic History: A Sociological, Historical, and Literary Introduction* (London and New York: T and T Clark, 2007).

and preceding 1–2 Chronicles, Ezra, Nehemiah, Tobit (in Roman Catholic Bibles), Judith (in Roman Catholic Bibles), and Esther. First–Second Samuel again recounts the origins of the Israelite monarchy following the periods of the conquest of Canaan (Joshua) and the period of the Judges (Judges and Ruth), and prior to the subsequent history of Israel and Judah as recounted in 1–2 Chronicles, Ezra, Nehemiah, Tobit, Judith, and Esther through the Persian period. Roman Catholic and Eastern Orthodox Bibles read 1–2 Maccabees as part of the Historical Books, extending the history into the Hellenistic period immediately preceding the time of Jesus, but 1–2 Maccabees are generally read as prophetic books following the Additions to Daniel in the Protestant Apocrypha because they anticipate further prophets from G-d. Insofar as the Prophets are read as the fourth and concluding segment of the Old Testament, the Christian Bible is organized to emphasize that the New Testament completes and fulfills the Old Testament in Jesus Christ. Consequently, the formation of the monarchy in 1–2 Samuel and 1–2 Chronicles points to the origins of the House of David, of which Jesus is considered to be a descendant.

TEXTUAL VERSIONS

Samuel appears in a variety of textual versions, including the Masoretic Hebrew Text, the various forms of the Septuagint Greek texts, the Syriac Peshiṭta, the Latin Vulgate, the Aramaic Targum Jonathan, the Coptic versions, the Ethiopian (Ge'ez) Bible, and many others. The Scrolls from the Judean Wilderness, also known as the Dead Sea Scrolls, include three major textual witnesses, namely, 4QSamuel[a], 4QSamuel[b], and 4QSamuel[c], and the text quoted by Josephus appears to have major affinities with the Old Latin version that preceded the Vulgate.[2]

Only the Hebrew Masoretic Text functions as sacred scripture in Judaism, and the Targums function as important witnesses to the interpretation of the Bible together with the rest of the Rabbinic literature. Some versions, such as the Septuagint, the Dead Sea Scrolls, and possibly the Peshiṭta, were originally written by Jews, but they are not considered as authoritative in Judaism.

All of the above-mentioned versions of the Bible in Christianity are considered as witnesses to sacred scripture, which resides with G-d.

---

[2]   Eugene Charles Ulrich, Jr., *The Qumran Text of Samuel and Josephus* (HSM 19; Missoula, MT: Scholars Press, 1978).

Consequently, interpreters frequently emend the biblical text, based on the versions, in an effort to reconstruct the presumed original text of the Bible. Such emendations inform Christian translations of the Bible, such as the New Revised Standard Version, which appears in the New Cambridge Bible Commentary.

The discovery of the Dead Sea Scrolls and the various textual versions, particularly the Greek Septuagint, indicate that there is a lengthy history of development of the biblical text. The earliest known manuscripts of the Masoretic Text appear in the Cairo Codex of the Prophets (896 CE or later), the Aleppo Codex of the Bible (920 CE), and the St. Petersburg or Leningrad Codex of the Bible (1008 or 1009 CE). No earlier manuscripts are available, apparently because worn-out manuscripts are buried in Judaism. Controversy between Rabbinic Jews and Karaite Jews, on the one hand, and polemics against Judaism by Muslim and Christian scholars, on the other hand, concerning the true reading of the Jewish Bible during the seventh and eighth centuries CE required the production of authoritative Masoretic manuscripts.

The Greek Septuagint version of the Bible originated in the third century BCE when Pharaoh Ptolemy II Philadelphus of Egypt (309–246 BCE) allegedly invited some seventy Jewish scholars to Alexandria to produce a Greek translation of the Torah for inclusion in the famed library at Alexandria. Although the account of this translation in the Letter of Aristeas may be legendary, the number of seventy Jewish or Rabbinic scholars remains in the term Septuagint, which identifies the Greek form of the Bible. The oldest extant manuscripts, Codex Vaticanus and Codex Sinaiticus, are Christian manuscripts that date to the fourth century CE.

The Septuagint version of 1–2 Samuel, known in the Septuagint as 1–2 Reigns or Kingdoms, is complicated.[3] The Greek form of 1–2 Reigns differs

---

[3] For discussion, see Emanuel Tov, *The Text-Critical Use of the Septuagint in Biblical Research* Jerusalem: Simor, 1997); Julio Trebolla Barrera, *The Jewish Bible and the Christian Bible: An Introduction to the History of the Bible* (Leiden: Brill/Grand Rapids, MI: Eerdmans, 1998); Natalio Fernández Marcos, *The Septuagint in Context: Introduction to the Greek Version of the Bible* (Atlanta: Society of Biblical Literature, 2000). For a critical edition of the Greek text of 1–2 Reigns (1–2 Samuel), see Alan E. Brooke, Norman McLean, and Henry St. John Thackeray, *The Old Testament in Greek, vol. II: The Later Historical Books. Part I: 1 and 2 Samuel* (London: Cambridge University Press, 1927); Natalio Fernández Marcos and José Ramon Busto Saiz, *El Texto Antioqueno de la Biblia Griega. I: 1–2 Samuel* (Madrid: Instituto de Filologia, C.S.I.C., 1989). For an up-to-date English translation of the Greek text, see Bernard Taylor "1 Reigns" and Bernard Taylor and Paul D. McLean, "2 Reigns," *A New English*

markedly from the Hebrew Masoretic form of Samuel, particularly in
1 Samuel 16–18, where the Greek text is much shorter, prompting scholars
to argue that the Hebrew *Vorlage* of the Greek text must be an earlier
version of these chapters than the Masoretic form. The Septuagint text fills
in gaps that appear in the often difficult Hebrew text, which has suggested
to some that scribal error might have affected the current text of Samuel or
that the older and potentially northern dialect of the Hebrew in some parts
of Samuel may have necessitated interpretative Greek renditions of the text
to present an esthetically coherent text for an educated Greek reader.

A major problem in the Greek text of Samuel is the presence of two
distinctive Greek versions of the text. The Greek of 1 Samuel 1–2 Samuel 9
(or 10) represents the so-called Old Greek, which many Septuagint
scholars judge to be an earlier Greek form of the text that in many cases
varies from the presumed proto-Masoretic text. The Old Greek is generally
coherent and well styled, which suggests that there are actually two issues
in this text. One is the question of the Hebrew *Vorlage*, which varies from
the Masoretic text, and the other is the translation technique employed by
the Greek translator to produce a coherent and esthetically pleasing Greek
text.[4] The other textual version is the so-called Kaige recension, derived
from the Greek wording *kai gē*, "and also," employed to render the Hebrew
waw-consecutive narrative tense characteristic of Samuel and most biblical
Hebrew narrative. Overall, the Kaige recension is very literal and stylistic-
ally deficient because it represents an effort by the translators to produce a
literal Greek reading of the underlying Hebrew text that contrasts markedly with the style of the Old Greek. The Kaige text begins in 2 Samuel 10
or 11 and continues all the way through the rest of Samuel and 1 Kings (3
Reigns) 1–2. In 1–2 Kings, the Old Greek resumes in 1 Kings (3 Reigns)
3–2 Kings (4 Reigns) 21, and the Kaige resumes once again in 2 Kings (4
Reigns) 22–24. Although the Kaige is supposedly intended to correct the
reading of the Old Greek in favor of the underlying Hebrew, the placement
of the Old Greek prior to the Kaige in 1–4 Reigns (Samuel and Kings)
suggests that the so-called Old Greek is an attempt to replace the Kaige
with a more coherent and esthetically pleasing form of Greek.

    Translation of the Septuagint, ed. Albert Pietersma and Benjamin G. Wright; New York
    and Oxford: Oxford University Press, 2007), 244–270, 271–296.
4   Anneli Aejmelaeus, "The Septuagint of 1 Samuel," *On the Trail of the Septuagint
    Translators: Collected Essays* (BET 50; Leuven: Peeters, 2007), 123–141.

The three major manuscripts of Samuel among the Dead Sea Scrolls show some correlation with the Septuagint manuscripts, although there is also considerable correlation with the presumed proto-Masoretic text. The first is 4QSamuel[a], a fragmentary manuscript that dates to 50–25 BCE and contains elements of 1 Samuel 1:9 through 24:16–22.[5] The Hebrew text agrees closely with the presumed *Vorlage* of the Old Greek in 1 Samuel 1–2 Samuel 9, but the text in 2 Samuel 10–24 displays far less agreement with the Kaige recension in 2 Reigns 10–24. Instead, this section shows closer correspondence to the Old Latin text and readings from Josephus, which prompted Tov to argue that it represents a combination of proto-Lucianic and late-Lucianic elements. The second is 4QSamuel[b], another fragmentary manuscript that preserves readings from 1 Samuel 12:3–23:23 and dates to approximately 225 BCE.[6] The manuscript displays extensive agreement with the Old Greek, but also substantive agreement with the proto-Masoretic text. The third is 4QSamuel[c], a very fragmentary manuscript that preserves 1 Samuel 25:30–32; 2 Samuel 14:7–21, 22–15:4; and 15:4–15.[7] The manuscript dates to the first quarter of the first century BCE. It shows greater conformity with the proto-Masoretic text, but there is substantive influence from the Old Greek. Overall, the three major Qumran scrolls of Samuel indicate eclectic texts that show influence from the Old Greek, the proto-Masoretic text, and the Lucianic Greek text that apparently stands behind the Old Latin and the citations of Josephus.

The Syriac Peshiṭta text may have originated as a Jewish Targum that was employed in early Christianity. It shows close adherence to the proto-Masoretic text, although there is some influence from the Septuagint tradition.[8] The Latin Vulgate was written in the fourth century CE by Jerome in consultation with Rabbinic authorities to bring the Bible closer to the presumed proto-Masoretic text of the day over against the variations found in the Greek translations.[9] The Aramaic Targum Jonathan to the

---

[5] For discussion, see Frank Moore Cross, Jr. et al., *Qumran Cave IV. XII. 1–2 Samuel* (DJD17; Oxford: Clarendon, 2005), 1–216, esp. 1–28.

[6] See Cross et al., *1–2 Samuel*, 219–246, esp. 219–224.

[7] Cross et al., *1–2 Samuel*, 247–267, esp. 247–254.

[8] For discussion, see M. P. Weitzman, *The Syriac Version of the Old Testament: An Introduction* (Cambridge: Cambridge University Press, 1999). For critical editions of the Syriac text, see P. A. H. De Boer, "Samuel," *The Old Testament in Syriac. Part II/2: Judges–Samuel* (Leiden: Brill, 1978); George A. Kiraz and Donald M. Walter et al., *The Syriac Peshiṭta with English Translation. Samuel* (Piscataway, NJ: Gorgias, 2015).

[9] See Benjamin Kedar, "The Latin Translations," *Mikra: Text, Translation, Reading and Interpretation of the Hebrew Bible in Ancient Judaism and Early Christianity*, ed.

Former Prophets is attributed to Jonathan ben Uzziel, the first century CE
Tanna and disciple of R. Hillel, but interpreters maintain that the authors
are unknown and that the period of composition extends from the second
through the seventh centuries CE.[10] Targum Jonathan adheres closely to
the proto-Masoretic text and offers a highly interpretative, midrashic
reading of the text.

This commentary is based on the Hebrew Masoretic Text of 1–2 Samuel,
with appropriate attention to variant readings in the text.

SYNCHRONIC LITERARY FORM

The synchronic literary form of literature refers to its literary structure,
plot development, and characterization without regard to diachronic or
historical considerations of authorship, historical setting, or compositional
history.[11] Consideration of the synchronic literary form of a biblical book
entails reading it strictly as literature.

Despite its narrative complexity, the Book of Samuel displays a very
simple synchronic literary structure: it recounts the successive reigns of the
ruling houses of Israel that emerged in the aftermath of the increasingly
chaotic rule of the Judges. The account begins in 1 Samuel 1–7 with the
rule of the priestly House of Eli, with which the priest and prophet Samuel
is affiliated, and it proceeds to recount the displacement of the
priestly house.

First Samuel 8–31 recounts the reign of the first King of Israel, King Saul
son of Kish, who failed in securing Israel from its enemies. The account
begins in 1 Samuel 8–15, which depict Saul's reign as an absolute failure
due to his inability to lead the nation and to observe YHWH's expectations. It continues in 1 Samuel 16–31 with the rise of David son of Jesse,

M. J. Mulder; Assen/Maastrict: Van Gorcum/Philadelphia: Fortress, 1988), 299–338,
esp. 313–334; for a critical edition of the Latin text, see Robertus Weber, *Biblia Sacra
iuxta Vulgatum Versionem* (Stuttgart: Deutsche Bibelgesellschaft, 1983).
[10] Daniel J. Harrington and Anthony J. Saldarini, *Targum Jonathan of the Former Prophets*
(Aramaic Bible 10; Collegeville, MN: Liturgical, 1987), 1–15, 101–208. For a critical
Aramaic edition of the text, see Alexander Sperber, *The Bible in Aramaic. II: The Former
Prophets According to Targum Jonathan* (Leiden: Brill, 1959), 94–211.
[11] For discussion of the critical methodology employed in this commentary, see Marvin A.
Sweeney, "Form Criticism," *To Each Its Own Meaning: An Introduction to Biblical
Criticisms and Their Application*, ed. S. L. McKenzie and S. R. Haynes (Louisville, KY:
Westminster John Knox, 1999), 58–89.

depicted as an ideal leader for Israel who enjoyed the favor of YHWH and thereby united the country against the Philistines. Saul ultimately committed suicide in a failed battle against the Philistines that resulted in Israel's subjugation to Philistia.

Second Samuel 1–24 recounts the reign of David son of Jesse. The narrative begins with 2 Samuel 1–9, which narrates David's rise to kingship in Judah, his victory over King Ish-Bosheth (Esh-Baal) son of Saul of Israel at Gibeon, and his selection as King of Israel. It continues with his victories over the Philistines, his selection of Jerusalem as his capital, his return of the Ark of G-d to Jerusalem, the account of YHWH's promise to grant David eternal kingship, his rule over Israel and Judah and the surrounding nations, and his care for Mephibosheth son of Jonathan.

Second Samuel 10–24 narrates David's failures as king, beginning with his adulterous affair with Bath Sheba and the murder of her husband, Uriah the Hittite. Although David repented of his sins, subsequent chapters demonstrate how Nathan's condemnation of David and David's failures as a father functioned to destroy his Hebron-based family and ultimately brought Solomon to the throne.

Samuel's accounts of the reigns of the House of Eli, the House of Saul, and the House of David constitute a study in leadership, including depictions of how a proper leader should exercise power, especially as exemplified by Samuel and David during his rise to power, and how a leader may fail, especially as exemplified by Eli, Saul, and David, whose failure to discipline his own sons produced catastrophic results.[12]

The Former Prophets do not depict the ultimate failure and exile of Israel and Judah as ends in themselves. Rather, the Former Prophets impress upon its readers the necessity to observe the commandments of YHWH that constitute the basis for YHWH's grant of the land of Israel to the people of Israel and Judah. Insofar as Samuel focuses on the leadership of the nation, it is especially incumbent upon the Kings of Israel and Judah and other leaders to exercise their power appropriately in accordance with the principles laid down in YHWH's commandments.[13] Samuel functions much like later works focused on leadership, such as Sun Tzu's *Art of War*

---

[12] See my study, "Rethinking Samuel," *Visions of the Holy* (SBL ResBibS, 2 vols.; Atlanta, GA: Society of Biblical Literature Press, in press).

[13] Sweeney, "Rethinking Samuel"; Moshe Halbertal and Stephen Holmes, *The Beginning of Politics: Power in the Biblical Book of Samuel* (Princeton and Oxford: Princeton University Press, 2017).

or Machiavelli's *The Prince*.[14] The Former Prophets anticipate a return of the exiles to Jerusalem, Judah, and Israel and a restoration of Jewish life in the land of Israel. Sun Tzu's *Art of War*, written in China during the fifth century BCE, advises the reader on strategic thinking for attaining goals in military campaigns and leadership in general. Niccolò Machiavelli's *The Prince*, written in 1513 by a senior Florentine Republic official but published posthumously in 1532, is a highly influential political manual that advises the reader on political strategic thinking and leadership in general. The Book of Samuel differs in genre but nevertheless illustrates principles of political and military leadership in its portrayals of Samuel, Saul, David, and the other major figures presented in the book.

DIACHRONIC CONSIDERATIONS

As an important component of the Former Prophets, Samuel functions as part of the so-called Deuteronomistic History. The Deuteronomistic History is a scholarly construct that is based on the final form of the Former Prophets read in diachronic perspective. The model for the Deuteronomistic History was first proposed by Martin Noth in 1943 to assess the literary form, theological outlook, and compositional history of the Former Prophets when read together as a whole.[15] Noth argued that the Deuteronomistic History (DtrH) was a historical work formed through a process of tradition history that attempted to assess the history of Israel from the perspective of the Babylonian Exile. Older tradition-historical textual units, such as major elements of the Book of Samuel and the Elijah–Elisha narratives in 1 Kings 17–2 Kings 13, were incorporated into the largely DtrH narrative framework. Noth argued that the Babylonian Exile marked the end of Israel's history, and the DtrH attempted to explain that end by charging that it presented a history of divine judgment against Israel for violating the covenant in Deuteronomy.

Subsequent studies grounded in continental scholarship, such as the work of Walter Dietrich, Rudolf Smend, and Timo Veijola, argue for an exilic-period model for the formation of the DtrH from its basic edition (DtrG), through a prophetic edition (DtrP), and a nomistic or legal edition

---

[14] Sun Tzu, *The Art of War*, trans. and ed. Ralph D. Sawyer (New York: Basic Books, 1994); Niccolò Machiavelli, *The Prince*, with an introduction by Christian Gauss (New York and Scarborough, Ontario; Mentor, 1952).
[15] Martin Noth, *The Deuteronomistic History* (JSOTSup 15; Sheffield: JSOT Press, 1981).

(DtrN).[16] American scholars, such as Frank Moore Cross, Jr., Richard D. Nelson, and Gary N. Knoppers, argue that an earlier edition of the DtrH, written during the reign of King Josiah of Judah (r. 640–609 BCE), points to Josiah as the righteous Davidic King who would restore the ideal of a united Davidic empire until his unexpected death at the hands of Pharaoh Necho of Egypt.[17] The exilic expansion of the DtrH points especially to the sins of King Manasseh of Judah (r. 687/6–642 BCE) to explain the destruction of Jerusalem and the Babylonian Exile.

Discussion of the DtrH has largely settled in support of the American model of a late-seventh-century BCE Josianic edition that was revised after Josiah's death to present a sixth-century exilic version of the work. But issues remain. Halpern and Vanderhooft posit a late-eighth-century BCE Hezekian edition of the work.[18] Campbell and O'Brien posit a late-ninth-century Prophetic Record that originated in northern Israel to point to the emergence of the Jehu dynasty.[19] McCarter posits a Solomonic Apology that culminates in the reign of Solomon and his building of the Jerusalem Temple.[20] Römer generally accepts the American model but raises

---

[16] Walter Dietrich, *Prophetie und Geschichte. Eine redaktionsgeschichtliche Untersuchung zum deuteronomistischen Geschichtswerk* (FRLANT 108; Göttingen: Vandenhoeck & Ruprecht, 1972); Walter Dietrich, *David, Saul und die Propheten* (BWANT 122; Stuttgart: Kohlhammer, 1989); Rudolf Smend, "Die Gesetz und die Völker. Eine Beitrag zum deuteronomischen Redaktionsgeschichte," in *Probleme Biblischer Theologie*, ed. H. W. Wolff (Fs. G. von Rad; Munich: Chr. Kaiser, 1971), 494–509; Timo Veijola, *Das Königtum in der Beurteilung der deuteronomistischen Historiographie. Eine redaktionsgeschichtliche Untersuchung* (Helsinki: Suomalainen Tiedeakatemia, 1977); Timo Veijola, *Die ewigen Dynastie. David und die Entstehung seiner Dynastie nach der deuteronomistischen Darstellung* (Helsinki: Suomalainen Tiedeakatemia, 1975).

[17] Frank Moore Cross, Jr., The Themes of the Books of Kings and the Structure of the Deuteronomistic History," in *Canaanite Myth and Hebrew Epic* (Cambridge, MA: Harvard University Press, 1973), 274–289; Richard D. Nelson, *The Double Redaction of the Deuteronomistic History* (JSOTSup 18; Sheffield: JSOT Press, 1981); Gary N. Knoppers, *Two Nations under G-d: The Deuteronomistic History of Solomon and the Duel Monarchies* (HSM 52–53; Atlanta, GA: Scholars Press, 1993–94).

[18] Baruch Halpern and David Vanderhooft, "The Editions of Kings in the 7th–6th Centuries," *HUCA* 62 (1991): 179–244; cf. Iain W. Provan, *Hezekiah and the Books of Kings: A Contribution to the Debate about the Deuteronomistic History* (BZAW 172; Berlin and New York: Walter de Gruyter, 1988).

[19] Antony F. Campbell, SJ, *Of Prophets and Kings: A Late-Ninth Century Document* (CBQMS 17; Washington, DC: The Catholic Biblical Association, 1986); Mark A. O'Brien, *The Deuteronomistic History Hypothesis: A Reassessment* (OBO 92; Freiburg: Universitätsverlag/Göttingen: Vandenhoeck & Ruprecht, 1989).

[20] P. Kyle McCarter, Jr., *2 Samuel* (AB 9; Garden City, NY: Doubleday, 1984), 11–16.

questions about the Deuteronomistic character of the whole.[21] And some contemporary scholars reject Noth's model altogether.[22] The present commentary posits a model of the composition of the DtrH that builds upon the scholarship outlined here and the author's work on the role of King Josiah's influence in the composition of the DtrH and the prophetic literature, as well as a detailed commentary on Kings.[23] The model largely accepts the hypotheses of an Exilic DtrH, a Josianic DtrH, and a Hezekian DtrH with minor modifications and explanations, It modifies the hypothesis of a ninth-century Prophetic Record offered by Campbell and O'Brien to point instead to an eighth-century Jehu Dynastic History that culminates in the reign of King Jeroboam ben Jehoash of Israel, who ruled a kingdom that extended from Lebo-Hamath in Aram to the Sea of the Arabah (the Red Sea), much like the kingdom of Solomon (to 2 Kgs 14:23–29).[24] The present commentary accepts much of McCarter's hypothesis of a Solomonic Apology, although it modifies the hypothesis with a great deal of further elaboration concerning its contents and theological outlook and relabels it as the Solomonic History.

The Book of Samuel shows little evidence of DtrH composition. Interpreters point to 1 Samuel 8, which presents Samuel's warnings concerning the nature of kingship that show some affinities with the Torah of the King in Deuteronomy 17:14–20, and 1 Samuel 12, in which Samuel's farewell speech calls upon the people to observe YHWH's commandments, as examples of DtrH composition.[25] First Samuel 8's warnings concerning

---

[21]   Thomas Römer, *The So-Called Deuteronomistic History* (New York and London: T and T Clark, 2007); see also the essays in Cynthia Edenburg and Juha Pakkala, eds., *Is Samuel among the Deuteronomists? Current Views on the Place of Samuel in a Deuteronomistic History* (AIL 16; Atlanta, GA: Society of Biblical Literature, 2013).

[22]   See the essays in Edenburg and Pakkala, eds., Is Samuel among the Deuteronomists? for a full discussion of contemporary issues.

[23]   Sweeney, *King Josiah of Judah*; Marvin A. Sweeney, *1-2 Kings: A Commentary* (OTL; Louisville, KY: Westminster John Knox, 2007).

[24]   Although Sweeney, *King Josiah of Judah*, 93–109 earlier posited that the so-called Succession Narrative in 2 Samuel 9:11–24 originated with the Josianic DtrH due to its critique of David in comparison to Josiah, study of this material in the present commentary prompted a change of view that includes the Succession Narrative as part of the Jehu Dynastic History to account for its anti-Davidic and pro-northern viewpoints. Even as part of an earlier Jehu Dynastic History, the Succession Narrative continues to lend itself easily to the Josianic DtrH's efforts to portray Josiah as a righteous Davidic King who corrected the problems of earlier kings of Israel and Judah.

[25]   For example, Hans Jochen Boecker, *Die Beurteilung der Anfänge des Königstums in den deuteronomistischen Abschnitten des 1. Samuelbuches* (WMANT 31; Neukirchen-Vluyn: Neukirchener Verlag, 1969), 10–34.

kingship do not match entirely the concerns expressed in Deuteronomy 17:14–20, but they anticipate Solomon's rule of northern Israel, especially imposition of the *mas*, "tax," or "corvée" upon the northern tribes in 1 Kings 4–5. Concern with observance of YHWH's commandments in 1 Samuel 12 gives cogent expression to the concerns of the DtrH.[26] Some argue that Nathan's prophecy of eternal kingship for the House of David in 2 Samuel 7 is a DtrH composition,[27] but the references to the dynastic oracle in 1 Kings 2:1–4; 8:14–26; and 9:1–9 all characterize the Davidic promise as conditional, insofar as the sons of David are adjured to observe YHWH's commandments in order to retain the throne. Such an under- standing explains why the House of David no longer rules Israel in Jerusalem at the end of Kings.

The compositional model for the Book of Samuel in modern scholarship is heavily indebted to the work of Leonhard Rost, who in 1926 proposed the model of the Succession Narrative to explain the composition of the Book of Samuel.[28] Second Samuel 10–20 and 1 Kings 1–2 constitute a narrative written by an author who attempts to show that David's adultery with Bath Sheba and his role in the murder of her husband, Uriah the Hittite, prompt conflict within the House of David that ultimately results in the deaths of David's Hebron-born sons, Amnon, Abshalom, and Adonijah, and leads to the ascent of David's younger son, Solomon, to the throne of Israel. The Succession Narrative thereby provides a means to work earlier narratives concerning the House of Eli in 1 Samuel 1–3, 7; the Ark in 1 Samuel 4–6, 2 Samuel 6; the reign of Saul in 1 Samuel 8–15; the rise of David in 1 Samuel 16–2 Samuel 8 or 9; and the appendices concerning David in 2 Samuel 21–24 into the present form of the Book of Samuel. Later interpreters retitle it as the Court History, but the foundations for their analyses continue to rest on the work of Rost.[29]

There are two fundamental problems with the work of Rost: first, the separation of 1 Kings 1–2 from the rest of the proposed Succession Narrative/Court History by the so-called Appendices in 2 Samuel 21–24, and second, the indications of northern dissatisfaction with the House of

[26]   Boecker, *Die Beurteilung*, 61–88.
[27]   Dennis J. McCarthy, "II Samuel 7 and the Structure of the Deuteronomistic History," *JBL* 84 (1965): 131–138.
[28]   Leonhard Rost, *The Succession to the Throne of David* (Sheffield, UK: Almond, 1982, German original, 1926).
[29]   For example, John Van Seters, *In Search of History* (New Haven, CT, and London: Yale University Press, 1983), 77–91.

David in the accounts of the revolts by Abshalom and Sheba against David in 2 Samuel 15–20 and the Appendices in 2 Samuel 21–24. Both call for reconsideration of Rost's hypothesis and the modifications made to it by later scholars.

Rost's argument that 1 Kings 1–2, in which Solomon supplants David's Hebron-born son, Adonijah, has been separated from the rest of the Succession Narrative by the introduction of the Appendices in 2 Samuel 21–24 raises questions. It is true that 1 Kings 1–2 is concerned with the issue of Davidic succession, but it presents an inherent critique of Solomon, who is born as a result of David's sins in committing adultery with Solomon's mother, Bath Sheba, and his role in murdering her husband, Uriah the Hittite, in a failed attempt to cover up his crime. Although David repented of his sins in 2 Samuel 10–12 prior to Solomon's birth, the narrative hardly represents an account of a royal birth that would have been propagated by the House of David. Furthermore, Solomon's execution of his brother Adonijah, based on the account of Adonijah's request to Bath Sheba for David's concubine, Abishag; his expulsion of the high priest, Abiathar; and his compliance with David's advice to eliminate Joab and Shimei indicate a purge of the House of David that eliminated David's Hebron-based family and supporters in favor of a Jerusalem-based faction that did not participate in David's rise to power. The narrative appears to recount a coup within the House of David that raises suspicions about the character of Solomon's reign. Solomon's reign is presented in adulatory terms in 1 Kings 3–10, but the accounts of Solomon's ascent to the throne in 1 Kings 1–2, his apostasy on behalf of his foreign wives in 1 Kings 11, and the subsequent references to his harsh rule over the north in the account of the failure of his son, Rehoboam, to be named king of northern Israel in 1 Kings 12, present a critique of Solomon that undermines the adulation in 1 Kings 3–10.[30]

Furthermore, the so-called Appendices in 2 Samuel 21–24 likewise indicate critique of David, which suggests that they have something in common with the critique of David evident in 2 Samuel 10–20. The account of David's handing over the sons of Saul to the Gibeonites for execution in 2 Samuel 21 critiques David for enabling the deaths of the royal House of Saul into which he married. The demand of the Gibeonites presupposes a relationship with David that would have been concluded

---

[30]   See Sweeney, *1–2 Kings*, 1–71, 152–161.

following his victory over northern Israel in 2 Samuel 2 and a prior relationship with the House of Saul.[31] Unfortunately, the Samuel narratives provide no account of Saul's relationship with the Gibeonites, although there are hints of such a relationship when the Ark of G-d appears with the army of Saul in 1 Samuel 14:18 at his victory over the Philistines. Prior to this battle, the Ark had been kept at Kiriath Jearim, apparently an ally of Gibeon. Otherwise, the only hint of a relationship between the House of Saul and Gibeon appears in Joshua 9–10, which recounts the Gibeonites' alliance with Israel in the time of Joshua, although the narrative may have once had the alliance with the House of Saul in mind. Likewise, the account of the exploits of David's warriors in 2 Samuel 21:15–22 includes mention of Elhanan son of Jaar-Oregim, who killed Goliath, which suggests that David may have taken credit for the exploits of one of his warriors.[32]

Second Samuel 22, David's psalm of thanksgiving to YHWH, and 23:1–7, David's last words, offer no critique of David, but the latter refers to YHWH's *běrît 'ôlām*, "eternal covenant," with David, which has affinities with 2 Samuel 7 but not with 1 Kings 2:1–4; 8:14–26; and 9:1–9. This suggests that 2 Samuel 22 and 23:1–7 once concluded an adulatory account of David's rise to power that did not include 2 Samuel 10–20 or 1 Kings 1–2. Second Samuel 23:8–39 presents David's warriors, which also upholds David's reputation for leadership.

Finally, 2 Samuel 24 includes an account of David's purchase of the threshing floor of Araunah as the site for the future Temple in Jerusalem. Although such an account might appear adulatory, the fact that the purchase was motivated by YHWH's punishment against David for taking a census of the people suggests critique of David, particularly since a census would provide the basis for imposing a tax on the people, as exemplified by Solomon's tax or corvée upon the people of northern Israel, mentioned in 1 Kings 4–5.

Consequently, the so-called Appendix in 2 Samuel 21–24 appears to have a central core in 2 Samuel 22–23, which honors David and upholds

---

[31] See also Joseph Blenkinsopp, *Gibeon and Israel: The Role of Gibeon and the Gibeonites in the Political and Religious History of Early Israel* (SOTSMS 2; Cambridge: Cambridge University Press, 1972), esp. 28–40; cf. Israel Finkelstein, *The Forgotten Kingdom: The Archaeology and History of Northern Israel* (ANEM 5; Atlanta, GA: Society of Biblical Literature, 2013), esp. 1–61, although he dates the Gibeonite/Gibeah polity to the mid-tenth century based largely on the account of Pharaoh Sheshonq's invasion of Israel in the late tenth century BCE.

[32] See Fritz Stolz, *Das erste und zweite Buch Samuel* (ZBK/AT 9; Zürich: Theologischer Verlag, 1981), 283; cf. McCarter, *2 Samuel*, 450.

his reputation, whereas the framework in 2 Samuel 21 and 24 presents critique of David and suggests that he is an inadequate monarch.

The second problem with Rost's work is the role that northern critique plays in the account of David's reign in 2 Samuel 10–20. Here, David appears as a king who is willing to betray one of his own loyal warriors, Uriah the Hittite (2 Sam 23:39), by having an affair with his wife, Bath Sheba, and arranging his murder with Joab in an effort to cover up the affair. The later marriage between David and Bath Sheba produces Solomon, which would indicate that Solomon would not be highly regarded by those who would read the account of his origins, particularly northern Israelites, who would bear the burden of supporting his royal house, according to 1 Kings 4–5, from which his home tribe of Judah was excused. The consequent chaos in the House of David would lead ultimately to the revolt of Abshalom, the son of David's wife Maacah daughter of Telmai, King of Geshur. Geshur was an Aramean kingdom situated along the northern and eastern shores of the Kinnereth, Sea of Galilee, and would have been part of the orbit of northern Israel. Apparently, David's marriage to Maacah sealed a treaty with Geshur that would have enabled David to keep northern Israel in check. Abshalom's revolt built on dissatisfaction with David's rule in both northern Israel and southern Judah, but when the revolt concluded, the men of Judah quickly resumed their allegiance with David, whereas the men of Israel did not, according to 2 Samuel 19, especially verses 42–44. Immediately following these verses, 2 Samuel 20 recounts the failed revolt against David led by Sheba son of Bichri of the tribe of Benjamin. Although his revolt failed, his call to revolt in 2 Samuel 20:1 presages the northern revolt against Rehoboam ben Solomon in 1 Kings 12:16. Such a correlation indicates a relationship between the revolts recounted in 2 Samuel 15–20 and the later revolt by the northern tribes of Israel against the House of David in 1 Kings 12.

The revolts of Abshalom son of David and Shebna son of Bichri were precursors to the later revolt of the northern tribes against Rehoboam. Such a scenario indicates that the critical account of David's reign in 2 Samuel 10–24 once formed a part of the Jehu Dynastic History.[33] The Jehu Dynastic History relates dissatisfaction with the House of David (and Saul) by the northern tribes of Israel that ultimately culminated in the rule of the House of Jehu, whose fourth king, Jeroboam son of Joash, ruled a

[33] See Sweeney, *1–2 Kings*, 26–30.

kingdom like that of Solomon, which extended from Lebo-Hamath in northern Aram to the Sea of the Arabah (Red Sea) to the south of Judah.

The remaining narrative in 1 Samuel 1–2 Samuel 9 presents an adulatory account of the rise of the House of David that would not only honor David as the founder of a new dynastic house in Judah and Israel but also culminate in the adulatory account of the reign of David's son, Solomon, in 1 Kings 3–10. Although the present form of the account of Solomon's ascent to the throne and rule in 1 Kings 1–11 is framed with critical accounts in 1 Kings 1–2 and 11 (12), 1 Kings 3–10 presents Solomon as a wise, wealthy, and powerful king who kept Israel and Judah united, built the Jerusalem Temple, engaged in international trade that made his kingdom wealthy, and kept the peace by maintaining extensive and friendly relations with the surrounding nations, including Egypt, as indicated by his many marriages to foreign women. McCarter has already demonstrated the foundations for such a hypothesis in his arguments for naming the account "the Solomonic Apology."[34]

McCarter built upon Grønbæk's analysis of the so-called history of the rise of David in 1 Samuel 16–2 Samuel 5 as well as earlier work on the origins of the so-called Saul Cycle in 1 Samuel 1–15 by Hylander and the Ark Narrative in 1 Samuel 4–6; 2 Samuel 6 by Campbell.[35] Hylander demonstrated how the present form of the Eli narratives in 1 Samuel 1–3 originally formed an introduction to the rise of Saul by pointing to the inadequacies of the rule of the House of Eli as well as the hints in the narrative concerning the coming appearance of Saul (Hebrew *šā'ûl*, which means literally "requested, asked"), as indicated by the verbal hints of the son "requested" by Hannah, namely, the prophet (and priest) Samuel, who would play the key role in bringing Saul to power at the end of his lifetime (see 1 Sam 1:20, 28; 2:20; 8:10; 12:13, 17, 19). Campbell pointed to the role played by the Ark Narrative in providing an account of the Philistine capture of the Ark in 1 Samuel 4–6 and the role played by 2 Samuel 6 in redactionally joining the account of Saul's rise to power to the accounts of David's rise. The account of Saul's reign has clearly been edited to serve the purposes of the Solomonic History by framing adulatory accounts of Saul's

---

[34] McCarter, *2 Samuel*, 9–16.

[35] Ivar Hylander, *Der literarische Samuel-Saul-Komplex (1 Sam. 1–15). Traditionsgeschichtlich Untersucht* (Uppsala: Alquist & Wiksell/Leipzig: Otto Harrassowitz, 1932); Antony F. Campbell, *The Ark Narrative* (SBLDS 16; Missoula, MT: Scholars Press, 1975); Jakob H. Grønbæk, *Die Geschichte vom Aufstieg Davids (1. Sam. 15–2. Sam. 5). Tradition und Komposition* (Copenhagen: Prostant Apud Munksgaard, 1971).

rise to kingship in 1 Samuel 9:1–10:16 and his rescue of the city of Jabesh Gilead in 1 Samuel 11 with critical accounts in 1 Samuel 8; 10:10–17; 12; 13–14; and 15. The Book of Judges, which portrays a steady decline of Israel during the period of the Judges from Othniel of Judah in Judges 3 to the rape and murder of the Levite's concubine in Judges 19–20, constitutes a critique of Saul, his capital at Gibeah, and his home tribe of Benjamin.[36]

Although the current form of the Saul Cycle serves the interests of the Solomonic History, it is clear that there was once an underlying narrative that provided an adulatory account of the rise of Saul to kingship and his heroism in delivering the city of Jabesh Gilead in 1 Samuel 1–7; 9:1–10:9; and 11. Portions of the narrative may be lost to us, but the interest in honoring Saul as the first King of Israel is clear.

THEOLOGICAL AND HISTORICAL CONSIDERATIONS

The Book of Samuel is first and foremost a work of literature, which means that the reader will play a decisive role in its interpretation.[37] Samuel is written to depict the changes of leadership in Israel during its early history, specifically the transition from tribal-based leadership in the period of the Judges to monarchies as the tribes undergo a process of unification.

The Book of Samuel portrays YHWH's interrelationship with the various agents of leadership during this period: the House of Eli, the House of Saul, and the House of David.[38] Apart from Samuel and other biblical sources, there is virtually no ancient literature that depicts Israel and Judah during this time. Insofar as Samuel provides the fullest depiction of Israel and Judah during this period, it is crucial for readers to understand its rhetorical aims, its plot development, and its characterization – or caricaturization – of the major players in the narrative. As Whybray demonstrates, Samuel is heavily

[36] Sweeney, *King Josiah of Judah*, 110–124.
[37] For foundational methodological perspective in reading Samuel as literature, see Sweeney, "Form Criticism"; Robert Alter, *The Art of Biblical Narrative* (New York: Basic, 1981); Meir Sternberg, *The Poetics of Biblical Narrative: Ideological Literature and the Drama of Reading* (Bloomington, IN: Indiana University Press, 1987); and Phyllis Trible, *Rhetorical Criticism: Context, Method, and the Book of Jonah* (Minneapolis, MN: Fortress, 1994); see also W. Lee Humphreys, *The Character of G-d in the Book of Genesis* (Louisville, KY: Westminster John Knox, 2001); Mignon R. Jacobs, *Gender, Power, and Persuasion: The Genesis Narratives and Contemporary Portraits* (Grand Rapids, MI: Baker, 2007); Keith Bodner and Benjamin J. M. Johnson, eds., *Characters and Characterization in the Book of Samuel* (LHBOTS 669; London: T and T Clark, 2020).
[38] Sweeney, "Rethinking Samuel."

influenced by wisdom motifs, and one must understand both the character of YHWH and the character of the book's human protagonists to comprehend its lessons concerning YHWH and Israel's human leadership.[39]

YHWH is a key character in Samuel, insofar as YHWH both plays a major role in bringing the various ruling houses to power to provide leadership for the people, and YHWH also plays a major role in passing judgment upon them.[40] YHWH is obviously dissatisfied with the House of Eli in 1 Samuel 1–7, and YHWH's dissatisfaction is justified by the characterization of Eli and his sons: Eli is portrayed as an incompetent priest who does not recognize a woman, Hannah, at prayer; does not train his sons, Hophni and Phineas, in proper conduct; and does not recognize YHWH when the deity speaks with young Samuel before the Ark. The result is a catastrophe when Israel goes to battle against the Philistines at Aphek and loses everything, including the Ark of G-d and their freedom from Philistine domination. YHWH nevertheless appears triumphant when the idol of the Philistine god, Dagon, falls before the Ark when it is placed in the temple before Dagon and must be sent to Kiriath Jearim for safekeeping because the Philistines are unable to endure the power of the presence of YHWH.

The accounts of the rise of the House of Saul in 1 Samuel 8–15 are heavily polemical, in that they are designed to portray Saul as an incompetent leader who will ultimately be overshadowed and replaced by David. The narrative warns Israel – and the reader – about the cost of kingship. Although 1 Samuel 9:1–10:16 and 11:1–15 portray Saul as a handsome young man of destiny and a hero who saves Jabesh Gilead, 1 Samuel 8; 10:17–27; 12:1–25; 13:1–14:52; and 15:1–35 work together to undermine the positive portrayal of Saul. The people's desire for a king represents their rejection of YHWH (1 Sam 8); Saul is unable to function publicly as a leader who inspires confidence in the people (1 Sam 10:17–27); Saul and the people must obey YHWH's commandments (1 Sam 12); Saul is a tragic figure who oversteps his bounds by acting as a priest and by inadvertently cursing his own son (1 Sam 13–14); and Saul is a dangerous figure who refuses to obey YHWH's commandments and threatens Samuel (1 Sam 15).

---

[39] R. Norman Whybray, *The Succession Narrative: A Study of II Sam. 9–20 and 1 Kings 1 and 2* (SBT II/9; Naperville, IL: Allenson, 1968).

[40] Stephen B. Chapman, "Worthy to Be Praised: G-d as Character in the Book of Samuel," *Characters and Characterization*, ed. Bodner and Johnson, 25–41.

The depiction of the rise of David during the reign of Saul continues to denigrate Saul as it builds up the character of David, who can do no wrong and who enjoys the favor of YHWH in 1 Samuel 16–31. YHWH selects David, the youngest of Jesse's sons, as the favored future King of Israel. David soothes Saul with his music; he kills the Philistine giant, Goliath, when Saul and the rest of the men of Israel are too afraid to challenge him; Saul's son and heir, Jonathan, and his daughter, Michal, love David, despite the fact that he represents a threat to their own interests as children of the House of Saul; David constantly shows loyalty to Saul when he has the opportunity to kill him; Nabal conveniently drops dead, enabling David to marry his widow, Abigail, thereby marrying into the power structure of the tribe of Judah; David eventually becomes a Philistine vassal when Saul, unable to defeat the Philistines, spends his time unsuccessfully trying to subdue David; and David is absent when Saul commits suicide as the Philistines overwhelm him at Mt. Gilboa.

David continues to enjoy the favor of YHWH in 2 Samuel 1–9 as he continues his rise to kingship following the death of Saul, but he is also helped by the competence and loyalty of his general, Joab. David constantly asserts his innocence in the death of Saul by condemning those who raise their hand against YHWH's anointed, despite the fact that David has so much to gain from Saul's death. David becomes King of Judah – thanks in part to his marriage to Abigail – and goes to war against Ish-Bosheth (i.e., Esh-Baal), the son of Saul, who succeeds his father as King of Israel. David defeats Israel at Gibeon and deftly handles – with the assistance of Joab – the effort by Abner, Ish-Bosheth's general, who betrays his master in a failed attempt to ally with David. Following the assassinations of both Abner and Ish-Bosheth/Esh-Baal, David becomes King of Israel as well as King of Judah, and he deftly defeats the Philistines – again, with the help of Joab – and conquers Jerusalem – with the help of Joab again – to serve as his capital over both Judah and Israel. David makes Jerusalem the holy center of Israel by moving the Ark from Kiriath Jearim to Jerusalem, and he also manages to ensure that Michal, who had given David everything over against her own father, was left childless, ensuring that David could found his own dynasty rather than serve as a monarch of the House of Saul. Through all of this, David receives the eternal covenant of kingship from YHWH, becomes the ruler of a vast empire, and even manages to look after Mephibosheth (Merib-Baal), the son of David's close friend, Jonathan, the son of Saul, who should have been king after his father.

But the favor of YHWH slips away as David acts in a despicable manner in his adulterous affair with Bath Sheba and his role in the murder of her husband, Uriah the Hittite, in 2 Samuel 10–24. Although David eventually repents of his sins, the damage is done as Solomon, the future king, is born, and David's older sons born in Hebron indulge themselves in sins reminiscent of those of their father. Amnon, David's presumed heir, rapes his half-sister, Tamar, and in retaliation, her brother, Abshalom, murders him when David fails to do anything about it. Abshalom flees Jerusalem but returns at the insistence of Joab, only to lead a revolt against his father that tears the kingdom apart. The revolt only ends when Joab kills Abshalom, something David should have done in the first place, although David never realizes just how Joab had saved his kingdom. David suffers another revolt by Shebna son of Bichri, which portends the later revolt of the northern tribes of Israel against David's grandson, Rehoboam son of Solomon. Otherwise, David turns the sons of Saul over to the Gibeonites for execution; continues to praise YHWH in 2 Samuel 22 and 23:1–7; sees his heroes named, including Elhanan, the man who really killed Goliath, and Uriah the Hittite, the man whom David betrayed, in 2 Samuel 23:8–39; and draws YHWH's ire by engaging in a census of Israel, thereby necessitating the purchase of the threshing floor of Araunah to serve as the site of the future Temple to assuage YHWH's anger.

These narratives illustrate three key lessons. One is that YHWH appears to make mistakes, in that the House of Eli, the House of Saul, and in many respects, David, constitute questionable choices to serve as the leaders of Israel.[41] Whatever their initial merits might have been, they prove to be inadequate in the cases of Eli and Saul and of questionable character in the case of David. But this leads to the other key lesson, that YHWH works through questionable human beings to achieve divine purposes. In Samuel, human characters have free will – and they exercise it vociferously. But this points to a third lesson, that Samuel is a study in leadership that teaches its readers the qualities and responsibilities necessary for just and effective leadership and the mistakes that leaders may make, thereby leading them to consequences that readers would do well to avoid.[42]

Given the theological and narrative interests in the Book of Samuel, one may wonder about its historical veracity, specifically, were Eli and Saul

[41] Cf. Marvin A. Sweeney, *Reading the Hebrew Bible after the Shoah: Engaging Holocaust Theology* (Minneapolis, MN: Fortress, 2008).
[42] Sweeney, "Rethinking Samuel."

incompetent leaders? Was David a brilliant leader who could also engage
in despicable behavior? Lacking supporting records from the ancient Near
East that would confirm or contradict what readers find in Samuel, there is
no way to know. Contemporary scholarship raises questions about the
history of the narratives in Samuel, due largely to the lack of inscriptional,
literary, and archeological evidence concerning Israel, Eli, Saul, and David
in this period,[43] but the general picture of Israel and Judah nevertheless
appears at least plausible. Israel evolved from a semi-nomadic, tribal
society that migrated into Canaan and merged with the local Canaanite
population in the hill country at the same time as the Sea Peoples entered
the coastal plain and merged with the Canaanite population there to
become the Philistines of the Bible. In the following struggle for dominance,
Israel and Judah eventually triumphed over the Philistines, even though they
later succumbed to the Arameans, Assyrians, and Babylonians. David was
not a builder, and so it is difficult to point to major building projects as he
appears to have taken over a Canaanite culture that had already built its
cities, towns, and edifices. Interpreters may note, nevertheless, that there is
some evidence of standardization in the building of smaller cities that
suggests the presence and influence of a minor monarchy that acted to unite
the land.[44] David may well have been politically astute, but the empire
claimed in 2 Samuel 8 may actually represent a web of alliances that would
have secured David's position as a minor monarch in the region.

---

[43]   See, for example, Finkelstein, *The Forgotten Kingdom*, esp. 1–61; see also the essays in
        Joachim J. Krause et al., eds., *Saul, Benjamin, and the Emergence of Monarchy in Israel:
        Biblical and Archeological Perspectives* (AIL 40; Atlanta: Society of Biblical Literature, 2020).
[44]   Yosef Garfinkel et al., *In the Footsteps of King David: Revelations from an Ancient
        Biblical City* (London: Thames and Hudson, 2018).

2 Suggested Readings on Samuel

The following bibliography is hardly comprehensive, insofar as a wealth of material is available for Samuel. These works would be especially helpful to introduce the interpretation of the book, including its literary, historical, and theological contexts, and its various components.

COMMENTARIES

Perhaps the most comprehensive and up-to-date contemporary commentary on the Book of Samuel is the currently four-volume work of Walter Dietrich in the German Biblischer Kommentar Series, *Samuel* (BKAT VIII; Neukirchen-Vluyn: Neukirchener Verlag/Göttingen: Vandenhoeck & Ruprecht, 2011–2021), including, *1 Samuel 1–12* (BKAT VIII/1; Neukirchen-Vluyn: Neukirchener Verlag, 2011); *1 Samuel 13–26* (BKAT VIII/2; Neukirchen-Vluyn: Neukirchener Verlag, 2015); *1 Samuel 27–2 Samuel 8* (BKAT VIII/3; Göttingen: Vandenhoeck & Ruprecht, 2019); and *2 Samuel 9–14* (BKAT VIII/4; Göttingen: Vandenhoeck & Ruprecht, 2021). Dietrich's work continues to indicate his roots in the Continental model for the composition of the Deuteronomic History, but he has succeeded in adapting his model to the current consensus as part of his magisterial and comprehensive treatment of Samuel. P. Kyle McCarter's two-volume Anchor Bible Commentary (now Yale Anchor Bible), *1 Samuel* (AB 8; Garden City, NY: Doubleday, 1980); *2 Samuel* (AB 9; Garden City, NY: Doubleday, 1984), has served as the primary commentary on Samuel for some forty years, with its focus on reconstructing the text of Samuel based on the Old Greek and the Dead Sea Scrolls and its philological and historical perspectives. David Toshio Tsumura's two-volume Samuel commentary in the New International Commentary on the Old Testament series, *The First Book of Samuel* (NICOT; Grand

Rapids, MI, and Cambridge, UK: Eerdmans, 2007); *The Second Book of Samuel* (NICOT; Grand Rapids, MI: Eerdmans, 2019), is filled with philological and comparative Semitic insight. The two volumes on Samuel in the Word Biblical Commentary series, Ralph W. Klein, *1 Samuel* (WBC 10; Grand Rapids, MI: Zondervan, 2000), and A. A. Anderson, *2 Samuel* (WBC 11; Grand Rapids, MI: Zondervan, 2000), also offer a wealth of textual, philological, and historical interpretation. The two-volume Forms of the Old Testament Literature Commentary on Samuel by Antony F. Campbell, S.J., *1 Samuel* (FOTL VII; Grand Rapids, MI, and Cambridge, UK: Eerdmans, 2003), and *2 Samuel* (FOTL VIII; Grand Rapids, MI, and Cambridge, UK: Eerdmans, 2005), presents a largely synchronic reading of the text that is also informed with diachronic insight into its history of composition.

Interpreters will also benefit from the many commentaries on Samuel published during the twentieth and twenty-first centuries:

Alter, Robert. *The David Story: A Translation with Commentary of 1 and 2 Samuel* (New York and London: Norton, 1999).
Arnold, Bill T. *1 and 2 Samuel: The NIV Application Commentary* (Grand Rapids, MI: Zondervan, 2003).
Auld, A. Graeme. *I and II Samuel: A Commentary* (Old Testament Library; Louisville, KY: Westminster John Knox, 2011).
Driver, Samuel Rolles. *Notes on the Hebrew Text and Topography of the Books of Samuel* (Oxford: Clarendon, 1960).
Fokkelman, J. P. *Narrative Art and Poetry in the Books of Samuel. Volume 1: King David (II Sam. 9–20 & 1 Kings 1–2)* (Assen: Van Gorcum, 1981).
Fokkelman, J. P. *Narrative Art and Poetry in the Books of Samuel. Volume 2: The Crossing Fates (1 Sam. 13–31 & II Sam. 1)* (Assen/Maastricth: Van Gorcum, 1986).
Fokkelman, J. P. *Narrative Art and Poetry in the Books of Samuel. Volume 3: Throne and City (II Sam. 2–8 & 21–24)* (Assen/Maastricth: Van Gorcum, 1990).
Fokkelman, J. P. *Narrative Art and Poetry in the Books of Samuel. Volume 4: Vow and Desire (1 Sam. 1–12)* (Assen: Van Gorcum, 1993).
Rosenberg, A. J. *The Book of Samuel 1* (Judaica Books of the Bible; Brooklyn, NY: Judaica, 1976).
Rosenberg, A. J. *The Book of Samuel 2* (Judaica Books of the Bible; Brooklyn, NY: Judaica, 1986).
Stoebe, Hans-Joachim. *Das Erste Buch Samuelis* (Kommentar zum Alten Testament VIII/1; Gütersloh: Gerd Mohn, 1973).
Stoebe, Hans-Joachim. *Das Zeite Buch Samuelis* (Kommentar zum Alten Testament VIII/2; Gütersloh: Gütersloher Verlaghause, 1994).
Van Wijk-Bos, Johanna. *Reading Samuel: A Literary and Theological Commentary* (Reading The Old Testament; Macon, GA: Smyth and Helwys, 2011).

SURVEYS OF RESEARCH

Although both of these studies are dated, Walter Dietrich and Thomas Naumann, *Die Samuelbücher* (Erträge der Forchungen 287; Darmstadt: Wissenschaftlichebuchgesellschaft, 1995), and R. P. Gordon, *1 and 2 Samuel* (OT Guides; Sheffield: Sheffield Academic Press, 1984), remain very valuable for modern research.

TEXT EDITIONS AND STUDIES

The most useful and up-to-date introductions to the study of the textual versions of the Bible and text criticism are Emanuel Tov, *Textual Criticism of the Hebrew Bible* (3rd ed.; Minneapolis, MN: Fortress, 2012) and Julio Trebolle Barrera, *The Jewish Bible and the Christian Bible: An Introduction to the History of the Bible* (Leiden: Brill/Grand Rapids, MI, and Cambridge, UK: Eerdmans, 1998).
The following will also be very useful.

Brooke, Alan England, McLean, Norman, and St. John Thackeray, Henry. *The Old Testament in Greek. Volume II. The Later Historical Books. Part I: I and II Samuel* (London: Cambridge University Press, 1927).

Cross, Frank Moore et al. *Qumran Cave 4. XII: 1–2 Samuel* (DJD XVII. Oxford: Clarendon, 2005).

Elliger, K., and Rudolph, W. *Biblia Hebraica Stuttgartensia* (Stuttgart: Deutsche Bibelstiftung, 1977).

Fernández Marcos, Natalio. *The Septuagint in Context: Introduction to the Greek Version of the Bible* (Atlanta: Society of Biblical Literature, 2000).

Fernández Marcos, Natalio, and Busto Saiz, José Ramón, *El Texto Antioqueno de la Biblia Griega I: 1–2 Samuel* (Madrid: Instituto de Filología. C.S.I.C., 1989).

Harrington, Daniel J., and Saldarini, Anthony J. *Targum Jonathan of the Former Prophets: Introduction, Translation, and Notes* (Collegeville, MN: Liturgical, 1987).

Rahlfs, Alfred. *Septuaginta*, 2 vols. (Stuttgart: Württembergische Bibelanstalt, 1935).

Sperber, Alexander. *The Bible in Aramaic II: The Former Prophets according to Targum Jonathan* (Leiden: Brill, 1959).

Ulrich, Eugene Charles, Jr. *The Qumran Text of Samuel and Josephus*. (HSM 19; Missoula, MT: Scholars Press, 1978).

Wellhausen, Julius. *Der Text der Bücher Samuelis* (Göttingen: Vandenhoeck & Ruprecht, 1871).

FORMER PROPHETS/DEUTERONOMISTIC HISTORY

The most useful introductions to the Deuteronomistic History are Thomas C. Römer, *The So-Called Deuteronomistic History* (New York and London: T and T Clark, 2007), and Antony F. Campbell and Mark A. O'Brien, *Unfolding the Deuteronomistic History: Origins, Upgrades, Present Test* (Minneapolis, MN: Fortress, 2000).
The following will also be very helpful.

Edenburg, Cynthia, and Pakkala, Juha, eds. *Is Samuel Among the Deuteronomists? Current Views on the Place of Samuel in a Deuteronomistic History* (AIL 16; Atlanta, GA: Society of Biblical Literature, 2013).

Noth, Martin. *The Deuteronomistic History* (JSOTSup 15; Sheffield: JSOT Press, 1981).

Polzin, Robert. *David and the Deuteronomist: A Literary Study of the Deuteronomistic History. Part III: 2 Samuel* (Bloomington and Indianapolis, IN: Indiana University Press, 1993).

Polzin, Robert. *Samuel and the Deuteronomist: A Literary Study of the Deuteronomistic History. Part II: 1 Samuel* (Bloomington and Indianapolis, IN: Indiana University Press, 1989).

Sweeney, Marvin A. *King Josiah of Judah: The Lost Messiah of Israel* (Oxford and New York: Oxford University Press, 2001).

METHODOLOGICAL ISSUES

Alter, Robert. *The Art of Biblical Narrative* (New York: Basic Books, 1981).
Bodner, Keith, and Johnson, Benjamin J. M. *Characters and Characterization in the Book of Samuel* (LHBOTS 669; London and New York: T and T Clark, 2020).
Bar-Efrat, Shimon. *Narrative Art in the Bible* (JSOTSup 70; Sheffield: Sheffield Academic Press, 2000).
Green, Barbara. *Mikhail Bakhtin and Biblical Scholarship: An Introduction* (Semeia Series 38; Atlanta, GA: Society of Biblical Literature, 2000).
Halbertal, Moshe, and Holmes, Stephen. *The Beginning of Politics: Power in the Biblical Book of Samuel* (Princeton and Oxford: Princeton University Press, 2017).
Sternberg, Meir. *The Poetics of Biblical Narrative: Ideological Literature and the Drama of Reading* (Bloomington, IN: Indiana University Press, 1987).
Sweeney, Marvin A. "Form Criticism," *To Each Its Own Meaning: An Introduction to Biblical Criticisms and Their Application*, ed. S. L. McKenzie and S. R. Haynes (Louisville, KY: Westminster John Knox, 1999), 58–89.

HISTORICAL AND ARCHEOLOGICAL STUDIES

Blenkinsopp, Joseph. *Gibeon and Israel: The Role of Gibeon and the Gibeonites in the Political and Religious History of Early Israel* (SOTSMS 2; London and New York: Cambridge University Press, 1972).
Finkelstein, Israel. *The Forgotten Kingdom: The Archaeology and History of Northern Israel* (ANEM 5; Atlanta: Society of Biblical Literature, 2013).
Garfinkel, Yosef et al. *In the Footsteps of King David: Revelations from an Ancient Biblical City* (London: Thames and Hudson, 2018).
Halpern, Baruch. *David's Secret Demons: Messiah, Murderer, Traitor, King.* (Grand Rapids, MI, and Cambridge, UK: Eerdmans, 2001).
Krause, Joachim J. et al., eds. *Saul, Benjamin, and the Emergence of Monarchy in Israel: Biblical and Archaeological Perspectives* (AIL 40; Atlanta, GA: Society of Biblical Literature, 2020).
McKenzie, Steven L. *King David: A Biography* (Oxford: Oxford University Press, 2000).
Wright, Jacob L. *David, King of Israel, and Caleb in Biblical Memory* (Cambridge and New York: Cambridge University Press, 2014).

OTHER USEFUL STUDIES

Auld, A. Graeme, and Eynikel, Erik, eds. *For and Against David. Story and History in the Books of Samuel* (BETL 132; Leuven: Peeters, 2010).
Bietenhard, Sophia Katharina. *Des Königs General. Die Heerführertraditionen in der Vorstaatlichen und Frühen staatlichen Zeit und die Joabgestalt in 2 Sam 2–20; 1 Kön 1–2* (OBO 163; Freiburg: Universitätsverlag/Göttingen: Vandenhoeck & Ruprecht, 1998).
Carlson, R. A. *David the Chosen King. A Traditio-Historical Approach to the Second Book of Samuel* (Stockholm: Alqvist & Wiksell, 1964).
Dietrich, Walter. *Historiographie und Erzäahlkunst in den Samuelbüchern* (BWANT 221; Stuttgart: Kohlhammer, 2019).
Green, Barbara. *David's Capacity for Compassion: A Literary-Hermeneutical Study of 1–2 Samuel* (LHBOTS 641; London and New York: Bloomsbury T and T Clark, 2017).
Green, Barbara. *How Are the Mighty Fallen? A Dialogical Study of King Saul in 1 Samuel* (JSOTSup 365; Sheffield: Sheffield Academic Press, 2003).
Grønbæk, Jakob H. *Die Geschichte vom Aufstieg Davids (1. Sam. 15–2. Sam. 5). Tradition und Komposition* (Copenhagen: Prostant apud Munksgaard, 1971).
Hylander, Ivar. *Der literarische Samuel-Saul-Komplex (1. Sam. 1–15). Traditionsgeschichtlich Untersucht* (Uppsala: Alqvist & Wiksell/Leipzig: Otto Harrassowitz, 1932).

Leuchter, Mark. *Samuel and the Shaping of Tradition* (Oxford: Oxford University Press, 2013).

Mettinger, Tryggve N. D. *King and Messiah: The Civil and Sacral Legitimation of the Israelite Kings* (ConBibOT; Lund: Gleerup, 1976).

Rost, Leonhard. *The Succession to the Throne of David*. Sheffield: Almond, 1982).

Westbrook, April D. *"And He Will Take Your Daughters ..."* Woman Story and the Ethical Evaluation of Monarchy in the David Narrative (LHBOTS 610; London and New York: Bloomsbury T and T Clark, 2015).

Whybray, R. N. *The Succession Narrative: A Study of II Sam. 9-20 and 1 Kings 1 and 2* (SBT II/9; Naperville, IL: Allenson, 1968).

3 Commentary Part I: The Rule of the House of Eli – 1 Samuel 1–7

The first major component of the Book of Samuel is 1 Samuel 1–7, which recounts the rule of the House of Eli.[1] This unit provides an assessment of the House of Eli as an incompetent ruling house that must be cast aside to make way for the House of Saul, which is ultimately cast aside to make way for the House of David.[2] Due to the incompetence of Eli and his sons, Hophni and Phineas, Israel is defeated by the Philistines at Aphek; the Ark is captured by the Philistines; Hophni and Phineas are killed in battle; and Eli dies suddenly upon hearing the news. The deaths of Eli and his sons leave Samuel as the only Elide figure left to lead the nation.

First Samuel 1–7 is demarcated by the introductory notice in 1 Samuel 1:1–3 concerning Samuel's father, Elkanah, and his wives, Hannah and Peninnah, and the sons of Eli, Hophni and Phineas, who served as priests at Shiloh. The segment concludes with the summation of Samuel's rule in 1 Samuel 7:15–17, where he is named as a Judge. The Hebrew word, šōpēṭ, generally translated in the NRSVue as "judge," which suggests a judicial figure, actually presumes a much broader meaning as "ruler," as illustrated by Samuel's activities in 1 Samuel 7 and those of the Judges.[3] First Samuel 1–7 comprises three major sub-units, including the Account of Samuel's Introduction to the House of Eli in 1 Samuel 1:1–4:1a, the account of the Philistine Defeat of Israel at Aphek and the Capture of the Ark of the Covenant in 1 Samuel 4:1b–7:1, and the account of Samuel's rule over Israel in 1 Samuel 7:2–17.

---

[1] Marvin A. Sweeney, *Tanak: A Theological and Critical Introduction to the Jewish Bible* (Minneapolis: Fortress, 2012), 208–211.

[2] Marvin A. Sweeney, "Eli: A High Priest Thrown under the Wheels of an Ox Cart," *Characters and Characterization in The Book of Samuel*, ed. K. Bodner and B. J. M. Johnson (LHBOTS 609; London: Bloomsbury T and T Clark, 2020), 59–75.

[3] H. Niehr, "*šāpaṭ*; *šōpēṭ*," *TDOT* 15 (2006), 411–431.

SAMUEL'S INTRODUCTION TO THE HOUSE OF ELI – 1 SAMUEL
1:1–4:1A

1 ¹ There was a certain man of Ramathaim, a Zuphite from the hill country of Ephraim, whose name was Elkanah son of Jeroham son of Elihu son of Tohu son of Zuph, an Ephraimite.

² He had two wives; the name of one was Hannah, and the name of the other Peninnah. Peninnah had children, but Hannah had no children.

³ Now this man used to go up year by year from his town to worship and to sacrifice to the LORD of hosts at Shiloh, where the two sons of Eli, Hophni and Phinehas, were priests of the LORD.

⁴ On the day when Elkanah sacrificed, he would give portions to his wife Peninnah and to all her sons and daughters,

⁵ but to Hannah he gave a double portion because he loved her, though the LORD had closed her womb.

⁶ Her rival used to provoke her severely, to irritate her, because the LORD had closed her womb.

⁷ So it went on year by year; as often as she went up to the house of the LORD, she used to provoke her. Therefore Hannah wept and would not eat.

⁸ Her husband Elkanah said to her, "Hannah, why do you weep? Why do you not eat? Why is your heart sad? Am I not more to you than ten sons?"

⁹ After they had eaten and drunk at Shiloh, Hannah rose and presented herself before the LORD. Now Eli the priest was sitting on the seat beside the doorpost of the temple of the LORD.

¹⁰ She was deeply distressed and prayed to the LORD and wept bitterly.

¹¹ She made this vow: "O LORD of hosts, if only you will look on the misery of your servant and remember me and not forget your servant but will give to your servant a male child, then I will set him before you as a nazirite until the day of his death. He shall drink neither wine nor intoxicants, and no razor shall touch his head."

¹² As she continued praying before the LORD, Eli observed her mouth.

¹³ Hannah was praying silently; only her lips moved, but her voice was not heard; therefore Eli thought she was drunk.

¹⁴ So Eli said to her, "How long will you make a drunken spectacle of yourself? Put away your wine."

¹⁵ But Hannah answered, "No, my lord, I am a woman deeply troubled; I have drunk neither wine nor strong drink, but I have been pouring out my soul before the LORD.

¹⁶ Do not regard your servant as a worthless woman, for I have been speaking out of my great anxiety and vexation all this time."

¹⁷ Then Eli answered, "Go in peace; the God of Israel grant the petition you have made to him."

¹⁸ And she said, "Let your servant find favor in your sight." Then the woman went her way and ate and drank with her husband, and her countenance was sad no longer.[]]

¹⁹ They rose early in the morning and worshiped before the LORD; then they went back to their house at Ramah. Elkanah knew his wife Hannah, and the LORD remembered her.

²⁰ In due time Hannah conceived and bore a son. She named him Samuel, for she said, "I have asked him of the LORD."

²¹ The man Elkanah and all his household went up to offer to the LORD the yearly sacrifice and to pay his vow.

²² But Hannah did not go up, for she said to her husband, "As soon as the child is weaned, I will bring him, that he may appear in the presence of the LORD and remain there forever; I will offer him as a nazirite for all time."

²³ Her husband Elkanah said to her, "Do what seems best to you; wait until you have weaned him; only, may the LORD establish your word." So the woman remained and nursed her son until she weaned him.

²⁴ When she had weaned him, she took him up with her, along with a three-year-old bull, an ephah of flour, and a skin of wine. She brought him to the house of the LORD at Shiloh, and the child was young.

²⁵ Then they slaughtered the bull and brought the child to Eli.

²⁶ And she said, "Oh, my lord! As you live, my lord, I am the woman who was standing here in your presence praying to the LORD.

²⁷ For this child I prayed, and the LORD has granted me the petition that I made to him.

²⁸ Therefore I have lent him to the LORD; as long as he lives, he is given to the LORD." And they worshiped the LORD there.

2 ¹ Hannah prayed and said,

"My heart exults in the LORD;

my strength is exalted in my God.

My mouth derides my enemies
   because I rejoice in your victory.
² There is no Holy One like the LORD,
   no one besides you;
   there is no Rock like our God.
³ Talk no more so very proudly;
   let not arrogance come from your mouth,
for the LORD is a God of knowledge,
   and by him actions are weighed.
⁴ The bows of the mighty are broken,
   but the feeble gird on strength.
⁵ Those who were full have hired themselves out for bread,
   but those who were hungry are fat with spoil.
The barren has borne seven,
   but she who has many children is forlorn.
⁶ The LORD kills and brings to life;
   he brings down to Sheol and raises up.
⁷ The LORD makes poor and makes rich;
   he brings low; he also exalts.
⁸ He raises up the poor from the dust;
   he lifts the needy from the ash heap
to make them sit with princes
   and inherit a seat of honor.
For the pillars of the earth are the LORD's,
   and on them he has set the world.
⁹ He will guard the feet of his faithful ones,
   but the wicked will perish in darkness,
   for not by might does one prevail.
¹⁰ The LORD! His adversaries will be shattered;
   the Most High will thunder in heaven.
The LORD will judge the ends of the earth;
   he will give strength to his king
   and exalt the power of his anointed."

¹¹ Then they left him there before the LORD and went home to Ramah, while the boy remained to minister to the LORD in the presence of the priest Eli.

¹² Now the sons of Eli were scoundrels; they had no regard for the LORD

¹³ or for the duties of the priests to the people. When anyone offered sacrifice, the priest's servant would come, while the meat was boiling, with a three-pronged fork in his hand,

¹⁴ and he would thrust it into the pan, kettle, caldron, or pot; all that the fork brought up the priest would take for himself. This is what they did at Shiloh to all the Israelites who came there.

¹⁵ Moreover, before the fat was burned, the priest's servant would come and say to the one who was sacrificing, "Give meat for the priest to roast, for he will not accept boiled meat from you but only raw."

¹⁶ And if the man said to him, "Let them burn the fat first and then take whatever you wish," he would say, "No, you must give it now; if not, I will take it by force."

¹⁷ Thus the sin of the young men was very great in the sight of the LORD, for they treated the offerings of the LORD with contempt.

¹⁸ Samuel was ministering before the LORD, a boy wearing a linen ephod.

¹⁹ His mother used to make for him a little robe and take it to him each year when she went up with her husband to offer the yearly sacrifice.

²⁰ Then Eli would bless Elkanah and his wife and say, "May the LORD repay you with children by this woman for the loan that she made to the LORD," and then they would return to their home.

²¹ And the LORD took note of Hannah; she conceived and bore three sons and two daughters. And the boy Samuel grew up in the presence of the LORD.

²² Now Eli was very old. He heard all that his sons were doing to all Israel and how they lay with the women who served at the entrance to the tent of meeting.

²³ He said to them, "Why do you do such things? For I hear of your evil dealings from all these people.

²⁴ No, my sons; it is not a good report that I hear the people of the LORD spreading abroad.

²⁵ If one person sins against another, someone can intercede for the sinner with the LORD, but if someone sins against the LORD, who can

make intercession?" But they would not listen to the voice of their father, for it was the will of the LORD to kill them.

²⁶ Now the boy Samuel continued to grow both in stature and in favor with the LORD and with the people.

²⁷ A man of God came to Eli and said to him, "Thus the LORD has said: I revealed myself to the family of your ancestor in Egypt when they were slaves to the house of Pharaoh.

²⁸ I chose him out of all the tribes of Israel to be my priest, to go up to my altar, to offer incense, to wear an ephod before me, and I gave to the family of your ancestor all my offerings by fire from the Israelites.

²⁹ Why then look with greedy eye at my sacrifices and my offerings and honor your sons more than me by fattening yourselves on the choicest parts of every offering of my people Israel?

³⁰ Therefore the LORD the God of Israel declares: I promised that your family and the family of your ancestor should go in and out before me forever, but now the LORD declares: Far be it from me, for those who honor me I will honor, and those who despise me shall be treated with contempt.

³¹ See, a time is coming when I will cut off your strength and the strength of your ancestor's family.

³² No one in your family shall ever live to old age.

³³ The only one of you whom I shall not cut off from my altar shall be spared to weep out his eyes and grieve his heart; all the members of your household shall die by the sword.

³⁴ The fate of your two sons, Hophni and Phinehas, shall be the sign to you: both of them shall die on the same day.

³⁵ I will raise up for myself a faithful priest who shall do according to what is in my heart and in my mind. I will build him a sure house, and he shall go in and out before my anointed one forever.

³⁶ Everyone who is left in your family shall come and prostrate himself before him for a piece of silver or a loaf of bread and shall say, 'Please put me in one of the priest's places, that I may eat a morsel of bread.'"

3 ¹ Now the boy Samuel was ministering to the LORD under Eli. The word of the LORD was rare in those days; visions were not widespread.

² At that time Eli, whose eyesight had begun to grow dim so that he could not see, was lying down in his room;

³ the lamp of God had not yet gone out, and Samuel was lying down in the temple of the LORD, where the ark of God was.

⁴ Then the LORD called, "Samuel! Samuel!" and he said, "Here I am!"

⁵ and ran to Eli and said, "Here I am, for you called me." But he said, "I did not call; lie down again." So he went and lay down.

⁶ The LORD called again, "Samuel!" Samuel got up and went to Eli and said, "Here I am, for you called me." But he said, "I did not call, my son; lie down again."

⁷ Now Samuel did not yet know the LORD, and the word of the LORD had not yet been revealed to him.

⁸ The LORD called Samuel again, a third time. And he got up and went to Eli and said, "Here I am, for you called me." Then Eli perceived that the LORD was calling the boy.

⁹ Therefore Eli said to Samuel, "Go, lie down, and if he calls you, you shall say, 'Speak, LORD, for your servant is listening.'" So Samuel went and lay down in his place.

¹⁰ Now the LORD came and stood there, calling as before, "Samuel! Samuel!" And Samuel said, "Speak, for your servant is listening."

¹¹ Then the LORD said to Samuel, "See, I am about to do something in Israel that will make both ears of anyone who hears of it tingle.

¹² On that day I will fulfill against Eli all that I have spoken concerning his house, from beginning to end.

¹³ For I have told him that I am about to punish his house forever for the iniquity that he knew, because his sons were blaspheming God, and he did not restrain them.

¹⁴ Therefore I swear to the house of Eli that the iniquity of Eli's house shall not be expiated by sacrifice or offering forever."

¹⁵ Samuel lay there until morning; then he opened the doors of the house of the LORD. Samuel was afraid to tell the vision to Eli.

¹⁶ But Eli called Samuel and said, "Samuel, my son." He said, "Here I am."

¹⁷ Eli said, "What was it that he told you? Do not hide it from me. May God do so to you and more also, if you hide anything from me of all that he told you."

¹⁸ So Samuel told him everything and hid nothing from him. Then he said, "It is the LORD; let him do what seems good to him."

¹⁹ As Samuel grew up, the LORD was with him and let none of his words fall to the ground.

²⁰ And all Israel from Dan to Beer-sheba knew that Samuel was a trustworthy prophet of the LORD.

²¹ **The LORD continued to appear at Shiloh, for the LORD revealed himself to Samuel at Shiloh by the word of the LORD.**

4 ¹ᵃ And the word of Samuel came to all Israel.

Samuel's Birth and Placement at Shiloh – 1 Samuel 1:1–2:11

First Samuel 1:1–2:11 is a birth report that relates the birth of a key figure in biblical literature.[4] It begins with the introductory notice in 1 Samuel 1:1–3 concerning Samuel's father, Elkanah, his two wives, Hannah and Peninnah, and the two sons of Eli, Hophni and Phineas, who served as priests at Shiloh. Elkanah's home town is Ramathaim Zophim or Ramathaim of the Zuphites "Heights of the Watchers," located in the hill country of Ephraim.[5] First Samuel 1:19 and 2:11 (cf. 1 Sam 7:17) identify Elkanah's home city as Ramah, "Height," which may be a shortened name of Ramathaim. Ramathaim Zophim likely refers to Ramah, located in the territory of Benjamin (Josh 18:25) and identified with modern Er-Ram, just over four miles north of Jerusalem.

Elkanah's identity as an Ephraimite poses questions, insofar as Samuel is raised in the Shiloh temple to serve as a priest. First Chronicles 6:1–15 identifies Elkanah and Samuel as Levites, which prompts traditional interpreters to understand Elkanah's Ephraimite identity as an indication of his domicile rather than his tribal affiliation.[6] Chronicles is well known for stating that the identities of non-Levitical figures are Levite when they have some priestly association (cf. the prophets in 2 Kgs 23:2 who are priests and the Levites in 2 Chr 34:20).[7] Some explain Samuel's Ephraimite identity as an instance of a Nazirite vow because Hannah vowed to give him to YHWH and allow no razor to touch his head (Num 6:1–21),[8] but a Nazirite vow is only for a specified term, whereas Samuel's priestly service is for a lifetime.

Samuel's priestly service is better explained as an example of priestly service in northern Israel prior to the institution of the Levitical priesthood.

---

4   Cf. Timothy D. Finlay, *The Birth Report Genre in the Hebrew Bible* (FAT 2:12; Tübingen: Mohr Siebeck, 2005), 138–146.

5   P. A. Arnold, "Ramah," *ABD* 5 (1992), 613–614; Walter Dietrich, *Samuel: 1 Samuel 1–12* (BKAT 8:1; Neukirchen-Vluyn: Neukirchener Verlag, 2011), 33–35.

6   See the comments of Rashi, Rabbi Solomon ben Isaac, and Kimḥi, Rabbi David Kimḥi, A. J. Rosenberg, *1 Samuel* (Judaica Books of the Bible; Brooklyn, NY: Judaica, 1976), 3.

7   David L. Petersen, *Late Israelite Prophecy: Studies in Deuteroprophetic Literature and in Chronicles* (SBLMS 23; Missoula, MT: Scholars Press, 1977), 55–96, esp. 85.

8   Dietrich, *1 Samuel 1–12*, 45–46.

Numbers explains a major change in the designation of priests in ancient Israel. YHWH states to Moses in Numbers 3:11–14; 3:40–43; and 8:13–19 that the Levites would be designated for priestly service in Israel in place of the first-born sons, and the tribe of Levi is formally designated for priestly service in Numbers 17–18. Exodus 34:19–20 (cf. Exod 13:13) states that the first-born of the womb is YHWH's and that the first-born of Israel must be redeemed. It appears that Samuel serves as an example of priestly identity for the first-born son of a mother in early Israel. Such a case would explain the practice of King Jeroboam son of Nebat of Israel, who appointed non-Levites as priests in 1 Kings 12:31.[9]

First Samuel 1:1–3 also introduces the sons of Eli, Hophni and Phineas, who served as priests before YHWH at Shiloh.[10] Their names are actually Egyptian, which provides a clue to their characterization in Samuel as incompetent priests who abuse their holy duties.[11]

First Samuel 1:1–2:11 is fundamentally about Hannah and her role in giving birth to Samuel.[12] Elkanah had two wives: Hannah, who was loved by her husband but remained childless, and Peninnah, the second wife, who bore him children. Ancient Near Eastern law presumed that a wife would provide children for her husband. The concern for children was important in the ancient world, insofar as they provided security for their parents in old age as well as heirs for their land and property. If the wife failed to do so, the husband could divorce her or bring a second wife or concubine into the household to ensure the birth of children (CH 138;

---

[9]   Marvin A. Sweeney, "Samuel's Institutional Identity in the Deuteronomistic History," *Constructions of Prophecy in the Deuteronomistic History and Other Texts*, ed., L. L. Grabbe and M. Nissinen (ANEM 4; Atlanta: Society of Biblical Literature, 2011), 165–174; Sweeney, "The Literary-Historical Dimensions of Intertextuality in Exodus-Numbers," *Second Wave Intertextuality and the Hebrew Bible*, ed. M. Grohmann and H. C. P. Kim (SBL ResBibS 93; Atlanta: Society of Biblical Literature, 2019), 41–52; Sweeney, *Reading the Hebrew Bible after the Shoah: Engaging Holocaust Theology* (Minneapolis, MN: Fortress, 2008), 67–72.

[10] See Aharon Kempinski and Israel Finkelstein, "Shiloh," *NEAEHL* 4:1364–1370; cf. Baruch Halpern, "Shiloh," *ABD* 5:1213–1215.

[11] For example, P. Kyle McCarter, *1 Samuel* (AB 8; Garden City, NY: Doubleday, 1980), 59.

[12] For example, Johanna W. H. van Wijk-Bos, *Reading Samuel: A Literary and Theological Commentary* (ROT; Macon, GA: Smyth and Helwys, 2011), 19–36; J. P. Fokkelman, *Narrative Art and Poetry in the Books of Samuel. Volume 4: Vow and Desire* (Assen: Van Gorcum, 1993), 1–111.

145–147).[13] The first wife had the right to return the second woman to slave status if she attempted to claim equality (cf. Gen 16; 21).

The rivalry between Hannah and Peninnah comes to the forefront in 1 Samuel 1:4–28. The rivalry between a first wife who was barren and a second wife who was fertile indicates a narrative motif to signal that the birth of a son to the barren wife would become a major figure in Israel (cf. Isaac or Joseph). Hannah's misery then provides the basis for demonstrating Eli's incompetence to serve as the high priest at the Shiloh temple. When Elkanah brings his wives and children to Shiloh to observe the holiday, perhaps Sukkot or Passover, Hannah refuses to eat or drink at the festival meal due to Peninnah's taunts. When she walks away from her family to pray to YHWH, Eli takes her to be drunk due to her silent but moving lips. Eli is unable to recognize Hannah's prayer to YHWH, thereby demonstrating his priestly incompetence.

First Samuel 1:20–28 relates how Hannah bore a son and vowed to dedicate him to the service of YHWH. She named the boy Samuel, explaining that she had "asked" YHWH for a son, but this explanation does not represent the meaning of the Hebrew name, Samuel, which is "G-d (El) has granted" or "His Name is G-d (El)." Insofar as the Hebrew verb, *š'l*, "to ask, request," also stands as the basis of the name of Saul (Hebrew, *šā'ûl*), some argue that the Hannah narrative was composed to anticipate the birth and kingship of Saul.[14] It is possible that the narrative was originally concerned with Saul because the focus on Samuel is key to Saul's kingship. Examples of the verb, *š'l*, appear in verses 20, 27 ("asked"), 28 ("lent"), and a second time in verse 28 ("given," the passive form, *šā'ûl*, i.e., the name Saul), but they are all applied to Samuel. After weaning Samuel, Hannah dedicates him to holy service at Shiloh forever (v. 22).

First Samuel 2:1–11 presents Hannah's song as her prayer of thanksgiving to YHWH. First Samuel 2:1a introduces the song in 1 Samuel 2:1b–10, and 1 Samuel 2:11 relates the family's return to Ramah and Samuel's service to YHWH.

---

[13]   G. R. Driver and John C. Miles, *The Babylonian Laws* (2 vols.; Oxford: Clarendon, 1955), 1:290–306; 2:220–221, 2:226–227; J. B. Pritchard, *ANET*, 172.

[14]   Ivar Hylander, *Der literarische Samuel-Saul-Komplex (1. Sam. 1–15) traditionsgeschichtlich untersucht* (Uppsala: Almqvist & Wiksell/Leipzig: Otto Harrassowitz, 1932).

Interpreters view Hannah's song in 1 Samuel 2:1b–10 as a thanksgiving song, a hymn of praise, or a combination of the two.[15] The psalm comprises ten basic strophes in verses 1b, 2, 3, 4, 5, 6, 7, 8, 9, and 10, which display thematic cohesion but variable indication of line and stanza number and length.[16] The strophes appear in three major groupings with distinctive content.

First Samuel 2:1b–2 comprises two first person singular strophes in which Hannah states her praise for YHWH together with the reasons for her praise in 1 Samuel 2:1b. First Samuel 2:2 continues with three statements concerning YHWH's incomparable holiness and strength.

First Samuel 2:3–5 shifts to Hannah's address to her enemies, in which she describes the consequences of YHWH's actions against them. First Samuel 2:3 employs second person masculine plural address forms to warn her enemies against speaking arrogantly, together with reasons for her warnings. First Samuel 2:4 describes the fall of enemy warriors, and 1 Samuel 2:5 describes their desperation for food and the plight of their mothers, who mourn for their sons.

First Samuel 2:6–10 presents a direct statement by Hannah concerning what YHWH has done. First Samuel 2:6 identifies YHWH as the one who brings death and life (Sheol is the underworld of the dead). First Samuel 2:7–8 describes YHWH as the true power over human life and the one who set the world on its pillars. First Samuel 2:9 states that YHWH guards the pious and causes the wicked to perish. First Samuel 2:10 refers to YHWH, whose opponents are shattered by YHWH's thundering and who will rule/judge the earth by supporting the king.

The reference to YHWH's king in 1 Samuel 2:10 looks forward to Samuel's role in anointing Saul (1 Sam 9–11) and later David as king (1 Sam 16). The focus on the king indicates that the song of Hannah may have played a role in an earlier narrative that anticipated Saul as the first King of Israel but was later reworked to anticipate the birth of Samuel.

YHWH's Condemnation of the House of Eli – 1 Samuel 2:12–4:1a

YHWH's condemnation of the House of Eli in 1 Samuel 2:12–4:1a continues the characterization of Eli as an incompetent priest in preparation

---

[15]   Antony F. Campbell, *1 Samuel* (FOTL 7; Grand Rapids, MI/Cambridge, UK: Eerdmans, 2003), 44; cf. Dietrich, *1 Samuel 1–12*, 70.
[16]   Contra Fokkelman, *Vow and Desire*, 75–111.

for the transition in Israel's leadership.[17] It culminates in Samuel's visionary experience, in which he is designated as YHWH's prophet. The text
comprises four major sub-units concerning the sons of Eli in 1 Samuel
2:12–17; Samuel in 1 Samuel 2:18–21; Eli in 1 Samuel 2:22–36; and Samuel
again in 1 Samuel 3:1–4:1a.

First Samuel 2:12–17 is demarcated at the outset by a conjunctive
phrase, "now the sons of Eli were scoundrels," literally, "and the sons of
Eli were sons of Belial (Hebrew, *bĕlîyāʿal*)," in 1 Samuel 2:12. The term
Belial combines two Hebrew elements (i.e., *bĕlî*, "without," and *yāʿal*,
"worth") to create a term that means "worthless." In later texts from the
Dead Sea Scrolls, Pseudepigrapha, and elsewhere, Belial (Greek, Beliar)
functions as a name for an evil angel.[18] The passage focuses on Hophni and
Phineas, who demonstrate their worthless characters by abusing the meat
offerings brought by the people (cf. Lev 7:28–36; Deut 18:3). The text
implicitly condemns Eli for not ensuring that his sons properly carry out
their holy functions.

First Samuel 2:18–21 follows with an introductory conjunctive statement that Samuel was ministering before YHWH, a boy wearing a linen
ephod. The ephod is a linen garment worn by the priests. Exodus
28 describes the ornate ephod worn by the high priest, but the ephod worn
by Eli's sons would have been much simpler.[19] The text emphasizes on a
regular basis that Hannah made her son a little robe, again a reference to a
priestly garment (Exod 28:4, 31–35). Exodus 23:14–17, from an early
Israelite law code,[20] specifies the three major festivals when Elkanah and
his family would travel to Shiloh: Pesach (Passover or Unleavened Bread),
Shavuot (Weeks, Pentecost, or Harvest), and Sukkot (Booths, Tabernacles,
or Ingathering). Whereas Eli was an inadequate father and priest, Hannah
was an ideal mother and adherent of YHWH.

First Samuel 2:22–36 turns to Eli with the introductory conjunctive
statement that Eli was very old, which leads the reader to consider how
he failed to train his sons properly. The text charges them with having sex
with the women who assembled at the door of the sanctuary. Although the
functions of these women are not specified, their assembly at the sanctuary

---

[17]   Sweeney, "Samuel's Institutional Identity"; Sweeney, "Eli: A High Priest."
[18]   T. J. Lewis, "Belial," *ABD* 1:654–656.
[19]   C. Meyers, "Ephod," *ABD* 2:550.
[20]   Cf. C. Meyers, *Exodus*, (New Cambridge Bible Commentary; Cambridge: Cambridge
       University Press, 2005) 156–205.

suggests a role for women at Shiloh and other northern sanctuaries.[21] The text raises theological questions by stating that the reason for the sons' failure to listen to Eli was because YHWH intended to kill them, much as YHWH hardened Pharaoh's heart in the Exodus narrative (see also Isa 6) in order to punish them.[22] First Samuel 2:26 accentuates the difference between the sons of Eli and Samuel, and 1 Samuel 2:27–36 follows with an account of how an unnamed man of G-d condemned Eli and his house for his failure properly to carry out his priestly duties. The man of G-d's oracle is a typical prophetic judgment speech, including the prophetic messenger formula and the grounds for punishment in verses 27–29 and the announcement of judgment, introduced by *lākēn*, "therefore," in verses 30–36.[23] YHWH's statement of the grounds for punishment notes the promise that Eli's ancestor, Aaron, would ascend the altar, offer incense, and wear the ephod before YHWH forever (Exod 28:43; Num 17–18). But the abuse of the sacrificial offerings, particularly taking meat from the offerings before it is presented to YHWH, is the sin for which the House of Eli is to be punished when it Solomon displaces it for the priestly House of Zadok (1 Kgs 1–2, esp. 1 Kgs 2:26–27). Many view this passage as a work of the Deuteronomistic History (DtrH),[24] but it is likely the work of the Solomonic History.[25]

First Samuel 3:1–4:1a returns to a focus on Samuel with an introductory conjunctive verbal statement that the boy Samuel was ministering to YHWH under Eli. Interpreters differ widely on the generic character of this narrative.[26] Some argue that it is a prophetic call narrative,[27] but the account does not include the typical elements of the genre. Others argue

[21]   Marvin A. Sweeney, "Israelite and Judean Religions," *The Cambridge History of Religions in the Ancient World. Volume 1: From the Bronze Age to the Hellenistic Age*, ed. M. Salzman and M. A. Sweeney (Cambridge: Cambridge University Press, 2013), 151–173, esp. 169–170.

[22]   Sweeney, *Reading the Hebrew Bible after the Shoah*, 84–103.

[23]   Marvin A. Sweeney, *Isaiah 1–39, with an Introduction to Prophetic Literature* (FOTL 16; Grand Rapids, MI, and Cambridge, UK: Eerdmans, 1996), 23–25, 533–534.

[24]   Dietrich, *1 Samuel 1–12*, 125–128.

[25]   Marvin A. Sweeney, *1-2 Kings: A Commentary* (OTL; Louisville, KT: Westminster John Knox, 2007), 31–32.

[26]   Dietrich, *1 Samuel 1–12*, 167–169; Victor Avigdor Hurowitz, "Eli's Adjuration of Samuel (1 Samuel III 17–18) in the Light of a 'Diviner's Protocol' from Mari (AEM I/1, 1)," *VT* 44 (1994) 483–497.

[27]   Norman Habel, "The Form and Significance of the Call Narrative," *ZAW* 77 (1965) 297–323; Hurowitz, "Eli's Adjuration of Samuel."

that it is a dream theophany,[28] but there is no clear indication that Samuel is dreaming.

A Closer Look at Samuel's Ordination

The role of Samuel as a first-born son dedicated to priestly service at Shiloh provides the basis for understanding this text as an account of priestly ordination. Priestly ordination accounts appear in Exodus 29 and Leviticus 8, and a Levitical ordination account appears in Numbers 8; indeed, Numbers 8 specifies that the Levites are to be ordained for priestly service in place of the first-born sons of Israel (Num 8:13–19). Exodus 29 and Leviticus 8 specify a seven-day period of ordination in which the ordinands enter the Tent of Meeting, dress in holy vestments, and eat from the ram of ordination, the sin offerings, and other offerings to consecrate themselves and the altar.[29] Numbers 8 specifies that the Levites will purify themselves by washing and appearing before the Tent of Meeting to eat from the Tenuphah offering, the "wave offering" or "elevation offering," which is then dedicated to them for their service in the sanctuary. First Samuel 3:1–4:1a has analogies to all three ordination ceremonies, including the role of the first-born that will be replaced by the Levites, as specified in Numbers 8, and the seven-day incubation for the sons of Aaron in Exodus 29 and Leviticus 8.

But 1 Samuel 3:1–4:1a differs in that Samuel, a first-born son in Israel, incubates in the Shiloh sanctuary, where he has a visionary experience of YHWH. The narrative employs elements of the priestly and Levitical ordination ceremonies to focus on YHWH's plans to decommission the priestly House of Eli. Indeed, other prophetic figures associated with northern Israel also served in priestly functions. Examples include Moses, who is identified as a prophet in Deuteronomy and a Levite in Exodus and Numbers, engages in priestly functions, such as the teaching of Torah and the offering of sacrifices; Elijah, who is identified in 1 Kings 17–2 Kings 2 as a man of G-d, presides over a Sukkot offering at Mt. Carmel in 1 Kings 18; and Elisha, who is also identified as a man of G-d in 2 Kings 2–14, functions as a priestly musician in 2 Kings 3 when he presents oracles during Israel's march against Moab.[30] Likewise, YHWH appears before the high priest when he enters the Holy

---

[28] Robert Gnuse, *The Dream Theophany of Samuel: Its Structure in Relation to Ancient Near Eastern Dreams and Its Theological Significance* (Lanham, MD: University Press of America, 1984).

[29] See also Zechariah 3, in which Joshua ben Jehozadak is dressed in pure garments (i.e., holy vestments) as part of his ordination as high priest in the Jerusalem Temple.

[30] Marvin A. Sweeney, "Prophets and Priests in the Deuteronomistic History: Elijah and Elisha," *Israelite Prophecy and the Deuteronomistic History: Portrait, Reality, and the Formation of a History*, ed. M. R. Jacobs and R. F. Person, Jr.; AIL 14; Atlanta: Society of Biblical Literature, 2013), 35–49.

of Holies on Yom Kippur in Leviticus 16:2. Samuel's visionary experience is configured as an analogy to the accounts of priestly and Levitical ordination in Exodus 29, Leviticus 8, and Numbers 8, thereby enabling him to serve as YHWH's prophet, as indicated in 1 Samuel 3:19–4:1a, as well as YHWH's priest, as indicated by his presentation of holy offerings in 1 Samuel 9:1–10:16 and 13–14.[31]

THE PHILISTINE DEFEAT OF ISRAEL AT APHEK AND THE CAPTURE OF THE ARK – 1 SAMUEL 4:1B–7:17

First Samuel 4:1b–7:1 recounts how Eli and his sons died in Israel's battle with the Philistines at Aphek, during which the Philistines captured the Ark of G-d. The formal structure of the narrative comprises three major sub-units. First Samuel 4:1b–22 recounts the Philistine victory over Israel at Aphek and the capture of the Ark. The narrative begins the *waw*-consecutive verbal statement that "Israel went out to battle against them" (Hebrew, "the Philistines"), which indicates that it follows the account of YHWH's judgment against the House of Eli in 1 Samuel 2:12–4:1a. The second major element appears in 1 Samuel 5:1–7:1, which recounts the Ark's sojourn among the Philistines, including the narrative concerning the inability of the Philistines to subjugate YHWH in 1 Samuel 5:1–12 and the narrative concerning the Philistines' return of the Ark to Israel at Kiriath Jearim in 1 Samuel 6:1–7:1. First Samuel 5:1 begins with a conjunctive *waw*-statement, which shifts the passage from the experience of Israel at the battle of Aphek to an account of the experience of the Philistines after the battle. First Samuel 6:1–7:1 is introduced by the *waw*-consecutive statement, "and the Ark of YHWH was in the country of the Philistines seven months," which indicates that it follows from 1 Samuel 5:1–12. First Samuel 7:2–17 recounts how Samuel protected Israel from the Philistines and judged Israel for the rest of his life.

The Ark narrative concludes in 2 Samuel 6:1–23, which recounts David's transfer of the Ark from Kiriath Jearim to Jerusalem and his refusal to have further marital relations with Michal, thereby ensuring that his own dynastic house would be independent from that of Saul. This episode takes place in the aftermath of his victory over northern Israel at Gibeon and his

---

[31] Sweeney, "Samuel's Institutional Identity"; Sweeney, "Intertextuality in Exodus–Numbers."

reunification of Israel in 2 Samuel 3–4 and following his establishment of Jerusalem as his capital and his defeat of the Philistines in the Emeq Rephaim in 2 Samuel 5. The bifurcated character of the Ark narrative indicates that it serves a redactional function in that 1 Samuel 4:1b–7:1(17) relates the consequences of YHWH's decision to reject the House of Eli. It provides the initial literary frame for the account of Saul's reign by demonstrating that YHWH was absent from Israel until David reunited Israel and transferred the Ark to Jerusalem. Second Samuel 6:1–23 then serves as the concluding frame of the account of Saul's kingdom and David's rise to power by demonstrating how David provided a place for YHWH's presence in Jerusalem following the destruction of the Shiloh temple and thereby enabled YHWH to promise him an eternal dynasty.

Many interpreters follow Rost in arguing that the Ark narrative in 1 Samuel 4–6 and 2 Samuel 6 is an originally independent cultic legend that was incorporated into the larger framework of Samuel and the DtrH, but even those scholars recognize that the present form of the narrative is closely tied to the larger narrative context.[32] The Ark narrative builds upon the condemnation of the House of Eli in 1 Samuel 1–3 and anticipates the establishment of the House of David in 2 Samuel 7.[33]

A Closer Look at the Ark Narrative

The Ark represents the presence of YHWH in Israel. It is described in Exodus 25 as a chest of acacia wood overlaid with gold in which the tablets of the covenant are placed. Two rings are built into each of the long sides of the Ark to enable the Levites to carry the Ark with poles, although 2 Samuel 6 depicts the Ark borne by a wheeled cart. Two cherubs are built atop the cover of the ark; cherubs are composite animal figures that frequently appear alongside royal thrones, city gates, or the entrance to the Holy of Holies of the Jerusalem Temple to represent quasi-divine creatures that guard the throne of the monarch, the city itself, or the inner sanctum of the Temple. Although the Ark functions like an idol in depicting the presence of YHWH, it does not portray YHWH per se. Rather, it represents the throne where YHWH is seated.

Reconstruction of the presumed underlying form of the Ark narrative has proved to be difficult, if not impossible, because it presents the transfer of the Ark from

---

[32] Leonhard Rost, *The Succession to the Throne of David* (Sheffield: Almond Press, 1982, German original, 1926); Antony F. Campbell, *The Ark Narrative* (SBLDS 16; Missoula, MT: Scholars Press, 1975); Campbell, *1 Samuel*, 60–84.

[33] For example, Campbell, *The Ark Narrative*, 165–178; Campbell, *1 Samuel*, 64–69.

Shiloh to the Philistines, from the Philistines to Kiriath Jearim, and finally from Kiriath Jearim to Jerusalem. But scholars point to ancient Near Eastern narratives that portray deities who abandon their home cities and temples when defeated by an enemy; indeed, their idols are typically carried off to the victorious city to celebrate the defeat of the city in question and the subjugation of the defeated deity.[34] Such an agenda underlies the initial account in 1 Samuel 4:1b–22, but the following elements in 1 Samuel 5–6 portray the failure of the Philistines and their gods to subjugate YHWH, prompting them to return the Ark to Israel in Kiriath Jearim. Blenkinsopp demonstrates that Kiriath Jearim is part of a Canaanite coalition led by Gibeon.[35] When David, acting as King of Judah and vassal of the Philistines, defeats the northern Israelite army at Gibeon in 2 Samuel 3, David establishes his own royal house over Judah and Israel and as suzerain over the Philistines, which results in the transfer of the Ark to Jerusalem in Samuel 4–7.

The Account of the Philistines' Defeat of Israel and Capture of the Ark of the Covenant – 1 Samuel 4:1b–22

4 [1b] In those days the Philistines mustered for war against Israel, and Israel went out to battle against them; they encamped at Ebenezer, and the Philistines encamped at Aphek.

[2] The Philistines drew up in line against Israel, and when the battle was joined, Israel was defeated by the Philistines, who killed about four thousand men on the field of battle.

[3] When the troops came to the camp, the elders of Israel said, "Why has the LORD put us to rout today before the Philistines? Let us bring the ark of the covenant of the LORD here from Shiloh, so that he may come among us and save us from the power of our enemies."

[4] So the people sent to Shiloh and brought from there the ark of the covenant of the LORD of hosts, who is enthroned on the cherubim. The two sons of Eli, Hophni and Phinehas, were there with the ark of the covenant of God.

[5] When the ark of the covenant of the LORD came into the camp, all Israel gave a mighty shout, so that the earth resounded.

[34] Campbell, *The Ark Narrative*, 179–191; Patrick D. Miller, Jr., and J. J. M. Roberts, *The Hand of the L-rd: A Reassessment of the Ark Narrative in 1 Samuel* (Baltimore and London: The Johns Hopkins University Press, 1977).

[35] Joseph Blenkinsopp, *Gibeon and Israel: The Role of Gibeon and the Gibeonites in the Political and Religious History of Early Israel* (SOTSMS 2; Cambridge: Cambridge University Press, 1972).

⁶ When the Philistines heard the noise of the shouting, they said, "What does this great shouting in the camp of the Hebrews mean?" When they learned that the ark of the LORD had come to the camp,

⁷ the Philistines were afraid, for they said, "Gods have come into the camp." They also said, "Woe to us! For nothing like this has happened before.

⁸ Woe to us! Who can deliver us from the power of these mighty gods? These are the gods who struck the Egyptians with every sort of plague in the wilderness.

⁹ Take courage, and be men, O Philistines, in order not to become slaves to the Hebrews as they have been to you; be men and fight."

¹⁰ So the Philistines fought; Israel was defeated, and they fled, everyone to his home. There was a very great slaughter, for there fell of Israel thirty thousand foot soldiers.

¹¹ The ark of God was captured, and the two sons of Eli, Hophni and Phinehas, died.

¹² A man of Benjamin ran from the battle line and came to Shiloh the same day, with his clothes torn and with earth upon his head.

¹³ When he arrived, Eli was sitting upon his seat by the road watching, for his heart trembled for the ark of God. When the man came into the city and told the news, all the city cried out.

¹⁴ When Eli heard the sound of the outcry, he said, "What is this uproar?" Then the man came quickly and told Eli.

¹⁵ Now Eli was ninety-eight years old, and his eyes were set, so that he could not see.

¹⁶ The man said to Eli, "I have just come from the battle; I fled from the battle today." He said, "How did it go, my son?"

¹⁷ The messenger replied, "Israel has fled before the Philistines, and there has also been a great slaughter[j] among the troops; your two sons also, Hophni and Phinehas, are dead, and the ark of God has been captured."

¹⁸ When he mentioned the ark of God, Eli fell over backward from his seat by the side of the gate, and his neck was broken, and he died, for he was an old man and heavy. He had judged Israel forty years.

¹⁹ Now his daughter-in-law, the wife of Phinehas, was pregnant, about to give birth. When she heard the news that the ark of God was captured and that her father-in-law and her husband were dead, she bowed and gave birth, for her labor pains overwhelmed her.

²⁰ As she was about to die, the women attending her said to her, "Do not be afraid, for you have borne a son." But she did not answer or give heed.

²¹ She named the child Ichabod, meaning, "The glory has departed from Israel," because the ark of God had been captured and because of her father-in-law and her husband.

²² She said, "The glory has departed from Israel, for the ark of God has been captured."

First Samuel 4:1b–22 recounts the Philistine defeat of Israel in two engagements and the capture of the Ark near Aphek. Aphek is located near the sources of the Yarkon River in the southern Sharon plain at Tel Ras el-ʿAin, some eight miles east of modern Tel Aviv. The site would have been a Philistine city in the eleventh century BCE. It supplies abundant water and overlooks the Aphek Pass, through which the Way of the Sea, the major north–south trade route in the coastal plain, would have lain.[36] Most interpreters identify Ebenezer with Izbet Sartan, ten miles east from modern Tel Aviv across the Aphek Pass near the eastern edge of the Ephraimitic hills, where it guarded the road that leads to Shiloh.[37]

First Samuel 4:1b–22 is demarcated initially by the phrase, "and Israel went out to battle against the Philistines" (NRSVue, "them"), a *waw*-consecutive phrase that shifts the subject from the word of Samuel in 1 Samuel 4:1a to the impending battle between the Philistines and Israel. Many interpreters adapt the reading of the Septuagint, "in those days the Philistines mustered for war against Israel (NRSVue)," based on the contention that the Greek text represents an earlier Hebrew text lost to scribal error.[38] But such a view ignores the fact that the Septuagint's longer and smoother text represents an attempt to correct the problematic Hebrew text in keeping with Hellenistic views concerning the need for a logical and esthetically pleasing text. The text concludes in 1 Samuel 4:22 with the notice that Phineas' daughter-in-law stated that "the glory has departed from Israel for the Ark of G-d has been captured" as she lay dying

[36] David Toshio Tsumura, *The First Book of Samuel* (NICOT; Grand Rapids, MI, and Cambridge, UK: Eerdmans, 2007), 188–189; Pirhiya Beck and Moshe Kochavi, "Aphek," *NEAEHL* 1:62–72; Rafael Frankel, "Aphek," *ABD* 1;275–277, esp. 276; Yigal Levin, "Aphek," *EBR* 2:303–308, esp. 305–307.
[37] Dietrich, *1 Samuel 1–12*, 225; Moshe Kochavi, "Izbet Sartah," *NEAEHL* 2:652–654; Israel Finkelstein, "Izbet Sartah," *ABD* 3:588–589.
[38] For example, McCarter, *1 Samuel*, 103, cf. 97.

following the birth of her son Ichabod. First Samuel 5:1 then employs a conjunctive clause to introduce the account of the Ark's travels in Philistine territory.

First Samuel 4:1b–22 comprises two major sub-units. First Samuel 4:1b–11 recounts Israel's military loss to the Philistines, and 1 Samuel 4:12–22 recounts the consequences of the loss when it is reported to Eli. Upon hearing the bad news, Eli drops dead. His daughter-in-law dies giving birth to a son named Ichabod ("no glory") to signify the loss of the Ark.[39]

First Samuel 4:1b–2 briefly recounts the Philistine victory. By attacking across the Aphek gap, the Philistines seek to take full control of the Way of the Sea and push up the road toward Shiloh to threaten and destroy Israel's central sanctuary. Israel plans to stop them, but there is little indication that the Israelite plan is well thought out and executed. The account mentions about four thousand Israelite casualties, which most interpreters think is exaggerated.[40]

The narrative indicates no real plan of defense other than to react to the Philistines. No leader is mentioned, and the lower casualty count of the first encounter suggests that a relatively small force was sent to counter the Philistines. Israel underestimated the threat posed by the Philistines, who were better equipped with iron weapons, better organized, and likely better trained and led. The Israelite reaction to the initial defeat shows no serious leadership.

The use of literary characterization – or better, caricaturization – becomes evident in the account of the second encounter between Israel and the Philistines in 1 Samuel 4:5–11. Israel brings the Ark to the battle, and the men of Israel break out in shouts of adulation. But the text indicates that the Philistines understand the nature of the threat posed by the presence of YHWH as well. Their fear of YHWH – in contrast to Hophni and Phineas (1 Sam 2:12–26) – motivates the Philistines to fight harder even though they expect to die. The result is a resounding victory for the Philistines; they defeat Israel, kill thirty thousand men, capture the Ark, and kill Hophni and Phineas, as previously determined by YHWH in

[39]   Cf. Campbell , *1 Samuel*, 60–63.

[40]   George E. Mendenhall, "The Census Lists of Numbers 1 and 26," *JBL* 77 (1958) 52–66; McCarter, *1 Samuel*, 105, 107.

1 Samuel 2:12–26. The casualty count is again exaggerated.[41] The larger number suggests that the Israelites took the Philistines more seriously for the second encounter, but there is still no sign of effective leadership or planning.

The account of the consequences of the defeat in 1 Samuel 4:12–22 demonstrates the impact on the House of Eli. Eli is sitting on his seat by the side of the road, apparently at the entrance to Shiloh, awaiting news of the battle and the Ark. As high priest, Eli is responsible for the Ark, but this notice demonstrates his incompetence; he knew the Ark would be in danger, but he was never able to discipline his sons or to talk them – or anyone else – into planning effectively for the defense of the nation. When the Benjaminite runner arrived with his clothing torn and dirt upon his head – both signs of mourning for the loss – Eli, ninety-eight years old and blind, heard the outcry in the city and the messenger's report and fell backward in shock. Because of his excessive weight, he broke his neck and died as a result. The use of the Hebrew term, *kābēd*, "heavy," is telling here, because the term literally means heavy, but it is a play on words with *kābôd*, "honor(ed)," which figures prominently in the next verses. A regnal summation in verse 18b indicates that Eli had ruled/judged Israel for forty years. The formula is analogous to those employed for the years that the land had peace during the time of the Judges (e.g., Judg 3:11; 3:30; 8:28) and the reigns of the Kings of Israel and Judah (e.g., 1 Kgs 2:11; 11:42; 14:21).

First Samuel 4:19–22 recounts the death of Eli's daughter-in-law, the wife of Phineas, as she died in childbirth upon hearing the news. As she lay dying, she heard from the women attending her that she had given birth to a son, and she named the boy Ichabod (Hebrew *'î-kābôd*, "no/without glory") because "the glory has departed from Israel." From a literary standpoint, the deaths of Eli, Hophni, and Phineas, fulfill the prophecy in 1 Samuel 2:12–26 that the men of the House of Eli would not reach old age. It also shows the irony that the death of the "heavy (Hebrew, *kābēd*)" Eli represents the departure of "glory (Hebrew, *kābôd*) from Israel."

Jeremiah mentions the destruction of YHWH's sanctuary at Shiloh in his famous Temple Sermon in Jeremiah 7 (especially Jer 7:12–15). Jeremiah is a priest of the line of Eli, and ultimately Ithamar ben Aaron, due to his descent from Abiathar, who was expelled by Solomon to

---

[41]   McCarter, *1 Samuel*, 107.

Anathoth in 1 Kings 2:26–27 (cf. Jer 1:1–3). The excavations at Sailun, identified as the site of Shiloh, provide clear evidence that Shiloh was destroyed in the mid-eleventh century BCE, although the site of the Israelite temple has not been identified.[42]

The Sojourn of the Ark in Philistine Territory – 1 Samuel 5:1–12

5 **¹ When the Philistines captured the ark of God, they brought it from Ebenezer to Ashdod;**

² then the Philistines took the ark of God and brought it into the house of Dagon and placed it beside Dagon.

³ When the people of Ashdod rose early the next day, there was Dagon, fallen on his face to the ground before the ark of the LORD. So they took Dagon and put him back in his place.

⁴ But when they rose early on the next morning, Dagon had fallen on his face to the ground before the ark of the LORD, and the head of Dagon and both his hands were lying cut off upon the threshold; only the trunk of Dagon was left to him.

⁵ This is why the priests of Dagon and all who enter the house of Dagon do not step on the threshold of Dagon in Ashdod to this day.

⁶ The hand of the LORD was heavy upon the people of Ashdod, and he terrified and struck them with tumors, both in Ashdod and in its territory.

⁷ And when the inhabitants of Ashdod saw how things were, they said, "The ark of the God of Israel must not remain with us, for his hand is heavy on us and on our god Dagon."

⁸ So they sent and gathered together all the lords of the Philistines and said, "What shall we do with the ark of the God of Israel?" The inhabitants of Gath replied, "Let the ark of God be moved on to us." So they moved the ark of the God of Israel to Gath.

⁹ But after they had brought it to Gath, the hand of the LORD was against the city, causing a very great panic; he struck the inhabitants of the city, both young and old, so that tumors broke out on them.

¹⁰ So they sent the ark of the God of Israel to Ekron. But when the ark of God came to Ekron, the people of Ekron cried out, "Why have they brought around to us the ark of the God of Israel to kill us and our people?"

---

[42] Kempinski and Finkelstein, "Shiloh."

¹¹ They sent therefore and gathered together all the lords of the Philistines and said, "Send away the ark of the God of Israel, and let it return to its own place, that it may not kill us and our people." For there was a deathly panic throughout the whole city. The hand of God was very heavy there;

¹² those who did not die were stricken with tumors, and the cry of the city went up to heaven.

First Samuel 5:1–12 recounts the sojourn of the Ark in Philistine territory, during which the Philistines are unable to subjugate YHWH. The narrative is ironically constructed in that the Ark, that is, the presence of YHWH, is taken captive by the Philistines, but YHWH displays mastery over the Philistines and their deities. The Ark's sojourn constitutes a tour of three major inland Philistine cities, Ashdod, Gath, and Ekron, whereas the two coastal cities, Ashkelon and Gaza, are not included. YHWH's tour appears to be analogous to the annual *palu* campaigns conducted by the late-eighth-century Assyrian King Sargon II (721–705 BCE), in which he would gather his army following the conclusion of the harvest and march to each of the major cities subject to his authority to collect their annual tribute.[43] In the end, the Ark would be sent back to Israel in 1 Samuel 6:1–22 with tribute to placate YHWH and to prevent further harm to the Philistines.

The narrative comprises two major parts. The first recounts the interaction between YHWH and the Philistine god, Dagon, in 1 Samuel 5:1–5, in which Dagon repeatedly falls over before the Ark. The second recounts the Ark's tour of the Philistine cities of Ashdod, Gath, and Ekron in 1 Samuel 5:6–12 and the consequences suffered due to the presence of YHWH. The site of ancient Ashdod is located inland from the Mediterranean coast, three and a half miles south of modern Ashdod in Israel. The tell has suffered considerably from modern agricultural work, although the site appears to have flourished from the Middle Bronze and Iron Ages. The site includes a well-fortified and planned city with an acropolis and a lower city; the remains of a small temple and altar date to the late eighth century BCE.[44]

---

[43] Hayim Tadmor, "The Campaigns of Sargon II of Assur: A Chronological Historical Study," *JCS* 12 (1958) 22–40, 77–100.

[44] Moshe Dotan, "Ashdod," *NEAEHL* 1:93–102; David Ben-Shlomo, "Ashdod," *EBR* 2:968–972.

A Closer Look at YHWH and Dagon

YHWH's interaction with Dagon in 1 Samuel 5:1–5 is formulated ironically to demonstrate Dagon's submission to YHWH rather than YHWH's submission to Dagon. Dagon is the chief deity of Ashdod, although he was known in Canaan, Syria, and Mesopotamia from the third through the first millennia BCE.[45] When the Sea Peoples failed in their attempted invasion of Egypt during the reign of Pharaoh Rameses III in 1198–1196 BCE, they withdrew to the Mediterranean coast of south Canaan to meld with the local population and establish the Philistine pentapolis, which proved to be a major rival to ancient Israel during Israel's pre-monarchic period. There is disagreement concerning the meaning of the name Dagon. Some derive it from the Semitic noun *dāg*, "fish," because Dagon is often portrayed with features of a fish. The more commonly accepted explanation, however, is that the name is derived from the Semitic root *dgn*, "grain," insofar as Dagon is a fertility god who provides rain and grain.

The narrative portrays the Philistine capture of the Ark at Ebenezer and its transfer to Ashdod. The Ark was placed next to the statue of Dagon overnight, but in the morning Dagon's statue was found lying face down before the Ark of YHWH in a position that would suggest that Dagon was bowing down to YHWH in worship. Dagon's statue was set aright, but the next morning it was found face down once again. This time, the head and hands of Dagon were broken off, suggesting the damage done to ancient idols when their cities were captured by invaders; the absence of the head and hands imply that the deity in question is no longer able to speak or act, thereby depriving it of divine power. Insofar as the head and hands were lying on the threshold of the temple, the narrative explains that this is the origin of the Philistine practice of avoiding the threshold when entering the temple. More likely, the practice was due to the belief that the threshold was holy due to the presence of divine figures, perhaps understood to be cherubim, who guarded city entrances and royal or divine thrones in the ancient Near East.

The account of the Ark's tour of Ashdod, Gath, and Ekron portrays the consequences for the Philistines of YHWH's presence in the land. The narrative begins with a reference to the "hand of the L-rd" being heavy upon the people of Ashdod. YHWH's punishment against the Philistines appears as the infliction of "tumors" or "hemorrhoids" upon them. The portrayal of such an anal affliction is apparently based on an attempt to mock the Philistines with a malady that would have presented them in an undignified state, although some point to the potential resemblance

---

[45] Lluis Feliu, "Dagon," *EBR* 6:1–3.

between these "tumors" or "hemorrhoids" and the buboes (i.e., swelling of the lymph nodes) characteristic of the bubonic plague in fourteenth-century Europe.[46]

As the "tumors," "hemorrhoids," or "plague" spread among the people of Ashdod, the Ark was sent to Gath, another Philistine city, identified with Tel es-Safi (Zafit), located at the border of the coastal plain and the Judean Shephelah (foothills) by the southern bank of the Elah River, some twelve miles east-southeast of ancient Ashdod.[47] When Gath likewise suffered the outbreak of "tumors" or "hemorrhoids," the Ark was sent to Ekron, a third Philistine city, identified with the site of Tel Miqne, located twenty-two miles southwest of Jerusalem, twelve miles east-northeast of ancient Ashdod and ten miles north of Gath, also on the border between the coastal plain and the Judean Shephelah.[48] When the "tumors" or "hemorrhoids" again broke out among the people of Ekron, the Ark was sent back to "its own place" in Israel because the Philistines were no longer able to withstand the power of YHWH. The panic and outcry to heaven among the Philistines resembles the panic and outcry among the Egyptians during the plagues sent by YHWH that prompted Pharaoh to let the people of Israel go (Exod 12:29–36).[49]

The Philistines' Return of the Ark to Israel – 1 Samuel 6:1–7:1

6 **¹** **The ark of the LORD was in the country of the Philistines seven months.**

² Then the Philistines called for the priests and the diviners and said, "What shall we do with the ark of the LORD? Tell us what we should send with it to its place."

³ They said, "If you send away the ark of the God of Israel, do not send it empty, but by all means return it with a guilt offering. Then you will be healed and forgiven; will not his hand then turn from you?"

⁴ And they said, "What is the guilt offering that we shall send to him?" They answered, "Five gold tumors and five gold mice, according to the

[46]   Ralph W. Klein, *1 Samuel* (WBC 10; Grand Rapids, MI: Zondervan, 2000), 50–51.
[47]   Aren M. Maeir, "Gath," *EBR* 9:1021–1023; Ephraim Stern, "Tel Zafit," *NEAEHL*, 4:1522–1524.
[48]   Trude Dotan and Seymour Gitin, "Tel Miqne (Ekron)," *NEAEHL* 4:1051–1059; Seymour Gitin and Trude Dotan, "Ekron," *EBR* 7:556–560.
[49]   Cf. David Daube, *The Exodus Pattern in the Bible* (London: Faber and Faber, 1963), 73–88.

number of the lords of the Philistines, for the same plague was upon all of you and upon your lords.

5 So you must make images of your tumors and images of your mice that ravage the land and give glory to the God of Israel; perhaps he will lighten his hand on you and your gods and your land.

6 Why should you harden your hearts as the Egyptians and Pharaoh hardened their hearts? After he had made fools of them, did they not let the people go, and they departed?

7 Now then, get ready a new cart and two milch cows that have never borne a yoke, and yoke the cows to the cart, but take their calves home, away from them.

8 Take the ark of the LORD and place it on the cart, and put in a box at its side the figures of gold that you are sending to him as a guilt offering. Then send it off, and let it go its way.

9 And watch: if it goes up on the way to its own land, to Beth-shemesh, then it is he who has done us this great harm; but if not, then we shall know that it is not his hand that struck us; it happened to us by chance."

10 The men did so; they took two milch cows and yoked them to the cart and shut up their calves at home.

11 They put the ark of the LORD on the cart and the box with the gold mice and the images of their tumors.

12 The cows went straight in the direction of Beth-shemesh along one highway, lowing as they went; they turned neither to the right nor to the left, and the lords of the Philistines went after them as far as the border of Beth-shemesh.

13 Now the people of Beth-shemesh were reaping their wheat harvest in the valley. When they looked up and saw the ark, they went with rejoicing to meet it.

14 The cart came into the field of Joshua of Beth-shemesh and stopped there. A large stone was there; so they split up the wood of the cart and offered the cows as a burnt offering to the LORD.

15 The Levites took down the ark of the LORD and the box beside it in which were the gold objects and set them on the large stone. Then the people of Beth-shemesh offered burnt offerings and presented sacrifices on that day to the LORD.

16 When the five lords of the Philistines saw it, they returned that day to Ekron.

¹⁷ These are the gold tumors that the Philistines returned as a guilt offering to the LORD: one for Ashdod, one for Gaza, one for Ashkelon, one for Gath, one for Ekron;

¹⁸ also the gold mice, according to the number of all the cities of the Philistines belonging to the five lords, both fortified cities and unwalled villages. The great stone, beside which they set down the ark of the LORD, is a witness to this day in the field of Joshua of Beth-shemesh.

¹⁹ The descendants of Jeconiah did not rejoice with the people of Beth-shemesh when they greeted the ark of the LORD, and he killed seventy men of them. The people mourned because the LORD had made a great slaughter among the people.

²⁰ Then the people of Beth-shemesh said, "Who is able to stand before the LORD, this holy God? To whom shall he go so that we may be rid of him?"

²¹ So they sent messengers to the inhabitants of Kiriath-jearim, saying, "The Philistines have returned the ark of the LORD. Come down and take it up to you."

7 ¹ And the people of Kiriath-jearim came and took up the ark of the LORD and brought it to the house of Abinadab on the hill. They consecrated his son, Eleazar, to have charge of the ark of the LORD.

First Samuel 6:1–7:1 recounts the Philistines' urgent return of the Ark to Israel at Kiriath Jearim. First Samuel 6:1–7:1 is joined to 1 Samuel 5:1–12 by a *waw*-consecutive verbal formation, "(and) the ark of YHWH was in the country of the Philistines seven months." This sub-unit concludes in 1 Samuel 7:1 with the notice that the people of Kiriath Jearim took the Ark, placed it in the house of Abinadab, and consecrated his son, Eleazar, to oversee the Ark. The narrative comprises two major sub-units: 1 Samuel 6:1–12, which recounts the Philistine return of the Ark to Israel, and 1 Samuel 6:13–7:1, which recounts the reception of the Ark by Israel, first by the people of Beth Shemesh in 1 Samuel 16:13–18, who then sent it to Kiriath Jearim following the deaths of seventy men by the hand of YHWH in 1 Samuel 6:19–7:1.

The account of the Philistines' return of the Ark to Israel is formulated as an ironic and somewhat comical narrative. One form of irony is the characterization of the Philistine priests as diviners in verse 2, an example of caricaturization. The Philistine priests are not true priests in the view of the narrative. Rather, they are "diviners," Hebrew, *qōsĕmîm*, a form of ancient Near Eastern holy men and women whom Israel would consider as illegitimate (Deut 18:9–14).

Another form of irony is the accentuation of the urgency of the Philistines' actions. English readers will not see the distinctive use of the Piel form of the verb *šālaḥ* in verses 2, 3 (twice), 6, and 8. The verb *šālaḥ* normally means "to send" when conjugated in the simple Qal verbal form, but the instances in this text are conjugated in the intensive Piel verbal form, which indicates a sense of urgency that is not represented in the NRSVue and other English translations. Indeed, this urgency in sending the Ark away builds upon the irony and comical portrayal of Dagon falling on his face as if bowing before YHWH's Ark and the Philistines suffering from tumors or bowel afflictions in 1 Samuel 5:1–12. The use of the Piel form of *šālaḥ* indicates that the Philistines cannot wait to get rid of the Ark!

Other elements of irony begin with the characterization of the Ark's sojourn in Philistine territory in verse 1. Although the Philistines had defeated Israel, the tour of the Ark among the Philistine cities takes on the character of a *palu* campaign in which YHWH and the Ark make their rounds to demonstrate YHWH's power over the Philistines. For their part, the Philistines would pay a form of tribute to YHWH as a "guilt offering" when they returned the Ark to Israel. Insofar as the Philistines had defiled the Ark by placing it in the sanctuaries of Dagon, their presentation of the golden "tumors" and "mice" are characterized in verses 4–5 as a "guilt offering", which would then be understood as a form of Philistine atonement for their sins against YHWH. The portrayal of the guilt offering employs a classic Israelite and Judean offering known in Hebrew as the *'āšam*, "guilt offering" (Lev 5:1–13; 7:1–10). The guilt offering is analogous to the *ḥaṭṭā'at*, "sin offering" (Lev 4:1–35; 6:17–23). Whereas the sin offering entails an offense against one of the commandments of YHWH (Lev 4:2), the guilt offering entails a sin of omission, for example, failing to testify when one has knowledge of a case, unknowingly touching the carcass of an unclean animal, or unknowingly touching human uncleanness (Lev 5:1–4). The guilt of the Philistines is that they placed the holy Ark of YHWH in a foreign sanctuary that would be considered unclean in Israel.

The form of the offering (i.e., five "tumors" and five "mice, rats," corresponding to each of the five rulers of the five cities constituting the Philistine pentapolis) is telling because it considers the five lords of the Philistines to be guilty of an offense against YHWH. The Hebrew words employed for these offering (i.e., "tumors" and "mice, rats") are also important. The Hebrew word for "tumor" is a special case of ketiv/qere (i.e., a case where one word is "written," *ketiv.* in Hebrew consonants, but the vowels for another word in Hebrew is "read," *qere,* in its place). The Hebrew word written for "tumors" is *'ōpālîm,* which means "hills, mounds," to indicate a euphemistic reference to "tumors," or "hemorrhoids," whereas the Hebrew word read in its place is *ṭĕḥōrîm,* which means specifically "tumors" or "hemorrhoids." Such a rendition gives greater emphasis to an affliction of the buttocks and thereby contributes to the caricaturization of the Philistines and their suffering.[50] The Hebrew term, *'akbĕrîm,* "mice," may also refer to rats and other vermin, although it is lacking in the LXX.

The reference to mice, rats, or vermin appears to be related to the narrative's use of the Exodus tradition in characterizing YHWH's plagues against the Philistines. The terminology employed in 1 Samuel 6 differs from that of Exodus, but there seems to be some correspondence between the tumors inflicted upon the Philistines, the boils inflicted upon the Egyptians in Exodus 9:8–12, and the role of the vermin or lice in Exodus 8:16–25. The key indication of the use of the Exodus motif is the reference to the hardening of the hearts of the Egyptians and the Pharaoh in verse 6, which is applied to the Philistines in the present text.[51] This reference introduces the suggestion to prepare a new cart of wood pulled by two milch cows that had never borne a yoke and who would be separated from their calves. The new cart would be a suitable conveyance for the Ark of YHWH and the golden guilt offerings. The choice of the two milch cows appears to be conceived by an interest in determining if the plagues and their consequent offerings would in fact be attributed to the will of YHWH. If the cows had never been yoked, they might resist being hitched to the cart, and if their calves were separated from them, they might not proceed to Israel and instead return to their young. But the narrative ensures that the will of YHWH was involved here as the milch cows head immediately for Beth Shemesh.

First Samuel 6:13–7:1 recounts the reception of the Ark of YHWH by Israel, beginning at Beth Shemesh and then Kiriath Jearim. Beth Shemesh is identified with Tel Rumeilah, located by the village of 'Ain Shems, in the northern Shephelah that marks the border between Israel or Judah and the

---

[50]   Tsumura, *1 Samuel,* 208; McCarter, *1 Samuel,* 123.
[51]   Daube, *The Exodus Pattern,* 73–88.

Philistines.[52] The site overlooks the Sorek Valley to its north, which indicates that Beth Shemesh was placed to defend the hill country of Judah from the coastal plain of Philistia. The city is Canaanite in origin, and it was apparently dedicated to the worship of the sun, given the meaning of its name in Hebrew. Its location fifteen miles east of Ekron and twelve and a half miles west of Jerusalem enabled it to protect Judah and Jerusalem from the Philistines.

When the Ark arrived at Beth Shemesh, the people were reaping the wheat harvest. This suggests a time before the festival of Shavuot, "Weeks, Pentecost," which celebrates the conclusion of the wheat harvest (Exod 23:16; Lev 23:15–22; Num 23:26–31; Deut 16:9–12). But the site was unsuitable for YHWH, who struck down seventy men in a town of fifty thousand. Fifty thousand is too large, although it may refer to a district or tribal population.

The choice of Kiriath Jearim for the placement of the Ark is a strategic decision, the significance of which will ultimately be realized with the accession of David to the throne in 2 Samuel 1–8. Kiriath Jearim was located in the Judean hill country about six miles west of Jerusalem at the site of Deir el-`Azar, overlooking modern Abu Ghosh.[53] Formerly known as Kiriath Baal (Josh 15:60; 18:14) or Baalah (Josh 15:9–10; 1 Chr 13:6), Kiriath Jearim is part of a coalition of Canaanite cities led by Gibeon (Josh 9:17), which is depicted in Joshua 9–10 as a Canaanite city that tricked Joshua and Israel into an alliance. That alliance ultimately enabled Israel to conquer southern Canaan, including Jerusalem, according to Joshua 9–10. Gibeon and Kiriath Jearim play an important role in David's rise to power. Following his accession as King of Judah while still a Philistine vassal in 1 Samuel 1–2, David fought a battle with northern Israel, led by Abner under the authority of King Ish-Bosheth (Esh-Baal) ben Saul, at Gibeon in 2 Samuel 3. David's victory at Gibeon led to the assassinations of both Abner by Joab and Ish-Bosheth by two of his Gibeonite army officers and ultimately to Israel's request that he serve as their king. David's victory prompted Gibeon to form an alliance with the newly forming House of David.[54] An important clue to this shift is the Gibeonite demand that

---

[52]   Shlomo Bunimovitz and Zvi Lederman, "Beth Shemesh," *NEAEHL* 1:249–253; Won Lee, "Beth Shemesh," *EBR* 3:1020–1024.
[53]   Ido Koch, "Kiriath Jearim," *EBR* 15:344.
[54]   Blenkinsopp, *Gibeon and Israel*.

David turn over the sons of Saul for execution due to Saul's attempt to destroy them, apparently an attempt to force them into his coalition (2 Sam 21). Once David secured the support of Gibeon, he was able to prompt Israel to submit to his rule. When he secured Jerusalem as his capital to rule both Israel and Judah – and the Gibeonite coalition – David was able to move the Ark from Kiriath Jearim to Jerusalem and thereby declare Jerusalem to be both his holy city and his political capital. The importance of Gibeon to the House of David is evident in 1 Kings 3, where David's son and successor, Solomon, has a vision of YHWH at Gibeon that promises him wisdom, wealth, and power over his enemies at the outset of his reign.

The Ark is placed in the house of Abinadab (1 Sam 7:1), a local Canaanite who lived on a hill. A hill is a suitable site for a sanctuary because it allows for wind to separate grain from chaff when the grain offerings are processed. Abinadab's son, Eleazar, is consecrated as a priest to guard the sanctity of the Ark. Although Eleazar is neither a priest nor a Levite, neither was Samuel (1 Sam 1:1). Insofar as Gibeon and its allies became part of Israel, Eleazar's consecration may provide insight into the evolving Israelite or Judean priesthood.

Samuel's Rule over Israel – 1 Samuel 7:2–17

7 ² From the day that the ark was lodged at Kiriath-jearim, a long time passed, some twenty years, and all the house of Israel lamented after the LORD.

³ Then Samuel said to all the house of Israel, "If you are returning to the LORD with all your heart, then put away the foreign gods and the Astartes from among you. Direct your heart to the LORD and serve him only, and he will deliver you out of the hand of the Philistines."

⁴ So Israel put away the Baals and the Astartes, and they served the LORD only.

⁵ Then Samuel said, "Gather all Israel at Mizpah, and I will pray to the LORD for you."

⁶ So they gathered at Mizpah and drew water and poured it out before the LORD. They fasted that day and said, "We have sinned against the LORD." And Samuel judged the Israelites at Mizpah.

⁷ When the Philistines heard that the Israelites had gathered at Mizpah, the lords of the Philistines went up against Israel. And when the Israelites heard of it, they were afraid of the Philistines.

⁸ The Israelites said to Samuel, "Do not cease to cry out to the LORD our God for us, and pray that he may save us from the hand of the Philistines."

⁹ So Samuel took a sucking lamb and offered it as a whole burnt offering to the LORD; Samuel cried out to the LORD for Israel, and the LORD answered him.

¹⁰ As Samuel was offering up the burnt offering, the Philistines drew near to attack Israel, but the LORD thundered with a mighty voice that day against the Philistines and threw them into confusion, and they were routed before Israel.

¹¹ And the men of Israel went out of Mizpah and pursued the Philistines and struck them down as far as beyond Beth-car.

¹² Then Samuel took a stone and set it up between Mizpah and Jeshanah and named it Ebenezer, for he said, "Thus far the LORD has helped us."

¹³ So the Philistines were subdued and did not again enter the territory of Israel; the hand of the LORD was against the Philistines all the days of Samuel.

¹⁴ The towns that the Philistines had taken from Israel were restored to Israel, from Ekron to Gath, and Israel recovered their territory from the hand of the Philistines. There was peace also between Israel and the Amorites.

¹⁵ Samuel judged Israel all the days of his life.

¹⁶ He went on a circuit year by year to Bethel, Gilgal, and Mizpah, and he judged Israel in all these places.

¹⁷ Then he would come back to Ramah, for his home was there; he administered justice there to Israel and built there an altar to the LORD.

First Samuel 7:2–17 recounts the rule of Samuel over Israel following the deaths of Eli, Hophni, and Phineas at the hands of the Philistines. Many interpreters maintain that 1 Samuel 7:2–17 functions as the introduction to the account of the institution of the monarchy under Saul in 1 Samuel 8–12, largely on the presence of the temporal statement in 1 Samuel 7:1 that some twenty years passed while the Ark remained at Kiriath Jearim and the concern with the leadership of Samuel.[55] But Samuel's rule marks

---

[55]   E.g., Bruce C. Birch, *The Rise of the Monarchy: The Growth and Development of 1 Samuel 7–17* (SBLDS 27; Missoula, MT: Scholars Press, 1976).

the conclusion of the rule of the House of Eli. First Samuel 7:15–17 presents a regnal summary of Samuel's role as ruler of Israel akin to those of the Judges. The failure of his sons to serve adequately as Judges provides the premise for the people's demand for a king in 1 Samuel 8.

First Samuel 7:2–17 comprises three major sub-units: 1 Samuel 7:2–6 recounts Samuel's assumption of leadership following Israel's return to YHWH; 1 Samuel 7:7–14 recounts Samuel's defeat of the Philistines; and 1 Samuel 7:15–17 presents the regnal summary of Samuel's rule. The Deuteronomistic elements in the passage suggest that it was composed as a redactional text that would incorporate the Ark narrative into the larger presentation of the emergence of the monarchy in Israel. Insofar as 1 Samuel shows marked favoritism to David, it would have been composed as part of the Solomonic History.[56]

First Samuel 7:2–6 begins with the notice that the Ark of YHWH remained for twenty years at Kiriath Jearim. Such a period anticipates 2 Samuel 6, when David removes the Ark from Kiriath Jearim and relocates it to Jerusalem, thereby claiming legitimacy for his newly forming dynastic house. The absence of the Ark – and therefore the presence of YHWH – from Israel during the selection and reign of Saul indicates judgment against the House of Saul. Although Saul was selected by YHWH as king, the Bible's recognition of human free will allows Saul to demonstrate his inadequacy for the role and the need for his replacement.

The reference to Israel's lamenting for YHWH in 1 Samuel 7:2 presents a leitmotif for this narrative. Interpreters have struggled over the interpretation of this passage insofar as the verb *nhh* means "to lament." But the significance of the conjugation of this verb in a *waw*-consecutive imperfect niphal form, *wayyinnānû*, appears to have been lost on interpreters. The niphal verb indicates a passive understanding of the verb root (i.e., "and they were lamented"), which indicates that the house of Israel "was aggrieved" at the absence of YHWH from Israel.

Samuel's role in calling for the people to return to YHWH constitutes a first step in the process to address the mourning of Israel over the loss of the battle with the Philistines at Aphek, the deaths of Eli, Hophni, and Phineas, and the absence of the Ark. The first step is to remove the foreign gods (i.e., the Baals and the Astartes) that the people would have followed after the failure of YHWH to deliver them from the Philistines. Baal and

---

[56] Sweeney, *1 and 2 Kings*, 31–32.

Astarte are the Canaanite fertility gods; Baal is the male god of storm and rain, through which he metaphorically impregnates the female Astarte, the goddess of the earth, thereby enabling the growth of agricultural produce, animals, and human beings. These deities also entail political significance, insofar as Israel would have submitted to the rule of foreigners symbolized by adherence to foreign gods.

The assembly at Mizpah is generally identified with Tell en-Naṣbeh, some eight miles northwest of Jerusalem in the territory of Benjamin, although others identify it with Nebi Samwil, located west of Jerusalem near Gibeon.[57] Tell en-Naṣbeh is the more likely location due to its suitability to protect Judah from Israelite encroachment during the reign of King Asa of Judah (1 Kgs 15:22; 2 Chr 16:6). The water libations and fasting also create difficulties. Water libations are associated with Sukkot, "Booths, Tabernacles," to symbolize the onset of the fall rains. Fasting is characteristic of Yom Kippur, observed on 10 Tishri some five days prior to Sukkot on 15 Tishri. It is possible that the account conflated these observances.

The notice that Samuel judged the people at Mizpah in 1 Samuel 7:6 indicates a combined judicial, political, and administrative role, like that of the Judges. The Hebrew verb *šāpaṭ* means "to judge (judicially)" and "to rule (politically and administratively)" in keeping with the Akkadian cognate *shappatum*.

The account of Samuel's defeat of the Philistines in 1 Samuel 7:7–14 points to his political and military role as ruler of Israel. Samuel acts as a priest in presenting an offering to YHWH in keeping with the conceptualization of a holy war fought by Israel. The offering of a suckling lamb as a whole burnt offering is intended to honor YHWH and request YHWH's support for Israel (Lev 1). The route of the Philistine assault may run from the vicinity of Beth Shemesh and up the Emeq Rephaim past Jerusalem and on to Mizpah. YHWH's thundering against the Philistines metaphorically depicts YHWH's fighting on behalf of Israel. The site of Beth Car may be identified with 'Ain Karim three miles west of Jerusalem or Beth Horon twelve miles northwest of Jerusalem.[58] The reference to Ebenezer (i.e., "the stone of help") would have been written as a response to the earlier Philistine defeat of Israel from their camp at Ebenezer in 1 Samuel 4:1;

---

[57] Jeffrey Zorn, "Tell en-Naṣbeh," *NEAEHL* 3:1098-11-2; Patrick M. Arnold, "Mizpah," *ABD* 4:879–881.

[58] McCarter, *1 Samuel*, 146.

5:1. The location of Shen is uncertain, although it might indicate Jeshanah, mentioned in 2 Chronicles 13:19, identified with Burj el-Isaneh located seventeen miles north of Jerusalem on the border between Judah and Israel during the reigns of Abijah of Judah and Jeroboam ben Nebat of Israel.[59] Samuel's victory ensured security for Israel during his rule.

Finally, the regnal summary of Samuel's rule is an adaptation of the regnal résumés of the Kings of Israel and Judah in the Book of Kings.[60] Its appearance here suggests Deuteronomistic authorship, perhaps as part of the Solomonic History. Samuel exercises his rule by making the rounds of his territory at Beth El, Gilgal, and Mizpah, all of which are located in the Ephraimitic and Benjaminite hill country. He asserts his authority much like the later Assyrian rulers did during their *palu* campaigns. His home and capital remain at Ramah.

SAMUEL'S INSTITUTION OF KINGSHIP UNDER SAUL BEN KISH –
1 SAMUEL 8–12

First Samuel 8–12 recounts Samuel's institution of kingship under Saul. This unit is transitional in that it marks the shift in leadership of Israel from the leadership of the priestly House of Eli at Shiloh to a royal dynasty based in the House of Saul ben Kish from the tribe of Benjamin. With the deaths of Eli and his sons, Hophni and Phineas, Samuel emerged as the last ruler of the House of Eli. By the time he reached old age, there was need for a transition in leadership, particularly because Samuel's sons, Joel and Abijah, based in Beer Sheba, proved to be unfit. Saul, however, was selected by YHWH as a concession to the people, who demanded to be ruled by a king like the nations around them. The narratives concerning his selection and reign would ultimately portray him as unfit for his role as king.

A Closer Look at the Emergence of Kingship in Benjamin

The shift in the institutional identity of the leadership of Israel from a priestly house to a royal house is consistent with the evolving character and needs of early Israel. Israel initially comprises a tribal confederation with unstable leadership based upon

---

[59]   Jeffries M. Hamilton, "Jeshanah," *ABD* 3:769.
[60]   Burke O. Long, *1 Kings, with an Introduction to Historical Literature* (FOTL 9; Grand Rapids, MI: Eerdmans, 1984), 259.

local Judges who would emerge in a time of crisis to deliver Israel from a foreign threat. Such a model of leadership is reactive to emergency and demonstrates little sense of appreciation or reflection upon the political, economic, and military needs of a growing nation; indeed, the institution of the Judges evolved from local tribal leadership, particularly as each Judge represents a limited tribal grouping, although the framework narrative of the book of Judges portrays each Judge as the leader of all Israel. But as Israel grew and faced sustained threats from the Philistines and other semi-nomadic peoples who would attack Israel's borders, the need for a more stable and permanent form of leadership became apparent.

The choice of a king from Benjamin makes eminent sense for a tribal federation that potentially includes a number of powerful tribes, such as Ephraim and Judah.[61] Benjamin appears as the smallest of the tribes in Judges 19–21, and it is located between the two major power tribes of the Israelite federation, south of Ephraim and north of Judah. The choice of such a small tribe for royal status creates a balance in power between potentially dominant tribes in that neither Ephraim nor Judah can then control the monarchy; rather, they must compete for influence with other tribes. Such a model is known in medieval Japan, in which the small Yamato clan emerged as the royal clan in the midst of more powerful clans (e.g., the Fujiwara, Tokugawa, and other clans or tribal groups that constituted the Japanese federation). In both Israel and Japan, however, the larger clans would undermine the system by marrying into the royal house, thereby gaining influence and ultimately control over the monarchy. Such would be the case in Israel when David married Michal daughter of Saul and thereby became a member of the House of Saul. David's marriage to Michal would produce no royal heirs, but the absence of Saulide sons for David put him in a position to establish his own dynastic house following the deaths of Saul, Jonathan, and other sons in battle against the Philistines at Mt. Gilboa. The assassination of Esh-Baal, known as Ish-Bosheth son of Saul in 2 Samuel 3, and the Gibeonite demand for the lives of Saul's heirs in 2 Samuel 20, likewise helped to clear the way for David to take control of Israel as a surviving member of the House of Saul who would establish his own dynastic house through the births of sons to his other wives.

First Samuel 8–12 appears to be a redactional unit in which very favorable accounts of Saul in 1 Samuel 9:1–10:16 and 11:1–15 are framed with critical accounts in 1 Samuel 8:1–22; 10:17–27; and 12:1–25. Many

---

[61]   Marvin A. Sweeney, "The Origins of Kingship in Israel and Japan: A Comparative Analysis," *Occasional Papers of the Institute for Antiquity and Christianity* 33 (1995), to be republished in *Visions of the Holy* (ResBibS XX; vol. 2; Atlanta: Society of Biblical Literature, in press).

interpreters follow Noth in viewing the resulting narrative as a Deuteronomistic composition based on its hostility to kingship in general and Saul in particular, as well as its emphasis on the need for the king to observe YHWH's expectations.[62] Although some Deuteronomistic influence is apparent, particularly in 1 Samuel 12, the text does not appear to have been edited in its entirety to serve the needs of the DtrH. The portrayal of the people's demand for a king as a rejection of YHWH's rule and the demands of the king for military and palace service, taxation of produce, flocks, and property is not fully consistent with Deuteronomic concerns. The so-called Torah of the King in Deuteronomy 17:14–20 does not view kingship as a rejection of YHWH's rule, although it does stipulate that the king should study YHWH's Torah daily under the supervision of the Levitical priests. Furthermore, it does not object to the needs of the state as depicted in 1 Samuel 8; rather, it points to the potential excesses of a king for gold, women, horses, etc., such as those demonstrated by Solomon in 1 Kings 3–11, and it thereby holds out for righteous kingship. Indeed, the critique of Saul inherent in the present form of 1 Samuel 8–12 appears to prepare the reader for the rejection of Saul and the rise of David. The foundational editing of 1 Samuel 8–12, which undermines the positive portrayals of Saul, appears to be the work of the Solomonic History, insofar as Solomon is the beneficiary of the rejection of the House of Saul and the establishment of the House of David. Later editions of Israel's history, such as the Jehu Dynastic History and the Deuteronomistic, Hezekian, Josian, and Exilic Histories would have viewed the rejection of Saul as essential to their own interests.[63]

First Samuel 8–12 is demarcated by the introductory notice concerning Samuel's old age and the disqualification of his sons for Israel's leadership in 1 Samuel 8:1–3.[64] The sequence concludes with Samuel's farewell speech in 1 Samuel 12 and the introductory regnal formula for Saul's reign in 1 Samuel 13:1, which introduces the account of Saul's reign. The unit comprises three major sub-units, namely, the people's demand for a king in 1 Samuel 8; the selection of Saul as king in 1 Samuel 9–11; and Samuel's farewell speech in 1 Samuel 12. First Samuel 9–11, in turn, includes three

---

[62]   Martin Noth, *The Deuteronomistic History* (JSOTSup 15; Sheffield: JSOT Press, 1981), 47–48; cf. Hans Jochen Boecker, *Die Beurteilung des Königtums in den deuteronomistischen Abschnitten des 1. Samuelbuches* (WMANT 31; Neukirchen-Vluyn: Neukirchener Verlag, 1969).
[63]   Sweeney, *1 and 2 Kings*, 4–32.
[64]   Sweeney, *Tanak*, 207–214.

sub-units: Samuel's anointing of Saul in 1 Samuel 9:1–10:16; the people's selection of Saul in 1 Samuel 10:17–27; and Saul's deliverance of Jabesh Gilead in 1 Samuel 11.

The People's Demand for a King – 1 Samuel 8:1–22

8 ¹ When Samuel became old, he made his sons judges over Israel.

² The name of his firstborn son was Joel, and the name of his second was Abijah; they were judges in Beer-sheba.

³ Yet his sons did not follow in his ways but turned aside after gain; they took bribes and perverted justice.

⁴ Then all the elders of Israel gathered together and came to Samuel at Ramah

⁵ and said to him, "You are old, and your sons do not follow in your ways; appoint for us, then, a king to govern us, like other nations."

⁶ But the thing displeased Samuel when they said, "Give us a king to govern us." Samuel prayed to the LORD,

⁷ and the LORD said to Samuel, "Listen to the voice of the people in all that they say to you, for they have not rejected you, but they have rejected me from being king over them.

⁸ Just as they have done to me from the day I brought them up out of Egypt to this day, forsaking me and serving other gods, so also they are doing to you.

⁹ Now then, listen to their voice; only, you shall solemnly warn them and show them the ways of the king who shall reign over them."

¹⁰ So Samuel reported all the words of the LORD to the people who were asking him for a king.

¹¹ He said, "These will be the ways of the king who will reign over you: he will take your sons and appoint them to his chariots and to be his horsemen, and to run before his chariots,

¹² and he will appoint for himself commanders of thousands and commanders of fifties and some to plow his ground and to reap his harvest and to make his implements of war and the equipment of his chariots.

¹³ He will take your daughters to be perfumers and cooks and bakers.

¹⁴ He will take the best of your fields and vineyards and olive orchards and give them to his courtiers.

¹⁵ He will take one-tenth of your grain and of your vineyards and give it to his officers and his courtiers.

¹⁶ He will take your male and female slaves and the best of your cattle and donkeys and put them to his work.

¹⁷ He will take one-tenth of your flocks, and you shall be his slaves.

¹⁸ And on that day you will cry out because of your king, whom you have chosen for yourselves, but the LORD will not answer you on that day."

¹⁹ But the people refused to listen to the voice of Samuel; they said, "No! We are determined to have a king over us,

²⁰ so that we also may be like other nations and that our king may govern us and go out before us and fight our battles."

²¹ When Samuel heard all the words of the people, he repeated them in the ears of the LORD.

²² The LORD said to Samuel, "Listen to their voice and set a king over them." Samuel then said to the Israelites, "Each of you return home."

First Samuel 8:1–22 presents the people's demand for a king when Samuel grows old and his sons are unfit for rule. This chapter portrays the people's demand for a king as a rejection of YHWH's rule, thereby influencing the reader's view of the positive narratives concerning Saul's anointing by Samuel in 1 Samuel 9:1–10:6 and his deliverance of Jabesh Gilead in 1 Samuel 11.

The narrative begins in 1 Samuel 8:1–3, which states the need for transition by noting Samuel's old age and his sons' lack of qualification for leadership. The narrative does not mention how old Samuel might be, but Numbers 4:3, 23, 25, 30 specify that the age of priestly service for those priestly families that perform the service of the Tent of Meeting is thirty to fifty years, and Numbers 8:23–26 specifies that the Levites who assist their brothers serve from age twenty-five through age fifty. The texts from Numbers agree that the age of priestly retirement is fifty. The passage notes that Samuel's sons, Joel and Abijah, who judged in Beer Sheba, were unfit for office. Their presence in Beer Sheba suggests some effort by northern Israel to extend its rule over all of Judah, insofar as Beer Sheba marks the southern boundary of the tribe of Judah.⁶⁵

---

⁶⁵ Ze'ev Herzog, "Tel Beersheba," *NEAEHL* 1:167–173; cf. 1 Sam 3:2; 2 Sam 3:3:10; 17:11; 24:15; 1 Kgs 5:5.

A Closer Look at the People's Demand for a King

First Samuel 8:4–22 presents the people's demand for a king when the elders of Israel travel to Ramah to meet with Samuel. The elders of Israel are a body of tribal representatives who serve alongside the king and the priests of northern Israel to make covenants with G-d, king, and perhaps others (Exod 24:1–11; Num 11:16–30; Deut 27:1; 31:9; 2 Sam 5:3; 2 Kgs 23:1–3).[66] They number seventy members and may be the precursors to the Rabbinic Sanhedrin. The first stage of the encounter appears in verses 4–9, in which the elders make their demand for a king because Samuel's sons are corrupt. Their demand greatly disturbs Samuel, who is compelled to consult with YHWH by prayer concerning the matter. YHWH instructs Samuel to grant their demand, but the passage hardly configures YHWH's acquiescence as approval of the elders' request. YHWH reassures Samuel that they are not rejecting him as leader but rejecting YHWH. YHWH's response is apparently tied to an understanding of Israel's resistance to YHWH, first through the wilderness rebellion tradition in Exodus 15–16; 32–34; and Numbers 11–25, and later through the repeated instances of apostasy on the part of Israel as presented throughout the book of Judges. It is noteworthy that Israel's apostasy in Judges is motivated by their failure to eliminate all the Canaanites as instructed by YHWH and YHWH's decision to leave the Canaanites as a snare to Israel to follow foreign gods (Judg 3:1–4).

Samuel's response to the elders in verses 10–18 points out the practices of a king, beginning with drafting Israel's sons for military service. The king will appoint them as commanders of military units, including cavalry and charioteers who will provide a royal entourage. The king will require their sons to plow his fields, reap the king's harvest, and manufacture weapons and equipment for the military. The daughters of Israel will be pressed into royal service as perfumers to make cosmetics for the royal household and to serve as cooks and bakers. The king will tax the fields, orchards, and vineyards, taking a ten percent share of all the people's produce. He will take the people's own slaves (i.e., debt slaves; Exod 21:1–11) for royal service. He will also take one tenth of the people's flocks and herds.

Many view Samuel's statements about the monarchy as a critique of an oppressive institution. But Samuel states the necessary support due to a monarchy that is responsible for the defense and well-being of its subjects. Given the threat posed to Israel by the Philistines, the establishment of a royal administration provides a more stable organization for the nation that facilitates self-defense. Samuel's warnings do not correspond to the issues named in Deuteronomy 17:14–20, which takes up the excesses and abuses in which a king might engage.

---

[66] Timothy M. Willis, "Elders," *EBR* 7:585–586.

The response of the elders, here identified as "the people," appears in verses 19–22 in the form of a firm rejection of Samuel's warnings. YHWH advises Samuel to grant their demand, and the next episodes present his efforts to appoint Saul ben Kish as King of Israel.

Samuel's Anointing of Saul as King of Israel – 1 Samuel 9:1–10:16

9 ¹ There was a man of Benjamin whose name was Kish son of Abiel son of Zeror son of Becorath son of Aphiah, a Benjaminite, a man of wealth.

² He had a son whose name was Saul, a handsome young man. There was not a man among the Israelites more handsome than he; he stood head and shoulders above everyone else.

³ Now the donkeys of Kish, Saul's father, had strayed. So Kish said to his son Saul, "Take one of the young men with you; go and look for the donkeys."

⁴ He passed through the hill country of Ephraim and passed through the land of Shalishah, but they did not find them. And they passed through the land of Shaalim, but they were not there. Then he passed through the land of Benjamin, but they did not find them.

⁵ When they came to the land of Zuph, Saul said to the young man who was with him, "Let us turn back, or my father will stop worrying about the donkeys and worry about us."

⁶ But he said to him, "There is a man of God in this town; he is a man held in honor. Whatever he says always comes true. Let us go there now; perhaps he will tell us about the journey on which we have set out."

⁷ Then Saul replied to the young man, "But if we go, what can we bring the man? For the bread in our sacks is gone, and there is no present to bring to the man of God. What have we?"

⁸ The young man answered Saul again, "Here, I have with me a quarter shekel of silver; I will give it to the man of God, to tell us our way."

⁹ (Formerly in Israel, anyone who went to inquire of God would say, "Come, let us go to the seer," for the one who is now called a prophet was formerly called a seer.)

¹⁰ Saul said to the young man, "Good; come, let us go." So they went to the town where the man of God was.

¹¹ As they went up the hill to the town, they met some young women coming out to draw water and said to them, "Is the seer here?"

¹² They answered, "Yes, there he is just ahead of you. Hurry; he has come just now to the town because the people have a sacrifice today at the shrine.

¹³ As soon as you enter the town, you will meet him before he goes up to the shrine to eat. For the people will not eat until he comes, since he must bless the sacrifice; afterward those eat who are invited. Now go up, for you will meet him immediately."

¹⁴ So they went up to the town. As they were entering the town, they saw Samuel coming out toward them on his way up to the shrine.

¹⁵ Now the day before Saul came, the LORD had revealed to Samuel:

¹⁶ "Tomorrow about this time I will send to you a man from the land of Benjamin, and you shall anoint him to be ruler over my people Israel. He shall save my people from the hand of the Philistines, for I have seen the suffering of my people, because their outcry has come to me."

¹⁷ When Samuel saw Saul, the LORD told him, "Here is the man of whom I spoke to you. He it is who shall rule over my people."

¹⁸ Then Saul approached Samuel inside the gate and said, "Tell me, please, where is the house of the seer?"

¹⁹ Samuel answered Saul, "I am the seer; go up before me to the shrine, for today you shall eat with me, and in the morning I will let you go and will tell you all that is on your mind.

²⁰ As for your donkeys that were lost three days ago, give no further thought to them, for they have been found. And on whom is all Israel's desire fixed, if not on you and on all your ancestral house?"

²¹ Saul answered, "I am only a Benjaminite, from the least of the tribes of Israel, and my family is the humblest of all the families of the tribe of Benjamin. Why then have you spoken to me in this way?"

²² Then Samuel took Saul and the young man and brought them into the hall and gave them a place at the head of those who had been invited, of whom there were about thirty.

²³ And Samuel said to the cook, "Bring the portion I gave you, the one I asked you to put aside."

²⁴ The cook took up the upper thigh and set it before Saul. Samuel said, "See, what was reserved is set before you. Eat, for it was kept for you for this appointed time, so that you might eat with the guests."

So Saul ate with Samuel that day.

²⁵ When they came down from the shrine into the town, a bed was spread for Saul on the roof, and he lay down to sleep.

²⁶ Then at the break of dawn Samuel called to Saul upon the roof, "Get up, so that I may send you on your way." Saul got up, and both he and Samuel went out into the street.

²⁷ As they were going down to the outskirts of the town, Samuel said to Saul, "Tell the young man to go on before us, and when he has passed on, stop here yourself for a while, that I may make known to you the word of God."

10 ¹ Samuel took a vial of oil and poured it on his head and kissed him; he said, "The LORD has anointed you ruler over his people Israel. You shall reign over the people of the LORD, and you will save them from the hand of their enemies all around. Now this shall be the sign to you that the LORD has anointed you ruler over his heritage:

² When you depart from me today you will meet two men by Rachel's tomb in the territory of Benjamin at Zelzah; they will say to you, 'The donkeys that you went to seek are found, and now your father has stopped worrying about them and is worrying about you, saying: "What shall I do about my son?"'

³ Then you shall go on from there further and come to the oak of Tabor; three men going up to God at Bethel will meet you there: one carrying three kids, another carrying three loaves of bread, and another carrying a skin of wine.

⁴ They will greet you and give you two loaves of bread, which you shall accept from them.

⁵ After that you shall come to Gibeath-elohim, at the place where the Philistine garrison is; there, as you come to the town, you will meet a band of prophets coming down from the shrine with harp, tambourine, flute, and lyre playing in front of them; they will be in a prophetic frenzy.

⁶ Then the spirit of the LORD will possess you, and you will be in a prophetic frenzy along with them and be turned into a different person.

⁷ Now when these signs meet you, do whatever you see fit to do, for God is with you.

⁸ And you shall go down to Gilgal ahead of me; then I will come down to you to present burnt offerings and offer sacrifices of well-being. Seven days you shall wait, until I come to you and show you what you shall do."

⁹ As he turned away to leave Samuel, God gave him another heart, and all these signs were fulfilled that day.

¹⁰ When they were going from there to Gibeah, a band of prophets met him, and the spirit of God possessed him, and he fell into a prophetic frenzy along with them.

¹¹ When all who knew him before saw how he prophesied with the prophets, the people said to one another, "What has come over the son of Kish? Is Saul also among the prophets?"

¹² A man of the place answered, "And who is their father?" Therefore it became a proverb, "Is Saul also among the prophets?"

¹³ When his prophetic frenzy had ended, he went home.

¹⁴ Saul's uncle said to him and to the young man, "Where did you go?" And he replied, "To seek the donkeys, and when we saw they were not to be found, we went to Samuel."

¹⁵ Saul's uncle said, "Tell me what Samuel said to you."

¹⁶ Saul said to his uncle, "He told us that the donkeys had been found." But about the matter of the kingship, of which Samuel had spoken, he did not tell him anything.

First Samuel 9:1–10:16 presents a favorable account of Samuel's anointing of Saul son of Kish as the first King of Israel. The narrative has a mythic quality: it presents Saul as an unknowing hero who sets out on a journey to find his father's lost asses but instead finds himself selected by YHWH to serve as Israel's first king.⁶⁷ There is an atmosphere of anticipation and hope built around the new king; Saul will surely deliver Israel from its Philistine oppressors. YHWH could not be wrong in selecting this handsome and tall young man from a leading family in Benjamin.

The narrative appears to have been written for a very different context. Whereas 1 Samuel 7 presents a critical account of the people's demand for a king as a rejection of YHWH, this account portrays the selection of Saul as a favorable move by YHWH and Samuel that will result in freedom for Israel from Philistine oppression. This narrative must have appeared in an earlier written or oral form that celebrated the selection of Saul as King of Israel. It builds upon 1 Samuel 1–3; 7, where the portrayal of Samuel's birth to his previously barren mother, Hannah, includes numerous references to Hannah's "asking" for a son from YHWH, a word play on Saul's Hebrew name, *šā'ûl*, which appears in several noun and verb forms in the narrative,

---

⁶⁷ Cf. Joseph Campbell, *The Hero with a Thousand Faces* (Princeton: Princeton University Press, 1968).

indicating that it was originally written about Saul (1 Sam 1:17 [twice], 27 [twice], 28; 2:20).

A Closer Look at Saul's Lack of Qualities for Leadership

Saul would prove to be a failure as the King of Israel as he was unable to defend his people from the Philistines, threatened Samuel, spent his time in futile attempts to subjugate David, and ultimately prompted YHWH to recognize the need to select David as Israel's king in Saul's place. Saul's naïve character already appears in this account. He displays little in the way of leadership qualities, appears to be clueless about his selection as king, and needs to take advice from the servant boy who accompanies him on the search for his father's lost asses. The seeds of Saul's failure are already apparent in this narrative, although elements of the surrounding literary context (e.g., Saul's reluctance to come forward when selected as king in 1 Samuel 10:17–27, Samuel's warnings to observe YHWH's expectations in 1 Samuel 12, and Saul's poor judgment and willful disregard of YHWH's expectations in 1 Samuel 13–15) make it clear that YHWH must have been wrong in selecting Saul as king. Although 1 Samuel 9:1–10:16 may well have originated in the court of King Saul, the critique of Saul evident in 1 Samuel appears to be the product of the Solomonic History.

The narrative includes three major sub-units. First is the introduction to Saul in 1 Samuel 9:1–2. Second is Saul's pursuit of his father's lost asses and his anointing as king by Samuel in 1 Samuel 9:3–10:9. This sub-unit is further divided into three episodes: Saul's search for his father's lost asses in 1 Samuel 9:3–14; YHWH's communication with Samuel concerning Saul in 1 Samuel 9:15; and Samuel's meeting with Saul in 1 Samuel 9:16–10:9. The third sub-unit presents Saul's departure from Samuel, his prophesying, and his return home in 1 Samuel 10:10–16.

The introduction to the narrative in 1 Samuel 9:1–2 makes several important points concerning the identity of Saul. His father is Kish, a man of wealth from the tribe of Benjamin who is descended from a long line of ancestors, identified as Abiel, Zeror, Becorath, and Aphiah. Kish's identity as a man of wealth indicates that he possesses substantial holdings in land, cattle, and sheep. It provides no details concerning his ancestors other than that they may be traced back for four generations, which suggests that they had the opportunity to secure their property and resources. Kish is from Benjamin, the smallest tribe in Israel, and both Kish and his tribal peers would have to defend their interests against incursions by other more powerful tribes, such as Ephraim, located immediately to the north of Benjamin, and Judah, located immediately to the south. The name Benjamin means "son of the south," which suggests that it is positioned on the southernmost boundaries of what would later be known as the northern kingdom of Israel; indeed, when David takes control of Judah and goes to war with Israel in 2 Samuel 2–5, Israel appears already to constitute the northern tribes of Israel. The introduction describes Saul as a handsome young man, but it says nothing about his intelligence or his capacity to lead.

The account of Saul's search for his father's lost asses and his anointing by Samuel comprises three major episodes, each of which is defined by the focus on a major character. Saul is the focus of attention in the account of his search for his father's lost asses in 1 Samuel 9:3–14. YHWH is the focus of attention in 1 Samuel 9:15–16, informing Samuel that the future King of Israel, a man from Benjamin, will arrive the following day. And Samuel is the focus in his anointing of Saul in 1 Samuel 9:17–10:9.

Saul's search for his father's lost asses in 1 Samuel 9:3–14 posits a mythic journey for a relatively common and mundane purpose that ultimately surprises Saul, with the unexpected outcome of being chosen by YHWH as the King of Israel. Kish shows a commanding presence by giving relatively direct and brief commands to his son: "take one of the boys with you, go look for the donkeys." Kish perhaps already understands from experience that his son needs clear and concise direction, just as the reader will come to understand his lack of leadership skills. The Hebrew term na'ar, "boy," generally refers to an adolescent who would have been a servant in the extended family of Kish. Although such a figure would have been normally subservient to the family, he appears as more of a peer to the young Saul and even takes charge of the search when they are not able to find the lost asses even after a lengthy journey through the land. The search extends through several regions that begin in the southern portions of the territory of Ephraim, including Shalishah and Shaalim, before extending south into Benjamin, until they return to Zuph in the hills of Ephraim, where Samuel's father, Elkanah, lived (cf. 1 Sam 1:1).[68]

The arrival of Saul and his servant in the territory of Zuph provides the opportunity to consult a seer. The boy makes this proposal; Saul does not come up with the idea. It is striking that the boy has some money with him. As a servant of the household, he would not likely have his own money to

---

[68] See McCarter, *1 Samuel*, 163, who provides a convenient map that traces the route taken by Saul and his servant.

spend on an attempt to retrieve his master's lost asses. It seems more likely that Kish gave him the money in case the two needed cash for some purpose. The fact that Saul has no money – or at least does not volunteer to spend any – might suggest that his father would not trust him with cash. Cash economies were already known in international trade during the Assyrian period; local cash transactions cannot be excluded for earlier periods.[69]

The narrative explains the reference to the man of G-d, which is especially associated with northern peripheral prophets or mantic figures, such as Elijah and Elisha.[70] Insofar as their purpose is to make an inquiry of the man of G-d to ascertain the location of the lost asses, the title fits. But the narrative would be read by southern Judean readers as well, who would be better acquainted with terms such as the earlier "seer" and the later "prophet."

The episode in 1 Samuel 9:11–14, in which Saul and the servant encounter girls coming out to draw water as they climb the ascent to the city, identifies Samuel as the "man of G-d." The approach to an ancient city would typically be an ascent as ancient Israelite cities were generally situated on tells, mounds formed by the repeated process of building and rebuilding a city atop the ruins of its older layers. Indeed, such a structure enhances the defenses of the city as attackers would need to advance uphill, subjecting themselves to the arrows, spears, and slings of the defenders. Talmud b. Berakot 48b characterizes the girls as "talkative" due to Saul's good looks.[71] Alter deems such a comment to be "misogynist," but young men are rarely shy about chatting up girls. What better way is there for travelers to find a prominent figure?

First Samuel 9:15–16 focuses on YHWH's communication with Samuel on the previous day to alert him to the fact that the Benjaminite man who is about to visit him is to be anointed as the new King of Israel. YHWH's expressed confidence in Saul's ability to deliver the nation is especially striking, particularly since he will ultimately fail to do so. But the narrative

---

[69] Contra. A. Graeme Auld, *1 and 2 Samuel: A Commentary* (OTL; Louisville, KY: Westminster John Knox, 2011), 104.

[70] Cf. David L. Petersen, *The Roles of Israel's Prophets* (JSOTSup 17; Sheffield: JSOT Press, 1981), 40–50, who notes that later literature in Deuteronomy, Joshua, Chronicles, and Ezra-Nehemiah identify figures such as Moses and David as men of G-d. Earlier prophetic legends employ the term for Elijah, Elisha, and other figures.

[71] Robert Alter, *The David Story* (New York and London: Norton, 1999), 49.

allows for human free will; humans have the capacity to act as they will, and Saul is no exception.

First Samuel 9:17–10:13 focuses on Samuel and his anointing of Saul as the new King of Israel. YHWH informs Samuel that Saul is the man mentioned the day before. Hence, Samuel approaches Saul knowing who he is, but Saul does not know who Samuel is, insofar as he asks Samuel how to find the seer. Samuel identifies himself and immediately assures Saul that the lost asses have been found. And why not? He is a seer, and he knows everything, including the fact that Saul's father is now worried because his son has not yet returned home. Even when Samuel suggests that all Israel awaits him, Saul diminishes himself by claiming that he is from the smallest clan of the smallest tribe in Israel (i.e., Benjamin). Why would anyone think him to be worthy of attention? Saul's characterization in 1 Samuel portrays him as a man who does not provide adequate leadership for his people – and he knows it.

Samuel does not answer Saul's question but takes him into the hall where approximately thirty invited guests have come to eat the sacrifice made that day. This would be a *zebah šĕlāmîm*, "a sacrifice of well-being" or "peace offering," from which the priests and people may eat (Lev 3), or perhaps a votive offering. Although Samuel is a member of the House of Eli, he treats Saul not only as a favored guest but as a priest who has the right to the right thigh portion normally reserved for YHWH and the priests (Exod 29:22; Lev 7:34). The kings of northern Israel, such as David's sons (2 Sam 8:18), Solomon (1 Kgs 8), and Jeroboam ben Nebat (1 Kgs 13), are sometimes named as priests or conduct themselves as such. Insofar as northern Israel had somewhat different practices from those of southern Judah, it may well be that Samuel acts in his capacity as a priest to give the priestly portion to Saul as the next King of Israel.[72]

Once the invited guests depart, Samuel anoints Saul with oil as the next King of Israel. Olive oil is a cleansing agent in the ancient world, especially when sweet-smelling spices are mixed in. Anointing is a symbol of purity and status. He then informs Saul of signs that will verify his new-found and unexpected status. Saul will pass by the Tomb of Rachel in the territory of Benjamin. Although the site of the Tomb of Rachel is south of Jerusalem on the way to Bethlehem in Judah (Gen 35:19), Joshua 18:28 claims that Jebus or Jerusalem is part of the territory of Benjamin, whereas Joshua

---

[72] Cf. Sweeney, "Israelite and Judean Religions."

15:63 indicates that Judah possessed Jerusalem, even though they were unable to expel the Jebusites.[73] Apparently, Jerusalem shifted hands at some point in Israel's history from Benjamin to Judah, perhaps at the outset of David's reign when he made Jerusalem his capital. The exact location is identified as Zelzah, which is unknown. Samuel tells Saul that there he will meet two men who will inform him that his father's lost asses have been found and that Kish is now worried about his son, who has been absent for far too long. Second, Saul will continue to the Oak of Tabor in Benjamin, where the tomb of Deborah, Rachel's nurse, is located (Gen 35:8). There, three men carrying three goats, three squares of bread, and a jar of wine on their way to Beth El will meet him and offer him two squares of bread, which he should take. Once again, he is given the portion of a priest (Num 18, esp. v. 11). From there, he will continue to Gibeath-Elohim, likely identified with Gibeah, Saul's capital in Benjamin. Gibeah is often identified with Tel el-Ful, located three miles north of Jerusalem, although this identification is disputed.[74] Gibeah is also the site of the rape and murder of the Levite's concubine in Judges 19–21, a narrative composed to discredit Saul.[75] It is the site of the Philistine prefect or garrison, indicating Philistine subjugation of Israel. There, Saul will meet a band of prophets who will play music and prompt Saul to be overtaken with prophetic ecstasy on the way to Gilgal. The site of Gilgal remains unknown.[76] The text indicates that YHWH will give Saul another heart and that Saul will become another man and prophesy, an indication of prophetic trance possession, which was well known in the ancient world. Here, it functions as a sign that G-d is with Saul. When Saul departs from Samuel, all of these signs are fulfilled. When he falls to the ground and prophesies in prophetic ecstasy, the people ask, "Is Saul also among the prophets?" giving rise to a popular association of Saul with prophetic circles (cf. 1 Sam 19:19–24). The question, "who are their fathers?" suggests that Saul was one of the prophets. Together, these signs fulfill Samuel's anointing of Saul as King of Israel. Although NRSVue states that "Saul

---

[73] Joshua 15:8 indicates that Judah's northern boundary is located along the southern flank of Jerusalem along the Hinnom Valley and the northern edge of the Rephaim Valley.

[74] Patrick M. Arnold, *Gibeah: The Search for a Biblical City* (JSOTSup 79; Sheffield: JSOT Press, 1990).

[75] Marvin A. Sweeney, "Davidic Polemics in the Book of Judges," *VT* 47 (1997) 517–529; Sweeney, *King Josiah of Judah: The Lost Messiah of Israel* (Oxford and New York: Oxford University Press, 2001), 110–124.

[76] McCarter, *1 Samuel*, 204; cf. E. A. Knauf, "Gilgal," *EBR* 10:277–279.

went home," the Hebrew text states that he went to the altar or shrine at Gilgal, where he presumably made the offering of bread to YHWH.

The final episode in 1 Samuel 10:14–16 portrays Saul's return to his family. Instead of his father, he meets his uncle; there is no satisfactory explanation as to why Saul's uncle should be featured rather than his father. But Saul does not disclose his anointing, which apparently clears the way for his selection as king by lot in 1 Samuel 10:17–27.

The People's Choice of Saul at Mizpah – 1 Samuel 10:17–27

10 ^{17} Samuel summoned the people to the LORD at Mizpah

^{18} and said to the Israelites, "Thus says the LORD, the God of Israel, 'I brought up Israel out of Egypt, and I rescued you from the hand of the Egyptians and from the hand of all the kingdoms that were oppressing you.'

^{19} But today you have rejected your God, who saves you from all your calamities and your distresses, and you have said, 'No, but set a king over us.' Now, therefore, present yourselves before the LORD by your tribes and by your clans."

^{20} Then Samuel brought all the tribes of Israel near, and the tribe of Benjamin was taken by lot.

^{21} He brought the tribe of Benjamin near by its families, and the family of the Matrites was taken by lot. Finally he brought the family of the Matrites near man by man, and Saul the son of Kish was taken by lot. But when they sought him, he could not be found.

^{22} So they inquired again of the LORD, "Did the man come here?" And the LORD said, "See, he has hidden himself among the baggage."

^{23} Then they ran and brought him from there. When he took his stand among the people, he was head and shoulders taller than any of them.

^{24} Samuel said to all the people, "Do you see the one whom the LORD has chosen? There is no one like him among all the people." And all the people shouted, "Long live the king!"

^{25} Samuel told the people the rights and duties of the kingship, and he wrote them in a book and laid it up before the LORD. Then Samuel sent all the people back to their homes.

^{26} Saul also went to his home at Gibeah, and with him went warriors whose hearts God had touched.

^{27} But some worthless fellows said, "How can this man save us?" They despised him and brought him no present. But he held his peace.

> Now Nahash, king of the Ammonites, had been grievously oppressing
> the Gadites and the Reubenites. He would gouge out the right eye of
> each of them and would not grant Israel a deliverer. No one was left of
> the Israelites across the Jordan whose right eye Nahash, king of the
> Ammonites, had not gouged out. But there were seven thousand men
> who had escaped from the Ammonites and had entered Jabesh-gilead.

First Samuel 10:17–27 recounts Saul's selection by lot as king by the people
of Israel at Mizpah, a strategically placed fortress located at the site of Tell
en-Naṣbeh, some eight miles northwest of Jerusalem in the territory of
Benjamin.[77] Its name, derived from the root *sph*, "to watch, guard,"
suggests that it was a defensive position that guarded the southern
approaches through Benjamin to northern Israel and later the northern
territory of southern Judah and Benjamin. According to 1 Kings 15:16–22,
King Asa of Judah repulsed efforts by King Baasha of Israel to encroach
upon Judean territory from Ramah. Asa took Ramah, dismantled its
fortifications, and used them to fortify Mizpah and Geba to protect
Jerusalem and Judah from northern attack. In 582 BCE, Gedaliah ben
Ahikam ben Shaphan, installed by Babylon as Governor of Judah in
Mizpah following the destruction of Jerusalem in 588–586 BCE, was
assassinated in a failed revolt (2 Kgs 25:23; Jer 40:1–41:16).

Mizpah's strategic position makes it an obvious choice to defend
Benjamin and to locate the first public efforts to select a king for Israel
in 1 Samuel 10:17–27 (cf. 1 Sam 7:5–17). But this narrative also plays a key
strategic literary role in that is placed to contextualize the very affirmative
accounts of Saul concerning his anointing by Samuel in 1 Samuel 9:1–10:16
and his relief of Jabesh Gilead in 1 Samuel 11:1–15 with its highly critical
account of Saul's selection by lot as King of Israel at Mizpah. When the
tribes are gathered at Mizpah and lots are drawn to discern YHWH's will
for the selection of the first King of Israel, the tribe of Benjamin is selected
in the first lot, the Matrite clan is selected in the second lot, and Saul ben
Kish is selected in the third lot. But when the people look for Saul, they find
him hiding in the baggage brought by the people when they gathered at
Mizpah, not a very flattering portrayal of the man chosen by YHWH to
lead Israel against the Philistines.

When Saul is finally brought before the people, the description of him as
taller than anyone among the people was apparently written to show that he

---

[77]   Zorn, "Tell en-Naṣbeh," *NEAEHL* 3:1098-11-02; cf. P. M. Arnold, "Mizpah,"
       ABD 4:879–881.

was an ideal leader in the eyes of the people. But leadership requires more than just physical height or good looks; it requires good judgment and the capacity to take responsibility, qualities that are not mentioned in the narrative and apparently contradicted by Saul's presumed efforts to "hide" by the baggage at a time of national crisis. First Samuel 10:25–27 stresses that after Samuel announced the "law of the monarchy," some worthless men, literally "sons of Belial" (Hebrew *bĕlîya'al*, "without worth/profit"), among the people raised questions about Saul's leadership abilities, stating, "How shall this one deliver us?" A competent and politically astute ruler would have quieted such scorn by demonstrating his leadership qualities from the start, but the narrative merely states that Saul remained silent, just as he did when he returned to Gibeah in 1 Samuel 10:14–16.

Many interpreters follow Noth in arguing that 1 Samuel 10:17–27 is a Deuteronomistic composition that is hostile to the monarchy.[78] But these interpreters mistakenly take the passage to be anti-monarchic. The DtrH is not anti-monarchic in principle; rather, it expects righteous and just kingship, not incompetent kingship that fails to recognize YHWH. First Samuel 10:17–27 is anti-Saul, and it therefore serves the interests of the Solomonic redaction that dismisses Saul and promotes David as YHWH's chosen monarch.[79]

Saul's Deliverance of Jabesh Gilead – 1 Samuel 11:1–15

11 ¹ About a month later,[1] Nahash the Ammonite went up and besieged Jabesh-gilead, and all the men of Jabesh said to Nahash, "Make a treaty with us, and we will serve you."

² But Nahash the Ammonite said to them, "On this condition I will make a treaty with you, namely, that I gouge out everyone's right eye and thus put disgrace upon all Israel."

³ The elders of Jabesh said to him, "Give us seven days' respite that we may send messengers through all the territory of Israel. Then, if there is no one to save us, we will give ourselves up to you."

---

[78] Noth, *The Deuteronomistic History*, 47–53; see also Hans Jochen Boecker, *Die Beurteilung der Anfänge des Königtums in den deuteronomistischen Abschnitten des 1. Samuelbuches* (WMANT 31; Neukirchen-Vluyn: Neukirchener Verlag, 1969), 35–60; cf. Timo Veijola, *Das Königtum in der Beurteilung der deuteronomistischen Historiographie* (Helsinki: Suomalainen Tiedeakatemia, 1977), 39–52, who argues that it is part of his proposed Deuteronomistic Nomistic redaction.

[79] Sweeney, *1 and 2 Kings*, 31–32.

⁴ When the messengers came to Gibeah of Saul, they reported the matter in the hearing of the people, and all the people wept aloud.

⁵ Now Saul was coming from the field behind the oxen, and Saul said, "What is the matter with the people, that they are weeping?" So they told him the message from the inhabitants of Jabesh.

⁶ And the spirit of God came upon Saul in power when he heard these words, and his anger was greatly kindled.

⁷ He took a yoke of oxen and cut them in pieces and sent them throughout all the territory of Israel by the messengers, saying, "Whoever does not come out after Saul and Samuel, so shall it be done to his oxen!" Then the dread of the LORD fell upon the people, and they came out as one.

⁸ When he mustered them at Bezek, those from Israel were three hundred thousand and those from Judah seventy thousand.

⁹ They said to the messengers who had come, "Thus shall you say to the inhabitants of Jabesh-gilead: Tomorrow, by the time the sun is hot, you shall have deliverance." When the messengers came and told the inhabitants of Jabesh, they rejoiced.

¹⁰ So the inhabitants of Jabesh said, "Tomorrow we will give ourselves up to you, and you may do to us whatever seems good to you."

¹¹ The next day Saul put the people in three companies. At the morning watch they came into the camp and cut down the Ammonites until the heat of the day, and those who survived were scattered, so that no two of them were left together.

¹² The people said to Samuel, "Who is it that said, 'Shall Saul reign over us?' Give them to us so that we may put them to death."

¹³ But Saul said, "No one shall be put to death this day, for today the LORD has brought deliverance to Israel."

¹⁴ Samuel said to the people, "Come, let us go to Gilgal and there renew the kingship."

¹⁵ So all the people went to Gilgal, and there they made Saul king before the LORD in Gilgal. There they sacrificed offerings of well-being before the LORD, and there Saul and all the Israelites rejoiced greatly.

First Samuel 15 presents an account of Saul's deliverance of Jabesh Gilead from Nahash, an Ammonite ruler who besieged the city. Jabesh Gilead is located in the northern Trans-Jordan. It was identified by Nelson Glueck with Tel Abu al-Kharaz in the Jordan Valley near the Wadi Jabesh, but Swedish excavations at the site have failed to confirm this identification.

Other possibilities include Deir el-Halawe, Miryamim, and Tel al-Maqlub, located further east along the Wadi, the last of which corresponds with Eusebius's statement that Jabesh Gilead was located by the sixth Roman milestone (*Onomastica* 110.11–13).[80] Jabesh Gilead appears earlier in Judges 21:8–14, where it is attacked for its refusal to join Israel's campaign against Benjamin for its role in the rape of the Levite's concubine (Judg 19–21), a clear polemic against Saul.[81] The people of the city were slaughtered, but 400 virgins were kept alive to be given as brides to the surviving men of Benjamin after the other tribes refused to marry their daughters to the Benjaminites. Later, in 1 Samuel 31, the men of Jabesh Gilead take Saul's body down from the wall of Beth Shean to give him a proper burial, and David later moves Saul's remains to the tomb of Kish in Zela (2 Sam 21:12–14; cf. 2 Sam 2:4–6).

A Closer Look at the LXX Text of 1 Reigns (Samuel) 11:1

The LXX text of 1 Reigns 11:1 adds the phrase "and it happened about a month later" to provide context for the opening statement of the verse, "Nahash the Ammonite went up and encamped against Jabesh Gilead." The text of 4QSam[a] 10:6–9 adds a much longer introduction, "And Nahash, King of the Sons of Ammon, oppressed the Sons of Gad and the Sons of Reuben in strength, and he gouged out for them every right eye, and he permitted no deliverer for Israel, and there was no man among the sons of Israel who were across the Jordan whom Nahash, the King of the Sons of Ammon, did not gouge out for him, every right eye to them, seven thousand men were delivered from the hand of the Sons of Ammon, and they came to Jabesh Gilead, and it was about a month (and Nahash went up against Jabesh, and all the men of Jabesh said to Nahash, King of the Sons of Ammon, 'Cut for us a treaty, and we will serve you,' But Nahash the Ammonite said to them, 'By this I will cut for you . . .").[82] The text shows close affinities to Josephus' *Ant.* 6.68–70, but it does not appear in the Lucianic text of 1 Reigns or in any other Septuagint version.[83] Most interpreters follow Cross and Ulrich in concluding that the text of Josephus presupposes a Hebrew *Vorlage* that was lost prior to the discovery of the Qumran manuscript. Nevertheless, the Qumran text does not

---

[80] Stéphanie Anthonioz, "Jabesh-Gilead," *EBR* 13:562–563.

[81] Sweeney, "Davidic Polemics"; Sweeney, *King Josiah*, 110–124.

[82] Frank Moore Cross et al., *Qumran Cave 4. XII. 1–2 Samuel* (DJD 17; Oxford: Clarendon, 2005), 66, Plate 10.

[83] Cross et al., *1–2 Samuel*, 66; Eugene Ulrich Jr., *The Qumran Text of Samuel and Josephus* (HSM 19; Missoula, MT: Scholars Press, 1978), 166–170.

present an original reading; nor does the brief Septuagint addition. The principle of *lectio difficilior* must be invoked here, in that the Qumran text and that employed by Josephus appear to have been written to address the rather abrupt statement now extant in MT 1 Samuel 11:1. The information contained in this reading (and the LXX text) is likely derived from the proto-Masoretic text of Samuel. There are also some minor variations from the MT that would suggest a rather free hand in rendering the text. It therefore appears to be a scribal expansion of the proto-Masoretic text that was designed to provide further contextualization for the introductory statement concerning Nahash's attack against Jabesh Gilead. Josephus appears to have had an expanded text like that at Qumran.

The account of the relief of Jabesh Gilead presents Saul as a hero who employs a well-thought-out plan of attack to save Jabesh Gilead from a humiliating and damaging submission to Nahash. Therefore, his kingship is "renewed" or confirmed at Gilgal. The narrative structure of 1 Samuel 11 falls into two major sub-units. First Samuel 11:1–4 portrays Nahash's advance against Jabesh Gilead and the negotiation concerning his terms of surrender. First Samuel 11:5–15 recounts Saul's defeat of Nahash in verses 5–11, his leniency for those who questioned his leadership in verses 12–13, and the renewal of his kingship at Gilgal in verses 14–15.

The account of Nahash's advance against Jabesh Gilead in 1 Samuel 11:1–4 presents a very plausible military situation. The earlier account of Israel's defeat by the Philistines at Aphek and the capture of the Ark in 1 Samuel 4–6 would have signaled Israel's vulnerability and prompted other adversaries, such as Nahash, to take advantage of the situation. Archeological evidence indicates that the Ammonites emerged in the Trans-Jordan during the Late Bronze Age in several locations, most notably Rabbath Ammon, the site of Amman, the present-day capital of Jordan. Inscriptional evidence is extant only from the late ninth century BCE, which makes historical reconstruction difficult. Nahash is not attested as King of the Ammonites outside of the Bible; his name means "snake" (cf. Gen 3:1), which suggests cleverness, power, and survivability insofar as snakes had eternal life because they shed their skins.

Biblical tradition indicates deep antipathy toward the Ammonites; Genesis 19:30–38 states that they originated as the result of incest between Lot and his daughters, and Deuteronomy 23:1–5 forbids the admission of the Ammonites to the congregation of Israel up to the tenth generation because they refused to share food with Israel during its journey through the wilderness and because they joined the Moabites in hiring Balaam ben Beor to curse them. Nevertheless, 1 Kings 14:21 states that King Rehoboam ben Solomon of Judah and Israel was the son of Solomon's wife, Naamah, an Ammonite woman. The outrageous demands made of Jabesh Gilead by Nahash compare to the Ammonite treatment of David's ambassadors in 2 Samuel 10. The treatment proposed by Nahash, gouging out the right eye, would impair the men of Jabesh Gilead from defending themselves in addition to serving as a very visible mark of their humiliation and subjugation. Josephus states (*Antiquities* 6.68) that they would be unable to see because the use of a shield would impair vision from the left eye.

The portrayal of Nahash suggests a caricature. Either he is a complete fool in contrast to the characteristics represented in his name, or he is entirely arrogant and overconfident in granting the men of Jabesh Gilead time to call for a deliverer to come to their aid.

Saul's deliverance of Jabesh Gilead in 1 Samuel 11:5–15 begins with a portrayal of his response and organization of a relief expedition in 1 Samuel 11:5–11. Saul responds to the situation like a true king, in contrast to the critical portrayal of his leadership qualities in 1 Samuel 9:1–10:16 and 10:17–27. He begins by slaughtering and cutting up the bovines that he was using to plow his field so that he could send the pieces out to the tribes of Israel to call them to battle. Such an act is characteristic of ancient Near Eastern treaty texts which call for the signatories to pass between the pieces of slaughtered offerings to declare that the same fate would await them if they failed to abide by the terms of the treaty.

Saul mustered the Israelite army at Bezek, an unidentified site, although it is presumed to have been within short marching range of Jabesh Gilead. Zertal proposes Khirbet Salhab, located in the Zebabdah Valley where the Manassite hills descend to the Jordan Valley near Jabesh Gilead. Excavations at the site produced pottery from the Iron I period (thirteenth–eleventh centuries BCE).[84] The numbers of men assembled, 300,000 from Israel and 30,000 from Judah, are clearly exaggerated. The men of Jabesh Gilead were informed that relief would come the next day when the sun grew hot, enabling Jabesh Gilead to inform Nahash that they would surrender the next day so that the ambush could be achieved. Such feints were often used in battle, such as the assault on Ai in Joshua 8, in which a small Israelite force attacked the city to lure its defenders out only to be ambushed by larger

---

[84]   Daniel D. Pioske, "Bezek," *EBR* 3:1060–1061.

Israelite forces who remained hidden until the moment that the trap closed. Nahash was completely deceived. Saul divided his forces into three columns to attack Nahash from three sides and cut off any chance of organized withdrawal.

First Samuel 11:12–13 recounts Saul's treatment of those who questioned his leadership (e.g., the Sons of Belial in 1 Samuel 10:27). Saul's leniency may seem to be admirable, but he needed to assert his authority even if he did not execute the culprits.

First Samuel 11:14–15 recounts the renewal of Saul's kingship at Gilgal as proposed by Samuel. The reference to the "renewal" of Saul's kingship is puzzling because nowhere does the text state that his kingship was rescinded until the accounts in 1 Samuel 13–14 and 15. The statement may reflect the editorial formation of the narrative insofar as it would presuppose that the Sons of Belial who questioned Saul's kingship may have been more successful than portrayed in the present form of the narrative. The location of Gilgal is unknown. Biblical accounts place it alternatively in the Jordan Valley near Jericho in Joshua 4–5 or in the Ephraimite hills near Beth El in 1 Samuel 7:16; 2 Kings 2:1–2; 4:38; Hosea 4:15; 9:15; Amos 4:4; 5:5.[85] Sacrifices of Well-Being or Peace Offerings were eaten by priests and people (Lev 3).

Because 1 Samuel 11 presents Saul as a hero, it appears to have originated in the court of King Saul, like 1 Samuel 9:1–10:16, perhaps as part of an early Saul narrative. But it has been edited together with critical accounts of the origins of his kingship in 1 Samuel 8; 10:17–27; and 12 to serve a later pro-Davidic account that was adapted for the DtrH.[86]

Samuel's Instruction Speech Concerning Obligations to YHWH – 1 Samuel 12:1–25

12 **¹ Samuel said to all Israel, "I have listened to you in all that you have said to me and have set a king over you.**

² See, it is the king who leads you now; I am old and gray, but my sons are with you. I have led you from my youth until this day.

³ Here I am; testify against me before the LORD and before his anointed. Whose ox have I taken? Or whose donkey have I taken? Or whom have I defrauded? Whom have I oppressed? Or from whose hand have

---

[85] Knauf, "Gilgal," *EBR* 10:277–279; Wade Kotter, "Gilgal," *ABD* 2:1022–1024.
[86] Sweeney, *1 and 2 Kings*, 1–32.

I taken a bribe to blind my eyes with it? Testify against me, and I will restore it to you."

⁴ They said, "You have not defrauded us or oppressed us or taken anything from the hand of anyone."

⁵ He said to them, "The LORD is witness against you, and his anointed is witness this day, that you have not found anything in my hand." And they said, "He is witness."

⁶ Samuel said to the people, "The LORD is witness, who appointed Moses and Aaron and brought your ancestors up out of the land of Egypt.

⁷ Now, therefore, take your stand so that I may enter into judgment with you before the LORD, and I will declare to you all the righteous acts of the LORD that he performed for you and for your ancestors.

⁸ When Jacob went into Egypt and the Egyptians oppressed them, then your ancestors cried to the LORD, and the LORD sent Moses and Aaron, who brought forth your ancestors out of Egypt and settled them in this place.

⁹ But they forgot the LORD their God, and he sold them into the hand of Sisera, commander of the army of King Jabin of Hazor, and into the hand of the Philistines, and into the hand of the king of Moab, and they fought against them.

¹⁰ Then they cried to the LORD and said, 'We have sinned, for we have forsaken the LORD and have served the Baals and the Astartes, but now rescue us out of the hand of our enemies, and we will serve you.'

¹¹ And the LORD sent Jerubbaal and Barak, and Jephthah, and Samson and rescued you out of the hand of your enemies on every side, and you lived in safety.

¹² But when you saw that King Nahash of the Ammonites came against you, you said to me, 'No, but a king shall reign over us,' though the LORD your God was your king.

¹³ See, here is the king whom you have chosen, for whom you have asked; see, the LORD has set a king over you.

¹⁴ If you will fear the LORD and serve him and heed his voice and not rebel against the commandment of the LORD, and if both you and the king who reigns over you will follow the LORD your God, it will be well;

¹⁵ but if you will not heed the voice of the LORD but rebel against the commandment of the LORD, then the hand of the LORD will be against you and your king.

[16] Now, therefore, take your stand and see this great thing that the L-RD will do before your eyes.

[17] Is it not the wheat harvest today? I will call upon the LORD, that he may send thunder and rain, and you shall know and see that the wickedness that you have done in the sight of the LORD is great in demanding a king for yourselves."

[18] So Samuel called upon the LORD, and the LORD sent thunder and rain that day, and all the people greatly feared the LORD and Samuel.

[19] All the people said to Samuel, "Pray to the LORD your God for your servants, so that we may not die, for we have added to all our sins the evil of demanding a king for ourselves."

[20] And Samuel said to the people, "Do not be afraid; you have done all this evil, yet do not turn aside from following the LORD, but serve the LORD with all your heart,

[21] and do not turn aside after useless things that cannot profit or save, for they are useless.

[22] For the LORD will not cast away his people, for his great name's sake, because it has pleased the LORD to make you a people for himself.

[23] Moreover as for me, far be it from me that I should sin against the LORD by ceasing to pray for you, and I will instruct you in the good and the right way.

[24] Only fear the LORD and serve him faithfully with all your heart, for consider what great things he has done for you.

[25] But if you still do wickedly, you shall be swept away, both you and your king."

First Samuel 12:1–25 recounts Samuel's farewell speech to the people as he instructs them on their obligations to YHWH now that Saul son of Kish has commenced his reign. The passage does not identify the location of Samuel's speech, and so a synchronic reading of the text requires that it be understood as Gilgal, based on prior mention of the site in 1 Samuel 11:14–15. Some interpreters see this passage as the conclusion of Samuel's leadership over Israel, but subsequent appearances by Samuel in the accounts of Saul's rejection as king in 1 Samuel 13–14 and 15 – as well as Samuel's clandestine role in anointing David as king in 1 Samuel 16 – make it clear that Samuel continues to serve as the prophet of YHWH. Given Samuel's priestly functions, his role as prophet represents an anticipation of the multifaceted leadership of Israel and Judah, which include both a king to govern and priests to oversee the major temples of each respective kingdom (i.e., Beth El and Dan in the later northern kingdom of Israel and Jerusalem in the southern kingdom of Judah). Unfortunately, interpreters know little concerning the functional relationship between king and priests in northern Israel – indeed, the king appears to function in a priestly role in the north – but Judah displays a very clear bifurcated division of power between the king and the high priest in the Jerusalem Temple.[87]

First Samuel 12 cannot be considered as Samuel's farewell speech; rather, it is Samuel's duty as prophet – or priest – to instruct the king and the people in their obligations to YHWH now that they have a king ruling them as YHWH's regent. Samuel's speech is comparable to the speeches given by Joshua to the people following the portrayal of the conquest of Canaan and the division of its land among the tribes of Israel in Joshua 23–24.[88]

First Samuel 12 comprises three narrative sub-units in 1 Samuel 12:1–5; 12:6–17; and 12:18–25, each of which presents a speech by Samuel to the people. First Samuel 12:1–5 presents Samuel's speech concerning the inauguration of Saul's role as King of Israel together with his own request for resolution of any outstanding issues or debts incurred during his own term as sole leader of Israel. First Samuel 12:6–17 presents Samuel's speech recounting the deeds that YHWH has performed on behalf of Israel from the time of Moses and Aaron. Finally, 1 Samuel 12:18–25 recounts Samuel's response to the people's request for intercession to YHWH by reminding them of their obligation to serve YHWH although they now have a king.

Following the initial narrative speech formula, "and Samuel said," Samuel's first speech account in 1 Samuel 12:1–5 begins with his initial statement that he has done what the people have asked of him in verse 1 followed by the statement in verse 2, "See, it is the king who leads you now" (NRSVue). The NRSVue is misleading here because the Hebrew verb, *mithallēk*, here translated as "leads," actually means "walks about." In contexts that refer to leaders, such as the king or the priest, it means

---

[87] Sweeney, "Israelite and Judean Religions."
[88] For full discussion of the interrelationship between 1 Samuel 12 and Joshua 24, see Dennis J. McCarthy, *Treaty and Covenant* (AnBib 21A; Rome: Biblical Institute Press, 1978), 206–242.

"serves" (i.e., to carry out the function of leadership). There is nothing exclusive about the term that would suggest that Samuel does not also continue in a recognized role as prophet or priest. Samuel himself notes his age and his sons, who remain with the people, but the earlier reference to Samuel's sons in 1 Samuel 8:1–3 indicates that they are entirely inadequate for their leadership roles. His questions to the people about whether he has stolen anything, defrauded anyone, or accepted a bribe is a legitimate attempt to enable anyone who requires restitution to demand it now. The people respond with a three-fold statement that Samuel has done nothing wrong, and they affirm that YHWH is witness to Samuel's integrity.

The account of Samuel's second speech in 1 Samuel 12:6–17 recounts YHWH's actions on behalf of Israel. The reference to Jacob in verse 8 indicates that this example of the historical review actually begins with Jacob's migration down to Egypt to escape famine, as narrated in Genesis 46. There is too little detail provided here to ensure that this is a direct reference to the Genesis narrative. Insofar as Jacob is the eponymous ancestor of Israel (Gen 32:23–33; 35:10–12), the reference in verse 8 indicates little more than Israel's journey to Egypt, where they would be oppressed (cf. Deut 26:5–10). Samuel's account actually focuses on YHWH's sending Moses and Aaron to deliver Israel from Egyptian oppression. But the NRSVue phrase concerning Egypt's oppression of Israel is derived from the Septuagint; the phrase does not appear in Hebrew. Samuel's speech ignores Joshua and instead turns directly to the period of the Judges to highlight YHWH's deliverance of Israel from Sisera, the commander of Hazor; the Philistines; and the King of Moab. These names presuppose the Judges Deborah and Barak, Samson (or maybe Samuel), and Eglon, but when the text actually names the Judges, Jerubbaal, Bedan, Jephthah, and Samuel appear. Jerubbaal is the Canaanite name of Gideon, who fought the Midianites (Judg 6–8); Bedan is unknown, although some suggest that it is a corruption of the name Barak (Judg 4–5; cf. 1 Chr 7:17, which mentions an otherwise unknown Bedan); Jephthah, who fought the Ammonites (Judg 10–12); and Samuel, who fought the Philistines. Interpreters have noted that this list shows little direct knowledge of the current form of the book of Judges or the DtrH at large, but instead must reflect a different source of knowledge for Israel's early history that is now unknown. The narrative knows Nahash, which presumes knowledge of the immediately preceding account in 1 Samuel 11. Indeed, the reference to Israel's sin in demanding a king does not presuppose the DtrH, as some interpreters argue.[89] The DtrH is not opposed to kingship in principle. As Deuteronomy 17:14–20 indicates, the DtrH looks for the righteous exercise of kingship, not the unjust and idolatrous exercise of kingship that it condemns throughout the Book of Kings. It appears that the statement concerning Israel's sin in demanding a king recalls the current literary context in 1 Samuel 8:4–9. Samuel's response to the people, reminding them of their obligations to YHWH, constitutes compliance with YHWH's instructions in 1 Samuel 8:4–9.

Finally, 1 Samuel 12:18–25 recounts Samuel's prayer to YHWH for rain to demonstrate once again YHWH's acts on behalf of the people. When the people ask him to intercede for them, he resumes his instructions to remain loyal to YHWH despite their alleged sins. Samuel reassures the people of YHWH's fidelity to them even as he warns them of impending punishment should they abandon YHWH. But a key point is Samuel's statement in verse 23 that he will continue to instruct the people in what is good and right, which is precisely the task of the priests (Lev 10:10–11). Samuel makes it clear that he is not giving up his sacred role. First Samuel 12 does not constitute a farewell speech; it is an account of Samuel's instructions to the people concerning their continuing obligations to YHWH now that they have a king.

First Samuel 12 is not a Deuteronomistic composition. It is hostile to the people's demand for a king, and the literary context indicates that Saul is the king in question, even if it does not mention him by name. This narrative takes up the concerns of 1 Samuel 8, undermines the heroic portrayal of Saul in 1 Samuel 11, and introduces the accounts of Saul's rejection as King of Israel in 1 Samuel 13–14 and 15. First Samuel 12 was written as part of the Solomonic History to justify the accession to kingship by David and his son, Solomon.[90]

---

[89] Boecker, *Beurteilung*, 61–88, who follows Noth, *Deuteronomistic History*, 51–52. For a full critique of this hypothesis, see Campbell, *1 Samuel*, 128–131.

[90] Sweeney, *1 and 2 Kings*, 31–32.

4 Commentary Part II: The Rule of King Saul ben Kish of Israel – 1 Samuel 13–31

First Samuel 13–31 presents an account of the rule of King Saul son of Kish of Israel. The account begins formally with the introductory regnal formula in 1 Samuel 13:1 that typically begins the regnal account genre in the book of Kings.[1] But 1 Samuel 13:1 presents a defective reading for Saul's age and the years of his reign: the Hebrew reads literally that Saul was one year old (Hebrew, *ben-šānâ*) when he became king, and the statement concerning the years of his reign employs a defective form of the number of years (Hebrew, *ûšĕnê šānîm*; cf. 2 Sam 2:10, *ûšĕtayîm šānîm*, "and two years"). Although some Greek Lucianic LXX texts of 1 Reigns 13:1 offer a variant reading, the difficulty of the Masoretic text indicates that it is the earlier version and that the Lucianic Greek attempts to correct a *lectio difficilior*.

Many interpreters consider 1 Samuel 13–15 to be an appendage to the account of Saul's anointing as it builds upon the overall negative impression of Saul in 1 Samuel 8–12. The focus on David beginning in 1 Samuel 16 characterizes 1 Samuel 16–2 Samuel 8 as the rise of the House of David.[2] But such a characterization ignores the fact that Saul is King of Israel from 1 Samuel 13 through 1 Samuel 31 and that David is a secondary figure in an account that depicts Saul as an incompetent and failed monarch. There is no typical closing regnal formula at the conclusion of Saul's reign. Instead, 1 Samuel 31:8–13 portrays the shameful treatment of his corpse and those of his three sons by the Philistines followed by the proper burial of their bodies by the men of Jabesh Gilead. Saul's son, Ish-Bosheth, which means "Man of Shame," ultimately succeeds his father on the throne, but

---

[1] Marvin A. Sweeney, *1–2 Kings: A Commentary* (OTL; Louisville, KY: Westminster John Knox, 2007), 31–32; Burke Long, *1 Kings, with an Introduction to Historical Literature* (FOTL 9; Grand Rapids, MI: Eerdmans, 1984), 259.

[2] Jakob Grønbæk, *Die Geschichte des Aufstieg Davids (1 Sam. 15–2 Sam. 5): Tradition und Komposition* (Acta Theologica Danica 10; Copenhagen: Munksgaard, 1971).

the notice of his succession appears only in 2 Samuel 2:8–11, and the account of his reign in 2 Samuel 2:8–4:8 is placed in relation to the reign of David beginning in 2 Samuel 2–4. Samuel's use of the name Ish-Bosheth for Saul's son and successor points to the polemical intent of the narrative. Chronicles uses his true name, Esh Baal, "fire of Baal," which suggests adherence to the Canaanite god of storm and fertility (1 Chr 8:33; 9:39).

Altogether, 1 Samuel 13–31 is a polemical account designed to demonstrate Saul's unfitness for rule and David's own political and military competence as well as YHWH's favor that will lead David to the thrones of Judah and Israel. Consequently, the account of Saul's reign in 1 Samuel 13–31 is best understood as the product of the Solomonic History that is written to celebrate and point to the reign of Solomon son of David as King of Israel.[3] The account includes three major components. The first is the account of Saul's rejection as king by YHWH and Samuel due to his failure to abide by YHWH's expectations in 1 Samuel 13–16:13. The second is the account of Saul's rivalry with David in 1 Samuel 16:14–27:12, which includes accounts of David's competence and adherence to YHWH together with Saul's incompetence and infidelity to YHWH, and the third is the account of Saul's demise in 1 Samuel 28–31.

SAUL'S REJECTION AS KING IN BATTLE AGAINST THE
PHILISTINES – 1 SAMUEL 13–14

13 **¹ Saul was ... years old when he began to reign, and he reigned ... and two years over Israel.**

² Saul chose three thousand out of Israel; two thousand were with Saul in Michmash and the hill country of Bethel, and a thousand were with Jonathan in Gibeah of Benjamin; the rest of the people he sent home to their tents.

³ Jonathan defeated the garrison of the Philistines that was at Geba, and the Philistines heard of it. And Saul blew the trumpet throughout all the land, saying, "Let the Hebrews hear!"

⁴ When all Israel heard that Saul had defeated the garrison of the Philistines and also that Israel had become odious to the Philistines, the people were called out to join Saul at Gilgal.

---

3 Sweeney, *1 and 2 Kings*, 31–32.

⁵ The Philistines mustered to fight with Israel: thirty thousand chariots, and six thousand horsemen, and troops like the sand on the seashore in multitude; they came up and encamped at Michmash, to the east of Beth-aven.

⁶ When the Israelites saw that they were in distress (for the troops were hard pressed), the people hid themselves in caves and in holes and in rocks and in tombs and in cisterns.

⁷ Some Hebrews crossed the Jordan to the land of Gad and Gilead. Saul was still at Gilgal, and all the people followed him trembling.

⁸ He waited seven days, the time appointed by Samuel, but Samuel did not come to Gilgal, and the people began to slip away from Saul.

⁹ So Saul said, "Bring the burnt offering here to me and the offerings of well-being." And he offered the burnt offering.

¹⁰ As soon as he had finished offering the burnt offering, Samuel arrived, and Saul went out to meet him and salute him.

¹¹ Samuel said, "What have you done?" Saul replied, "When I saw that the people were slipping away from me and that you did not come within the days appointed and that the Philistines were mustering at Michmash,

¹² I said, 'Now the Philistines will come down upon me at Gilgal, and I have not entreated the favor of the LORD,' so I forced myself and offered the burnt offering."

¹³ Samuel said to Saul, "You have done foolishly; you have not kept the commandment of the LORD your God, which he commanded you. The LORD would have established your kingdom over Israel forever,

¹⁴ but now your kingdom will not continue; the LORD has sought out a man after his own heart, and the LORD has appointed him to be ruler over his people because you have not kept what the LORD commanded you."

¹⁵ And Samuel left and went on his way from Gilgal. The rest of the people followed Saul to join the army; they went up from Gilgal toward Gibeah of Benjamin.

Saul counted the people who were present with him, about six hundred men.

¹⁶ Saul, his son Jonathan, and the people who were present with them stayed in Geba of Benjamin, but the Philistines encamped at Michmash.

¹⁷ And raiders came out of the camp of the Philistines in three companies; one company turned toward Ophrah to the land of Shual,

¹⁸ another company turned toward Beth-horon, and another company turned toward the mountain that looks down upon the valley of Zeboim toward the wilderness.

¹⁹ Now there was no smith to be found throughout all the land of Israel, for the Philistines said, "The Hebrews must not make swords or spears for themselves,"

²⁰ so all the Israelites went down to the Philistines to sharpen their plowshares, mattocks, axes, or sickles.

²¹ The charge was two-thirds of a shekel for the plowshares and for the mattocks and one-third of a shekel for sharpening the axes and for setting the goads.

²² So on the day of the battle neither sword nor spear was to be found in the possession of any of the people with Saul and Jonathan, but Saul and his son Jonathan had them.

²³ Now a garrison of the Philistines had gone out to the pass of Michmash.

14 ¹ One day Jonathan son of Saul said to the young man who carried his armor, "Come, let us go over to the Philistine garrison on the other side." But he did not tell his father.

² Saul was staying in the outskirts of Gibeah under the pomegranate tree that is at Migron; the troops who were with him were about six hundred men,

³ along with Ahijah son of Ahitub, Ichabod's brother, son of Phinehas son of Eli, the priest of the LORD in Shiloh, carrying an ephod. Now the people did not know that Jonathan had gone.

⁴ In the pass by which Jonathan tried to go over to the Philistine garrison there was a rocky crag on one side and a rocky crag on the other; the name of the one was Bozez, and the name of the other was Seneh.

⁵ One crag rose on the north in front of Michmash and the other on the south in front of Geba.

⁶ Jonathan said to the young man who carried his armor, "Come, let us go over to the garrison of these uncircumcised; it may be that the LORD will act for us, for nothing can hinder the LORD from saving by many or by few."

⁷ His armor-bearer said to him, "Do all that your mind inclines to. I am with you; as your mind is, so is mine."

⁸ Then Jonathan said, "Now we will cross over to those men and will show ourselves to them.

⁹ If they say to us, 'Wait until we come to you,' then we will stand still in our place, and we will not go up to them.

¹⁰ But if they say, 'Come up to us,' then we will go up, for the LORD has given them into our hand. That will be the sign for us."

¹¹ So both of them showed themselves to the garrison of the Philistines, and the Philistines said, "Look, Hebrews are coming out of the holes where they have hidden themselves."

¹² The men of the garrison hailed Jonathan and his armor-bearer, saying, "Come up to us, and we will show you something." Jonathan said to his armor-bearer, "Come up after me, for the LORD has given them into the hand of Israel."

¹³ Then Jonathan climbed up on his hands and feet, with his armor-bearer following after him. The Philistines fell before Jonathan, and his armor-bearer coming after him killed them.

¹⁴ In that first attack Jonathan and his armor-bearer killed about twenty men within an area about half a furrow long in an acre of land.

¹⁵ There was a panic in the camp, in the field, and among all the people; the garrison and even the raiders trembled; the earth quaked; and it became a very great panic.

¹⁶ Saul's lookouts in Gibeah of Benjamin were watching as the multitude was surging back and forth.

¹⁷ Then Saul said to the troops who were with him, "Call the roll and see who has gone from us." When they called the roll, Jonathan and his armor-bearer were not there.

¹⁸ Saul said to Ahijah, "Bring the ark of God here." For at that time the ark of God went with the Israelites.

¹⁹ While Saul was talking to the priest, the tumult in the camp of the Philistines increased more and more, and Saul said to the priest, "Withdraw your hand."

²⁰ Then Saul and all the people who were with him rallied and went into the battle, and every sword was against the other, so that there was very great confusion.

²¹ Now the Hebrews who previously had been with the Philistines and had gone up with them into the camp turned and joined the Israelites who were with Saul and Jonathan.

²² Likewise, when all the Israelites who had gone into hiding in the hill country of Ephraim heard that the Philistines were fleeing, they also followed closely after them in the battle.

²³ So the LORD gave Israel the victory that day.

The battle passed beyond Beth-aven, and the troops with Saul numbered altogether about ten thousand men. The battle spread out over the hill country of Ephraim.

²⁴ Now Saul committed a very rash act on that day. He had laid an oath on the troops, saying, "Cursed be anyone who eats food before it is evening and I have been avenged on my enemies." So none of the troops tasted food.

²⁵ All the troops came upon a honeycomb, and there was honey on the ground.

²⁶ When the troops came upon the honeycomb, the honey was dripping out, but they did not put their hands to their mouths, for they feared the oath.

²⁷ But Jonathan had not heard his father charge the troops with the oath, so he extended the staff that was in his hand and dipped the tip of it in the honeycomb and put his hand to his mouth, and his eyes brightened.

²⁸ Then one of the soldiers said, "Your father strictly charged the troops with an oath, saying, 'Cursed be anyone who eats food this day.' And so the troops are faint."

²⁹ Then Jonathan said, "My father has troubled the land; see how my eyes have brightened because I tasted a little of this honey.

³⁰ How much better if today the troops had eaten freely of the spoil taken from their enemies, for now the defeat of the Philistines has not been great."

³¹ After they had struck down the Philistines that day from Michmash to Aijalon, the troops were very faint,

³² so the troops flew upon the spoil and took sheep and oxen and calves and slaughtered them on the ground, and the troops ate them with the blood.

³³ Then it was reported to Saul, "Look, the troops are sinning against the LORD by eating with the blood." And he said, "You have dealt treacherously; roll a large stone before me here."

³⁴ Saul said, "Disperse yourselves among the troops and say to them: Let all bring their oxen or their sheep, and slaughter them here and eat, and do not sin against the LORD by eating with the blood." So all of the troops brought their oxen with them that night and slaughtered them there.

94

³⁵ And Saul built an altar to the LORD; it was the first altar that he built to the LORD.

³⁶ Then Saul said, "Let us go down after the Philistines by night and despoil them until the morning light; let us not leave one of them." They said, "Do whatever seems good to you." But the priest said, "Let us draw near to God here."

³⁷ So Saul inquired of God, "Shall I go down after the Philistines? Will you give them into the hand of Israel?" But he did not answer him that day.

³⁸ Saul said, "Come here, all you leaders of the people, and let us find out how this sin has arisen today.

³⁹ For as the LORD lives who saves Israel, even if it is in my son Jonathan, he shall surely die!" But there was no one among all the people who answered him.

⁴⁰ He said to all Israel, "You shall be on one side, and I and my son Jonathan will be on the other side." The people said to Saul, "Do what seems good to you."

⁴¹ Then Saul said, "O LORD God of Israel, why have you not answered your servant today? If this guilt is in me or in my son Jonathan, O LORD God of Israel, give Urim, but if this guilt is in your people Israel give Thummim." And Jonathan and Saul were indicated by the lot, but the people were cleared.

⁴² Then Saul said, "Cast the lot between me and my son Jonathan." And Jonathan was taken.

⁴³ Then Saul said to Jonathan, "Tell me what you have done." Jonathan told him, "I tasted a little honey with the tip of the staff that was in my hand; here I am; I will die."

⁴⁴ Saul said, "God do so to me and more also; you shall surely die, Jonathan!"

⁴⁵ Then the people said to Saul, "Shall Jonathan die, who has accomplished this great victory in Israel? Far from it! As the LORD lives, not one hair of his head shall fall to the ground, for he has worked with God today." So the people ransomed Jonathan, and he did not die.

⁴⁶ Then Saul withdrew from pursuing the Philistines, and the Philistines went to their own place.

⁴⁷ When Saul had taken the kingship over Israel, he fought against all his enemies on every side: against Moab, against the Ammonites, against Edom, against the kings of Zobah, and against the Philistines; wherever he turned he routed them.

⁴⁸ He did valiantly and struck down the Amalekites and rescued Israel out of the hands of those who plundered them.

⁴⁹ Now the sons of Saul were Jonathan, Ishvi, and Malchishua, and the names of his two daughters were these: the name of the firstborn was Merab, and the name of the younger was Michal.

⁵⁰ The name of Saul's wife was Ahinoam daughter of Ahimaaz. And the name of the commander of his army was Abner son of Ner, Saul's uncle;

⁵¹ Kish was the father of Saul, and Ner the father of Abner was the son of Abiel.

⁵² There was hard fighting against the Philistines all the days of Saul, and when Saul saw any strong or valiant warrior, he took him into his service.

The account of Saul's rejection as king in battle against the Philistines includes two basic components: YHWH's rejection of Saul as king proper in 1 Samuel 13:1–14 and the battle account in which Saul demonstrates his incompetence in 1 Samuel 13:15–14:52.

First Samuel 13:1–14 begins with the introductory regnal formula in 1 Samuel 13:1. This formula is defective insofar as it portrays Saul as one year old at the outset of his reign, and the report of the years of his reign employs a corrupted number in the form of a construct rendition of two years (Hebrew *ûšĕnê šānîm*). The Hebrew construct form *ûšĕnê* cannot stand alone and requires a numerical element to follow (e.g., Hebrew, *ûšĕnê 'eśreh*, "twelve"), but no such reading appears in any manuscript. The Greek text offers a more coherent reading. The LXX text of 1 Reigns 13:1 omits the verse altogether, but some manuscripts of the Lucianic text read, "Saul was thirty years old (Greek, *huios eniautou triakonta etōn*) in his reign, and he reigned for two years over Israel." Saul's son Ish-Bosheth was forty years old when he began his reign (2 Sam 2:10), but that figure was likely drawn from David's age at accession to the throne as stated in 2 Samuel 5:4. The reading does not satisfactorily account for the duration of Saul's reign. Josephus states at one point that Saul ruled for twenty years (*Antiquities* 10.143) and at another point for forty years (*Antiquities* 6.378; cf. Acts 13:21), based perhaps on 1 Samuel 7:2 (the Ark's twenty-year stay at Kiriath Jearim) and 2 Samuel 5:4 (David's forty-year reign).

The account of Saul's rejection as king in 1 Samuel 13:2–14 begins with the notice of Saul's placement of his forces with 2,000 men under his own command at Michmas(h) in the hill country of Beth El and 1,000 men under the command of his son and presumptive heir, Jonathan, in Gibeah of Benjamin. Michmash is identified with Khirbet el-Hara el-Fawqa, located about seven to eight miles northeast of Jerusalem along the northern side of the Wadi eṣ-Ṣuwenit (Naḥal Mikmas), which descends east from the Benjaminite hills to the Jordan Valley.[4] Verse 5 locates the site east of Beth Aven, "House of Iniquity," a pejorative name for Beth El. Gibeah of Benjamin, also known as Gibeah of Saul, is often identified with Tel el-Ful, but more likely is to be identified with the site of modern Jabaʿ, located five or six miles northeast of Jerusalem in Benjamin on the south side of the Wadi eṣ-Ṣuwenit (Naḥal Mikmas).[5] Such a position indicates that the Philistines had pushed deep into Israelite territory.

The account states that Jonathan killed the Philistine prefect in Geba, generally identified as a variant of Gibeah. The narrative indicates that Jonathan took the initiative to provoke combat, while Saul held back on the north side of the Wadi, perhaps to ambush any Philistine forces that might intervene. Saul then sounded the shofar (i.e., the ram's horn) to summon all Israel to battle. He retreated to Gilgal, the unidentified site of an Israelite sanctuary, perhaps in the eastern Israelite hill country or in the Jordan Valley, to gather his forces.[6] Philistine forces numbered 30,000 chariots (LXX reads 3,000), 6,000 horsemen, and foot soldiers as numerous as the sands of the seashore. These numbers are likely inflated, but they make the point that the Philistines came with a large army and camped at Michmash.

Saul waited seven days for Samuel. As a prophet and priest, Samuel would prepare the people for battle with an exhortative speech to assure them of YHWH's support (Deut 20:1–4). Samuel would also presumably present the whole burnt offering (Hebrew, *ʿōlâ*; Lev 1) and the sacrifice of well-being or peace (Hebrew, *zebaḥ šĕlāmîm*; Lev 3). But when Samuel failed to show and Saul's men begin to desert in droves, Saul took matters into his own hands and made the offerings himself to hold his army together. Ironically, Samuel arrives as Saul is completing the offerings to accuse Saul of disobeying YHWH's instructions by making the offerings himself. It is not clear that Saul was precluded from making the offerings; indeed, there is evidence that northern Israelite kings may also have served

---

[4]   Patrick M. Arnold, "Michmash," *ABD* 4:813–815.
[5]   Arnold, "Gibeah," *ABD* 2:1007–1008.
[6]   Wade R. Kotter, "Gilgal," *ABD* 2:1022–1024; Ernst Axel Knauf, "Gilgal," *EBR* 10:277–279.

in a priestly role (see 2 Sam 8:18; 1 Kgs 13).[7] Nevertheless, Samuel announces to Saul that had he obeyed, YHWH would have confirmed his dynasty forever, but now that Saul has disobeyed, YHWH will find another man, obviously David, who will observe YHWH's commands. The pro-Davidic perspective of this episode indicates that it is the product of the Solomonic History.

First Samuel 13:15–14:52 demonstrates Saul's incompetence as a military leader. The account also points to Saul's son, Jonathan, as a talented and courageous military leader who takes the initiative against significant odds to win a victory.

First Samuel 13:15–18 begins with a notice of Saul's movement from Gilgal to Gibeah of Benjamin, also known as Geba. Even in Gilgal, the Israelites saw the buildup of Philistine forces and deserted in droves, demonstrating their complete lack of confidence in Saul. When Saul moved up to Gibeah, he only had about 600 men left. His position on the southern side of the Naḥal Michmash/Wadi eṣ-Ṣuwenit protected him from a Philistine advance insofar as the Naḥal Michmash, a deep canyon, is difficult to traverse. The Philistines divided their forces, circa 3,000 men, into three columns.[8] One column advanced northeast on the Ophrah road toward Shual, east of Beth El. A second column advanced to the west along the Beth Ḥoron Road to protect their rear and ensure control of western Benjamin and southern Ephraim. The third column advanced southeast along the border road north of the Naḥal Michmash/Wadi eṣ-Ṣuwenit to overlook the Zeboim Valley and the eastern wilderness.

Saul was in no position to stop the Philistines, and his failure to move indicated his lack of confidence in his ability to overcome them. Having assassinated the Philistine prefect, Saul had painted himself into a very vulnerable corner. First Samuel 13:19–22 reports that the Philistines had ensured that no ironwork would be done in Israel, which meant that Saul's men had no weapons. They were forced to rely only on their agricultural tools, which they had to take to the Philistines for sharpening and repair. Only Saul and Jonathan had weapons (v. 22).

---

[7] Marvin A. Sweeney, "Israelite and Judean Religions," *The Cambridge History of Religions in the Ancient World. Volume 1: From the Bronze Age to the Hellenistic Age,* ed. M. Salzman and M. A. Sweeney; Cambridge: Cambridge University Press, 2013).

[8] For a convenient, but simple map, see P. Kyle McCarter, *1 Samuel* (AB 8; Garden City, NY: Doubleday, 1980), 231.

First Samuel 13:23 indicates that the Philistine garrison advanced directly against Saul at the Michmash Pass. The Michmash Pass is a location
in the Naḥal Michmash/Wadi eṣ-Ṣuwenit where it is possible to cross the
steep canyon dividing Michmash from Gibeah of Saul. The text gives no
indication that Saul did anything to counter the Philistine move.

First Samuel 14:1–15 recounts how Saul's son, Jonathan, took the
initiative. Together with his armor bearer, Jonathan descended into the
Naḥal Michmash/Wadi eṣ-Ṣuwenit to launch a two-man attack against the
Philistines before they could cross. The pass was marked by two rock
formations, Bozez, "Gleaming or Slippery," on the north by Michmash,
and Seneh, "Thorny," on the south by Gibeah. Each rock formation is
described as a "tooth" (Hebrew, *šēn*), but attempts to identify them today
have been futile.[9] He did not inform his father, who sat under a pomegran-
ate tree at Migron, outside of Gibeah, with Ahijah ben Ahitub, the brother
of Ichabod. Both Ahitub and Ichabod were the sons of Phineas ben Eli, the
priest (1 Sam 4:19–22), which meant that Ahijah was also a priest. Ahijah
had an ephod, a garment used for oracular inquiry of YHWH.[10]

Jonathan lays out his plan to attack "the uncircumcised," a derogatory
reference applied to the Philistines, who did not share the practice of the
Israelites and Judeans, Egyptians, Edomites, Moabites, Ammonites, and
the ancient Bedouin (Jer 9:25). Jonathan proposed that they cross the wadi,
clamber up on their hands and feet to the other side, and see how the
Philistine guards would react. If they said to wait while they came down to
attack the two Israelites, Jonathan and his armor bearer would stay where
they were because the Philistines would be too confident. If they said to
come on up, they would do so, but they would approach in a manner by
which they would not be seen to surprise the defenders. When they
appeared, the Philistines mocked them, which signaled that the
Philistines did not take the attack seriously. This enabled them to kill
twenty men in a narrow space that trapped the doomed Philistine camp.

With the Philistine camp in complete confusion, Saul noticed that his
son was gone. At first, Saul called for Ahijah to bring the Ark so that an
oracular inquiry might be made. This statement indicates that the present
story was an older narrative that was taken up into its present context

---

[9]   Ralph W. Klein, *1 Samuel* (WBC 10; Grand Rapids, MI: Zondervan, 2000), 135.
[10] See Exodus 28, esp. vv. 6–12, for the priestly understanding of the ephod; cf. 2 Samuel
      6:14, which describes it as a linen garment; see also Judges 8:27, which portrays it as a
      garment festooned with gold and precious stones.

without fully editing its content, insofar as the Ark was supposed to reside at Kiriath Jearim for twenty years following its capture by the Philistines (1 Sam 7:1–4).

But Saul demonstrated his lack of judgment. He commanded his men to swear that they would take no food whatsoever until the Philistines were completely routed. He apparently intended to ensure that the Philistines would not escape in case the starving Israelites stopped to eat the spoil of the Philistine camp. But it was foolish to make his men take such an oath, particularly since they obviously needed the food. And it was poor judgment because not everyone knew about it, most notably Jonathan, who stumbled upon some honey while pursuing the Philistines and ate. This would mean death for Jonathan as a result of his father's ill-considered oath (cf. Gen 31:32; 35:16–21).

First Samuel 14:31–35 illustrates the need of the Israelites to eat when the famished men rushed upon the spoils of the Philistine camp at Aijalon, located east of ancient Gezer where the Israelite hill country descends into the coastal plain.[11] The men took animals from the flock and herd, slaughtered them on the ground, and ate them with their blood, violating the dietary laws (Deut 12:16; cf. Lev 19:26). Upon hearing the report of his soldiers' sin, Saul ordered a large rock to be used as an altar for the proper slaughter of animals.

When Saul proposed further plundering and slaughtering of the Philistines that night in 1 Samuel 14:36–46, the priest, presumably Ahijah, ordered an inquiry of G-d to secure divine approval. Using the Urim and Thummim, a form of lots employed in ancient Israel for divine inquiry, Saul asked YHWH if he should go down after the Philistines. When YHWH did not respond, it was evident that there was a problem, thereby heightening the narrative tension. The inquiry indicated that Jonathan was the problem, and he admitted that he had eaten honey. When Saul announced that Jonathan should therefore die in accordance with his oath, Jonathan accepted the judgment of death. But the Israelite men rejected Saul's decision by insisting that Jonathan should not die after having won such an important victory for Israel.

First Samuel 14:47–48 states that Saul secured his kingship over Israel and protected his nation against Israel's enemies on all sides. First Samuel 14:49–51 identifies his family, including his sons, Jonathan, Ishvi, and

---

[11]   Stefan Münger, "Aijalon," *EBR* 1:682–683.

Malchishua; his daughters, Merab and Michal; his wife, Ahinoam bat
Ahimaaz; his army commander, Abner ben Ner, Saul's uncle; and Saul's
father, Kish ben Abiel. Abiel was the father of Kish and Ner (cf. 1 Sam 9:1;
10:14–16). First Samuel 14:52 states that the hard fighting throughout
Saul's reign prompted Saul to enlist any capable warrior.

Overall, 1 Samuel 14 portrays Saul as a willing but incompetent military
leader of his people who exercises poor judgment throughout the encounter. First Samuel 13–14 therefore appear to be the work of the Solomonic
History, which consistently critiques Saul and applauds David, thereby
preparing the way for the establishment of the House of David.[12]

SAUL'S REJECTION AS KING FOR DISOBEYING YHWH AND
SAMUEL'S SECRET ANOINTING OF DAVID – 1 SAMUEL
15:1–16:13

> 15 ¹ Samuel said to Saul, "The LORD sent me to anoint you king over his
> people Israel; now therefore listen to the words of the LORD.
>
> ² Thus says the LORD of hosts: I will punish the Amalekites for what
> they did in opposing the Israelites when they came up out of Egypt.
>
> ³ Now go and attack Amalek and utterly destroy all that they have; do
> not spare them, but kill both man and woman, child and infant, ox and
> sheep, camel and donkey."
>
> ⁴ So Saul summoned the people and numbered them in Telaim, two
> hundred thousand foot soldiers and ten thousand soldiers of Judah.
>
> ⁵ Saul came to the city of the Amalekites and lay in wait in the valley.
>
> ⁶ Saul said to the Kenites, "Go! Leave! Withdraw from among the
> Amalekites, or I will destroy you with them, for you showed kindness
> to all the Israelites when they came up out of Egypt." So the Kenites
> withdrew from the Amalekites.
>
> ⁷ Saul defeated the Amalekites, from Havilah as far as Shur, which is east
> of Egypt.
>
> ⁸ He took King Agag of the Amalekites alive but utterly destroyed all the
> people with the edge of the sword.
>
> ⁹ Saul and the people spared Agag and the best of the sheep and of the
> cattle and of the fatted calves, and the lambs, and all that was valuable

---

[12]   Sweeney, 1 and 2 Kings, 31–32.

and would not utterly destroy them; all that was despised and worthless they utterly destroyed.

¹⁰ The word of the LORD came to Samuel:

¹¹ "I regret that I made Saul king, for he has turned back from following me and has not carried out my commands." Samuel was angry, and he cried out to the LORD all night.

¹² Samuel rose early in the morning to meet Saul, and Samuel was told, "Saul went to Carmel, where he set up a monument for himself, and on returning he passed on down to Gilgal."

¹³ When Samuel came to Saul, Saul said to him, "May you be blessed by the LORD; I have carried out the command of the LORD."

¹⁴ But Samuel said, "What then is this bleating of sheep in my ears and the lowing of cattle that I hear?"

¹⁵ Saul said, "They have brought them from the Amalekites, for the people spared the best of the sheep and the cattle to sacrifice to the LORD your God, but the rest we have utterly destroyed."

¹⁶ Then Samuel said to Saul, "Stop! I will tell you what the LORD said to me last night." He replied, "Speak."

¹⁷ Samuel said, "Though you are little in your own eyes, are you not the head of the tribes of Israel? The LORD anointed you king over Israel.

¹⁸ And the LORD sent you on a mission and said, 'Go, utterly destroy the sinners, the Amalekites, and fight against them until they are consumed.'

¹⁹ Why then did you not obey the voice of the LORD? Why did you swoop down on the spoil and do what was evil in the sight of the LORD?"

²⁰ Saul said to Samuel, "I have obeyed the voice of the LORD. I have gone on the mission on which the LORD sent me. I have brought Agag the king of Amalek, and I have utterly destroyed the Amalekites.

²¹ But from the spoil the people took sheep and cattle, the best of the things devoted to destruction, to sacrifice to the LORD your God in Gilgal."

²² And Samuel said,

"Has the LORD as great delight in burnt offerings and sacrifices
  as in obedience to the voice of the LORD?
Surely, to obey is better than sacrifice
  and to heed than the fat of rams.

²³ For rebellion is no less a sin than divination,

and stubbornness is like iniquity and idolatry.

Because you have rejected the word of the LORD,

he has also rejected you from being king."

²⁴ Saul said to Samuel, "I have sinned, for I have transgressed the commandment of the LORD and your words because I feared the people and obeyed their voice.

²⁵ Now therefore, I pray, pardon my sin, and return with me, so that I may worship the LORD."

²⁶ Samuel said to Saul, "I will not return with you, for you have rejected the word of the LORD, and the LORD has rejected you from being king over Israel."

²⁷ As Samuel turned to go away, Saul caught hold of the hem of his robe, and it tore.

²⁸ And Samuel said to him, "The LORD has torn the kingdom of Israel from you this very day and has given it to a neighbor of yours who is better than you.

²⁹ Moreover, the Glory of Israel will not deceive or change his mind, for he is not a mortal, that he should change his mind."

³⁰ Then Saul said, "I have sinned; yet honor me now before the elders of my people and before Israel, and return with me, so that I may worship the LORD your God."

³¹ So Samuel turned back after Saul, and Saul worshiped the LORD.

³² Then Samuel said, "Bring Agag king of the Amalekites here to me." And Agag came to him haltingly. Agag said, "Surely death is bitter."

³³ Samuel said,

"As your sword has made women childless,

so your mother shall be childless among women."

And Samuel hewed Agag in pieces before the LORD in Gilgal.

³⁴ Then Samuel went to Ramah, and Saul went up to his house in Gibeah of Saul.

³⁵ Samuel did not see Saul again until the day of his death, but Samuel grieved over Saul. And the LORD was sorry that he had made Saul king over Israel.

16 ¹ The LORD said to Samuel, "How long will you grieve over Saul? I have rejected him from being king over Israel. Fill your horn with

oil and set out; I will send you to Jesse the Bethlehemite, for I have provided for myself a king among his sons."

² Samuel said, "How can I go? If Saul hears of it, he will kill me." And the LORD said, "Take a heifer with you and say, 'I have come to sacrifice to the LORD.'

³ Invite Jesse to the sacrifice, and I will show you what you shall do, and you shall anoint for me the one whom I name to you."

⁴ Samuel did what the LORD commanded and came to Bethlehem. The elders of the city came to meet him trembling and said, "Do you come peaceably?"

⁵ He said, "Peaceably. I have come to sacrifice to the LORD; sanctify yourselves and come with me to the sacrifice." And he sanctified Jesse and his sons and invited them to the sacrifice.

⁶ When they came, he looked on Eliab and thought, "Surely his anointed is now before the LORD."

⁷ But the LORD said to Samuel, "Do not look on his appearance or on the height of his stature, because I have rejected him, for the LORD does not see as mortals see; they look on the outward appearance, but the LORD looks on the heart."

⁸ Then Jesse called Abinadab and made him pass before Samuel. He said, "Neither has the LORD chosen this one."

⁹ Then Jesse made Shammah pass by. And he said, "Neither has the LORD chosen this one."

¹⁰ Jesse made seven of his sons pass before Samuel, and Samuel said to Jesse, "The LORD has not chosen any of these."

¹¹ Samuel said to Jesse, "Are all your sons here?" And he said, "There remains yet the youngest, but he is keeping the sheep." And Samuel said to Jesse, "Send and bring him, for we will not sit down until he comes here."

¹² He sent and brought him in. Now he was ruddy and had beautiful eyes and was handsome. The LORD said, "Rise and anoint him, for this is the one."

¹³ Then Samuel took the horn of oil and anointed him in the presence of his brothers, and the spirit of the LORD came mightily upon David from that day forward. Samuel then set out and went to Ramah.

First Samuel 15:1–35 recounts Saul's rejection as King of Israel due to his failure to obey YHWH's command to proscribe Agag and the Amalekites, followed by an account of the consequences in 1 Samuel 16:1–13, viz., the anointing of David as king.

The narrative comprises two major sub-units. The first appears in 1 Samuel 15:1–35, which recounts Saul's refusal to kill Agag, and the second appears in 1 Samuel 16:1–13, which recounts Samuel's secret anointing of David ben Jesse as King of Israel.

First Samuel 15:1–35 includes four sub-units. The first appears in 1 Samuel 15:1–9, which portrays Samuel's transmission to Saul of YHWH's instructions to proscribe Amalek in 1 Samuel 15:1–3 and Saul's failure to comply fully with YHWH's instructions in 1 Samuel 15:4–9. The second appears in 1 Samuel 15:10–31, in which Samuel confronts Saul with his failure to obey YHWH and announces YHWH's judgment against him. The third appears in 1 Samuel 15:32–33, in which Samuel kills Agag. And the fourth, in 1 Samuel 15:34–35, recounts Samuel's departure from Saul and the disruption of their relationship.

First Samuel 15:1–9 begins with an account of YHWH's speech to Samuel in 1 Samuel 15:1–3, in which YHWH instructs Samuel to speak to Saul. YHWH's first statement sets the agenda for the passage by emphasizing that YHWH made Saul King of Israel; therefore, Saul is obligated to obey YHWH's command. The second element of YHWH's speech then follows in 1 Samuel 15:2–3, introduced by the prophetic messenger formula, "Thus said YHWH of Hosts," which authenticates the following message as a statement by YHWH.[13] YHWH explains the instruction to destroy Amalek due to its efforts to destroy Israel in the Wilderness (Exod 17:8–16; Deut 25:17–19). Such an act is justified when facing an enemy who seeks complete destruction.

First Samuel 15:4–9 recounts Saul's actions against the Amalekites. The encounter takes place at Telaim (Hebrew, "lambs"), a site generally identified with Telem (Josh 15:24), identified with modern Khirbet ez-Zeifeh, approximately thirty-two miles south of Hebron, near Judah's border with Edom.[14] Although the LXX identifies the site as Gilgal, its decision appears to be based on perplexity as to why Saul would be campaigning in the Judean Negeb when his prior encounter with the Philistines had taken place near Gilgal. David's marriage to Saul's daughter Michal in 1 Samuel 18 signaled an alliance between Judah and Israel, but that alliance broke

---

[13]   Marvin A. Sweeney, *Isaiah 1–39, with an Introduction to Prophetic Literature* (FOTL 16; Grand Rapids, MI, and Cambridge, UK: Eerdmans, 1996), 546.

[14]   McCarter, *1 Samuel*, 261, 266.

down when Saul began to view David as a rival. The account notes Saul's consideration of the Kenites, who showed fidelity to the Israelites in the wilderness. This fidelity with Israel may be related to Moses' marriage to Zipporah, daughter of the Midianite priest, Jethro, insofar as the Midianites may be identified with the Kenites (Judg 1:16; 4:11, 17; 5:24; Num 10:29–32).[15]

Saul's attack against the Amalekites ranged from Havilah to Shur. The location of Havilah is uncertain, and the language here appears dependent in part on Genesis 25:18,[16] but the location of the Wilderness of Shur in the northern Sinai between the northeastern border of Egypt and the southern border of Canaan is far more secure (Gen 16:7; 20:1; 25:18; Exod 15:22).[17] The region was guarded by a string of Egyptian fortresses from Egypt to western Asia.

First Samuel 15:10–31 then takes up the consequences for Saul's decision not to kill Agag and the best of the cattle and sheep. The passage shows influence from the prophetic judgment speech genre because it takes up Saul's disobedience to YHWH and portrays a prophet, Samuel, who states the consequences.[18] The sub-unit begins in 1 Samuel 15:10–11, in which YHWH expresses regret to Samuel for having made Saul king due to Saul's failure to obey YHWH's command. YHWH's speech prompts Samuel to travel to Saul for a confrontation, but 1 Samuel 15:12 notes that Saul set up a monument to himself for defeating Amalek, which suggests that Saul is more interested in his own reputation than in obeying YHWH's commands as king.

First Samuel 15:13–31 relates Samuel's confrontation with Saul. The interchange presents Saul as either ignorant of what he has (not) done or disingenuous in blessing Samuel and stating that he had fulfilled YHWH's command. But Samuel challenges him immediately by asking rhetorically about the bleating of sheep and the lowing of cattle that should be dead had Saul indeed followed YHWH's instructions. Saul's explanation is that the Israelites, obviously at his command or acquiescence, had spared the best of the cattle as a sacrifice to YHWH. Samuel reminds Saul that he is King of Israel and that it is his responsibility to obey YHWH. Saul's insistence

[15]   Martin Leuenberger, "Kenites," *EBR* 15:111–112.
[16]   McCarter, *1 Samuel*, 261; Bryan Bibb, "Havilah," *EBR* 11:415–417.
[17]   David R. Seely, "Shur, Wilderness of," *ABD* 5:1230.
[18]   Bruce C. Birch, *The Rise of the Monarchy: The Growth and Development of 1 Samuel 7–17* (SBLDS 27; Missoula, MT: Scholars Press, 1976), 94–129; Sweeney, *Isaiah 1–39*, 533–534.

that he did obey YHWH's commands is unconvincing, particularly because he captured Agag but did not kill him as instructed. Samuel's retort that YHWH prefers obedience to sacrifices is often cited as a basis for the view that YHWH does not want sacrifice at all, but Samuel observes that sacrifice is useless unless one does YHWH's will (cf. Isa 1:10–17).

Saul asks for forgiveness, but Samuel does not let Saul off the hook. He charges Saul with rebellion against YHWH. Samuel then makes a formal announcement of judgment in v. 23.

Saul makes a further attempt to apologize and ask forgiveness, promising that if Samuel returns with him, he will bow down publicly to YHWH to beg forgiveness. But Samuel is having none of it, and he repeats his sentence of punishment. When Samuel turns to leave, Saul grabs Samuel's garment, accidentally tearing it. The NRSVue and NJPS add the name of Saul as the one to tear the garment even though it is not present in the text. Interpreters have therefore speculated that Samuel tore Saul's garment as part of a prophetic symbolic action to illustrate his announcement of punishment. The argument is based in part on the syntax of the passage: Samuel is the subject of the first verb in v. 27, "and he turned," and he must be the subject of the subsequent verb as well, "and he caught hold of the hem of his robe, and it tore" (cf. 1 Kgs 11:26–39). The statement in v. 28 that YHWH would give the kingdom to someone better than Saul is an obvious reference to David.

Samuel makes a further point in v. 29, that YHWH, identified as "the Glory of Israel," does not change his mind because he is not mortal. The text wrestles with the notion of YHWH's integrity by arguing that YHWH is not wrong. Saul had clearly disobeyed YHWH, thereby demonstrating to YHWH – and Samuel – that he was the wrong choice as King of Israel

The third major sub-unit, in 1 Samuel 15:32–33, briefly describes Samuel's execution of Agag at Gilgal. Agag's halting approach expresses some trepidation and perhaps the hope that his life might be spared as indicated by his statement translated literally, "perhaps the bitterness of death is turned aside." The book of Esther maintains that Haman was an Agagite (i.e., a descendant of Agag) and that Mordecai and Esther were descendants of Kish, the father of Saul, to illustrate the need to kill an unrelenting enemy like Haman or Agag. Rabbinic tradition states that Agag fathered a descendant between his capture and his execution.[19]

---

[19] See Targum Sheni to Esther 4:13; b. Megillah 13a.

Finally, 1 Samuel 15:34–35 relates Samuel's departure from Saul for his home in Ramah and Saul's return to his home in Gibeah of Saul. Although Samuel never saw Saul again (but see 1 Sam 28), he grieved for the rest of his life over his role in making Saul King of Israel.

First Samuel 16:1–13 is clearly related to 1 Samuel 15:1–35 by the introductory *waw*-consecutive verbal formation, "and YHWH said to Samuel," which asks if Samuel is still grieving over Saul. The passage includes two major sub-units. The first, in 1 Samuel 16:1–3, recounts YHWH's instructions to Samuel to travel to Beth Lehem to anoint David as king, and the second, in 1 Samuel 16:4–13, recounts Samuel's compliance with YHWH's instructions.

The account of YHWH's instructions to Samuel in 1 Samuel 16:1–3 builds upon the prior narrative in 1 Samuel 15:1–35 by emphasizing Samuel's anointing of David as a consequence of Saul's failure to obey YHWH's command to kill Agag. It also highlights Samuel's fear of the increasingly threatening Saul. Saul repeatedly claims that he did no wrong, and he makes a point of following Samuel back to the camp so that he might bow low before the elders of Israel. There is no explicit statement in 1 Samuel 15 that Saul threatens Samuel, but the threat becomes explicit in Samuel's response to YHWH's initial instruction to go to Jesse of Beth Lehem to anoint one of his sons as king. The emphasis placed on Samuel's fear of Saul suggests that 1 Samuel 16:1–13 is an interpretative expansion of 1 Samuel 15 that establishes a fault in Saul's character. Saul repeatedly threatens David – and his own son and presumed heir, Jonathan – which illustrates Saul's personality breakdown beginning in 1 Samuel 16:14–23 and continuing all the way through 1 Samuel 31, when Saul commits suicide at Mt. Gilboa.

YHWH's instruction to take a heifer and invite Jesse and sons to a sacrificial feast provides cover for Samuel's trip to Beth Lehem. The motif also appears in 1 Samuel 20, which explains David's absence from Saul's table due to a family feast in Beth Lehem (1 Sam 20:29). The explanation enrages Saul, who then throws a spear at his own son.

Samuel's compliance with YHWH's instructions follows in 1 Samuel 16:4–13. Samuel travels to Beth Lehem, some five and a half miles south of Jerusalem in Judah (Judg 17:7–9; 19:1–2, 18; cf. LXX Josh 15:59).[20] Upon arrival in 1 Samuel 16:4–5, Samuel instructs the elders as well as Jesse and

---

[20]   Sweeney, "Bethlehem," *EBR* 3:983–985; M. Stekelis et al., "Bethlehem," *NEAEHL* 1:203–210.

his sons to "sanctify" themselves for a sacrifice to YHWH. Their sanctifi-
cation would involve washing, donning clean clothing, and avoiding sexual
relations prior to engagement in holy sacrifice (see Exod 19:10, 14–15). The
choice of a heifer as the sacrificial offering suggests that it is a *zebaḥ
šělāmîm*, a "sacrifice of peace or well-being," which the priests and people
might share (Lev 3).

The narrative emphasizes several motifs. One is that YHWH sees
qualities in human beings beyond those that human beings might see.
When Jesse gathers seven of his sons to stand before Samuel in 1 Samuel
16:6–10, YHWH instructs Samuel not to consider the appearance of Jesse's
sons for YHWH "looks to the heart" (1 Sam 16:7). This is an interesting
statement insofar as the narrative later highlights David's good looks (1
Sam 16;12) and that David later commits the sins of adultery and murder
in relation to his affair with Bath Sheba and the murder of her husband,
Uriah the Hittite (2 Sam 10–12). But the point made here is that YHWH
looks for the qualities of leadership necessary for a king – even though
YHWH did not successfully do this in the case of Saul. YHWH apparently
sees those qualities in David but not in his brothers.

A second motif is that the younger prevails over the older in Israelite
folklore, as evidenced by the examples of Jacob, Joseph, Ephraim, and even
Israel itself.[21] Although the first-born is expected to be the major heir of
the family, younger siblings frequently prove to be more capable. The motif
is based in part on Israel's self-identity in relation to the early Canaanite
culture of the land and David's role in successfully founding a dynasty.

The third motif is David's qualities of leadership. When David is
brought before Samuel as Jesse's eighth and youngest son in 1 Samuel
16:11–13, YHWH instructs Samuel to anoint him. It is ironic that David is
described as "ruddy" (i.e., red-headed) with "beautiful eyes," which suggests a clear-eyed gaze lacking in shyness like Saul, and "handsome,"
literally "good appearance," the very qualities against which YHWH
warned Samuel in 1 Samuel 16:7. But an indication of David's qualities
appears in verse 11, which describes David as "keeping the sheep." Ancient
Near Eastern monarchs often portray themselves as shepherds, which
serves as a metaphorical portrayal of leadership in that the shepherd guides
and cares for the sheep, which cannot otherwise survive (cf. Isa 44:28).
Shepherds defend their flocks against predators, and kings portray

---

[21] Frederick E. Greenspahn, *When Brothers Dwell Together: The Preeminence of Younger
Siblings in the Hebrew Bible* (New York and Oxford: Oxford University Press, 1994).

themselves as lion hunters to demonstrate their capacities to protect their people.[22]

The last motif is that the "spirit of YHWH" was upon David "from that day on," which contrasts markedly with Saul as portrayed in 1 Samuel 16:14–23, from whom "the spirit of YHWH had departed" and who suffered from an evil spirit from YHWH. Throughout the narratives concerning the "rise of David," David constantly enjoys the favor of YHWH.[23]

SAUL'S DEPRESSION AND DAVID'S EFFORTS TO RELIEVE IT –
1 SAMUEL 16:14–23

16 [14] Now the spirit of the LORD departed from Saul, and an evil spirit from the LORD tormented him.

[15] And Saul's servants said to him, "See now, an evil spirit from God is tormenting you.

[16] Let our lord now command the servants who attend you to look for someone who is skillful in playing the lyre, and when the evil spirit from God is upon you, he will play it, and you will feel better."

[17] So Saul said to his servants, "Provide for me someone who can play well, and bring him to me."

[18] One of the young men answered, "I have seen a son of Jesse the Bethlehemite who is skillful in playing, a man of valor, a warrior, prudent in speech, and a man of good presence, and the LORD is with him."

[19] So Saul sent messengers to Jesse and said, "Send me your son David, who is with the sheep."

[20] Jesse took a donkey loaded with bread, a skin of wine, and a kid and sent them by his son David to Saul.

[21] And David came to Saul and entered his service. Saul loved him greatly, and he became his armor-bearer.

[22] Saul sent to Jesse, saying, "Let David remain in my service, for he has found favor in my sight."

---

[22] See also James B. Pritchard, *The Ancient Near East in Pictures* (Princeton: Princeton University Press, 1969) 184.

[23] Grønbæk, *Die Geschichte vom Aufstieg Davids*, 68–76.

²³ And whenever the evil spirit from God came upon Saul, David took the lyre and played it with his hand, and Saul would be relieved and feel better, and the evil spirit would depart from him.

First Samuel 16:24–23 is clearly related to 1 Samuel 16:1–13 by the concern with the spirit of YHWH, which "came mightily" upon David in 1 Samuel 15:25 but departed from Saul in 1 Samuel 16:1. But the absence of a clear syntactical relationship between verses 13 and 14 indicates that 1 Samuel 16:14–23 begins a new unit within the larger formal structure of the Saul and David narratives. The passage begins in 1 Samuel 16:14 with a conjunctive noun clause, "and (NRSVue, 'now') the spirit of YHWH departed from Saul, and an evil spirit from YHWH tormented him." The absence of a *waw*-consecutive verb at this point breaks the syntactical linkage to the preceding narrative and prompts the reader to pause and recognize something new.

Indeed, the passage introduces a major issue, Saul's depression. Saul's inadequacies have been displayed before in 1 Samuel 10:17–27; 1 Samuel 13–14; and 1 Samuel 15. But the departure of YHWH's spirit, apparently a reference to Saul's depression at the recognition that he has failed as King of Israel, is new. Saul's primary task is to defend the people of Israel against its enemies, but narrative context demonstrate that he is ill prepared to do so.

Ironically, the solution for Saul's depression prompts his servants to find someone to play music for Saul to relieve him from his depression – and that person is David. The lyre, Hebrew, *kinnôr*, is a stringed instrument known throughout the eastern Mediterranean world that has become the symbolic national instrument of Israel in modern times.[24] One of Saul's servants proposes David ben Jesse the Bethlehemite, whom he describes as "skillful in playing, a man of valor, a warrior, prudent in speech, and a man of good presence; and YHWH is with him." Saul is impressed with David and makes him an arms bearer. Apparently, the role is to serve as part of Saul's retinue or royal guard during battle (cf. Saul's "equipment bearer" in 1 Samuel 31).

When the evil spirit came to torment Saul, David would play the lyre and presumably sing for him so that the evil spirit would depart. Such

---

[24]   Marvin A. Sweeney, "The Kinnor in the Bible: Instrument of the Divine,"*Kinnor: The Biblical Lyre in History, Thought, and Culture*, ed. J. L. Friedmann and J. Gereboff (Claremont, CA; Claremont Press, 2021), 31–41.

action illustrates David's role in composing or authorizing many psalms in
the Book of Psalms.

DAVID'S VICTORY OVER GOLIATH – 1 SAMUEL 17:1–58

17 **¹ Now the Philistines gathered their armies for battle; they were
gathered at Socoh, which belongs to Judah, and encamped between
Socoh and Azekah, in Ephes-dammim.**

**² Saul and the Israelites gathered and encamped in the valley of Elah
and formed ranks against the Philistines.**

**³ The Philistines stood on the mountain on the one side, and Israel
stood on the mountain on the other side, with a valley between them.**

**⁴ And there came out from the camp of the Philistines a champion
named Goliath, of Gath, whose height was four cubits and a span.**

**⁵ He had a helmet of bronze on his head, and he was armed with a coat
of mail; the weight of the coat was five thousand shekels of bronze.**

**⁶ He had greaves of bronze on his legs and a javelin of bronze slung
between his shoulders.**

**⁷ The shaft of his spear was like a weaver's beam, and his spear's head
weighed six hundred shekels of iron, and his shield-bearer went before
him.**

**⁸ He stood and shouted to the ranks of Israel, "Why have you come out
to draw up for battle? Am I not a Philistine, and are you not servants
of Saul? Choose a man for yourselves, and let him come down to me.**

**⁹ If he is able to fight with me and kill me, then we will be your servants,
but if I prevail against him and kill him, then you shall be our servants
and serve us."**

**¹⁰ And the Philistine said, "Today I defy the ranks of Israel! Give me a
man, that we may fight together."**

**¹¹ When Saul and all Israel heard these words of the Philistine, they were
dismayed and greatly afraid.**

**¹² Now David was the son of an Ephrathite of Bethlehem in Judah
named Jesse, who had eight sons. In the days of Saul the man was
already old and advanced in years**

**¹³ The three eldest sons of Jesse had followed Saul to the battle; the
names of his three sons who went to the battle were Eliab the first-
born, and next to him Abinadab, and the third Shammah.**

[14] David was the youngest; the three eldest followed Saul,

[15] but David went back and forth from Saul to feed his father's sheep at Bethlehem.

[16] For forty days the Philistine came forward and took his stand, morning and evening.

[17] Jesse said to his son David, "Take for your brothers an ephah of this parched grain and these ten loaves, and carry them quickly to the camp to your brothers;

[18] also take these ten cheeses to the commander of their thousand. See how your brothers fare, and bring some token from them."

[19] Now Saul, and they, and all the men of Israel were in the valley of Elah fighting with the Philistines.

[20] David rose early in the morning, left the sheep with a keeper, took the provisions, and went as Jesse had commanded him. He came to the encampment as the army was going forth to the battle line, shouting the war cry.

[21] Israel and the Philistines drew up for battle, army against army.

[22] David left the things in charge of the keeper of the baggage, ran to the ranks, and went and greeted his brothers.

[23] As he talked with them, the champion, the Philistine of Gath, Goliath by name, came up out of the ranks of the Philistines and spoke the same words as before. And David heard him.

[24] All the Israelites, when they saw the man, fled from him and were very much afraid.

[25] The Israelites said, "Have you seen this man who has come up? Surely he has come up to defy Israel. The king will greatly enrich the man who kills him and will give him his daughter and make his family free in Israel."

[26] David said to the men who stood by him, "What shall be done for the man who kills this Philistine and takes away the reproach from Israel? For who is this uncircumcised Philistine that he should defy the armies of the living God?"

[27] The people answered him in the same way, "So shall it be done for the man who kills him."

[28] His eldest brother Eliab heard him talking to the men, and Eliab's anger was kindled against David. He said, "Why have you come down? With whom have you left those few sheep in the wilderness? I know your presumption and the evil of your heart, for you have come down just to see the battle."

²⁹ David said, "What have I done now? It was only a question."

³⁰ He turned away from him toward another and spoke in the same way, and the people answered him again as before.

³¹ When the words that David spoke were heard, they repeated them before Saul, and he sent for him.

³² David said to Saul, "Let no one's heart fail because of him; your servant will go and fight with this Philistine."

³³ Saul said to David, "You are not able to go against this Philistine to fight with him, for you are just a boy, and he has been a warrior from his youth."

³⁴ But David said to Saul, "Your servant used to keep sheep for his father, and whenever a lion or a bear came and took a lamb from the flock,

³⁵ I went after it and struck it down, rescuing the lamb from its mouth, and if it turned against me, I would catch it by the jaw, strike it down, and kill it.

³⁶ Your servant has killed both lions and bears, and this uncircumcised Philistine shall be like one of them, since he has defied the armies of the living God."

³⁷ David said, "The LORD, who saved me from the paw of the lion and from the paw of the bear, will save me from the hand of this Philistine." So Saul said to David, "Go, and may the LORD be with you!"

³⁸ Saul clothed David with his armor; he put a bronze helmet on his head and clothed him with a coat of mail.

³⁹ David strapped Saul's sword over the armor, and he tried in vain to walk, for he was not used to them. Then David said to Saul, "I cannot walk with these, for I am not used to them." So David removed them.

⁴⁰ Then he took his staff in his hand and chose five smooth stones from the wadi and put them in his shepherd's bag, in the pouch; his sling was in his hand, and he drew near to the Philistine.

⁴¹ The Philistine came on and drew near to David, with his shield-bearer in front of him.

⁴² When the Philistine looked and saw David, he disdained him, for he was only a youth, ruddy and handsome in appearance.

⁴³ The Philistine said to David, "Am I a dog, that you come to me with sticks?" And the Philistine cursed David by his gods.

⁴⁴ The Philistine said to David, "Come to me, and I will give your flesh to the birds of the air and to the wild animals of the field."

⁴⁵ But David said to the Philistine, "You come to me with sword and spear and javelin, but I come to you in the name of the LORD of hosts, the God of the armies of Israel, whom you have defied.

⁴⁶ This very day the LORD will deliver you into my hand, and I will strike you down and cut off your head, and I will give the dead bodies of the Philistine army this very day to the birds of the air and to the wild animals of the earth, so that all the earth may know that there is a God in Israel

⁴⁷ and that all this assembly may know that the LORD does not save by sword and spear, for the battle is the LORD's, and he will give you into our hand."

⁴⁸ When the Philistine drew nearer to meet David, David ran quickly toward the battle line to meet the Philistine.

⁴⁹ David put his hand in his bag, took out a stone, slung it, and struck the Philistine on his forehead; the stone sank into his forehead, and he fell face down on the ground.

⁵⁰ So David prevailed over the Philistine with a sling and a stone, striking down the Philistine and killing him; there was no sword in David's hand.

⁵¹ Then David ran and stood over the Philistine; he grasped his sword, drew it out of its sheath, and killed him; then he cut off his head with it.

When the Philistines saw that their champion was dead, they fled.

⁵² The troops of Israel and Judah rose up with a shout and pursued the Philistines as far as Gath and the gates of Ekron, so that the wounded Philistines fell on the way from Shaaraim as far as Gath and Ekron.

⁵³ The Israelites came back from chasing the Philistines, and they plundered their camp.

⁵⁴ David took the head of the Philistine and brought it to Jerusalem, but he put his armor in his tent.

⁵⁵ When Saul saw David go out against the Philistine, he said to Abner, the commander of the army, "Abner, whose son is this young man?" Abner said, "As your soul lives, O king, I do not know."

⁵⁶ The king said, "Inquire whose son the young man is."

⁵⁷ On David's return from killing the Philistine, Abner took him and brought him before Saul, with the head of the Philistine in his hand.

⁵⁸ Saul said to him, "Whose son are you, young man?" And David answered, "I am the son of your servant Jesse the Bethlehemite."

The account of David's victory over Goliath is one of the best-known narratives in Samuel, insofar as it presents David as a young shepherd boy who bravely takes on the heavily armed Philistine giant, Goliath, and kills him using his shepherd's sling. Nevertheless, the narrative poses some very serious critical problems, such as the demarcation of the unit as many interpreters define it as 1 Samuel 17:1–18:5, the earliest form of the unit. The Septuagint Greek Codex Vaticanus presents a much shorter text than the Masoretic version, and there is a question whether David actually killed Goliath, insofar as 2 Samuel 21:19 states that Elhanan son of Jaareoregim the Bethlehemite killed Goliath the Gittite.

The demarcation of the unit is tied up with the issue of the shorter text of Codex Vaticanus, which lacks 1 Samuel 17:12–31, 41, 48b, 50; 17:55–18:5; 18:6aα, 8a, 8b, 10–11, 12b, 17–19, 21b, and 29b–30, although the missing verses are found in Codex Alexandrinus and other Greek manuscripts. The absence of 1 Samuel 17:55–18:5 is a particularly important consideration in this discussion because it suggests that the LXX text of 1 Samuel (1 Reigns) binds 1 Samuel 18:1–5 to the preceding material in 1 Samuel 17. First Samuel 18:1–5 does indeed build upon the narrative in 1 Samuel 17 in that it mentions Jonathan's love for David in the aftermath of David's heroism in killing Goliath. But the notice concerning Jonathan's love for David provides the opening statement of an account of David's growing popularity and skill in defeating the Philistines in contrast to Saul's diminishing reputation and the onset of Saul's jealousy toward David. Jonathan's love for David is especially important for the motif of the growing rivalry between David and Saul because Jonathan is Saul's first-born son and heir to the throne of Israel, but the narrative makes it clear that Jonathan loves David because he recognizes David's leadership skills that Saul apparently lacks, as demonstrated in 1 Samuel 13–14 and 15. Although some have argued that Jonathan's love for David constitutes the foundation for a homosexual relationship between the two young men, such a view ignores the function of the Hebrew verb *'hb*, "to love," which is commonly used to portray the relationship between political allies in the ancient Near Eastern world.²⁵ Even Jonathan, Saul's son and heir,

---

²⁵   William L. Moran, "The Ancient Near Eastern Background of the Love of G-d in Deuteronomy," *CBQ* 25 (1963): 77–87.

recognizes David's leadership qualities in 1 Samuel 18:5, and this recognition introduces the motif of the rivalry between David and Saul that follows in 1 Samuel 18:6–30 and beyond.

The role of 1 Samuel 18:1–5 is bound up with the larger question of the interrelationship between the longer form of the MT of 1 Samuel 17–18 and the shorter form of 1 Samuel 17–18 in Codex Vaticanus.[26] Many scholars maintain that the so-called Old Greek of Vaticanus represents an earlier Hebrew *Vorlage* of the text and that the Masoretic version is a later expansion.[27] Others maintain that Vaticanus represents a text shortened in the interests of harmonizing the narrative.[28] The debate is based on a number of tensions evident in the present form of the Masoretic text: 1) David is introduced twice to Saul, in 1 Samuel 16:14–23 and 17:5–58/18:1–5, although Saul does not know him in the latter text; 2) David is introduced to the reader twice, in 1 Samuel 16:1–13 and 17:12–14; 3) the conflict with the Philistines is twice introduced, in 1 Samuel 17:13 and 17:19; 4) the Philistine, Goliath, is introduced twice, in 1 Samuel 17:4 and 17:23; 5) the portrayal of David's character differs in that he is an altruistic hero who relies on faith in YHWH in 1 Samuel 17:32–37, but he is concerned with reward in 1 Samuel 17:25–30; and 6) David kills Goliath twice, in 1 Samuel 17:50 and in 1 Samuel 17:51.

There is tension in that 1 Samuel 16:14–23 emphasizes David's musical skills in relation to Saul's deteriorating personality to explain Saul's jealousy of David and his attempts to kill him following David's victory over Goliath. But the narrative indicates Saul's close relationship with David, whereas 1 Samuel 17:55–58 indicates that Saul does not even know David. It seems likely that the two narratives presuppose different societal settings, viz., 1 Samuel 16:14–23 explains David's musical talents and thereby presupposes the setting of Jerusalemite worship and the role that David

---

[26] See Antony F. Campbell and Mark A. O'Brien, *Unfolding the Deuteronomistic History: Origins, Upgrades, and Present Text* (Minneapolis: Fortress, 2000) 259–265, who provide a convenient overview of the text that clearly identifies the portions missing in the Greek version of Vaticanus. For a full overview of the issue, see also Antony F. Campbell, *1 Samuel* (FOTL 7; Grand Rapids, MI/Cambridge, UK: Eerdmans, 2003), 171–184.

[27] See Klein, *1 Samuel*, 168–183; Dominique Barthélemy, D. W. Gooding, J. Lust, and Emanuel Tov, *The Story of David and Goliath: Textual and Literary Criticism* (OBO 73; Freiburg: Universitätsverlag; Göttingen: Vandenhoeck & Ruprect, 1986); McCarter, *1 Samuel*, 284–309; Hans Joachim Stoebe, *Das erste Buch Samuelis* (KAT VIII/1; Gütersloh: Gerd Mohn, 1973) 312–341; Walter Dietrich, *1 Samuel 13–26* (BKAT VIII/ 2; Neukirchen-Vluyn: Neukirchener Verlag, 2015), 289–392.

[28] See Barthélemy et al., *The Story of David and Goliath*.

plays as the author or patron of the writing of Psalms. First Samuel 17:1–58, however, presupposes a combat setting that aids in explaining David's military prowess and facility for leadership in defending the nation, a quality which Saul appears to lack. Second Samuel 16:14–23 appears to be redactional insertion before 1 Samuel 17:1–55 that contextualizes David's victory over Goliath by pointing to it as a key factor in Saul's progressing personality breakdown. Second Samuel 16:14–23 would then represent the Solomonic History, whereas 1 Samuel 17:1–58 represents an earlier pro-Davidic narrative.

A Closer Look at the Two Versions of 1 Samuel 17

The tensions within the text, particularly in regard to the shorter Vaticanus Greek text and the longer Masoretic text may also be explained. Earlier scholarship has presupposed that textual harmonization is the primary issue here, either to argue that the text was expanded by adding material from an alternative tradition to the presumed Hebrew *Vorlage* of the Vaticanus text or that the Hebrew proto-Masoretic text has been shortened to produce the Hebrew *Vorlage* for Vaticanus in order to remove tensions. But this is a far too mechanistic understanding of the process of textual formation. It is not entirely clear that the presumed expanded material in the Masoretic text presents a complete account that can stand by itself. The combat scenes, which appear in the supposed expansion, comprise only verses 41, 48b, 50 and are far too sparse for what should be the dramatic confrontation of the text. Something has dropped out, the texts have been somehow elided, or – more likely – prior scholarship has missed the mark in presuming textual harmonization to be the impetus behind the formation of the text.

Instead, the characterization of David appears to play a more important role. Prior scholarship has observed that David appears to be a selfless hero who fights a superior enemy based on his faith in YHWH in the shorter Vaticanus Greek version of the text, whereas David appears to be self-interested and ambitious in what he can gain should he defeat Goliath. Such a concern would be a problem in Vaticanus, an early fourth century CE Christian manuscript written in Greek, perhaps one of Epiphanius's fifty manuscripts commissioned at the beginning of the Constantinian Era. It would seem that the desire to present David, the founder of the Davidic line that led ultimately to Jesus Christ, as an altruistic hero who fights against overwhelming odds based on his faith in G-d would provide a more suitable account for how David ben Jesse demonstrated his worthiness before G-d to become the origin of the Messianic House of David. The proto-Masoretic text would be the earlier version – the Qumran 4Q Samuel a and b manuscripts provide no support for the shorter text in Vaticanus insofar as their fragmentary character does not preserve most of the missing Hebrew text for 1 Samuel 17.[29] 4QSamuel[a] presents small fragments of 1 Samuel 17:41 and 1 Samuel 18:4–5, which are missing in the Greek Vaticanus text. They therefore do not provide a textual witness to the Hebrew *Vorlage* of Vaticanus. Vaticanus would then present a later, shortened version of the text in 1 Samuel 17, to show David overcoming impossible odds based on his faith in G-d.

The other tensions mentioned above are then easily explained. 1) David's second introduction to Saul and Saul's failure to recognize him are due to the independent origin of the narrative in 1 Samuel 16:14–23. 2) Likewise, David's second introduction to the reader is due to the independent origin of 1 Samuel 16:14–23. 3) The two-fold introduction to the conflict with the Philistines in 1 Samuel 17:1–3 and 1 Samuel 17:19 is not a tension; 1 Samuel 17:19 is merely an incidental remark to explain why David must travel to the battle site to bring food to his brothers. 4) The two-fold introduction of the Philistine champion in 1 Samuel 17:4 and 1 Samuel 17:23 is a dramatic advance of the plot to indicate that Goliath of Gath steps forward while David talks with his brothers. 5) The differing characterizations of David as an altruistic hero and a self-interested warrior are artificial; David may have faith in G-d, but there is nothing wrong with finding out what there might be to gain. Such a portrayal of David's character entails both of these qualities throughout the Samuel narratives. 6) The presumed two-fold reference in 1 Samuel 17:50 and 1 Samuel 17:51 to David's killing Goliath is also artificial. When Goliath falls after having been struck with David's stone, he lays dying as a stone is not likely to kill him instantly. David must finish him with Goliath's own sword to ensure that he is dead and then cut off his head as a trophy to prove in graphic fashion what he has accomplished.

Overall, 1 Samuel 17:1–58 presents a dramatic account of David's celebrated victory over the Philistine giant, Goliath of Gath. It is not out of the question that David may have taken credit for a deed that should be attributed to Elhanan son of Jaareoregim of Bethlehem. The reference to David taking Goliath's head to Jerusalem suggests that the present form of the narrative was written far later than the event itself, insofar as David would not have taken Jerusalem until much later in his lifetime. Others explain the reference to Elhanan as an indication that this was David's name prior to his ascension to the throne with the throne name David, but this does not account for the father's name of Jaareoregim, although the

---

[29]   Frank Moore Cross, Jr. et al., *Qumran Cave 4. XII: 1–2 Samuel* (DJD 17; Oxford: Clarendon, 2005), esp. 78–81.

name does include a potential reference to Goliath's spear as the size of a weaver's (Hebrew,'*ōrĕgîm*, "weavers'") beam. David was not above setting up Uriah the Hittite, one of his own warriors (2 Sam 23:39), to be killed to get him out of the way following David's adultery with Bath Sheba; why would he not take credit for a victory won by another one of his own warriors?

The battle is set in the Valley of Elah, that is, the Valley of the Terebinth/ Oak (Hebrew,'*ēlâ*), known in Arabic as the *Wadi es-Sant*, "Valley of the Acacia," located some fifteen miles west-southwest of Bethlehem, running from Gath in the west to the base of the Judean Shephelah or hill country.[30] The sites mentioned in the text are located near a point when the Elah Valley turns north and then east again to present facing hillsides where the town sites are located. The Philistines encamp near Socoh (Josh 15:35; 2 Chr 28:18; cf. 2 Chr 11:6–10), a Judean walled town on the south side of Elah at the site of Khirbet ʿAbbad and near the site of Khirbet Suweikeh, which apparently preserves a rendition of the ancient Hebrew name, Sokoh.[31] Ephes Dammim (also known as Pas Dammim, see 1 Chr 11:13), the site of the Philistine camp, is identified with modern Damun, about four miles northeast of Sokoh.[32] Azekah, identified with Tell Zakariyah, is located on a hill overlooking the northern slope of the Elah Valley, about five and a half miles northeast of Beth Guvrin.[33] The sites indicate that the Philistines had advanced from Gath eastward to Judean territory near Sokoh on the south side of the Elah Valley, and the Israelites gathered to stop them on the north side of the Valley by Azekah.

The text refers to a "champion" named Goliath of Gath. Goliath is not a Semitic name. It is likely a Philistine name, perhaps with Anatolian roots.[34] The Hebrew term translated in the NRSVue as "champion" is *'îš habbēnayim*, literally, "a man between (two parties)." This term has been interpreted as a champion on the model of Homeric depictions that pit two champions from each army to fight each other to determine the outcome of a battle.[35] The concept is similar to the combat between Marduk and

---

[30] Jeffries Hamilton, "Elah, Valley of," *ABD* 2:423.
[31] H. Darrell Lance, "Socoh," *ABD* 6:99.
[32] Hamilton, "Ephes-Dammim," *ABD* 2:535.
[33] Ephraim Stern, "Azekah," *NEAEHL* 1:123–124.
[34] McCarter, *1 Samuel*, 291.
[35] Roland De Vaux, "Single Combat in the Old Testament," *The Bible and the Ancient Near East* (Garden City, NY: Doubleday, 1971) 122–135.

Tiamat in the Babylonian Enuma Elish or Creation Epic,[36] or the champions of Judah and Israel that fought each other at Gibeon in 2 Samuel 2. The portrayal of Goliath and his weapons and equipment appears to be hyperbole to impress the reader with the difficulty of overcoming such an enemy. Goliath's height of six cubits and a span is equivalent to about nine feet and nine inches, which is not impossible.[37] His bronze helmet is to be expected of a Philistine warrior insofar as the Philistines originated as the Sea Peoples from the Greek Islands or vicinity. His breastplate of scale armor is well known in the ancient world, although the 5,000-shekel weight would be the equivalent of about 125 pounds. Bronze greaves are to be expected, although the bronze javelin (Hebrew, *kîdôn*) is more likely to be a sword or a scimitar.[38] The shaft of his spear is likened to a weaver's beam (Hebrew, *měnôr 'ōrěgîm*) with an iron tip, all the better for piercing bronze armor, and weighs 600 shekels or fifteen pounds.[39] Goliath steps out to challenge the Israelite warriors twice per day, stating the terms that the winning side would be dominant and the losing side would then serve the winners. The Israelites are portrayed as terrified, and there are no takers.

First Samuel 17:12–15 portrays Israel's champion, David ben Jesse of Beth Lehem, the youngest of Jesse's eight sons. His older brothers, Eliab, Abinadab, and Shammah, have already been mentioned in 1 Samuel 16:1–13. Jesse had sent David, normally occupied with tending sheep, to take food, including an ephah of parched corn, ten loaves of bread for the brothers, and ten cuts of cheese for their commander. When David hears the challenge of Goliath, he asks about the reward for the man who might kill him. The response is that he would marry King Saul's daughter, receive riches, and be tax exempt. When Eliab, David's oldest brother, sees David, he scolds him for coming to watch the battle, but David responds in verse 29 like a normal teenager, "what have I done now? It was only a question!"

When Saul hears about the ruckus with Eliab, he has David brought to him for an explanation and a lecture that he cannot go to fight the Philistine. Although David is often understood to be a small boy, he

---

[36] Pritchard, *ANET*, 60–72.
[37] Qumran and LXX read four cubits.
[38] McCarter, *1 Samuel*, 292.
[39] McCarter, *1 Samuel*, 293.

responds with statements of his experience at defending the flock by killing lions and bears. When Saul attempts to give David his own armor and weapons, David complains that he cannot walk in the heavy equipment, and so with staff and sling in hand, he advanced toward Goliath. The most telling aspect of this encounter remains unspoken, however. Saul is the king, but Saul will not go out to meet Goliath's challenge. His failure to do so suggests that Saul might be a coward, but he is willing to send a teenage boy to his death.

David's approach to the Philistine in 1 Samuel 17:41–51a demonstrates David's skill and bravery. He is described as a ruddy (i.e., red-headed, handsome) youth. He carries a staff, but his sling is not mentioned. A sling is a weapon of war that is depicted in Assyrian reliefs of the siege of Lachish in 701 BCE,[40] but the weapon likely remains hidden behind David's back as he approaches so as not to alert his opponent. When Goliath curses him, David responds that he comes in the name of YHWH and that his victory will testify to the power of YHWH. As Goliath ran toward him, David picked a stone from his bag and slung it at Goliath, hitting him in the head and felling him. Without wasting any time, David ran forward, took Goliath's sword, and cut off his head, finishing him off. When the Philistines saw that Goliath was dead, they fled the field, and the Israelites pursued all the way to Gai, "Valley," although LXX reads, "Gath." The Elah Valley runs westward into Philistine territory, and the Philistine city of Gath lies on the south side of the Elah. The scenario portrays an extensive area into which the Israelites pursued the fleeing Philistines. Shaaraim may be identified with Tell Qeiyafa, located on the northern heights of the Elah Valley about midway between Azekah and Socoh on the southern side.[41]

The episode closes in 1 Samuel 17:54–58 with notices that David took Goliath's head to Jerusalem, which would have been a Jebusite city at the time, but he put Goliath's equipment in his own tent. The final notices indicate that neither Saul nor Saul's commander, Abner, have any idea who David is. From a literary standpoint, Saul should have known who David was.

[40] Pritchard, *The Ancient Near East* (Princeton: Princeton University Press, 2011), fig. 101.
[41] See Yosef Garfinkel et al., *In the Footsteps of King David: Revelations from an Ancient Biblical City* (New York: Thames and Hudson, 2018) 161–166.

THE LOVE OF SAUL'S OWN CHILDREN FOR DAVID IN CONTRAST
WITH SAUL'S JEALOUSY – 1 SAMUEL 18:1–30

18 ¹ When David had finished speaking to Saul, the soul of Jonathan was
bound to the soul of David, and Jonathan loved him as his own soul.

² Saul took him that day and would not let him return to his father's
house.

³ Then Jonathan made a covenant with David because he loved him as
his own soul.

⁴ Jonathan stripped himself of the robe that he was wearing and gave it
to David and his armor and even his sword and his bow and his belt.

⁵ David went out and was successful wherever Saul sent him; as a result,
Saul set him over the army. And all the people, even the servants of
Saul, approved.

⁶ As they were coming home, when David returned from killing the
Philistine, the women came out of all the towns of Israel, singing and
dancing, to meet King Saul, with tambourines, with songs of joy, and
with musical instruments.

⁷ And the women sang to one another as they made merry,

"Saul has killed his thousands
  and David his ten thousands."

⁸ Saul was very angry, for this saying displeased him. He said, "They
have ascribed to David ten thousands, and to me they have ascribed
thousands; what more can he have but the kingdom?"

⁹ So Saul eyed David from that day on.

¹⁰ The next day an evil spirit from God rushed upon Saul, and he raved
within his house, while David was playing the lyre, as he did day by
day. Saul had his spear in his hand,

¹¹ and Saul threw the spear, for he thought, "I will pin David to the
wall." But David eluded him twice.

¹² Saul was afraid of David because the LORD was with him but had
departed from Saul.

¹³ So Saul removed him from his presence and made him a commander
of a thousand, and David marched out and came in, leading the
army.

¹⁴ David had success in all his undertakings, for the LORD was with
him.

¹⁵ When Saul saw that he had great success, he stood in awe of him.

¹⁶ But all Israel and Judah loved David, for it was he who marched out and came in leading them.

¹⁷ Then Saul said to David, "Here is my elder daughter Merab; I will give her to you as a wife; only be valiant for me and fight the LORD's battles." For Saul thought, "I will not raise a hand against him; let the Philistines deal with him."

¹⁸ David said to Saul, "Who am I, and who are my kinsfolk, my father's family in Israel, that I should be son-in-law to the king?"

¹⁹ But at the time when Saul's daughter Merab should have been given to David, she was given to Adriel the Meholathite as a wife.

²⁰ Now Saul's daughter Michal loved David. Saul was told, and the thing pleased him.

²¹ Saul thought, "Let me give her to him that she may be a snare for him and that the hand of the Philistines may be against him." Therefore Saul said to David a second time,] "You shall now be my son-in-law."

²² Saul commanded his servants, "Speak to David in private and say, 'See, the king is delighted with you, and all his servants love you; now then, become the king's son-in-law.'"

²³ So Saul's servants reported these words to David in private. And David said, "Does it seem to you a little thing to become the king's son-in-law, seeing that I am a poor man and of no repute?"

²⁴ The servants of Saul told him, "This is what David said."

²⁵ Then Saul said, "Thus shall you say to David, 'The king desires no marriage present except a hundred foreskins of the Philistines, that he may be avenged on the king's enemies.'" Now Saul planned to make David fall by the hand of the Philistines.

²⁶ When his servants told David these words, David was well pleased to be the king's son-in-law. Before the time had expired,

²⁷ David rose and went, along with his men, and killed one hundred of the Philistines, and David brought their foreskins, which were given in full number to the king, that he might become the king's son-in-law. Saul gave him his daughter Michal as a wife.

²⁸ But when Saul realized that the LORD was with David and that Saul's daughter Michal loved him,

²⁹ Saul was still more afraid of David. So Saul was David's enemy from that time forward.

³⁰ Then the commanders of the Philistines came out to battle, and as often as they came out, David had more success than all the servants of Saul, so that his fame became very great.

A Closer Look at the Textual Versions of 1 Samuel 18

The absence of 1 Samuel 17:12–31, 41, 48b, 50; 17:55–18:5; 18:6aα, 8a, 8b, 10–11, 12b, 17–19, 21b, and 29b–30 likewise influences scholarly views of the integrity and demarcation of 1 Samuel 18. The missing text in 1 Samuel 18:1–5 prompts interpreters to view 1 Samuel 18:6 as the beginning of the new unit, due in part to its shift in focus from the account of Jonathan's love for David in the aftermath of his victory over Goliath and the shift in focus to the Israelite women lauding David for his victories, apparently more numerous than those of Saul. But just as the Greek text of 1 Samuel 17 appears to be a shortened text due to an interest in protecting the character of David, so the shorter text of 1 Samuel 18 in Codex Vaticanus appears to follow suit. The missing text in 1 Samuel 18:1–5, 6aα, 8a, 8b, 10–11, 12b, 17–19, 21b, and 29b–30 presents an account of Jonathan's love for David in 1 Samuel 18:1–5, which might be mistaken for a homosexual relationship between Jonathan and David for readers not familiar with the political function of the language of love in the ancient Near Eastern world.[42] The other elements in 1 Samuel 18:6aα, 8a, 8b, 10–11, 12b, 17–19, 21b, and 29b–30, eliminate any connection to the Goliath narratives (v. 6aα); redundancies, such as references to Saul's anger and the evil spirit influencing him (vv. 8a, 8b, 10–11, 12b); the references to Saul's first offer of his older daughter, Merab, to David for a wife which would highlight Saul's duplicity and illness (vv. 17–19, 21b); and the references to David's success in battle against the Philistines (vv. 29b–30). 4QSamuelᵃ preserves fragments of 1 Samuel 18:4–5, which are missing in Vaticanus. The Qumran scroll does not support the hypothesis that the shorter Greek text of Vaticanus is a witness to an earlier Hebrew *Vorlage* of 1 Samuel. Rather, Vaticanus and its associated manuscripts represent a shortened version of a proto-Masoretic text of 1 Samuel 17–18.[43]

First Samuel 18:1–5, which recounts Jonathan's love for David, serves as an introduction to 1 Samuel 18:1–30, which recounts the love for David by

---

[42]   Tom Horner, *Jonathan Loved David: Homosexuality in Biblical Times* (Philadelphia: Westminster, 1978); see also 1 Sam 20:17; 2 Sam 1:26. But see Moran, "The Ancient Near Eastern Background of the Love of G-d."

[43]   Cross et al., *Qumran Cave 4. XII: 1–2 Samuel*, esp. 78–81; see the discussion of 1 Sam 17.

both Jonathan, Saul's first-born son and presumed successor, and Michal, Saul's second-born daughter. The love of Saul's children for David then stands in striking contrast to the growing jealousy and animosity of Saul for David as he recognizes a figure far more capable than himself to serve as King of Israel. Neither Jonathan nor Michal is in a position to challenge the account, apparently written by Davidic supporters in the Solomonic edition of the text, which portrays them as willing partners with David in supplanting their father even though their support for David can cost them dearly. Jonathan is the presumed heir of Saul on the throne, but his love for David includes recognition that David will become the next King of Israel in his place. Michal loves David, marries him, and aids him in his efforts to resist her father, and thereby willingly participates in David's rise to power. As David's wife, Michal is in a position to bear sons to David who could succeed Saul should there be no sons born to Saul's own sons. But once Saul's sons are eliminated as potential heirs, David will eventually refuse to have marital relations with Michal, thereby enabling him to succeed Saul himself as son-in-law of the king (see 2 Sam 6).

The account in 1 Samuel 18:1–5 of Jonathan's love for David, so great that he strips off his own garments and weapons and presents them to David, provides motivation for Saul's jealousy of David and his growing anger toward him. First Samuel 18:1–5 makes it clear that David's victory over Goliath prompts Jonathan's love for David, but the following account of the women who sing accolades for David over Saul in 1 Samuel 18:6–7 likewise contribute to Saul's animosity. These texts shift the focus from David's battle with Goliath to Saul's battle with David, thereby presenting David with a more relentless foe than Goliath. David cannot kill Saul as he killed Goliath; the following narratives make it clear that David has no desire to kill Saul – even if Saul's death facilitates his rise to power – but Saul's animosity and efforts to kill David provide David with the opportunity to outmaneuver Saul as he displays the qualities of leadership that will eventually enable him to become King of Israel (2 Sam 5:1–3).

First Samuel 18:8–16 illustrates Saul's jealousy and anger against David due to David's success in winning the hearts of the women of Israel, who sing that David has killed his ten thousands while Saul has only killed his thousands, as well as the hearts of Jonathan and ultimately his own daughter Michal. But the sub-unit also recognizes the role that Saul's mental affliction, here noted in the form of an evil spirit from YHWH in 1 Samuel 18:10 (cf. 1 Sam 16:14–23), which prompts Saul to "rave" in his house while David plays the lyre (see NRSVue; NJPS). The translations are appropriate, but they obscure an essential element of this text, viz., the use of the verb *wayyitnabē'*, "and he prophesied," to portray his raving. The use of this verb indicates a very different dimension to Saul's prophesying in 1 Samuel 10:10 when he encountered a band of prophets on the road after having been anointed as King of Israel. That narrative is part of one of the laudatory accounts of the rise of King Saul in 1 Samuel 9:1–10:16, but the present text undermines the prior positive view of Saul with a notice that his "prophesying" presents a very different and dangerous dimension of Saul and the breakdown of his personality. It also points to a deceptive dimension of YHWH, who deliberately afflicts Saul with the evil spirit that undermines him and leads to his failure as King of Israel and tragic death by suicide on Mt. Gilboa in 1 Samuel 31.[44] As a result of his affliction, Saul throws a spear at David twice in an attempt to kill him. But David is so capable that he eludes both attempts and nevertheless continues to serve as a loyal servant to his king. Saul is incensed enough by his failure to kill David that he removes him from his presence and sends him out to war, perhaps with the intent to see him killed by the Philistines. But David succeeds at every turn against the Philistines – unlike Saul – and thereby continues to demonstrate his ability to surpass Saul as a leader qualified and capable to serve as King of Israel.

First Samuel 18:17–29 recounts Saul's efforts to marry one of his daughters to David, which entails that David would serve as a military commander, in the hope that his new role would lead to his death. Nevertheless, David shows both his mettle and his humility as a leader. Saul shows his inconsistency and duplicity in his treatment of David. When the time comes to marry off Merab, his oldest daughter, Saul gives her to Adriel the Meholathite, apparently another one of his officers whose marriage to the oldest daughter would signify higher rank among Saul's officers. The marriage of Adriel ben Barzillai (2 Sam 21:8) to Merab apparently seals an alliance with the town of Abel Meholah, the home of the prophet Elisha (1 Kgs 19:16), possibly identified with Tell Abu Sus, located about ten miles south of Beth Shean west of the Jordan River.[45] Saul's duplicity suggests his lack of integrity as a leader.

---

[44]   For another account of YHWH deliberately undermining a King of Israel, see 1 Kings 22, in which YHWH sends a lying spirit to deceive King Ahab of Israel, thereby leading to his death (Sweeney, *1 and 2 Kings*, 252–262).

[45]   Diana V. Edelman and Mark J. Fretz, "Adriel," *ABD* 1:81; Diana V. Edelman, "Abel Meholah," *ABD* 1:11–12.

With the marriage of Merab to Adriel, 1 Samuel 18:20 notes that Michal loved David and that Saul approved. But the text also makes it clear that Saul views Michal's marriage to David as an opportunity to kill him. When Saul's servants reported the king's invitation to David, David responded with humility, indicating that he was not able to provide an adequate bride's price for Michal. But this enabled Saul to propose that the bride's price be set at 100 Philistine foreskins, which presumes fully well that the Philistines are not going to give up their foreskins easily and that David will likely be killed in the effort to take them. David met the price and more by taking 200 Philistine foreskins, again demonstrating his military capabilities, his ability to outsmart Saul, and his capacity to serve as King of Israel. The episode notes that Saul recognizes David's abilities and therefore fears and hates him all the more.

The final statement in 1 Samuel 18:30 reiterates David's successes in battle against the Philistines and therefore his qualification to serve as king.

SAUL'S FURTHER ATTEMPT TO KILL DAVID – 1 SAMUEL 19:1–24

19 ¹ Saul spoke with his son Jonathan and with all his servants about killing David. But Saul's son Jonathan took great delight in David.

² Jonathan told David, "My father Saul is trying to kill you; therefore be on guard tomorrow morning; stay in a secret place and hide yourself.

³ I will go out and stand beside my father in the field where you are, and I will speak to my father about you; if I learn anything I will tell you."

⁴ Jonathan spoke well of David to his father Saul, saying to him, "The king should not sin against his servant David, because he has not sinned against you and because his deeds have been of good service to you,

⁵ for he took his life in his hand when he attacked the Philistine, and the LORD brought about a great victory for all Israel. You saw it and rejoiced; why then will you sin against an innocent person by killing David without cause?"

⁶ Saul heeded the voice of Jonathan; Saul swore, "As the LORD lives, he shall not be put to death."

⁷ So Jonathan called David and related all these things to him. Jonathan then brought David to Saul, and he was in his presence as before.

⁸ Again there was war, and David went out to fight the Philistines. He launched a heavy attack on them, so that they fled before him.

⁹ Then an evil spirit from the LORD came upon Saul as he sat in his house with his spear in his hand, while David was playing music.

¹⁰ Saul sought to pin David to the wall with the spear, but he eluded Saul, so that he struck the spear into the wall. David fled and escaped that night.

¹¹ Saul sent messengers to David's house to keep watch over him, planning to kill him in the morning. David's wife Michal told him, "If you do not save your life tonight, tomorrow you will be killed."

¹² So Michal let David down through the window; he fled away and escaped.

¹³ Michal took an idol and laid it on the bed; she put a net of goats' hair on its head and covered it with the clothes.

¹⁴ When Saul sent messengers to take David, she said, "He is sick."

¹⁵ Then Saul sent the messengers to see David for themselves. He said, "Bring him up to me in the bed, that I may kill him."

¹⁶ When the messengers came in, the idol was in the bed, with the covering of goats' hair on its head.

¹⁷ Saul said to Michal, "Why have you deceived me like this and let my enemy go, so that he has escaped?" Michal answered Saul, "He said to me, 'Let me go; why should I kill you?'"

¹⁸ Now David fled and escaped; he came to Samuel at Ramah and told him all that Saul had done to him. He and Samuel went and settled at Naioth.

¹⁹ Saul was told, "David is at Naioth in Ramah."

²⁰ Then Saul sent messengers to take David. When they saw the company of the prophets in a frenzy, with Samuel standing in charge of them, the spirit of God came upon the messengers of Saul, and they also fell into a prophetic frenzy.

²¹ When Saul was told, he sent other messengers, and they also fell into a frenzy. Saul sent messengers again the third time, and they also fell into a frenzy.

²² Then he himself went to Ramah. He came to the great well that is in Secu; he asked, "Where are Samuel and David?" And someone said, "They are at Naioth in Ramah."

²³ He went there, toward Naioth in Ramah, and the spirit of God came upon him. As he was going, he fell into a prophetic frenzy, until he came to Naioth in Ramah.

²⁴ **He, too, stripped off his clothes, and he, too, fell into a frenzy before Samuel. He lay naked all that day and all that night. Therefore it is said, "Is Saul also among the prophets?"**

First Samuel 19 continues with a focus on Saul's deteriorating mental state and his willingness to enlist his children, Jonathan and Michal, in his efforts to kill David. The narrative begins in 1 Samuel 19:1–7, which depicts Saul's open efforts to persuade Jonathan to kill David and Jonathan's loyalty to David. Jonathan immediately warns David of the danger and proposes a meeting with Saul that will clarify Saul's intentions. He tells David to hide himself in a field where he will bring Saul to discuss David's merits. He praises David to Saul and suggests that David has done no wrong to him. Saul agrees with Jonathan that David does not deserve death, but the following sub-units show that the evil spirit from YHWH continues to afflict Saul, who will once again engage in his irrational attempts to kill David.

First Samuel 19:8–10 turns to an account of such an attempt. The narrative notes that the evil spirit from YHWH again torments Saul, and he again throws a spear at David as he plays the lyre to soothe Saul. David easily dodges the spear, but the repetition of this motif builds the case that Saul's mental state is rapidly collapsing, posing a threat to David and Israel at large.

First Samuel 19:11–17 portrays Saul's attempt to send assassins to David's home in the city while he is asleep in bed. The city is presumably Gibeah of Saul, Saul's capital. Michal warns David of the threat and helps him to escape, again illustrating the premise that Saul's children, Michal and Jonathan, do everything they can to help David even though they have much to lose if David supplants their father as King of Israel. Michal places a family idol, named in Hebrew as *hattĕrāpîm*, "household idols" (cf. Gen 31:19–35). The presence of such family idols would illustrate the Canaanite background of Saul's family and northern Israel at large. Michal helps David escape out of the window, indicating that their house was built into the wall of the city (cf. Josh 2:15–21). She placed the household idol in the bed and disguised it to suggest that David was asleep in the bed. When Saul's men came for David, she replied that he was sick in bed. Not to be deterred, Saul ordered his men to bring David to him, even in his bed, so that he could kill him. But when the men discovered the ruse, Saul demanded an explanation from Michal, who responded that David threatened to kill her. Michal is under no moral obligation to sacrifice herself to an obviously dangerous Saul.

First Samuel 19: 18–24 portrays David's escape to Samuel at Ramah and their efforts to hide from Saul at Naioth. The location of Naioth is uncertain, although the narrative indicates that it is "in Ramah" (1 Sam 19:23). The Hebrew term, *nāyôt* (Qere reading of the Ketiv, *nĕwāyōt*), suggests that the term refers to the "pastures" (Hebrew, *nĕ'ôt*, derived from, *nāwâ*, "pasture") of Ramah, outside the city.[46] When Saul sent messengers to capture David, they encountered a band of prophets who were prophesying under the leadership of Samuel. As the spirit of G-d descended on Saul's men, they too started to prophesy, impeding them from carrying out their mission. Saul sent two further groups of messengers with the same result (cf. 2 Kgs 1). Saul finally traveled to Ramah to take care of matters himself, but when the spirit of G-d overcame him and prompted him to prophesy as well, Saul eventually stripped off his clothing to prophesy naked before Samuel all night. Saul's performance prompted witnesses to ask once again, "Is Saul also among the prophets?" as in 1 Samuel 10:9–13. Whereas in 1 Samuel 10:9–13 this question suggests approval or affirmation of Saul, here it suggests Saul's madness. The episodes illustrate Saul's deteriorating mental state and his incapacity to serve as King of Israel.

DAVID'S ESCAPE FROM SAUL – 1 SAMUEL 20:1–21:1

20 **¹ David fled from Naioth in Ramah. He came before Jonathan and said, "What have I done? What is my guilt? And what is my sin against your father that he is trying to take my life?"**

² He said to him, "Far from it! You shall not die. My father does nothing either great or small without disclosing it to me, and why should my father hide this from me? Never!"

³ But David also swore, "Your father knows well that you like me, and he thinks, 'Do not let Jonathan know this, or he will be grieved.' But truly, as the LORD lives and as you yourself live, there is but a step between me and death."

⁴ Then Jonathan said to David, "Whatever you say, I will do for you."

---

46   Hamilton, "Naioth," *ABD* 4:1001; McCarter, *1 Samuel*, 328–329; cf. Abraham Malamat, *Mari and the Early Israelite Experience* (Schweich Lectures; Oxford: The British Academy and Oxford University Press, 1989) 43–46.

⁵ David said to Jonathan, "Tomorrow is the new moon, and I should not fail to sit with the king at the meal, but let me go, so that I may hide in the field until the third evening.

⁶ If your father misses me at all, then say, 'David earnestly asked leave of me to run to Bethlehem his city, for there is a yearly sacrifice there for all the family.'

⁷ If he says, 'Good!' it will be well with your servant, but if he is angry, then know that evil has been determined by him.

⁸ Therefore deal kindly with your servant, for you have brought your servant into a sacred covenant with you. But if there is guilt in me, kill me yourself; why should you bring me to your father?"

⁹ Jonathan said, "Far be it from you! If I knew that it was decided by my father that evil should come upon you, would I not tell you?"

¹⁰ Then David said to Jonathan, "Who will tell me if your father answers you harshly?"

¹¹ Jonathan replied to David, "Come, let us go out into the field." So they both went out into the field.

¹² Jonathan said to David, "By the LORD, the God of Israel! When I have sounded out my father, about this time tomorrow or on the third day, if he is well disposed toward David, shall I not then send and disclose it to you?

¹³ But if my father intends to do you harm, the LORD do so to Jonathan and more also, if I do not disclose it to you and send you away, so that you may go in safety. May the LORD be with you, as he has been with my father.

¹⁴ If I am still alive, show me the faithful love of the LORD, but if I die,

¹⁵ never cut off your faithful love from my house, even if the L-RD were to cut off every one of the enemies of David from the face of the earth."

¹⁶ Thus Jonathan made a covenant with the house of David, saying, "May the LORD seek out the enemies of David."

¹⁷ Jonathan made David swear again by his love for him, for he loved him as he loved his own life.

¹⁸ Jonathan said to him, "Tomorrow is the new moon; you will be missed because your place will be empty.

¹⁹ On the day after tomorrow, you shall go a long way down; go to the place where you hid yourself earlier, and remain beside the stone there.

²⁰ I will shoot three arrows to the side of it, as though I shot at a mark.

²¹ Then I will send the boy, saying, 'Go, find the arrows.' If I say to the boy, 'Look, the arrows are on this side of you; collect them,' then you are to come, for, as the LORD lives, it is safe for you and there is no danger.

²² But if I say to the young man, 'Look, the arrows are beyond you,' then go, for the LORD has sent you away.

²³ As for the matter about which you and I have spoken, the LORD be between you and me forever."

²⁴ So David hid himself in the field. When the new moon came, the king sat at the feast to eat.

²⁵ The king sat upon his seat, as at other times, upon the seat by the wall. Jonathan stood, while Abner sat by Saul's side, but David's place was empty.

²⁶ Saul did not say anything that day, for he thought, "Something has befallen him; he is not clean; surely he is not clean."

²⁷ But on the second day, the day after the new moon, David's place was empty. And Saul said to his son Jonathan, "Why has the son of Jesse not come to the feast, either yesterday or today?"

²⁸ Jonathan answered Saul, "David earnestly asked leave of me to go to Bethlehem;

²⁹ he said, 'Let me go, for our family is holding a sacrifice in the city, and my brother has commanded me to be there. So now, if I have found favor in your sight, let me get away and see my brothers.' For this reason he has not come to the king's table."

³⁰ Then Saul's anger was kindled against Jonathan. He said to him, "You son of a rebellious woman! Do I not know that you have chosen the son of Jesse to your own shame and to the shame of your mother's nakedness?

³¹ For as long as the son of Jesse lives upon the earth, neither you nor your kingdom shall be established. Now send and bring him to me, for he shall surely die."

³² Then Jonathan answered his father Saul, "Why should he be put to death? What has he done?"

³³ But Saul threw his spear at him to strike him, so Jonathan knew that it was the decision of his father to put David to death.

³⁴ Jonathan sprang up from the table in fierce anger and ate no food on the second day of the month, for he was grieved for David and because his father had disgraced him.

³⁵ In the morning Jonathan went out into the field to the appointment with David, and with him was a little boy.

³⁶ He said to the boy, "Run and find the arrows that I shoot." As the boy ran, he shot an arrow beyond him.

³⁷ When the boy came to the place where Jonathan's arrow had fallen, Jonathan called after the boy and said, "Is the arrow not beyond you?"

³⁸ Jonathan called after the boy, "Hurry, be quick, do not linger." So Jonathan's boy gathered up the arrows and came to his master.

³⁹ But the boy knew nothing; only Jonathan and David knew the arrangement.

⁴⁰ Jonathan gave his weapons to the boy and said to him, "Go and carry them to the city."

⁴¹ As soon as the boy had gone, David rose from beside the stone heap and prostrated himself with his face to the ground. He bowed three times, and they kissed each other and wept with each other; David wept the more.

⁴² Then Jonathan said to David, "Go in peace, since both of us have sworn in the name of the LORD, saying, 'The LORD shall be between me and you and between my descendants and your descendants forever.'" He got up and left, and Jonathan went into the city.

21 ¹ David came to Nob to the priest Ahimelech. Ahimelech came trembling to meet David and said to him, "Why are you alone and no one with you?"

First Samuel 20:1–21:1 portrays Saul's willingness to engage in a blatant attempt to murder David and the willingness of Saul's son, Jonathan, to assist David in his efforts to escape from Saul. Jonathan is willing to deceive his father, despite the fact that he has much to lose if David becomes king. The narrative accentuates the portrayal of Saul's son as lacking confidence in his own father and giving his full support to David even as he fears Saul's retribution. Such a portrayal is all the more remarkable when read in relation to David's willingness to turn the descendants of Saul over to the Gibeonites for execution in 2 Samuel 21.

The demarcation of 1 Samuel 20:1–21:1 is based on the thematic focus of the narrative on David's escape from Saul's attempted murder with the support of Jonathan and Michal. This concern begins in 1 Samuel 20:1 with the notice of David's flight from Naioth in Ramah to Jonathan to ask for his assistance. Although the chapter division follows 1 Samuel 20:42, the narrative must include 1 Samuel 21:1, which narrates the departures of

David and Jonathan. The following verse in 1 Samuel 21:2 shifts to David's encounter with Ahimelech at Nob.

First Samuel 20:1–21:1 includes three episodic sub-units, including the account of David's conversation with Jonathan in 1 Samuel 20:1–23; the account of the results of Jonathan's plan to discover Saul's intentions and report them to David in 1 Samuel 20:24–34; and the account of Jonathan's warning to David in 1 Samuel 20:35–21:1.

The account of David's conversation with Jonathan concerning his problems with Saul raises a number of key issues. The location of the conversation is likely Saul's court at Gibeah of Saul. A key issue is Jonathan's belief that he has influence with his father, whom he thinks shares all his thoughts with him. But David's response to Jonathan persuades Jonathan to devise a plan to see if indeed Saul is concealing his animosity toward David. David lays out a plan to be absent from the king's table at the upcoming celebration of the New Moon (Num 28:11–15). David's plan calls for an explanation for his absence, viz., that his family requires him to be present for a sacrifice in Beth Lehem. David reminds Jonathan of the covenant that the two friends made in 1 Samuel 18:1–4 and proposes that Jonathan may kill him if David is wrong. Although Jonathan dismisses the threat, David's response intimates that Jonathan might be in danger if Saul reacts with anger. The earlier instances in which Saul cast a spear at David in 1 Samuel 18:8–16 and 19:8–10 would provide the basis for David's concern.

Jonathan responds to David by proposing a plan of his own. He will investigate the matter on the next day to see how Saul reacts to David's absence and inform David of the results on the following third day.[47] But Jonathan demands David's full loyalty, thereby specifying the terms of the covenant in 1 Samuel 18:1–4. This specification anticipates David's care for Jonathan's son, Mephibosheth, in 2 Samuel 9, even though David hands over Saul's other descendants for execution by the Gibeonites in 2 Samuel 21. Jonathan's plan to inform David includes a clandestine warning. David is to hide behind the Ezel Stone, an otherwise unknown location. The meaning of Ezel (Hebrew, *hā'āzel*) is uncertain,[48] although it may be

---

[47] There is controversy concerning the temporal language, viz., *māḥār*, "tomorrow," in v. 18, and *wešilaštā*, "and you shall (go on) the third day" (i.e., the day after tomorrow) in v. 19, but the terminology fits the temporal pattern proposed by Jonathan in the text.

[48] See the NRSVue note to v. 19. LXX refers simply to "that stone heap," apparently an interpretation of the Hebrew text. See Yoshitaka Kobayashi, "Ezel," *ABD* 2:722.

derived from the Aramaic root *'zl*, "to leave, go," or the Hebrew particle *'eṣel*, "beside," which appears in v. 19. On the third day, Jonathan will come to practice with his bow. If he shoots beside the stone, all is well, but if he shoots beyond the stone, David is in danger.

The account of Jonathan's test of Saul in 1 Samuel 20:24–34 confirms David's suspicions about Saul. While David hides in the field, Jonathan attends the festival dinner with Saul and Abner. The identity of the presumed four men at the table indicates the power structure in Saul's regime, including Saul as king, Jonathan as son and presumed heir to the throne, Abner as commander of the northern Israelite army, and David as commander of the Judean forces. This arrangement suggests that Saul's kingdom is a federation of tribes that will later form northern Israel and southern Judah. As a vassal to Saul and northern Israel, David's presence is expected. But when Jonathan explains David's absence as due to his need to attend a family festival in Beth Lehem, Saul flies into a rage. Saul's reaction on the second day portrays him as insanely overreacting when he exclaims in vv. 30–31 that Jonathan has chosen David over his own family. Saul is right about David; if David remains alive, Jonathan's kingdom is at risk. Saul's insanity then manifests itself in his attempt to kill Jonathan just as he had attempted to kill David. Jonathan now realizes the extent of Saul's madness and leaves the table in anger.

Jonathan proceeds to inform David in 1 Samuel 20:35–21:1. He goes to the Ezel Stone with a servant boy, and he shoots three arrows beyond the stone to warn David of the danger. David shows utmost respect and subservience to Jonathan by bowing three times and weeping even longer than Jonathan does at the realization of the situation. Jonathan's departing statements call for David to go in peace, but he reminds David of their obligation to protect their offspring. Jonathan returns to the city, but David heads south, Hebrew, *hannegeb*, toward the Negev Desert in southern Judah.

DAVID SEEKS ASSISTANCE FROM AHIMELECH OF NOB AND
ACHISH OF GATH – 1 SAMUEL 21:2–16

> **21 ² David said to the priest Ahimelech, "The king has charged me with a matter and said to me, 'No one must know anything of the matter about which I send you and with which I have charged you.' I have made an appointment with the young men for such and such a place.**

³ Now then, what have you at hand? Give me five loaves of bread or whatever is here."

⁴ The priest answered David, "I have no ordinary bread at hand, only holy bread – provided that the young men have kept themselves from women."

⁵ David answered the priest, "Indeed, women have been kept from us as always when I go on an expedition; the vessels of the young men are holy even when it is a common journey; how much more today will their vessels be holy?"

⁶ So the priest gave him the holy bread, for there was no bread there except the bread of the Presence, which is removed from before the LORD, to be replaced by hot bread on the day it is taken away.

⁷ Now a certain man of the servants of Saul was there that day, detained before the LORD; his name was Doeg the Edomite, the chief of Saul's shepherds.

⁸ David said to Ahimelech, "Is there no spear or sword here with you? I did not bring my sword or my weapons with me because the king's business required haste."

⁹ The priest said, "The sword of Goliath the Philistine, whom you killed in the valley of Elah, is here wrapped in a cloth behind the ephod; if you will take that, take it, for there is none here except that one." David said, "There is none like it; give it to me."

¹⁰ David rose and fled that day from Saul; he went to King Achish of Gath.

¹¹ The servants of Achish said to him, "Is this not David the king of the land? Did they not sing to one another of him in dances,

'Saul has killed his thousands

   and David his ten thousands'?"

¹² David took these words to heart and was very much afraid of King Achish of Gath.

¹³ So he changed his behavior before them; he pretended to be mad when in their presence. He scratched marks on the doors of the gate and let his spittle run down his beard.

¹⁴ Achish said to his servants, "Look, you see the man is mad; why then have you brought him to me?

¹⁵ Do I lack madmen, that you have brought this fellow to play the madman in my presence? Shall this fellow come into my house?"

First Samuel 21:2–16 narrates David's transition from his position as a member of the court of King Saul to become a fugitive, pursued by Saul and forced to become an ally of the Philistines. The narrative comprises two brief sub-units. First Samuel 21:2–10 presents an account of David's efforts to seek support from Ahimelech, the leading figure among the priests at Nob, who represent the surviving members of the Elide priestly line. First Samuel 21:10–16 recounts David's flight to King Achish of Gath in an attempt to seek support from the Philistines, the primary enemy of Israel. The preceding narratives have focused especially on Saul's emotional breakdown, caused by an evil spirit from YHWH, as the root cause of the rift between Saul and David. But Saul and David also have a political relationship in which Israel would serve as the suzerain power, whereas David's home tribe of Judah would serve as a vassal to northern Israel. David's maneuvering between Saul and the Philistines will ultimately enable him to become King of Judah, King of Israel, and suzerain ruler of Philistia (see 2 Sam 1–8).

The account of David's flight to Ahimelech takes him to Nob, which is associated with Mt. Scopus or Har ha-Tzophim, the present-day site of Hadassah Hospital, the Hebrew University Mt. Scopus campus, the German Archaeological Institute, and the Augusta Victoria Hospital. Mt. Scopus is situated across the Wadi el-Joz, immediately to the northeast of the site of Jerusalem during the transition from the Late-Bronze Age to the early Iron Age.[49] Most interpreters identify the site where Ahimelech resided as 'Isawiyeh, located immediately to the north of the present-day Mt. Scopus campus of Hebrew University.[50]

Ahimelech is the son of Ahitub (1 Sam 22:9, 10–11), and Ahitub is the brother of Ichabod ben Phineas ben Eli (1 Sam 14:3). This genealogy makes Ahimelech the great grandson of Eli. Eli is portrayed as a descendant of the line of Ithamar in 1 Chronicles 24:3.[51]

First Samuel 21:2–10 prepares the reader for the massacre of the priests of Nob recounted in 1 Samuel 22. David flees to Ahimelech in order to secure support, but he appears unsure if Ahimelech will help him. Ahimelech asks him why he is alone, indicating suspicion that David is a

---

[49] Hamilton, "Nob," *ABD* 4:1133.
[50] Walter Dietrich, *Samuel* (BKAT VIII; Neukirchen-Vluyn: Neukirchener Verlag/ Göttingen: Vandenhoeck & Ruprecht, 2011–2021), 573; David Toshio Tsumura, *The First Book of Samuel* (NICOT; Grand Rapids, MI, and Cambridge, UK: Eerdmans, 2007), 529; Klein, *1 Samuel*, 212.
[51] See William H. C. Propp, "Ithamar," *ABD* 3:579–581.

fugitive from the king. David recognizes the problem, which prompts him to claim that the king has sent him on a secret mission to explain why his men would have to hide.

David's request for food for himself and his unseen men elicits a reply from the priest that appears to be a dodge, viz., Ahimelech explains that no common bread is available at Nob, but consecrated bread is available. Consecrated bread is set out before the Holy of Holies in the Temple as an offering to YHWH (Num 15:17–21; Ezek 44:30). It may be eaten by the priests or those laypersons who have been consecrated for Temple service. David's explanation that his men were consecrated is based on his claim that they had not been around women (cf. Exod 19:14–15).

First Samuel 21:8 notes that Doeg the Edomite, Chief of the Shepherds to King Saul (Hebrew, *'abbîr hārō'îm*), was present during David's visit. Doeg likely oversaw the king's flocks and herds. Perhaps he was at Nob to claim the royal tithe on the offerings of the people.

David's request for a weapon also raises questions for Ahimelech, but again David deceives him by claiming that the urgency of his mission precluded carrying weapons. Such an assertion is hardly convincing, but Ahimelech readily accepts it – he had already fallen for David's earlier lie – and he tells David that he can take Goliath's sword, which is placed behind the ephod in the sanctuary. This offer raises questions because David supposedly put Goliath's equipment in his own tent according to 1 Samuel 17:53. Such a discrepancy suggests poor editing (cf. 1 Sam 14:18). The presence of Goliath's sword at Nob, however, is not entirely a surprise. Excavations at Vered Jericho uncovered a fortified building that apparently served as an administrative center in the seventh century BCE. Buried on the site with the corpse of a man was a sword approximately three feet long.[52]

First Samuel 21:11–16 recounts David's flight to King Achish of Gath following his brief stay at Nob. Gath, the home of Goliath, is an enemy city of Israel. The servants of Achish recognized David and repeated the chant of the women when David returned from his victory over Goliath in 1 Samuel 18:6–7. David understands his vulnerability and feigns madness by scratching on the doors of the city gate and slobbering down his beard.

[52]   Avraham Eitan, "Vered Yeriho," *NEAEHL* 5:2067–2068; Amihai Mazar, *Archaeology of the Land of the Bible, 10,000–586 BCE* (New York: Doubleday, 1990) 452; Ephraim Stern, *Archaeology of the Land of the Bible. Volume II: The Assyrian, Babylonian, and Persian Periods (732–332 BCE)* (New York: Doubleday, 2001) 134–135.

Achish's response in v. 16 is meant to elicit laughter: "(Do I) lack madmen that you bring this one to rant on me?"

SAUL'S PURSUIT OF DAVID AND SLAUGHTER OF THE PRIESTS OF NOB – 1 SAMUEL 22:1–23

22 ¹ David left there and escaped to the cave of Adullam; when his brothers and all his father's house heard of it, they went down there to him.

² Everyone who was in distress, and everyone who was in debt, and everyone who was discontented gathered to him, and he became captain over them. Those who were with him numbered about four hundred.

³ David went from there to Mizpeh of Moab. He said to the king of Moab, "Please let my father and mother come to you, until I know what God will do for me."

⁴ He left them with the king of Moab, and they stayed with him all the time that David was in the stronghold.

⁵ Then the prophet Gad said to David, "Do not remain in the stronghold; leave and go into the land of Judah." So David left and went into the forest of Hereth.

⁶ Saul heard that David and those who were with him had been located. Saul was sitting at Gibeah, under the tamarisk tree on the height, with his spear in his hand, and all his servants were standing around him.

⁷ Saul said to his servants who stood around him, "Hear now, you Benjaminites; will the son of Jesse give every one of you fields and vineyards? Will he make you all commanders of thousands and commanders of hundreds?

⁸ Is that why all of you have conspired against me? No one discloses to me when my son makes a league with the son of Jesse; none of you is sorry for me or discloses to me that my son has stirred up my servant against me to lie in wait, as he is doing today."

⁹ Doeg the Edomite, who was in charge of Saul's servants, answered, "I saw the son of Jesse coming to Nob, to Ahimelech son of Ahitub;

¹⁰ he inquired of the LORD for him, gave him provisions, and gave him the sword of Goliath the Philistine."

¹¹ The king sent for the priest Ahimelech son of Ahitub and for all his father's house, the priests who were at Nob, and all of them came to the king.

¹² Saul said, "Listen now, son of Ahitub." He answered, "Here I am, my lord."

¹³ Saul said to him, "Why have you conspired against me, you and the son of Jesse, by giving him bread and a sword and by inquiring of God for him, so that he has risen against me to lie in wait, as he is doing today?"

¹⁴ Then Ahimelech answered the king, "Who among all your servants is so faithful as David? He is the king's son-in-law and is quick to do your bidding and is honored in your house.

¹⁵ Is today the first time that I have inquired of God for him? By no means! Do not let the king impute anything to his servant or to any member of my father's house, for your servant has known nothing of all this, much or little."

¹⁶ The king said, "You shall surely die, Ahimelech, you and all your father's house."

¹⁷ The king said to the guard who stood around him, "Turn and kill the priests of the LORD, because their hand also is with David; they knew that he fled and did not disclose it to me." But the servants of the king would not raise a hand to attack the priests of the LORD.

¹⁸ Then the king said to Doeg, "You, Doeg, turn and attack the priests." Doeg the Edomite turned and attacked the priests; on that day he killed eighty-five who wore the linen ephod.

¹⁹ Nob, the city of the priests, he put to the sword; men and women, children and infants, oxen, donkeys, and sheep, he put to the sword.

²⁰ But one of the sons of Ahimelech son of Ahitub, named Abiathar, escaped and fled after David.

²¹ Abiathar told David that Saul had killed the priests of the LORD.

²² David said to Abiathar, "I knew on that day, when Doeg the Edomite was there, that he would surely tell Saul. I am responsible for the lives of all your father's house.

²³ Stay with me, and do not be afraid, for the one who seeks my life seeks your life; you will be safe with me."

First Samuel 22:1–23 recounts Saul's pursuit of David and slaughter of the priests of Nob. The narrative comprises three major components: David's escape to Adullam, where he began to build a following, to Mizpeh of Moab, where he hid his parents, and finally to the forest of Hereth in 1 Samuel 22:1–5; Saul's slaughter of the priests of Nob in 1 Samuel 22:6–19; and Abiathar's escape to David in 1 Samuel 22:20–23. These narratives point to the breakdown of Saul's capacity to serve as King of Israel and David's increasing capacity as a leader.

The account of David's escape from Saul begins with his flight to the cave of Adullam in 1 Samuel 22:1–5. Adullam is located in the Judean Shephelah approximately halfway between Gath (Tel Ṣafit) to the west and Beth Lehem to the east (Josh 15:35), about ten miles east-southeast of Gath.[53] Adullam is identified with Tel Esh Sheikh Madhkur, also known as 'Id El-mâ, located on a hilltop overlooking the Elah Valley near the boundary between Israel and the West Bank. The area around Adullam is known for its caves, which would have provided protection to David and his followers. The narrative indicates that David was joined by his brothers and the rest of his father's family, which suggests that the House of Jesse was viewed with hostility by Saul, as well as those who were in difficulty. Such an announcement suggests that the alliance between Judah and Saul had broken down. Saul appears determined to force Judah to submit to him, although the narrative portrays Saul as acting irrationally. Saul's actions again demonstrate that he is unfit for leadership insofar as he lashes out against those on whom he would rely for support. David's followers number 400, but the figure will later grow to 600 (1 Sam 23:13; 25:13; 27:2; 30:9, 10).

David's move to Mizpeh of Moab is intended to secure sanctuary for his parents. The site of Mizpeh of Moab is generally identified with either Kerak or Rujm el-Meshrefah, southwest of Madaba, in Jordan.[54] David's ability to move freely throughout Judah and into Moab indicates widespread support in both Judah and Moab. The need to hide his parents presupposes the threat that Saul poses to his family, apparently due to his interest in wiping out leadership in Judah to facilitate his own efforts to subjugate Judah. David's location in Moab also provides a basis for the much later narrative in Ruth that identifies Ruth as his great grandmother (Ruth 4:17–23). The prophet Gad, a supporter of David who was later supplanted by Nathan (2 Sam 24:11–19; cf. 1 Chr 21:9–19; 29:29; 2 Chr 29:25), advises him to return to Judah. Such a move would protect David's parents and enable him to build support in Judah.

David's final move to the forest of Hereth places him near Keilah, a Judean town in the Shephelah located to the south of Adullam, which

---

[53]   McCarter, 1 Samuel, 369; Jacques Briend, "Adullam," EBR 1:446–447; Hamilton, "Adullam," ABD 1:81.

[54]   Arnold, "Mizpah," ABD 4:880.

David would propose to protect from Philistine attack in 1 Samuel 23. Again, the move would provide protection from Saul and enable him to build his constituency as a protector of Judah from either Saul or the Philistines.

A Closer Look at the Massacre of the Priests of Nob

The account of Saul's massacre of the priests at Nob demonstrates the depths of Saul's breakdown and his failure of leadership, insofar as he attempted to destroy a priestly house on which he depended for the legitimacy of his rule. The narrative goes to great effort to portray Saul's paranoia when he demands to know from his own servants whether David would be capable of granting them land or office, thereby illustrating his belief that his own servants were conspiring against him in favor of David. Indeed, Saul cites the support of his own son Jonathan for David by referring to the pact made between Jonathan and David (1 Sam 18:1–16), but the narrative makes it clear that neither Jonathan nor David conspires against Saul.

Doeg the Edomite informs Saul that David had taken refuge with the priests at Nob and that Ahimelek ben Ahitub inquired of YHWH on David's behalf and gave him food and the sword of Goliath (1 Sam 21:2–10). Saul thereupon summons Ahimelek and the priests at Nob to explain themselves. When Saul accuses Ahimelek of supporting David, the priest responds by asserting that David is one of Saul's most trusted servants (1 Sam 18:17–30) and that he knows nothing of any conspiracy on the part of David against Saul. Saul responds by sentencing Ahimelek and the priests at Nob to death for treason, but Saul's men justifiably refuse to obey Saul's order. Saul then orders Doeg the Edomite to carry out the death sentence. As an Edomite, he would have no regard for the priests at Nob, and he complies by killing eighty-five priests, nearly wiping out the priestly House of Eli. Doeg then massacred Nob's inhabitants and cattle, something that Saul had earlier declined to do to Agag and the Amalekites (1 Sam 15). Saul's failure of leadership as King of Israel is clear.

The final episode in 1 Samuel 22:20–23 relates the escape of Abiathar ben Ahimelek ben Ahitub, the only survivor of the massacre, to David. When Abiathar reports the massacre to David, David's response illustrates his capacity to serve as the leader of Israel in place of the discredited Saul. David states that Doeg the Edomite was indeed at Nob when David stopped there (1 Sam 21:8), and that David himself is therefore to blame for the murder of the priestly house because he would have known that Doeg would report his presence to Saul. David takes responsibility for Abiathar's safety and thereby secures the support and legitimacy for his own claims to leadership from the survivor of the priestly House of Eli.

DAVID'S DEFENSE OF KEILAH AND SAUL'S CONTINUING PURSUIT
IN JUDAH – 1 SAMUEL 23:1–28

23 ¹ Now they told David, "The Philistines are fighting against Keilah and are robbing the threshing floors."

² David inquired of the LORD, "Shall I go and attack these Philistines?" The LORD said to David, "Go and attack the Philistines and save Keilah."

³ But David's men said to him, "Look, we are afraid here in Judah; how much more then if we go to Keilah against the armies of the Philistines?"

⁴ Then David inquired of the LORD again. The LORD answered him, "Yes, go down to Keilah, for I will give the Philistines into your hand."

⁵ So David and his men went to Keilah, fought with the Philistines, brought away their livestock, and dealt them a heavy defeat. Thus David rescued the inhabitants of Keilah.

⁶ When Abiathar son of Ahimelech fled to David at Keilah, he came down with an ephod in his hand.

⁷ Now it was told Saul that David had come to Keilah. And Saul said, "God has given him into my hand, for he has shut himself in by entering a town that has gates and bars."

⁸ Saul summoned all the people to war, to go down to Keilah, to besiege David and his men.

⁹ When David learned that Saul was plotting evil against him, he said to the priest Abiathar, "Bring the ephod here."

¹⁰ David said, "O LORD, the God of Israel, your servant has heard that Saul seeks to come to Keilah, to destroy the city on my account.

¹¹ And now, will Saul come down as your servant has heard? O LORD, the God of Israel, I beseech you, tell your servant." The LORD said, "He will come down."

¹² Then David said, "Will the men of Keilah surrender me and my men into the hand of Saul?" The LORD said, "They will surrender you."

¹³ Then David and his men, who were about six hundred, set out and left Keilah; they wandered wherever they could go. When Saul was told that David had escaped from Keilah, he gave up the expedition.

¹⁴ David remained in the strongholds in the wilderness, in the hill country of the wilderness of Ziph. Saul sought him every day, but the LORD did not give him into his hand.

[15] David was in the wilderness of Ziph at Horesh when he learned that Saul had come out to seek his life.

[16] Saul's son Jonathan set out and came to David at Horesh; there he strengthened his hand through the LORD.

[17] He said to him, "Do not be afraid, for the hand of my father Saul shall not find you; you shall be king over Israel, and I shall be second to you; my father Saul also knows that this is so."

[18] Then the two of them made a covenant before the LORD; David remained at Horesh, and Jonathan went home.

[19] Then some Ziphites went up to Saul at Gibeah and said, "David is hiding among us in the strongholds of Horesh, on the hill of Hachilah, which is south of Jeshimon.

[20] Now, O king, whenever you wish to come down, do so, and our part will be to surrender him into the king's hand."

[21] Saul said, "May you be blessed by the LORD for showing me compassion!

[22] Go and make sure once more; find out exactly where he is and who has seen him there, for I am told that he is very cunning.

[23] Look around and learn all the hiding places where he lurks and come back to me with sure information. Then I will go with you, and if he is in the land, I will search him out among all the thousands of Judah."

[24] So they set out and went to Ziph ahead of Saul.

David and his men were in the wilderness of Maon, in the Arabah to the south of Jeshimon.

[25] Saul and his men went to search for him. When David was told, he went down to the rock and stayed in the wilderness of Maon. When Saul heard that, he pursued David into the wilderness of Maon.

[26] Saul went on one side of the mountain and David and his men on the other side of the mountain. David was hurrying to get away from Saul, while Saul and his men were closing in on David and his men to capture them.

[27] Then a messenger came to Saul, saying, "Hurry and come, for the Philistines have made a raid on the land."

[28] So Saul stopped pursuing David and went against the Philistines; therefore that place was called the Rock of Escape.

First Samuel 23:1–28 presents an account of David's attempted defense of Keilah and Saul's continuing pursuit of David in Judah. The narrative comprises two major passages, each based on the geographical location of the episodes. The first is 1 Samuel 23:1–13, which recounts David's attempt to defend Keilah in southwestern Judah, and the second is 1 Samuel 23:14–28, which recounts Saul's continuing efforts to pursue David in the Judean wilderness.

David's attempt to defend Keilah in 1 Samuel 23:1–13 begins with a notice in verse 1 concerning the threat posed to Keilah by Philistine raids. Keilah was a fortified town located in the Judean Shephelah about seven miles east of Beth Guvrin and about eight and a half miles northwest of Hebron. Keilah is identified with Khirbet Qila to the north of Qila (Josh 15:44). It defends the Shephelah from the coastal plain, especially Gath.[55]

The first element of 1 Samuel 23:1–5 relates how the Philistines raided Keilah. Hearing this news, David inquired of YHWH whether he should go up to defend Keilah, and YHWH's answer was affirmative. David defeated the Philistines and saved Keilah, thereby demonstrating his capacity for leadership.

A second element in 1 Samuel 23:6 recounts that Abiathar ben Ahimelech fled to David at Keilah following Saul's massacre of the priests at Nob (1 Sam 22:20–23). The notice explains how David inquired of YHWH because Abiathar, a priest of the line of Eli, brought an ephod.

The third element in 1 Samuel 23:7–13 recounts how the inhabitants of Keilah turned against David due to fear of Saul. When Saul heard that David was at Keilah, he moved his army down to Keilah to capture David. The narrative suggests that Saul is an inadequate leader because he ruled by fear rather than by acting on behalf of the people. When David inquires of YHWH whether Saul will come down to Keilah, YHWH's answer is affirmative. When David then inquires whether the people will turn against him in favor of Saul, YHWH again answers in the affirmative. David and his now 600-man army abandon Keilah, but Saul does not pursue David, apparently because he accomplished his goal to control Keilah by intimidation.

The account of Saul's pursuit of David in the Judean wilderness stands in marked contrast with the prior sub-unit concerning Keilah in that Saul pursues David in the southeastern Judean wilderness but not in the south-western Judean Shephelah. The distinction suggests that these narratives once were independent, but in the present context they suggest

---

[55] La Moine F. DeVries, "Keilah," *ABD* 4:13–14; Istvan Karasszon, "Keilah," *EBR* 15:102.

inconsistency by Saul. Ironically, Saul will leave the Shephelah open to David when he submits to the Philistines in 1 Samuel 27. It also suggests that Saul is afraid to confront the Philistines, but he does not fear to pursue David in the Judean wilderness, where he is unlikely to confront a powerful enemy.

The narrative places the action in the wilderness of Ziph, identified as the Judean wilderness extending from the hill country of Judah east to the northwestern edges of the Dead Sea. The first segment in 1 Samuel 18:14–18 continues to show support for David from Jonathan (1 Sam 18; 20), insofar as Jonathan meets David at Horesh to make a covenant with him. The account reiterates Jonathan's support of David, and it reinforces that support with Jonathan's observation that he will serve as David's "second" when David becomes king. The meaning of the title "second to the king" is uncertain; it may suggest a deputy king, although no such office is known in Israel or Judah, or it may refer to an escort or close advisor for the king.[56] The site of Horesh on the Hill of Hachilah (v. 19) remains uncertain, although many identify it with Khirbet Khoreisa, five and a half miles south-southeast of Hebron. Others point out that Horesh (*ḥōrĕšâ*, lit., "toward Horesh") simply means "forest."[57]

The second segment in 1 Samuel 23:19–28 indicates that the Ziphites, like the people of Keilah, were willing to betray David to Saul. Such a scenario suggests that the Ziphites feared Saul more than David, insofar as Saul was king and had a large army, whereas David was a renegade with a small personal force. Saul choses subterfuge over open leadership by asking the Ziphites to spy on David to learn his whereabouts before Saul will bother to pursue him. The narrative nevertheless recognizes Saul as king, although it portrays Saul as judging David to be very cunning (v. 22; Hebrew, *'ārôm*), like the snake in Genesis 3:1.

When the Ziphites left Saul to carry out their orders, David and his men moved to the wilderness of Maon, located in the Arabah (desert) south of Jeshimon. The wilderness of Maon is apparently associated with the town of Maon, the home of Nabal and Abigail (1 Sam 25), approximately eight miles south-southeast of Hebron.[58] David's informants tell him of Saul's movements. As Saul's men search one side of a mountain, David and his

---

[56]　See Nili Sacher Fox, *In the Service of the King: Officialdom in Ancient Israel and Judah* (Cincinnati: Hebrew Union College Press, 2000) 128–132.

[57]　DeVries, "Horesh," *ABD* 3:288.

[58]　DeVries, "Maon," *ABD* 4:512–513.

men escape by moving to the other side. But when Saul receives a report that the Philistines are once again threatening the land, he breaks off his pursuit of David to confront the Philistines, but there is no account of this confrontation. The place where Saul gave up his pursuit of David is "the Rock of Escape" (NRSVue; Hebrew, *selaʿ hammaḥlĕqôt*, lit., "the rock of divisions" or "the rock of smoothnesses, slipperinesses").[59] The site is unknown.

DAVID'S ENCOUNTER WITH SAUL AT EIN GEDI – 1 SAMUEL 24:1–23

24 [1] When Saul returned from following the Philistines, he was told, "David is in the wilderness of En-gedi."

[2] Then Saul took three thousand chosen men out of all Israel and went to look for David and his men in the direction of the Rocks of the Wild Goats.

[3] He came to the sheepfolds beside the road, where there was a cave, and Saul went in to relieve himself. Now David and his men were sitting in the innermost parts of the cave.

[4] The men of David said to him, "Here is the day of which the LORD said to you, 'I will give your enemy into your hand, and you shall do to him as it seems good to you.'" Then David went and stealthily cut off a corner of Saul's cloak.

[5] Afterward David was stricken to the heart because he had cut off a corner of Saul's cloak.

[6] He said to his men, "The LORD forbid that I should do this thing to my lord, the LORD's anointed, to raise my hand against him, for he is the LORD's anointed."

[7] So David rebuked his men severely and did not permit them to attack Saul. Then Saul got up and left the cave and went on his way.

[8] Afterward David also rose up and went out of the cave and called after Saul, "My lord the king!" When Saul looked behind him, David bowed with his face to the ground and did obeisance.

[9] David said to Saul, "Why do you listen to the words of those who say, 'David seeks to do you harm'?

---

[59] DeVries, "Rock of Escape," *ABD* 5:788.

¹⁰ This very day your eyes have seen how the LORD gave you into my hand in the cave, and some urged me to kill you, but I spared you. I said, 'I will not raise my hand against my lord, for he is the LORD's anointed.'

¹¹ See, my father, see the corner of your cloak in my hand, for by the fact that I cut off the corner of your cloak and did not kill you, you may know for certain that there is no wrong or treason in my hands. I have not sinned against you, though you are hunting me to take my life.

¹² May the LORD judge between me and you! May the LORD avenge me on you, but my hand shall not be against you.

¹³ As the ancient proverb says, 'Out of the wicked comes forth wickedness,' but my hand shall not be against you.

¹⁴ Against whom has the king of Israel come out? Whom do you pursue? A dead dog? A single flea?

¹⁵ May the LORD, therefore, be judge and give sentence between me and you. May he see to it and plead my cause and vindicate me against you."

¹⁶ When David had finished speaking these words to Saul, Saul said, "Is this your voice, my son David?" Saul lifted up his voice and wept.

¹⁷ He said to David, "You are more righteous than I, for you have repaid me good, whereas I have repaid you evil.

¹⁸ Today you have explained how you have dealt well with me, in that you did not kill me when the LORD put me into your hands.

¹⁹ For who has ever found an enemy and sent the enemy safely away? So may the LORD reward you with good for what you have done to me this day.

²⁰ Now I know that you shall surely be king and that the kingdom of Israel shall be established in your hand.

²¹ Swear to me, therefore, by the LORD that you will not cut off my descendants after me and that you will not wipe out my name from my father's house."

²² So David swore this to Saul. Then Saul went home, but David and his men went up to the stronghold.

First Samuel 24:1–23 recounts David's encounter with Saul at Ein Gedi. The narrative is especially concerned with building up David and denigrating Saul by portraying David as a loyal servant of Saul who spared Saul's life when Saul stopped in a cave at Ein Gedi to relieve himself while on an expedition to capture or kill David.

There has been sustained discussion of the combined literary units in 1 Samuel 24–26, particularly because 1 Samuel 24 and 1 Samuel 26 portray David's refusal to harm Saul, which encase 1 Samuel 25. First Samuel 25 portrays David's marriage to Abigail, the widow of Nabal, a highly placed Judean figure, which advances David's political standing in Judah.[60]

The narrative begins in 1 Samuel 24:1 with a brief notice that David went up from the wilderness of Maon to the strongholds of Ein Gedi in an attempt to escape from Saul. Ein Gedi is the site of an oasis, including a spring and small waterfall, located along the western shore of the Dead Sea, east and slightly south of Hebron (Josh 15:61). Judean settlement appears in the late seventh century BCE and into the Second Temple and Roman-Byzantine periods, but 1 Samuel 24 requires only caves in the hills over-looking Ein Gedi.[61]

The main body of the narrative in 1 Samuel 24:2–23 includes two basic components: David's encounter with Saul in the cave in 1 Samuel 24:2–8a and David's encounter with Saul outside of the cave in 1 Samuel 24:8b–23.

First Samuel 24:2–8a states that Saul had gathered 3,000 chosen men to hunt down David in the wilderness of Ein Gedi. David has 600 men with him, and they take refuge in a large cave to hide from Saul. Saul happens upon the cave and steps inside "to cover his feet" (i.e., to relieve himself), which introduces an element of ridicule for Saul. While Saul is occupied with his own business, David and his 600 men have a conversation about what they should do with Saul in which David forbids his men to kill the anointed King of Israel. Apparently, Saul is so intent on what he is doing that he does not notice the conversation or that 601 men are present in the cave with him. Instead of killing Saul, David creeps forward and cuts off part of the hem of Saul's garment. Ancient texts from Mari indicate that the hem of a garment, a lock of hair, or a fingernail cutting were common ways to identify the writer of a document in the ancient world.[62]

First Samuel 24:8b–23 turns to David's encounter with Saul outside the cave. Once Saul exited the cave, David followed with the severed hem of Saul's garment. David makes appropriate obeisance to Saul to demonstrate his loyalty to the king. David then addresses Saul in verses 10–16 by asking a rhetorical question, viz., why Saul believes those who say that David intends to do him harm, especially when he just had the opportunity to kill

[60] Dietrich, *1 Samuel 13–26*, 688–698.
[61] Benjamin Mazar, "En Gedi," *NEAEHL* 2:399–405; Joe Uziel, "En-Gedi," *EBR* 7:883–884.
[62] Malamat, Mari and the Early Israelite Experience, 94–96.

Saul in the cave. The severed hem of Saul's garment provides conclusive evidence that David could had killed him! When David asks Saul to look at the severed hem as proof, he addresses Saul as "my father (Hebrew,'*ābî*)" to emphasize his close relationship to Saul as a son-in-law who has no interest in harming him even as his question suggests that Saul is in the wrong.

Saul accepts David's claims of loyalty and vows not to harm him in vv. 17–23. He addresses David as "my son" to accentuate the relationship between them, and he breaks down sobbing at what has just transpired. Saul then follows up by confessing that he is in the wrong and that David is right, and he affirms the fact that David did not kill him when he had the chance as proof of David's intentions. Saul very interestingly asserts that he knows that David will someday be King of Israel, and he therefore calls upon David to swear that he will not harm Saul's family. David agrees, but he does not keep this oath, with the exception of Jonathan's son, Mephibosheth (2 Sam 9; 19; 21). The fact that Mephibosheth goes on to father sons technically ensures that David will live up to his oath, but it is his oath to Jonathan and not to Saul. Saul's statement affirming David as king and asking that he spare his family are key to the narrative in that they add Saul to the list of those that recognize David as the future king. These characteristics identify the passage as part of the Solomonic History, which justifies the foundation of the House of David and Solomon's accession to the throne of Israel.

Saul returns home, and David returns to southeastern Judah in verse 23, but 1 Samuel 26 indicates that Saul continues to pursue David, thereby casting doubt on Saul's integrity.

DAVID'S MARRIAGE TO ABIGAIL THE WIDOW OF NABAL THE CALEBITE – 1 SAMUEL 25:1–44

25 Now Samuel died, and all Israel assembled and mourned for him. They buried him at his home in Ramah.

Then David got up and went down to the wilderness of Paran.

² There was a man in Maon whose property was in Carmel. The man was very rich; he had three thousand sheep and a thousand goats. He was shearing his sheep in Carmel.

³ Now the name of the man was Nabal, and the name of his wife was Abigail. The woman was clever and beautiful, but the man was surly and mean; he was a Calebite.

⁴ David heard in the wilderness that Nabal was shearing his sheep.

⁵ So David sent ten young men, and David said to the young men, "Go up to Carmel, and go to Nabal, and greet him in my name.

⁶ Thus you shall salute him, 'Peace be to you, and peace be to your house, and peace be to all that you have.

⁷ I hear that you have shearers; now your shepherds have been with us, and we did them no harm, and they missed nothing all the time they were in Carmel.

⁸ Ask your young men, and they will tell you. Therefore let my young men find favor in your sight, for we have come on a feast day. Please give whatever you have at hand to your servants and to your son David.'"

⁹ When David's young men came, they said all this to Nabal in the name of David, and then they waited.

¹⁰ But Nabal answered David's servants, "Who is David? Who is the son of Jesse? There are many servants today who are breaking away from their masters.

¹¹ Shall I take my bread and my water and the meat that I have butchered for my shearers and give it to men who come from I do not know where?"

¹² So David's young men turned away and came back and told him all this.

¹³ David said to his men, "Every man strap on his sword!" And every one of them strapped on his sword; David also strapped on his sword, and about four hundred men went up after David, while two hundred remained with the baggage.

¹⁴ But one of the young men told Abigail, Nabal's wife, "David sent messengers out of the wilderness to salute our master, and he shouted insults at them.

¹⁵ Yet the men were very good to us, and we suffered no harm, and we never missed anything when we were in the fields as long as we were with them;

¹⁶ they were a wall to us both by night and by day, all the while we were with them keeping the sheep.

¹⁷ Now, therefore, know this and consider what you should do, for evil has been decided against our master and against all his house; he is so ill-natured that no one can speak to him."

¹⁸ Then Abigail hurried and took two hundred loaves, two skins of wine, five sheep ready dressed, five measures of parched grain, one hundred

clusters of raisins, and two hundred cakes of figs. She loaded them on donkeys

¹⁹ and said to her young men, "Go on ahead of me; I am coming after you." But she did not tell her husband Nabal.

²⁰ As she rode on the donkey and came down under cover of the mountain, David and his men came down toward her, and she met them.

²¹ Now David had said, "Surely it was in vain that I protected all that this fellow has in the wilderness, so that nothing was missed of all that belonged to him, but he has returned me evil for good.

²² God do so to David and more also if by morning I leave so much as one male of all who belong to him."

²³ When Abigail saw David, she hurried and dismounted from the donkey and fell before David on her face, bowing to the ground.

²⁴ She fell at his feet and said, "Upon me alone, my lord, be the guilt; please let your servant speak in your ears and hear the words of your servant.

²⁵ My lord, do not take seriously this ill-natured fellow, Nabal, for as his name is, so is he; Nabal is his name, and folly is with him, but I, your servant, did not see the young men of my lord, whom you sent.

²⁶ "Now then, my lord, as the LORD lives and as you yourself live, since the LORD has restrained you from bloodguilt and from taking vengeance with your own hand, now let your enemies and those who seek to do evil to my lord be like Nabal.

²⁷ And now let this present that your servant has brought to my lord be given to the young men who follow my lord.

²⁸ Please forgive the trespass of your servant, for the LORD will certainly make my lord a sure house, because my lord is fighting the battles of the LORD, and evil shall not be found in you so long as you live.

²⁹ If anyone should rise up to pursue you and to seek your life, the life of my lord shall be bound in the bundle of the living under the care of the LORD your God, but the lives of your enemies he shall sling out as from the hollow of a sling.

³⁰ When the LORD has done to my lord according to all the good that he has spoken concerning you and has appointed you prince over Israel,

³¹ my lord shall have no cause of grief or pangs of conscience for having shed blood without cause or for having saved himself. And when the LORD has dealt well with my lord, then remember your servant."

³² David said to Abigail, "Blessed be the LORD, the God of Israel, who sent you to meet me today!

³³ Blessed be your good sense, and blessed be you, who kept me today from bloodguilt and from avenging myself by my own hand!

³⁴ For as surely as the LORD the God of Israel lives, who has restrained me from hurting you, unless you had hurried and come to meet me, truly by morning there would not have been left to Nabal so much as one male."

³⁵ Then David received from her hand what she had brought him; he said to her, "Go up to your house in peace; see, I have heeded your voice, and I have granted your petition."

³⁶ Abigail came to Nabal; he was holding a feast in his house like the feast of a king. Nabal's heart was merry within him, for he was very drunk, so she told him nothing at all until the morning light.

³⁷ In the morning, when the wine had gone out of Nabal, his wife told him these things, and his heart died within him; he became like a stone.

³⁸ About ten days later the LORD struck Nabal, and he died.

³⁹ When David heard that Nabal was dead, he said, "Blessed be the LORD, who has judged the case of Nabal's insult to me and has kept back his servant from evil; the LORD has returned the evildoing of Nabal upon his own head." Then David sent word to Abigail to make her his wife.

⁴⁰ When David's servants came to Abigail at Carmel, they said to her, "David has sent us to you to take you to him as his wife."

⁴¹ She rose and bowed down, with her face to the ground, and said, "Your servant is a slave to wash the feet of the servants of my lord."

⁴² Abigail got up hurriedly and rode away on a donkey; her five maids attended her. She went after the messengers of David and became his wife.

⁴³ David also married Ahinoam of Jezreel; both of them became his wives.

⁴⁴ Saul had given his daughter Michal, David's wife, to Palti son of Laish, who was from Gallim.

First Samuel 25 recounts David's marriage to Abigail, the widow of Nabal the Calebite, which advances David's political standing in the tribe of Judah.

The passage begins in 1 Samuel 25:1 with Samuel's death and David's move to the wilderness of Paran. First Samuel 25:1a is particularly important because it means that David no longer has a patron in Israel and that he will have to build a new power base to become king. First Samuel 25:43–44 makes it clear that Saul presumed that David had abandoned and therefore divorced Michal bat Saul, and that Saul had married his daughter off to another man, Palti ben Laish of Gallim. David no longer has political standing in Israel.

Many presume that David went to Ramah for the burial of Samuel, but 1 Samuel 25:1 presents no statement that he did so. Samuel was buried in his house, insofar as house burials were characteristic of pre-Israelite Canaanite culture. Israelite culture would have viewed a house in which a corpse was buried as unclean and unfit for human habitation (Num 19).

Many view the notice that David went to the wilderness of Paran in 1 Samuel 25:1b as corrupt insofar as Paran is often identified with the northern Sinai wilderness and the Arabah region south of Judah in the vicinity of the Red Sea. The usual solution is to follow the Septuagint text of 1 Reigns 25:1b, which reads "Maon" instead of "Paran."[63] But the LXX reading appears to be an ancient attempt to correct the text in keeping with 1 Samuel 25:2–41, which places David in Maon and Carmel in southern Judah. The precise boundaries of the wilderness of Paran remain uncertain. Texts such as Numbers 13:3, which portrays Moses' efforts to send spies into south Canaan from Paran, have prompted some to argue that Paran is south of Judah and west of Edom.[64]

Many view the account of David's marriage to Abigail in 1 Samuel 25:2–42 as a very well-developed example of Israelite or Judean storytelling, which is set off by an introductory noun clause, "there was a man in Maon, whose property was in Carmel," Hebrew, *wě'îš běmā'ôn ûma'ăśēhû bakarmel*. Another clause introduced by a noun in 1 Samuel 25:43, Hebrew, *wě'et 'ăhînō'am lāqah dāwid mmiyyizrě'ē'l*, "and Ahinoam David took from Jezreel" (cf. NRSVue: "David also married Ahinoam of Jezreel"), introduces the next sub-unit. Thus the narrative is set in the region of Maon in southern Judah, where the Judean town of Carmel, not to be confused with the northern Israelite site of Elijah's contest with the prophets of Baal (1 Kgs 18), was located some eight miles southeast of Hebron (Josh 15:55).[65] The narrative includes a sequence of episodes in verses 2–8, 9–13, 14–17, 18–35, 36–38, and 39–42.

---

[63] McCarter, *1 Samuel*, 388.
[64] Hamilton, "Paran," *ABD* 5:162; see also Yohanan Aharoni, *The Land of the Bible: A Historical Geography* (London: Burns and Oates, 1979) 31.
[65] DeVries, "Carmel," *ABD* 1:873.

The first episode, in 1 Samuel 25:2–8, describes Nabal as a very wealthy man in Carmel with 3,000 sheep, 1,000 goats, and a wife named Abigail. Whereas Abigail is portrayed as very intelligent and very beautiful, Nabal is described as "difficult" (Hebrew, *qāšeh*) and a man of "evil deeds" (Hebrew, *ra' ma'ălālîm*). But Nabal is also a Calebite, from the leading clan of Judah. The clan's founder, Caleb ben Jephunneh, is the only other spy besides Joshua ben Nun to bring back a favorable report of the situation in south Canaan in Numbers 13–14 (note that Wright reconstructs a historical scenario in which the Calebite clan settled in Judah at the outset of Israelite history).[66] The episode posits that Nabal was celebrating a sheep shearing festival when David sent ten young men to greet Nabal and to propose to him a defensive agreement in which David would protect his property in return for provisions for his men. Sheep shearing is an important occasion that calls for celebration in a pastoral society because it is a time when shepherds reap their profits in the form of wool for textiles. Although many complain that David is proposing a Mafia-like protection agreement, he is in fact asserting Judean control over the region as Saul had previously defeated the Amalekites and erected a stele proclaiming his mastery of the area (1 Sam 15, esp. v. 12). Nabal was a Calebite, but he had done nothing to assert Judean rights in the region and likely would have had to send provisions to King Saul of Israel as his overlord. David informed Nabal that he had been protecting the region – apparently from Saul and other enemies – and that Nabal had lost none of his flocks as a result. David exercises leadership in Judah that Nabal has failed to do despite his Calebite status.

The second episode, in 1 Samuel 25:9–13, recounts Nabal's response to David's overture and David's reaction. The passage illustrates Nabal's difficult character by his harsh response, which rejects David's proposal for protection in insulting terms. Nabal's response conveys some truth in that David is indeed Saul's loyal servant, vassal, and son-in-law, but he now seeks to rebel against Saul and set up his own protectorate in Judah at Saul's expense. Nabal's claim that he does not know who David is questions David's authority to act against his suzerain, King Saul of Israel. Why should he give meat and other provisions to David instead of to his own family and retainers, especially when he may well have already paid his

---

[66] Mark J. Fretz and Paphael I. Panitz, "Caleb," *ABD* 1:808–810; Jacob L. Wright, *David, King of Israel, and Caleb in Biblical Memory* (Cambridge and New York: Cambridge University Press, 2014).

tribute to Saul? David's division of his forces into 400 who would attack and 200 who would remain behind to guard the baggage makes eminent military sense (cf. 1 Sam 30).

The third episode, in 1 Samuel 25:14–17, recounts the report by one of Nabal's men to Abigail, who recognizes the stupidity and danger of Nabal's response. Abigail lives up to the standards of leadership articulated in Proverbs 31:1–31.

The fourth episode, in 1 Samuel 25:18–35, recounts Abigail's approach to David to head off the destruction that David will bring upon her house. She assembles provisions, namely, 200 breads (likely pita rather than loaves), two large jars of wine, five ready dressed (cooked) sheep, five measures (a seah is equal to about nine US quarts or 8.5 liters) of parched corn (grain), 100 raisin clusters, and 200 fig cakes, which she loads on donkeys for transport. These provisions will not feed David's 600 men for long, but they are an appropriate gift in return for the protection that David offers. By sending them ahead, Abigail intends to soften David's anger, much as Jacob does with Esau in Genesis 32:14–22. As for David's anger, the narrative aptly illustrates his intentions to destroy Nabal and his house in verses 21–22. David's vow not to leave a single male of Nabal's house alive, here expressed literally as "one who pisses against a wall" (Hebrew, *maštîn bĕqîr*) signals a potential literary relationship with the Elijah and Elisha narratives in 1 Kings 17–2 Kings 13, which employ the same terminology in 1 Kings 14:10; 16:11; 21:21; 2 Kings 9:8.[67] Abigail follows mounted on a donkey, but when she reaches David, she dismounts, bows low to the ground in appropriate submission to an overlord, and adds important touches, such as taking the blame for the situation upon herself, referring to herself as David's handmaiden (Hebrew, *'āmâ*, a female servant), and claiming that her husband is a fool. The Hebrew name *nābāl* means "fool" or "senseless," but this is apparently a pun on a name that has other meanings.[68] The related Hebrew term *nēbel* also refers to a (wine) jar or a musical instrument, such as a lute, which may suggest that his name was somehow linked to prosperity.

[67] E.g., Antony F. Campbell, *Of Prophets and Kings: A Late Ninth-Century Document (1 Samuel 1–2 Kings 10)* (CBQMS 17; Washington, DC: The Catholic Biblical Association of America, 1986) 63, who posits a ninth-century Prophetic Record in 1 Samuel 1–2 Kings 10; Timo Veijola, *Die Ewige Dynastie* (Helsinki: Suomalainen Tiedeakatemia, 1975) 51–55, esp. 55, ascribes 1 Samuel 25 and the phrase to Deuteronomistic redaction.
[68] BDB 614–615.

Abigail's language begins to shift in verses 25b–31. She now asserts that she did not see the men that David sent to Nabal, and she suggests that YHWH has restrained David from shedding blood, which functions as a proposal to an alternative means of settling the issue. She first mentions the blessing of the provisions that she has sent to feed David's men; David, having seen the provisions, will be well disposed to an alternative solution. He may also be influenced by a subtle shift in her reference to herself as David's maidservant, Hebrew, *'āmâ*, as noted above in verses 24 and 25, to Hebrew, *šipḥâ*, "servant" (NRSVue), in that the term indicates a maidservant who might also become a concubine.[69] Some might object that she is already married, but she is deliberately acting against her husband's wishes, and Nabal could decide to divorce for what she is doing. Whether she is making such an overture to David is uncertain, but she then suggests that YHWH will grant David a "secure house," Hebrew, *bayit ne'ĕmān*, which could simply indicate wishes for his success, although it also leaves open the role that she might play in securing that house. She continues with suggestions that YHWH will defeat David's enemies, and like Jonathan and Saul before her, she suggests that YHWH has appointed David as *nāgîd*, "prince" (NRSVue), or better, "designated ruler" of Israel. She closes with renewed appeals to desist from his planned slaughter of Nabal's house and to remember her as his maidservant.

Abigail's speech works. David praises her "good sense" (NRSVue; Hebrew, *ṭa'am*, "taste") and declares that he will desist from his plans to massacre Nabal's house. He accepts her gifts, releases her to return safely, and emphatically tells her that he has granted her petition.

The fifth episode, in 1 Samuel 25:36–38, briefly depicts Nabal's death. When Abigail returns home, she finds her husband feasting and drunk, apparently in celebration of the sheep shearing festival, and she therefore says nothing about what she has done. When she tells him the next morning about what had happened, verse 37 states that "his heart died within him, and he became like stone." Although many suspect that David colluded with Abigail to murder Nabal, the portrayal of his death appears to represent the effects of a stroke.

The sixth episode, in 1 Samuel 25:39–42, relates David's marriage to Abigail. After praising YHWH for supporting him and preventing him from killing Nabal himself, David sends messengers to Abigail to propose marriage.

---

[69] BDB 1046.

There is no indication of a mourning period for her dead husband, but she agrees readily and comes to David to marry him. This marriage is crucial. Abigail is the widow of Nabal the Calebite, from the key family in the power structure of Judah. The David narratives make it clear repeatedly that one who marries the widow of a king or other leader claims that role of leadership (2 Sam 3:6–11; 2 Sam 12:12:5–12; 2 Sam 16:20–23; 1 Kgs 2:13–25). David's marriage to Abigail gives him standing in the Calebite clan to claim kingship in Judah following the death of Saul and his sons (2 Sam 2:1–4a).[70]

First Samuel 25:43–44 closes the chapter by noting David's marriages to other women. He married Ahinoam of Jezreel, who happens to have the same name as Saul's wife. Although many speculate that Ahinoam of Jezreel was Saul's wife, Saul's wife is identified as Ahinoam bat Ahimaaz (1 Sam 14:50) and never as Ahinoam of Jezreel. Some speculate that Ahinoam of Jezreel was from the Jezreel Valley in northern Israel, but Jezreel is also the name of a town in Judah near Carmel (Josh 15:55, 56), which means that David gained further standing in Judah based on his marriage to her.[71] Political standing in Judah is now crucial to David, insofar as Saul had taken David's wife, Michal, and married her off to Palti ben Laish of Gallim, a location in Benjamin to the north of Jerusalem (Isa 10:30).

DAVID SPARES SAUL AT HACHILAH – 1 SAMUEL 26:1–25

26 **¹ Then the Ziphites came to Saul at Gibeah, saying, "David is in hiding on the hill of Hachilah, which is opposite Jeshimon."**

² So Saul rose and went down to the wilderness of Ziph, with three thousand chosen men of Israel, to seek David in the wilderness of Ziph.

³ Saul encamped on the hill of Hachilah, which is opposite Jeshimon, beside the road. But David remained in the wilderness. When he learned that Saul had come after him into the wilderness,

⁴ David sent out spies and learned that Saul had indeed arrived.

⁵ Then David set out and came to the place where Saul had encamped, and David saw the place where Saul lay, with Abner son of Ner, the commander of his army. Saul was lying within the encampment, while the army was encamped around him.

---

[70]   See Jon D. Levenson and Baruch Halpern, "The Political Import of David's Marriages," *JBL* 99 (1980) 507–518.
[71]   Edelman, "Ahinoam," *ABD* 1:117–118.

⁶ Then David said to Ahimelech the Hittite and to Joab's brother Abishai son of Zeruiah, "Who will go down with me into the camp to Saul?" Abishai said, "I will go down with you."

⁷ So David and Abishai went to the army by night; there Saul lay sleeping within the encampment, with his spear stuck in the ground at his head, and Abner and the army lay around him.

⁸ Abishai said to David, "God has given your enemy into your hand today; now, therefore, let me pin him to the ground with one stroke of the spear; I will not strike him twice."

⁹ But David said to Abishai, "Do not destroy him, for who can raise his hand against the LORD's anointed and be guiltless?"

¹⁰ David said, "As the LORD lives, the LORD will strike him down, or his day will come to die, or he will go down into battle and perish.

¹¹ The LORD forbid that I should raise my hand against the LORD's anointed, but now take the spear that is at his head and the water jar, and let us go."

¹² So David took the spear that was at Saul's head and the water jar, and they went away. No one saw it or knew it, nor did anyone awake, for they were all asleep, because a deep sleep from the LORD had fallen upon them.

¹³ Then David went over to the other side and stood on top of a hill far away, with a great distance between them.

¹⁴ David called to the army and to Abner son of Ner, saying, "Abner! Will you not answer?" Then Abner replied, "Who are you who calls to the king?"

¹⁵ David said to Abner, "Are you not a man? Who is like you in Israel? Why then have you not kept watch over your lord the king? For one of the people came in to destroy your lord the king.

¹⁶ This thing that you have done is not good. As the LORD lives, you deserve to die because you have not kept watch over your lord, the LORD's anointed. See now, where is the king's spear or the water jar that was at his head?"

¹⁷ Saul recognized David's voice and said, "Is this your voice, my son David?" David said, "It is my voice, my lord, O king."

¹⁸ And he added, "Why does my lord pursue his servant? For what have I done? What guilt is on my hands?

¹⁹ Now, therefore, let my lord the king hear the words of his servant. If it is the LORD who has stirred you up against me, may he accept an

offering, but if it is mortals, may they be cursed before the LORD, for they have driven me out today from my share in the heritage of the LORD, saying, 'Go, serve other gods.'

²⁰ Now therefore, do not let my blood fall to the ground away from the presence of the LORD, for the king of Israel has come out to seek a single flea, like one who hunts a partridge in the mountains."

²¹ Then Saul said, "I have done wrong; come back, my son David, for I will never harm you again, because my life was precious in your sight today; I have been a fool and have made a great mistake."

²² David replied, "Here is the spear, O king! Let one of the young men come over and get it.

²³ The LORD rewards everyone for his righteousness and his faithfulness, for the LORD gave you into my hand today, but I would not raise my hand against the LORD's anointed.

²⁴ As your life was precious today in my sight, so may my life be precious in the sight of the LORD, and may he rescue me from all tribulation."

²⁵ Then Saul said to David, "Blessed be you, my son David! You will do many things and will succeed in them." So David went his way, and Saul returned to his place.

First Samuel 26:1–25 recounts how David spared Saul's life at Hachilah and again demonstrated his loyalty to Saul. The narrative comprises three major sub-units: the report of the Ziphites to Saul that David is hiding in the hill of Hachilah, which faces Jeshimon in 1 Samuel 26:1; David's encounter with Saul at Hachilah in 1 Samuel 26:2–25a; and the departure of David and Saul from Hachilah in 1 Samuel 26:25b.

The first sub-unit, in 1 Samuel 26:1, recounts the report of the Ziphites to Saul that David was hiding in Hachilah. The Ziphites were a clan that apparently lived near the town of Ziph, identified with Tel Zif or Khirbet Zif, both of which are located some 4.2 miles south-southeast of Hebron in the eastern Judean hills descending down to the Dead Sea.[72] Jeshimon, which means "desert," is identified with this region,[73] although the site of Hachilah remains unidentified.[74] The name of the site may mean "to hide,"[75] which may explain the attempt of the LXX text to identify the site

---

[72]   Lance, "Ziph," *ABD* 6:1104.
[73]   DeVries, "Jeshimon," *ABD* 3:769.
[74]   DeVries, "Hachilah," *ABD* 3:10.
[75]   Ido Koch, "Hachilah," *EBR* 10:1057.

as Keilah in the Vaticanus Codex and as Ziklag in the Lucianic Greek text of 1 Samuel 26:4.[76] In either case, the LXX text of 1 Samuel 26:1 continues to identify the site as Hachilah (i.e., Greek, *Echela*). The Ziphites appear to be loyal to Saul, as they journey north to Gibeah to report David's presence in their region.

The second major sub-unit, in 1 Samuel 26:2–25a, portrays Saul's attempt to capture David and David's efforts to spare Saul's life and to assert his loyalty to the king.

First Samuel 26:2–3a recounts Saul's pursuit of David in the wilderness of Ziph and his encampment at Hachilah, which faces Jeshimon (i.e., the Judean wilderness near the Dead Sea).

First Samuel 26:3b–12 recounts David's dispatch of runners to confirm Saul's presence. He then saw where Saul was sleeping in a protected spot with his army commander, Abner ben Ner, and the rest of the army asleep around him. David asked two of his men, Ahimelech the Hittite and Abishai ben Zeruiah, to accompany him into Saul's camp. Abishai agreed, and men entered Saul's camp, where they found Saul sound asleep with his spear stuck in the ground by his head. Although Saul and his army are sound asleep – verse 12 states that YHWH had imposed a "deep sleep" (Hebrew, *tardēmâ*) like that imposed on Adam in Genesis 2:21 or Abram in Genesis 15:12 – Abishai, the brother of Joab ben Zeruiah, David's army commander, proposes to David that he will kill Saul with his own spear. But the narrative makes a special point of having David turn down Abishai's proposal, which enables David once again to assert his loyalty to the king. David states that it is up to YHWH to decide when and how Saul will die; he and Abishai should not incur guilt before YHWH. David instead proposes that they take Saul's spear and water bottle as proof that they were able to approach Saul and kill him but did not.

Once David and Abishai returned to the other side of the road, 1 Samuel 26:13–16 recounts David's speech. He loudly addresses Abner to shame him for not protecting his king, and then celebrates their penetration of Saul's camp and seizure of Saul's spear and water bottle.

Once Saul awakens and recognizes David's voice, 1 Samuel 26:17–25a focuses on David's conversation with Saul. Saul addresses David as "my son," which is true insofar as David is – or was – Saul's son-in-law, but it is also disingenuous in that it disarms David and suggests that he means

---

[76] McCarter, *1 Samuel*, 405.

David no harm – which is untrue. David can now seize the advantage with a rhetorical question that demands to know why Saul pursues him when in fact he is a loyal servant to the king. David continues that if YHWH has prompted Saul to hunt him down, perhaps YHWH will be satisfied with a *minḥah* offering ("grain offering," Lev 2). But if human beings have prompted Saul to chase down David, they will be cursed by YHWH for prompting Saul to drive David out so that he might be forced to worship other gods. David's concluding statement in verse 20 suggests that Saul would commit a crime if he were to shed David's blood.

The final exchange between Saul and David in 1 Samuel 26:21–25a makes the key points of the passage. Saul begins in verse 21 by stating that he has sinned against David (cf. Lev 4), and he asks that David return to him, swearing that he will never do David harm because David spared his life. David responds in verses 22–24 by first returning Saul's spear. He swears that he would never raise his hand against YHWH's anointed king, but he is careful enough to state his hope that just as he has spared Saul's life, so YHWH will rescue him from any trouble. Saul's final response in verse 25a is to bless David, "my son," and declaring that David will prevail.

The final sub-unit, in 1 Samuel 26:25b, states that David went on his way, and Saul went to his own place (i.e., Gibeah). From now on, David and Saul will never see each other again.

DAVID BECOMES A PHILISTINE VASSAL – 1 SAMUEL 27:1–12

27 **1** **David said in his heart, "I shall certainly perish one day by the hand of Saul; there is nothing better for me than to escape to the land of the Philistines; then Saul will despair of seeking me any longer within the borders of Israel, and I shall escape out of his hand."**

2 **So David set out and went over, he and the six hundred men who were with him, to King Achish son of Maoch of Gath.**

3 **David stayed with Achish at Gath, he and his troops, every man with his household, and David with his two wives, Ahinoam of Jezreel and Abigail of Carmel, Nabal's widow.**

4 **When Saul was told that David had fled to Gath, he no longer sought for him.**

5 **Then David said to Achish, "If I have found favor in your sight, let a place be given me in one of the country towns so that I may live there, for why should your servant live in the royal city with you?"**

⁶ So that day Achish gave him Ziklag; therefore Ziklag has belonged to the kings of Judah to this day.

⁷ The length of time that David lived in the country of the Philistines was one year and four months.

⁸ Now David and his men went up and made raids on the Geshurites, the Girzites, and the Amalekites, for these were the landed settlements from Telam on the way to Shur and on to the land of Egypt.

⁹ David struck the land, leaving neither man nor woman alive, but took away the sheep, the oxen, the donkeys, the camels, and the clothing and came back to Achish.

¹⁰ When Achish asked, "Against whom have you made a raid today?" David would say, "Against the Negeb of Judah," or "Against the Negeb of the Jerahmeelites," or "Against the Negeb of the Kenites."

¹¹ David left neither man nor woman alive to be brought back to Gath, thinking, "They might tell about us and say, 'David has done so and so.'" Such was his practice all the time he lived in the country of the Philistines.

¹² Achish trusted David, thinking, "He has made himself utterly abhorrent to his people Israel; therefore he shall always be my servant."

First Samuel 27 makes it clear that, despite Saul's pledges, he continues to pose a threat to David. David therefore became a Philistine ally who was expected to harass Judah from the town of Ziklag near the Philistine–Judean border. But the narrative recounts how David deceived his Philistine overlords by claiming to raid Judah while he was actually protecting it from various enemies in the wilderness south of Judean territory. David builds a constituency in Judah that will later facilitate his rise to power as King of Judah.

The narrative comprises three major sub-units: 1 Samuel 27:1–4 recounts David's defection to the Philistines; 1 Samuel 27:5–7 recounts David's request to King Achish ben Maoch of Gaza for a fiefdom outside of Gath; and 1 Samuel 27:8–12 recounts David's actions from Ziklag to deceive the Philistines and protect the people of Judah.

First Samuel 27:1–4 begins in verse 1 with David's recognition that he cannot be safe in his own land when Saul continues in his attempts to kill him. Such recognition indicates that his only hope is to seek protection from the Philistines. David therefore takes his 600 men and their families to Gath, where he seeks sanctuary from King Achish ben Maoch. Ironically, Gath is the home city of Goliath (1 Sam 17:4) and the major

staging point for Philistine attacks against Israel and Judah. The name
Achish appears to be an authentic Philistine name, based on the conjecture
that it is based on an Anatolian or Greek name (e.g., Anchises or
Achaios).[77] Indeed, the Philistine strategy appears to be based on an
attempt to divide Judah from the rest of Israel, which would be supported
by Philistine recognition of conflict between David and Saul as well as the
federated nature of the Israelite tribal confederation. David also brings his
wives, Ahinoam of Jezreel and Abigail, the wife (widow) of Nabal the
Carmelite. The identification of Abigail as the widow of Nabal the
Carmelite simply emphasizes the city of Nabal's residence as noted
throughout 1 Samuel 25. David's alliance with Achish indicates an important shift in power that will ultimately split Judah off from the Israelite
kingdom ruled by the House of Saul.

First Samuel 27:5–7 presents David's request to Achish for a city where he
can live. Achish grants David Ziklag, and this explains how Ziklag, originally
assigned to the tribe of Simeon (Josh 19:5; 1 Chr 4:3) but later assigned to
Judah (Josh 15:15:31), became a possession of the royal House of David. The
reference to Ziklag as a possession of the kings of Judah "to this day" in verse
6 would indicate a time during the Judean monarchy. The site of Ziklag is
not entirely certain. Most identify it with Tell esh-Sharia located along the
Naḥal Gerar, approximately fifteen and a half miles southeast of Gaza and
ten and a half miles due west of Tell el-Khuweilfah, which is also suggested
as a site for Ziklag.[78] The site is deep in Judean territory, which suggests a
Philistine incursion, and it threatens Beer Sheba, some 9.3 miles to the
southeast, which would serve Philistine interests. Verse 7 states that David
and his men stayed in Ziklag for a year, literally "days," a term which refers
to a year (cf. Judg 17:10; Lev 25:29) and four months.[79]

First Samuel 27:8–12 relates how David and his men used Ziklag as a
base from which to defend Judah against the various tribal groups that
inhabited the desert regions west and south of Judah. The reference to
Olam, generally corrected to Telem with the LXX, extends from the
Wilderness of Shur through the northern Sinai to Egypt. The LXX reading
presumes that Olam is a place name, but the MT in verse 8 actually reads,
"who were inhabitants from antiquity." The LXX reference to Telem

---

[77]   McCarter, 1 Samuel, 356; Tsumura, 1 Samuel, 536.
[78]   Wade R. Kotter and Eliezer D. Oren, "Ziklag," ABD 6:1090–1093.
[79]   Samuel R. Driver, Notes on The Hebrew Text and The Topography of the Books of
        Samuel (Oxford: Clarendon, 1960) 210.

reminds the reader of Saul's earlier encounter with Agag and the Amalekites at Telaim, an alternative name for Telem (1 Sam 15:4), which reiterates that David succeeded whereas Saul had failed.

The narrative explains David's strategy for dealing with the Philistines and other enemies in the region. David would attack an enemy, leaving no one alive, seize all of their property, and then report to Achish upon his return. Killing everyone among an enemy population was necessary so that no survivors could later report that David attacked Judah's enemies rather than Judah itself. David's statements that he had raided the Negev region to the south, where the Jerahmeelites and the Kenites lived, indicated that he was targeting hostile tribal groups from the Judean Negev, which suggested that David was actually encircling Judah. In fact, David was building a constituency among the Judeans that would enable him to rise to kingship in Judah. Verse 12 states that Achish was taken in by David's ruse, thinking that David had made himself odious (*hab'ēš hib'îš*; cf. NRSVue, "has made himself utterly abhorrent") to the Judeans.

SAUL'S ENCOUNTER WITH THE GHOST OF SAMUEL THROUGH THE WITCH OF ENDOR – 1 SAMUEL 28:1–25

28 **¹ In those days the Philistines gathered their forces for war, to fight against Israel. Achish said to David, "You know, of course, that you and your men are to go out with me in the army."**

² David said to Achish, "Very well, then you shall know what your servant can do." Achish said to David, "Very well, I will make you my bodyguard for life."

³ Now Samuel had died, and all Israel had mourned for him and buried him in Ramah, his own city. Saul had expelled the mediums and the wizards from the land.

⁴ The Philistines assembled and came and encamped at Shunem. Saul gathered all Israel, and they encamped at Gilboa.

⁵ When Saul saw the army of the Philistines, he was afraid, and his heart trembled greatly.

⁶ When Saul inquired of the LORD, the LORD did not answer him, not by dreams or by Urim or by prophets.

⁷ Then Saul said to his servants, "Seek out for me a woman who is a medium, so that I may go to her and inquire of her." His servants said to him, "There is a medium at Endor."

⁸ So Saul disguised himself and put on other clothes and went there, he and two men with him. They came to the woman by night. And he said, "Consult a spirit for me, and bring up for me the one whom I name to you."

⁹ The woman said to him, "Surely you know what Saul has done, how he has cut off the mediums and the wizards from the land. Why then are you laying a snare for my life to bring about my death?"

¹⁰ But Saul swore to her by the LORD, "As the LORD lives, no punishment shall come upon you for this thing."

¹¹ Then the woman said, "Whom shall I bring up for you?" He answered, "Bring up Samuel for me."

¹² When the woman saw Samuel, she cried out with a loud voice, and the woman said to Saul, "Why have you deceived me? You are Saul!"

¹³ The king said to her, "Have no fear; what do you see?" The woman said to Saul, "I see a divine being coming up out of the ground."

¹⁴ He said to her, "What is his appearance?" She said, "An old man is coming up; he is wrapped in a robe." So Saul knew that it was Samuel, and he bowed with his face to the ground and did obeisance.

¹⁵ Then Samuel said to Saul, "Why have you disturbed me by bringing me up?" Saul answered, "I am in great distress, for the Philistines are warring against me, and God has turned away from me and answers me no more, either by prophets or by dreams, so I have summoned you to tell me what I should do."

¹⁶ Samuel said, "Why then do you ask me, since the LORD has turned from you and become your enemy?

¹⁷ The LORD has done to you just as he spoke by me, for the LORD has torn the kingdom out of your hand and given it to your neighbor, David.

¹⁸ Because you did not obey the voice of the LORD and did not carry out his fierce wrath against Amalek, therefore the LORD has done this thing to you today.

¹⁹ Moreover, the LORD will give Israel along with you into the hands of the Philistines, and tomorrow you and your sons shall be with me; the LORD will also give the army of Israel into the hands of the Philistines."

²⁰ Immediately Saul fell full length on the ground filled with fear because of the words of Samuel, and there was no strength in him, for he had eaten nothing all day and all night.

²¹ The woman came to Saul, and when she saw that he was terrified, she said to him, "Your servant has listened to you; I have taken my life in my hand and have listened to what you have said to me.

²² Now, therefore, you also listen to your servant; let me set a morsel of bread before you. Eat, that you may have strength when you go on your way."

²³ He refused and said, "I will not eat." But his servants, together with the woman, urged him, and he listened to their words. So he got up from the ground and sat on the bed.

²⁴ Now the woman had a fatted calf in the house. She quickly slaughtered it, and she took flour, kneaded it, and baked unleavened cakes.

²⁵ She put them before Saul and his servants, and they ate. Then they rose and went away that night.

First Samuel 28:1–25 begins a narrative sequence in 1 Samuel 28–31 that portrays Saul's final battle against the Philistines near Beth Shean at Mt. Gilboa, in which Israel suffers a major defeat. Jonathan and two other sons of Saul are killed, and Saul commits suicide to avoid capture and humiliation by the Philistines. Saul's body is ultimately given a proper burial by the men of Jabesh Gilead, who remember Saul's deliverance of the city in 1 Samuel 11. Scholars have long recognized that the narrative is clearly the product of a Solomonic redaction, apparently due to its role in preparing the way for the rise of David as king over both Judah and Jerusalem, the double introduction to the Philistine threat in 1 Samuel 28:1–2 and 4, and the repeated reference to Samuel's death and burial in 1 Samuel 28:3 (cf. 1 Sam 25:1).

First Samuel 28 portrays Saul as a failed leader for his violation of his own decree prohibiting necromancy and to signal his impending demise at the hands of the Philistines.

The narrative comprises two major sub-units. First is the introduction to the narrative – and indeed, to the whole of 1 Samuel 28–31 – in 1 Samuel 28:1–2, which relates the gathering of the Philistines for war against Israel and the initial appointment of David and his men as bodyguards for King Achish of Gath. The second appears in 1 Samuel 28:3–25, introduced by a noun clause concerning Samuel's death and burial in verse 3, which recounts Saul's encounter with the ghost of the now dead Samuel through the agency of the witch at Endor. Following this introduction, 1 Sam 28:4–25 recounts Saul's visit with the witch at Endor and his encounter with the now dead Samuel. First Samuel 28:4–25 comprises five elements, including the notice in verse 4 of the Philistine camp at Shunem and the Israelite camp at Gilboa; the account of Saul's fear and his instructions to find a necromancer through whom to make an oracular inquiry when YHWH failed to answer him in verses 5–7; and Saul's encounter with Samuel through the witch at Endor in verses 9–25.

First Samuel 28:1–2 introduces 1 Samuel 28–31 with a notice of the Philistines gathering for an attack against Israel and the appointment of David and his men as bodyguards for King Achish of Gath. The notice of the Philistine preparations for war covers the entire narrative, which will only reach its culmination with Saul's death and burial in 1 Samuel 31, but the notice of David's appointment by Achish serves a different role. It raises narrative tension in that David and his men are about to join the Philistines in their war against Israel. It thereby builds upon the accounts of David's treason against Israel by switching his allegiance from Saul to Achish in 1 Samuel 21:11–16 and 27:1–12. The narrative will later explain in 1 Samuel 29 that David and his men would be left behind in Ziklag due to the recognition by the Philistine lords that David might turn against them in battle. Achish's proposal indicates that David had succeeded in deceiving him about his actions in Ziklag. His efforts to deceive Achish appear once again when he answers Achish's implicit question concerning David's actions as he marches to confront Saul. David's response is an example of evasion: "Very well then, you shall know what your servant can do." Achish falls for the bait and declares that David will be his bodyguard for life, a role that David apparently would have played in relation to Saul following the death of Goliath in 1 Samuel 18. The narrative thereby demonstrates that David is loyal to Saul and Israel despite Saul's efforts to kill him. David once again emerges as an ideal future leader of Israel and Judah.

The notice in 1 Samuel 28:3 of Samuel's death and burial in Ramah may well indicate the introduction to the earlier underlying narrative in 1 Samuel 28. It repeats information given already in 1 Samuel 25:1, but in the present context it reminds the reader that Samuel is dead and that he therefore can be conjured up from the netherworld in the following account. But it also undermines Saul by noting that Saul had forbidden "mediums" (Hebrew, 'ōbôt, "necromancers" or "ghosts") and "wizards" (Hebrew, yiddĕ'ōnîm, "soothsayers" or "familiar spirits"). The Covenant Code in Exodus 22:17 calls for the execution of a witch (Hebrew, mĕkaššēpâ, "sorceress"). The presence of necromancers and soothsayers appears to be a holdover from pre-Israelite Canaanite culture that continued to serve as a challenge to YHWH and Israelite or Judean authority (see Deut 18:9–14).

The account of Saul's encounter with the witch at Endor in 1 Samuel 4–25 begins with a notice in verse 4 that the Philistines were encamped at Shunem and Israel were encamped at Gilboa. Shunem is identified with modern Solem, located at the foot of the Moreh Hill in the midst of the Jezreel Valley just east of modern Afula. It was part of the tribal territory of Issachar (Josh 19:18), and it is known for its women, such as David's concubine Abishag (1 Kgs 1–2) and the woman who fed and housed Elisha (2 Kgs 4:8–27).[80] The location of Shunem on the Hill of Moreh provides an ideal position from which to control the Jezreel Valley and thereby cut off the northern Israelite hill country from Galilee. Control of the Jezreel would also assure control of the trade routes to Aram and Mesopotamia. Mt. Gilboa is located to the south of Mt. Moreh across the Jezreel and to the west of Beth Shean. It is the logical place from which to defend the Jezreel from the Philistine attack and to protect Beth Shean, which guards the eastern entrance to the Jezreel Valley and therefore the trade route to Aram and Mesopotamia.[81]

First Samuel 28:5–7 recounts Saul's reaction to the sight of the Philistine camp. It is never wise for a leader to display fear before the people. Saul's decision to consult a necromancer, contrary to his own decree noted in verse 9 (and Exod 22:17; Deut 18:9–14) demonstrates his desperation, his failure in leadership, and his own betrayal of YHWH. Endor is located in Galilee, north of the Jezreel Valley. Endor, Hebrew, *'ên dôr*, "spring of settlement" or "spring of divine assembly," is identified with Khirbet Ṣafṣâfeh in the northern Jezreel Valley, about 4.2 miles northeast of modern Solem.[82]

First Samuel 28:8–25 relates Saul encounter with the witch at Endor and with Saul per se. He disguises himself, apparently due to his order banning consultation with necromancers on pain of death. But once the séance begins and Samuel begins to appear, Saul's true identity is revealed to her. When he asks what she sees, she describes Samuel as "a divine being" (i.e., Hebrew, *'ělōhîm*, "god(s)"), who looks like an old man wrapped in a robe.

Samuel demands in verses 15–21 to know why he has been disturbed. When Saul explains to him that he needs Samuel's help because YHWH

---

[80] Elizabeth F. Huwiler, "Shunem," *ABD* 5:1228–1229.
[81] Hamilton, "Gilboa, Mount," *ABD* 2:1019.
[82] Edelman, "En-Dor," *ABD* 2:499–501.

will no longer answer him, Samuel chastises him by asking why Saul should call on him when YHWH has already become his enemy. Samuel reiterates his point by declaring that YHWH has done what YHWH promised to do, viz., YHWH has torn the kingdom away from Saul and given it to David instead when Saul failed to follow YHWH's instructions concerning the Amalekites in 1 Samuel 15.

Saul's desperation is underscored by the observation that Saul had not eaten all day and night. When the woman saw Saul's condition, she slaughtered a fattened calf, cooked it, and baked bread as well, all of which must have taken a few hours of work, and fed the desperate king and his retinue. Saul and his party then left without so much as a single word of thanks for what she had done. Saul's lack of leadership continues to be clear.

THE PHILISTINES' DISMISSAL OF DAVID – 1 SAMUEL 29:1–11

29 ¹ Now the Philistines gathered all their forces at Aphek, while the Israelites were encamped by the spring that is in Jezreel.

² As the lords of the Philistines were passing on by hundreds and by thousands and David and his men were passing on in the rear with Achish,

³ the commanders of the Philistines said, "What are these Hebrews doing here?" Achish said to the commanders of the Philistines, "Is this not David, the servant of King Saul of Israel, who has been with me now for days and years? Since he deserted to me I have found no fault in him to this day."

⁴ But the commanders of the Philistines were angry with him, and the commanders of the Philistines said to him, "Send the man back, so that he may return to the place that you have assigned to him; he shall not go down with us to battle, or else he may become an adversary to us in the battle. For how could this fellow reconcile himself to his lord? Would it not be with the heads of the men here?

⁵ Is this not David, of whom they sing to one another in dances,

'Saul has killed his thousands

    and David his ten thousands'?"

⁶ Then Achish called David and said to him, "As the LORD lives, you have been honest, and to me it seems right that you should march out

and in with me in the campaign, for I have found nothing wrong in you from the day of your coming to me until today. Nevertheless, the lords do not approve of you.

⁷ So go back now, and go peaceably; do nothing to displease the lords of the Philistines."

⁸ David said to Achish, "But what have I done? What have you found in your servant from the day I entered your service until now, that I should not go and fight against the enemies of my lord the king?"

⁹ Achish replied to David, "I know that you are as blameless in my sight as an angel of God; nevertheless, the commanders of the Philistines have said, 'He shall not go up with us to the battle.'

¹⁰ Now then, rise early in the morning, you and the servants of your lord who came with you, and go to the place that I appointed for you. As for the evil report, do not take it to heart, for you have done well before me. Start early in the morning, and leave as soon as you have light."

¹¹ So David set out with his men early in the morning, to return to the land of the Philistines. But the Philistines went up to Jezreel.

First Samuel 29:1–11 demonstrates that David will not be a part of the Philistine army that will be responsible for the defeat of Israel and the deaths of Saul and his sons. It also prepares the reader for the following chapter in 1 Samuel 30, in which he defeats the Amalekites, something Saul was never able to do fully, thereby protecting the people of Judah and sharing the spoils of his victory with them. First Samuel 29 shows David as a capable leader who is able to deceive the Philistines and act on behalf of his own people even when he functions as a Philistine vassal.

The narrative has two major sub-units. The first appears in 1 Samuel 29:1–5, in which the Philistine leaders object to the presence of David and his 600 men as they gather their forces at Aphek in preparation for the attack against Israel in the Jezreel Valley. The basis for their objection is that David is a "Hebrew" who has served King Saul of Israel, and they therefore doubt his loyalty. The second major sub-unit appears in 1 Samuel 29:6–11, in which David's suzerain, King Achish of Gath, informs him that the Philistine lords oppose his presence in the army even though Achish trusts him unconditionally. David returns to Ziklag.

Aphek, the site of Philistia's earlier defeat of Israel in the time of Eli (1 Sam 4), is identified with the site of Ras el-'Ain, located at the source of the Yarkon River to the east of modern Petaḥ Tiqva.[83] This site differs from Shunem, which 1 Samuel 28:4 reports as the site of the Philistine camp. Although some see this as evidence of redactional activity, it merely represents the retrospective narrative viewpoint of 1 Samuel 29 in that the Philistines would have initially gathered at Aphek before advancing forward to Shunem.[84] David had convinced Achish of his loyalty due to his prior service, as noted in 1 Samuel 27, but the Philistine lords were not convinced. As a former officer of Saul, David's loyalty would be suspect, despite the clear tension between them. They cite the song of the women, "Saul has killed his thousands, and David his ten thousands," in 1 Samuel 29:5, which recalls their chant in 1 Samuel 18:7 when David killed the Philistine giant, Goliath, and ensured Israel's victory over Philistia.

Achish's discussion with David of the Philistine lords' rejection of his presence in the army demonstrates both Achish's confidence in David and the degree to which he has been taken in by David's deception. David clearly serves his own interests, particularly the protection of his own people. He answers Achish in 1 Samuel 29:8, "But what have I done? What have you found in your servant from the day I entered your service until now, that I should not go and fight against the enemies of my lord the king?" much as he answered Saul in 1 Samuel 24:10–16 when he declined to kill Saul in the cave at Ein Gedi or in 1 Samuel 26:17–20, when he again declined to kill Saul at Hachilah. David's statements are included to convince the reader that David is innocent of any interest in killing Saul and that he is the appropriate leader for Israel.

David returns to Ziklag, where he can continue to protect Judah and avoid any blame for the defeat of Israel or the deaths of Saul and his sons at the hands of the Philistines.

DAVID'S DEFENSE OF ZIKLAG – 1 SAMUEL 30:1–31

30 ¹ **Now when David and his men came to Ziklag on the third day, the Amalekites had made a raid on the Negeb and on Ziklag. They had attacked Ziklag, burned it down,**

---

[83]　Rafael Frankel, "Aphek," *ABD* 1:276; Yigal Levin, "Aphek," *EBR* 2:305–308.
[84]　See discussion in McCarter, *1 Samuel*, 426; Walter Dietrich, *1 Samuel 27–2 Samuel 8* (BKAT 8/3; Göttingen: Vandenhoeck & Ruprecht, 2019) 101–103.

² and taken captive the women and all who were in it, both small and great; they killed none of them but carried them off and went their way.

³ When David and his men came to the city, they found it burned down and their wives and sons and daughters taken captive.

⁴ Then David and the people who were with him raised their voices and wept until they had no more strength to weep.

⁵ David's two wives also had been taken captive, Ahinoam of Jezreel and Abigail the widow of Nabal of Carmel.

⁶ David was in great danger, for the people spoke of stoning him because all the people were bitter in spirit for their sons and daughters. But David strengthened himself in the LORD his God.

⁷ David said to the priest Abiathar son of Ahimelech, "Bring me the ephod." So Abiathar brought the ephod to David.

⁸ David inquired of the LORD, "Shall I pursue this band? Shall I overtake them?" He answered him, "Pursue, for you shall surely overtake and shall surely rescue."

⁹ So David set out, he and the six hundred men who were with him. They came to the Wadi Besor, where those stayed who were left behind.

¹⁰ But David went on with the pursuit, he and four hundred men; two hundred stayed behind, too exhausted to cross the Wadi Besor.

¹¹ In the open country they found an Egyptian and brought him to David. They gave him bread, and he ate; they gave him water to drink;

¹² they also gave him a piece of fig cake and two clusters of raisins. When he had eaten, his spirit revived, for he had not eaten bread or drunk water for three days and three nights.

¹³ Then David said to him, "To whom do you belong? Where are you from?" He said, "I am a young man of Egypt, servant to an Amalekite. My master left me behind because I fell sick three days ago.

¹⁴ We had made a raid on the Negeb of the Cherethites and on that which belongs to Judah and on the Negeb of Caleb, and we burned Ziklag down."

¹⁵ David said to him, "Will you take me down to this raiding party?" He said, "Swear to me by God that you will not kill me or hand me over to my master, and I will take you down to them."

¹⁶ When he had taken him down, they were spread out all over the ground, eating and drinking and dancing, because of the great

amount of spoil they had taken from the land of the Philistines and from the land of Judah.

[17] David attacked them from twilight until the evening of the next day. Not one of them escaped, except four hundred young men, who mounted camels and fled.

[18] David recovered all that the Amalekites had taken, and David rescued his two wives.

[19] Nothing was missing, whether small or great, sons or daughters, spoil or anything that had been taken; David brought back everything.

[20] David also captured all the flocks and herds, which were driven ahead of the other cattle; people said, "This is David's spoil."

[21] Then David came to the two hundred men who had been too exhausted to follow David and who had been left at the Wadi Besor. They went out to meet David and to meet the people who were with him. When David drew near to the people, he saluted them.

[22] Then all the corrupt and worthless fellows among the men who had gone with David said, "Because they did not go with us, we will not give them any of the spoil that we have recovered, except that each man may take his wife and children and leave."

[23] But David said, "You shall not do so, my brothers, with what the L-RD has given us; he has preserved us and handed over to us the raiding party that attacked us.

[24] Who would listen to you in this matter? For the share of the one who goes down into the battle shall be the same as the share of the one who stays by the baggage; they shall share alike."

[25] From that day forward he made it a statute and an ordinance for Israel; it continues to the present day.

[26] When David came to Ziklag, he sent part of the spoil to his friends, the elders of Judah, saying, "Here is a present for you from the spoil of the enemies of the LORD."

[27] It was for those in Bethel, in Ramoth of the Negeb, in Jattir,

[28] in Aroer, in Siphmoth, in Eshtemoa,

[29] in Racal, in the towns of the Jerahmeelites, in the towns of the Kenites,

[30] in Hormah, in Bor-ashan, in Athach,

[31] in Hebron, all the places where David and his men had roamed.

First Samuel 30:1–31 recounts David's defense of Ziklag in the aftermath of the Amalekite sack of the city. The narrative is especially important for several key reasons. First, it portrays David's efforts to build a constituency for himself in Judah by sending portions of the spoil to the various cities of Judah. This motif had been addressed before in 1 Samuel 27 when King Achish of Gath first granted him Ziklag. But several other aspects of David's actions in 1 Samuel 30 indicate that David also demonstrates his capacity for leadership. The second reason for its importance is the portrayal of David's defeat of the Amalekites, something that Saul had failed fully to accomplish in 1 Samuel 15 when he failed to carry out Samuel's orders to kill Agag and therefore lost the support of YHWH and Samuel for the kingship. A third reason is David's principle that men who guard the baggage – or otherwise defend home territory in a time of war – share equally in the booty with those who actually fight the battle. David demonstrates his capacity as a leader by granting equal shares of the booty to those who stayed behind to defend baggage or home territory, thereby correcting the mistake of leaving Ziklag unguarded.

The narrative comprises five major sub-units, each of which is defined by the sequence of narrative action. The first appears in 1 Samuel 30:1–6, which recounts the return of David and his men to Ziklag following their departure from Aphek in 1 Samuel 29 only to find the city sacked and a potential revolt among David's men. The second appears in 1 Samuel 30:7–8, in which David makes an oracular inquiry of YHWH, who authorizes David's pursuit of the Amalekites. The third appears in 1 Samuel 30:9–20, which recounts David's enlistment of an Egyptian slave left behind by the Amalekites, who enabled David to find and defeat the Amalekites. The fourth appears in 1 Samuel 30:21–25, which recounts David's stipulation that those men who remained behind to guard the baggage would share equally in the spoils of the victory. And the fifth appears in 1 Samuel 30:26–31, which recounts David's dispatch of spoils to Judah to build a constituency that would ultimately lead him to the throne of Judah.

The first episode, in 1 Samuel 30:1–6, establishes the problematic premise of the narrative by recounting the Amalekite sack of Ziklag and the potential for revolt against David by his own men. While David and his men were north at Aphek, the Amalekites, the major traditional enemy of Israel during the period of Wilderness Wandering in Exodus 17:8–16; Deuteronomy 25:17–19 and the enemy that Saul failed to destroy in 1 Samuel 15, had taken the opportunity to sack and burn the undefended city, to take the women and children as captives, and to take the livestock and other goods as spoils of war. Ahinoam of Jezreel and Abigail the wife of Nabal from Carmel were among the captives. Things began to turn ugly for David as his men were ready to stone him to death for enabling the Amalekites to make off with their families and property as well as to destroy their homes. The narrative does not immediately provide a solution; instead, it states that David "strengthened himself" with YHWH, his G-d. It thereby demonstrates how YHWH showed favor to David, and David adhered to YHWH.

The second episode, in 1 Samuel 30:7–8, portrays David's oracular inquiry of YHWH by means of the ephod brought by Abiathar the priest. Abiathar was the surviving member of the House of Eli from the massacre of the priests at Nob in 1 Samuel 22. His presence with David indicates that David continues to enjoy the support of the House of Eli, even in its present weakened state, where Saul had already been informed by the now dead Samuel in 1 Samuel 28 that Saul and his sons would join him in Sheol in the coming battle against the Philistines. David inquired of YHWH whether he should pursue and overtake the enemies responsible for the sack of Ziklag. YHWH's positive response indicated YHWH's authorization and support for David's proposed actions, again emphasizing YHWH's favor for David.

The third episode, in 1 Samuel 30:9–20, recounts David's pursuit and defeat of the Amalekites. He initially leads his men to the Wadi Besor, likely identified with the Wadi Gazzeh or possibly the Wadi Gerar (esh-Sharia), which flow west and then north from the vicinity of Beer Sheba to the Mediterranean coast south of present-day Gaza and north of Khan Yunis in the Gaza strip.[85] Although David marched with his entire 600-man force, 200 men were too exhausted to continue when they reached the Wadi Besor to the south of Ziklag. They picked up a young Egyptian man in the open country who had not eaten or drunk in three days since he was abandoned by the Amalekites. Once he was given food and water, he identified himself as an Egyptian slave of the Amalekites who was abandoned after he became ill while raiding Ziklag and other areas of the Negev, including the regions of the Cherithites, apparently Cretans associated with the Philistines,[86] and the Calebites, a Judean clan.[87] He agreed to lead David and his men to the Amalekites on the condition that they would not

---

[85] DeVries, "Besor, The Brook," *ABD* 1:679–680; Münger, "Besor," *EBR* 3:935.
[86] Carl S. Ehrlich, Cherethites," *ABD* 1:898–899; André Lemaire, "Cherethites," *EBR* 5:54.
[87] Mark J. Fritz and Raphael I. Panitz, "Caleb," *ABD* 1:808–810; Dennis T. Olson, "Caleb," *EBR* 4:779–781.

kill him or return him to his former Amalekite captors. David defeated the Amalekites, except for 400 young men who escaped on their camels. All the captives, including David's two wives, and all the booty was recovered, which would resolve the brewing opposition to David among his men. Verse 20 notes that the livestock driven ahead of the captured livestock would belong to David; it must have been the property of the Amalekites prior to their Negev raids.

The fourth episode, in 1 Samuel 30:21–25, recounts one of the major results of David's victory, his stipulation that the 200 men who stayed behind to protect the baggage will receive an equal share of the spoils. The stipulation thereby resolves the problem with which the narrative began, that Ziklag was sacked because it was left undefended when David and his men traveled north to join the Philistine forces at Aphek. The assertion that only the attacking warriors should share in the spoils was made by evil men who were called "sons of Belial" (i.e., "worthless fellows") among David's men in verse 22. Whereas Saul had never been able to answer such "worthless fellows" in 1 Samuel 10:27, David answers easily by asking rhetorically how anyone could listen to such nonsense in verse 24, again demonstrating his capacity for leadership. The stipulation in verse 26 that this principle remains in force "until this day" indicates that the narrative was composed during the monarchic period and not during the exilic or post-exilic periods when Judah was subject to Babylonia and later to Persia. The favorable portrayal of David suggests the Solomonic narrative that was later incorporated into the Jehu Dynastic History and the Josian DtrH.

Finally, the fifth episode in 1 Samuel 30:26–31 recounts how David sent portions of his share of the spoils to the elders and allies of the various cities of Judah, thereby securing their support for his own rise to kingship in 2 Samuel 1–8 following Saul's death at Mt. Gilboa in 1 Samuel 31. The cities and regions to which David sent shares included Bethel, an unknown location in Judah;[88] Ramot-Negev, an unknown location in Judah;[89] Jattir, identified with Khirbet 'Attir, approximately fifteen and a half miles northeast of Beer Sheba;[90] Aroer, identified with Tel Esdar, north of 'Ar'arah, roughly 12 miles southeast of Beer Sheba;[91] Siphmoth, an unknown

---

[88] Harold Brodsky, "Bethel (Place)," *ABD* 1:710–712; Henrik Pfeiffer, "Bethel," *EBR* 3:967.
[89] McCarter, *1 Samuel*, 436.
[90] John L. Peterson, "Jattir," *ABD* 3:649–650; Ralph K. Hawkins, "Jattir," *EBR* 13:789.
[91] Gerald L. Mattingly, "Aroer," *ABD* 1:399–400; Levin, "Aroer," *EBR* 2:803–804.

location in Judah;[92] Eshtemoa, identified with Tell es-Samu', located five miles northeast of Khirbet 'Attir and 8.7 miles southwest of Hebron;[93] Racal, an unknown location in Judah, although LXX identifies it with Carmel;[94] the cities of the Jerahmeelites, a clan region in the Negev that was absorbed into Judah;[95] the cities of the Kenites, a tribal region in the southeastern Negev of Judah;[96] Hormah, identified with a number of sites in the southern Negev;[97] Bor-Ashan, a site in Judah or Simeon associated with Khirbet Ashan five miles northwest of Beer Sheba;[98] Athach, a Judean city sometimes identified with Ether in Joshua 15:42; 19:7 and possibly identified with Khirbet el-'Ater, approximately fifteen miles northwest of Hebron;[99] and Hebron, the capital city of the tribe of Judah, identified with Tell er-Rumedie in modern Hebron, located nineteen miles south-southeast of Jerusalem and twenty-three miles northeast of Beer Sheba.[100] The locations mentioned here indicate that David built his base of support in southern and southwestern Judah. Although his home town of Bethlehem was located north of Hebron and south of Jerusalem, it appears that Saul controlled northern Judah, even though David could easily turn it to support his own claims.

SAUL'S TRAGIC DEATH AT MT. GILBOA – 1 SAMUEL 31:1–13

31 [1] **Now the Philistines fought against Israel, and the men of Israel fled before the Philistines, and many fell on Mount Gilboa.**

[2] **The Philistines overtook Saul and his sons, and the Philistines killed Jonathan and Abinadab and Malchishua, the sons of Saul.**

[3] **The battle pressed hard on Saul, and the archers found him, and he was badly wounded by them.**

[4] **Then Saul said to his armor-bearer, "Draw your sword and thrust me through with it, so that these uncircumcised may not come and thrust**

[92] Kotter, "Siphmoth," *ABD* 6:51.
[93] Peterson, "Eshtemoa," *ABD* 2:617–618.
[94] Hamilton, "Racal," *ABD* 5:605.
[95] Roger W. Uitti, "Jerahmeel," *ABD* 3:683–684.
[96] Baruch Halpern, "Kenites," *ABD* 4:17–22; Leuenberger, "Kenites," *EBR* 15:111–112.
[97] Hamilton, "Hormah," *ABD* 3:288–289; Jaeyoung Jeon, "Hormah," *EBR* 12:293–294.
[98] Hamilton, "Ashan," *ABD* 1:476–477; Kah-Jin Jeffrey Kuan, "Ashan," *EBR* 2:967.
[99] McCarter, *1 Samuel*, 434; Kuan, "Athach," *EBR* 2:1181–1182.
[100] Paul Wayne Ferris, Jr., "Hebron," *ABD* 3:107–108; Jeffrey R. Chadwick, "Hebron," *EBR* 11:694–697.

me through and make sport of me." But his armor-bearer was unwilling, for he was terrified. So Saul took his own sword and fell on it.

⁵ When his armor-bearer saw that Saul was dead, he also fell on his sword and died with him.

⁶ So Saul and his three sons and his armor-bearer and all his men died together on the same day.

⁷ When the men of Israel who were on the other side of the valley and those beyond the Jordan saw that the men of Israel had fled and that Saul and his sons were dead, they forsook their towns and fled, and the Philistines came and occupied them.

⁸ The next day, when the Philistines came to strip the dead, they found Saul and his three sons fallen on Mount Gilboa.

⁹ They cut off his head, stripped off his armor, and sent messengers throughout the land of the Philistines to carry the good news to the houses of their idols and to the people.

¹⁰ They put his armor in the temple of Astarte, and they fastened his body to the wall of Beth-shan.

¹¹ But when the inhabitants of Jabesh-gilead heard what the Philistines had done to Saul,

¹² all the valiant men set out, traveled all night long, and took the body of Saul and the bodies of his sons from the wall of Beth-shan. They came to Jabesh and burned them there.

¹³ Then they took their bones and buried them under the tamarisk tree in Jabesh and fasted seven days.

First Samuel 31 recounts Saul's tragic suicide at Mt. Gilboa together with his failed attempt to defend the Jezreel Valley against the Philistine attack. As a result, the Philistines were able to take control of the entire Jezreel Valley, thereby dividing the Israelite hill country to the south from the Galilee region to the north and leaving Israel to Philistine domination. With the deaths of Saul and his three sons, Jonathan, Abinadab, and Malchishua, the royal House of Saul was left in a very weak position with only Ish-Bosheth, also known as Esh Baal but generally identified with Ishvi (see 1 Sam 14:49; cf. 2 Sam 2:8). But then, David was also a member of the House of Saul due to his earlier marriage to Michal (see 1 Sam 18:17–29; cf. 1 Sam 25:44).

First Samuel 31:1–13 comprises two major sub-units: the account of Israel's defeat and Saul's death in 1 Samuel 31:1–7 and the account of Saul's burial in 1 Samuel 31:8–13.

The account of Israel's defeat and Saul's death in 1 Samuel 31:1–7 is very straightforward. It begins with a brief notation of the Philistine attack against Israel at Mt. Gilboa, situated on the southwestern boundary of the Jezreel Valley as part of the Israelite hill country, resulting in many Israelite casualties. The narrative focuses on the Philistine pursuit of Saul and his sons, Jonathan, Abinadab, and Malchishua. Philistine archers wounded Saul. The verb, *wayyāḥel*, "and he was badly wounded," is generally repointed as a passive form of the verb,[101] but the phrase reads literally, "and he writhed very much (in pain) from the archers." Mortally wounded and in fear of capture, death, and humiliation at the hands of the Philistines, Saul asks his arms bearer to finish him off with his sword. But the arms bearer is afraid to kill YHWH's anointed, leaving Saul to grab the sword and commit suicide by falling on it himself. Once the arms bearer sees that Saul has killed himself, he follows suit. Verse 7 states that the men on the other (north) side of the (Jezreel) Valley and across the Jordan River then fled.

A Closer Look at Saul's Suicide

Many interpreters view Saul's actions as heroic.[102] There is no doubt that Saul is portrayed as courageous in his final battle, but Jewish tradition forbids suicide, based on Genesis 9:5.[103] Only two other instances of suicide are presented in the Hebrew Bible, Samson in Judges 16:23–31 and Ahitophel in 2 Samuel 17:23. The view that Saul's suicide is heroic is based on a Greek ideal of self-sacrifice in the face of adversity, but the Jewish notion of suicide is that no human is permitted to take the life that G-d has given him or her; indeed, the Jewish ideal calls for one to overcome adversity rather than to succumb to it with suicide. Saul's task was to save his people from its enemies – most notably, the Philistines – and he failed miserably at his task due to his ineptitude as a leader who spent his time in envious attempts to kill David rather than enlisting him as his closest ally. Elements of the narrative suggest that ineptitude even in Saul's last battle. Why were Israelite men left on the north side of the Jezreel or beyond the Jordan when Saul should have rallied them to his cause? Where was Abner, Saul's general, throughout the battle? Saul, with only one part of his army, was left to face the Philistines alone when he should have had his entire force at his disposal. Saul appears to be a victim of his own poor capacity at leadership, which left him to end his life as a suicide when he was unable to rally his full army to his side.

---

[101] Driver, *Notes*, 228.
[102] E.g., Hertzberg, *1 and 2 Samuel*, 231–232; Klein, *1 Samuel*, 288.
[103] Rosenberg, *1 Samuel*, 248.

First Samuel 31:8–13 then recounts the disgraceful treatment of Saul's body by the Philistines and the efforts by the men of Jabesh Gilead to give their king a proper burial. The Philistines reportedly found the bodies of Saul and his sons lying on Mt. Gilboa on the day following the battle. They cut off Saul's head, thereby replicating what David had earlier done to Goliath in 1 Samuel 17, stripped him of his armor, and sent both for public display in the temples dedicated to their own gods.[104] The men of Jabesh Gilead, whom Saul had saved from Nahash the Ammonite in 1 Samuel 11, took down the bodies of Saul and his sons, burned them, buried them under a tamarisk tree near Jabesh Gilead, and fasted for seven days in mourning for their dead king. Canaanite and Israelite–Judean burial practices indicate that bodies were in some cases burned or allowed to decompose until the flesh was gone, and then the bodies were placed in stone burial coffins within the tomb.[105] Second Samuel 21:12–14 reports that David took the bones of Saul and his sons from Jabesh Gilead to Zela, an unknown site located in the territory of Benjamin,[106] where he buried them in the tomb of Saul's father, Kish.

---

[104] Amihai Mazar, "Beth Shean," *NEAEHL* 1:214–223.
[105] Elizabeth Bloch-Smith, *Judahite Burial Practices and Beliefs about the Dead* (JSOTSup 123; Sheffield: Sheffield Academic Press, 1992).
[106] Edelman, "Zela," *ABD* 6:1072.

5 Commentary Part III: David's Rise to Power as King of Judah and Israel – 2 Samuel 1:1–5:3

David's mourning for the deaths of Saul and Jonathan begins the account of David's rise to kingship over Judah and Israel in 2 Samuel 1–7. Second Samuel 1 does not close the account of the reign of the House of Saul. Saul's only surviving son, identified as Ish-Bosheth in Samuel and Esh-Baal in Chronicles, would rule over Israel after his father, and David, a member of the House of Saul due to his marriage to Michal, would also emerge as a contender for the throne.

An additional key element in the recognition that 2 Samuel 1 begins the account of David's rise to kingship over Judah and Israel is David's handling of the Amalekite threats to Israel. Second Samuel 1 anticipates the account of David's pursuit of the Amalekites who had razed Ziklag; kidnapped his wives, Ahinoam of Jezreel and Abigail, the widow of Nabal of Carmel, as well as the wives and children of his men; and plundered their wealth, in 1 Samuel 30. Interpreters frequently underestimate the reasons why Saul was rejected as King of Israel in the earlier narratives of 1 Samuel 13–14, where he usurped Samuel's role as priest and pronounced a death sentence on his son Jonathan for eating food before the victory over the Philistines was complete, and 1 Samuel 15, where Samuel condemned Saul for failing to follow YHWH's instructions to destroy the Amalekites entirely. Both narratives factor in here, particularly the death sentence against Jonathan in 1 Samuel 13–14, which would undermine the House of Saul, and the failure to destroy the Amalekites, Israel's unrelenting enemy that threatened its very existence, in 1 Samuel 15. Whereas Saul expected that Jonathan would succeed him on the throne, his own pronouncement of a death sentence for Jonathan ended that possibility – and that of his brothers Abinadab and Malchishua – at Mt. Gilboa, leaving only the incompetent Ish-Bosheth to succeed his father. And whereas Saul showed no willingness to destroy Amalek completely by sparing Agag and the Amalekite flocks and herds that had been taken as booty, David did not hesitate to kill the Amalekites and their flocks and herds in 1 Samuel 30 as well as the Amalekite who claimed to have killed Saul in 2 Samuel 1.

Because of his marriage to Michal daughter of Saul, David is a son-in-law of the House of Saul. As such, he is perfectly capable of succeeding his father-in-law if no other sons are available. David will further demonstrate his qualification to ascend the throne of Israel by building upon his power base to become King of Judah (2 Sam 2), defeating Ish-Bosheth's forces led by Abner at Gibeon (2 Sam 2), eliminating Abner as a potential contender for the Israelite throne (2 Sam 3), and following the assassination of Ish-Bosheth by Gibeonite army officers (2 Sam 4), David accepted the invitation of the elders of Israel to serve as King of Israel (2 Sam 5:1–3). A further qualification is David's consistent and loud respect for YHWH's anointed King of Israel and his punishment of those who would strike YHWH's anointed, beginning with the Amalekite in 2 Samuel 1. Indeed, 2 Samuel 1:1–5:3 demonstrates that David – like Saul before him in 1 Samuel 8–12 – will be the next King of Israel. The introductory regnal formula in 2 Samuel 5:4–5 begins the account of David's reign in 2 Samuel 5:4–24:25.

DAVID'S MOURNING FOR THE DEATHS OF SAUL AND JONATHAN – 2 SAMUEL 1:1–27

1 ¹ After the death of Saul, when David had returned from defeating the Amalekites, David remained two days in Ziklag.

² On the third day, a man came from Saul's camp with his clothes torn and dirt on his head. When he came to David, he fell to the ground and did obeisance.

³ David said to him, "Where have you come from?" He said to him, "I have escaped from the camp of Israel."

⁴ David said to him, "How did things go? Tell me!" He answered, "The army fled from the battle, but also many of the army fell and died, and Saul and his son Jonathan also died."

⁵ Then David asked the young man who was reporting to him, "How do you know that Saul and his son Jonathan died?"

⁶ The young man reporting to him said, "I happened to be on Mount Gilboa, and there was Saul leaning on his spear, while the chariots and the horsemen drew close to him.

7 When he looked behind him, he saw me and called to me. I answered, 'Here, sir.'

8 And he said to me, 'Who are you?' I answered him, 'I am an Amalekite.'

9 He said to me, 'Come, stand over me and kill me, for convulsions have seized me, and yet my life still lingers.'

10 So I stood over him and killed him, for I knew that he could not live after he had fallen. I took the crown that was on his head and the armlet that was on his arm, and I have brought them here to my lord."

11 Then David took hold of his clothes and tore them, and all the men who were with him did the same.

12 They mourned and wept and fasted until evening for Saul and for his son Jonathan and for the army of the Lord and for the house of Israel, because they had been struck down by the sword.

13 David said to the young man who had reported to him, "Where do you come from?" He answered, "I am the son of a resident alien, an Amalekite."

14 David said to him, "Were you not afraid to lift your hand to destroy the Lord's anointed?"

15 Then David called one of the young men and said, "Come here and strike him down." So he struck him down, and he died.

16 David said to him, "Your blood be on your head, for your own mouth has testified against you, saying, 'I have killed the Lord's anointed.'"

17 David intoned this lamentation over Saul and his son Jonathan.

18 (He ordered that The Song of the Bow be taught to the people of Judah; it is written in the Book of Jashar.) He said,

19 "Your glory, O Israel, lies slain upon your high places!

How the mighty have fallen!

20 Tell it not in Gath;

proclaim it not in the streets of Ashkelon,

or the daughters of the Philistines will rejoice;

the daughters of the uncircumcised will exult.

21 You mountains of Gilboa,

let there be no dew or rain upon you

nor bounteous fields!

For there the shield of the mighty was defiled,

the shield of Saul, anointed with oil no more.

²² From the blood of the slain,
   from the fat of the mighty,
   the bow of Jonathan did not turn back,
   nor the sword of Saul return empty.
²³ Saul and Jonathan, beloved and lovely!
   In life and in death they were not divided;
   they were swifter than eagles;
   they were stronger than lions.
²⁴ O daughters of Israel, weep over Saul,
   who clothed you with crimson, in luxury,
   who put ornaments of gold on your apparel.
²⁵ How the mighty have fallen
   in the midst of the battle!
   Jonathan lies slain upon your high places.
²⁶ I am distressed for you, my brother Jonathan;
   greatly beloved were you to me;
   your love to me was wonderful,
   passing the love of women.
²⁷ How the mighty have fallen,
   and the weapons of war perished!"

Second Samuel 1 begins the account of David's rise to power as King of Judah and Israel. The narrative is demarcated at the outset by the introductory temporal statement in 2 Samuel 1:1, which refers to the deaths of Saul and Jonathan in 1 Samuel 31 and David's defeat of the Amalekites in 1 Samuel 30. It includes three major sub-units: the initial temporal statement in 2 Samuel 1:1, which introduces the narrative; the account of David's reception of the news of the deaths of Saul and Jonathan from the Amalekite in 2 Samuel 1:2–10; and David's reactions to the terrible news in 2 Samuel 2:11–27. Second Samuel 2:11–27 in turn comprises two sub-units, the account of David's decision to execute the Amalekite for his role in killing Saul, YHWH's anointed King of Israel, in 2 Samuel 2:11–16 and David's very public lament for Saul and Jonathan in 2 Samuel 1:17–27. The temporal statement in 2 Samuel 2:1, introduces David's actions, beginning with his journey to Hebron, that leads him to the thrones of Judah and Israel.

The temporal formula in 2 Samuel 1:1 looks back to the accounts of the deaths of Saul and Jonathan at Mt. Gilboa in 1 Samuel 31 and to David's defeat of the Amalekites who had raided Ziklag in 1 Samuel 30. The temporal formula, "and it came to pass after the death of Saul," begins a *waw*-consecutive narrative chain that introduces the action of the narrative, viz., David's subsequent actions, beginning with the finite verbal clause based on the perfect verbal phrase, "David returned (Hebrew, *šāb*) from defeating (Hebrew, *mēhakkôt*, lit., "from striking") the Amalekites" and the following statement based on the *waw*-consecutive verb, *wayyēšeb*, "and David remained (lit., "stayed") two days in Ziklag."

A second *waw*-consecutive formula, "and it came to pass (Hebrew, *wayěhî*) on the third day," introduces the narrative action of 2 Samuel 1:2–10, which recounts David's reception of the news of the deaths of Saul and Jonathan from the Amalekite man, who reportedly comes to David from the camp of Saul. His clothing is torn and he has dirt on his head in a typical depiction of mourning. He bows low to the ground in a typical sign of subservience to a superior, and David begins an interrogation in which the Amalekite identifies himself and reports the news of the deaths of Saul and Jonathan. When David asks the man how he knows about their deaths, he reports that he was with Saul at the end. Both the NRSVue and NJPS translations underplay the Hebrew in the narrative when they state that the man "happened" to be on Mt. Gilboa in verse 6; the Hebrew employs an infinitive absolute, *niqrō' niqrêtî*, which emphatically states, "I definitely happened to be" on Mt. Gilboa, which would lend credence to the man's statements and alert David to the possibility of deception, especially since the man was an Amalekite, the unremitting enemies of Israel that David had just returned from attacking. The man states that Saul asked him who he was, to which he responded "an Amalekite," and that Saul asked the man to finish him off to end his suffering. The man claims that he then killed Saul and took the crown and armlet from Saul's body that identified Saul as King of Israel.

Most interpreters focus on whether or not the man was lying.[1] This is a valid question, but it is not the fundamental question to be asked here. The narrative in 1 Samuel 31 makes it clear that Saul committed suicide and that everyone with Saul, including his three sons, died beside him. The

---

[1]   E.g., A. A. Anderson, *2 Samuel* (WBC 11; Grand Rapids, MI: Zondervan, 2000) 5–6.

question as to whether the man was lying is an attempt to discern what really happened. Several facts emerge from David's interrogation. For example, the man says that he was there, so why did he not defend Saul in the first place or die in an attempt to do so? His self-identification as an Amalekite suggests that he was an enemy of Israel, and this would indicate that he more likely served with the Philistines than with the Israelites; his presence at the battle would not have been happenstance. Second, he states that he killed Saul; that is reason to doubt his sincerity and motives, especially since he was an Amalekite, from a people who specialized in killing Israelites. Third, he took the trouble to recover the royal crown and armlet and brought them to David. Was this a chance to claim a reward by bringing the symbols of Israelite royal authority to a man widely understood to possess the leadership qualities necessary to be king and the ambition to do so? And there is the question of an appointment as one of David's officers. But the man is an Amalekite, an enemy of Israel, who was likely at the battle as an enemy. His story does not make sense. What is David going to do about this?

David's reactions appear in 2 Samuel 1:11–27. The first sub-unit in 2 Samuel 1:11–16 begins with a notice of David's own signs of mourning for his dead king and father-in-law as well as his dead friend and brother-in-law. Although David appears to be overcome with grief, he does not lose his wits, and with the suspicions generated by his first round of interrogation of the Amalekite, he resumes his interrogation in verse 13. David now asks, "Where do you come from?" The repetition of this issue gives David and the narrative a chance to delve deeper into the man's identity, but it also accentuates the issue of the man's Amalekite identity beyond what had been stated before. The man answers that he is the son of a resident alien, an Amalekite. The man's response might be an appeal for favor – at least from a literary standpoint – because the reader may well know that the book of Deuteronomy and the Covenant Code in Exodus 20–23 (esp. Exod 22:20; 23:9) require that Israelites (and Judeans) treat resident aliens, Hebrew, *gērîm*, justly and hospitably. But the man's answer to David's question highlights once again his Amalekite identity, which means that he is an enemy whom YHWH requires to be destroyed. Upon ascertaining the man's Amalekite identity publicly and clearly, David orders him executed, thereby fulfilling YHWH's orders that Saul had failed to fulfill and demonstrating his fitness to be king. The sub-unit concludes with David's statement in verse 16 that the man confessed to killing the King of Israel and therefore deserved death.

David's second reaction appears in 2 Samuel 1:17–27, in which he leads
the people in singing a lamentation or dirge for the dead Saul and
Jonathan. A lament or dirge is a form of psalm called *qînâ*, "lament, dirge"
in Hebrew, which is sung to mourn the death of someone.[2] It employs a
typical 3/2 Qinah meter, which represents the halting march of three steps
followed by two more that those who carry a body to its burial spot would
employ as they march, weep, and cry out in mourning for the dead (see
1 Kgs 18:25–29, esp. verse 26, in which the prophets of Baal perform a
limping march around the altar to mourn for the god Baal, who lies dead in
the netherworld until he is brought back to life to commence the rainy
season in the fall). The other identifying mark of the Qinah is the Hebrew
particle *'êk*, "how!" here repeated three times in the phrase, "how (*'êk*) the
mighty have fallen!" in verses 19, 25, and 27 (cf. Lam 1:1). The text labels
David's lament as "the Song of the Bow," insofar as the song makes
mention of the loss of weapons employed by the dead in defense of the
land of Israel in verses 21–22. The song is said to be included in "the Book
of Jashar," generally understood as a proper name, but it is better translated as "the Book of the Righteous," based on the Hebrew word *hayyāšār*,
"righteous" (see Josh 10:13). Some suggest that the term *hayyāšār* may be a
corrupted form of the verb *yāšār*, "he sings," based on the notice in the
3 Kingdoms 8:53 (= 1 Kgs 8:12) in the Septuagint, which cites Solomon's
psalm at the dedication of the Jerusalem Temple as a work from a book of
songs, but this appears unlikely due to the conjugated verbal form of *yāšār*.
Greek, *oidēs*, in 3 Kingdoms 8:53 may be an alternative reference to
Psalms, *psalmoi* in Greek.[3]

The lament presents a series of poetic strophes that express grief at the
deaths of Saul and Jonathan. Verse 19 exclaims grief at the glory of Israel,
Saul, Jonathan, and the rest of Israel's warriors, lying dead on the high
places, better, "heights," presumably a reference to Mt. Gilboa where the
battle took place. Verse 20 warns against proclaiming the defeat in Gath,
one of the principal cities of the Philistines, from which Goliath came, or in
Ashkelon, another major Philistine city, because the uncircumcised
Philistines will celebrate the deaths of Israel's finest. The verse refers to

---

[2]   Erhard S. Gerstenberger, *Psalms, Part 1, with an Introduction to Cultic Poetry* (FOTL 14;
      Grand Rapids, MI: Eerdmans, 1984) 10–11; see esp. Hedwig Jahnow, *Das Hebräische
      Leichenlied im Rahmen deer Völkerdichtung* (BZAW 36; Giessen: A. Töpelmann, 1923)
      133–157. Jahnow, a student of Hermann Gunkel and a lecturer at Marburg University,
      was murdered by the Nazis at Theresienstadt in 1944 because her father was Jewish.
[3]   P. Kyle McCarter, *2 Samuel* (AB 9; Garden City, NY: Doubleday, 1984) 74.

the singing of the Philistine women, much like the Israelite women sang for David and Saul (1 Sam 18:7; 21:12; cf. Exod 15:20–21). Verse 21 calls for no dew or rain to fall on Mt. Gilboa, the site of the defeat and the deaths of Saul and Jonathan, because rain brings new growth in the land, but Mt. Gilboa is a place of death and mourning, where the shield of Saul lies cast away and unoiled (apparently a means to keep a shield made of leather and wood supple enough to give protection in battle), never to be used again in the defense of Israel. Verse 22 refers to the blood of the slain and the fat or liveliness of the dead warriors, whose weapons, the Bow of Jonathan, after which the Qinah is named, and the Sword of Saul never turned back from confronting Israel's oppressors. Verse 23 celebrates Saul and Jonathan, who were not parted even in death, who were swifter than eagles and stronger than lions in their defense of the homeland. Verse 24 recounts how the women of Israel will now mourn for Saul, who made it possible for them to live in safety and wealth, clad in crimson garments and jewels. The last stanzas in verses 25–27 are devoted to Jonathan, David's friend. Verse 25 raises the refrain again, "How the mighty have fallen," and verse 26 expresses David's personal grief at the death of Jonathan, his brother, whose love he describes as surpassing the love of women. Although some see this as a reference to a homosexual relationship between David and Jonathan,[4] the word "love" is typically used in reference to the relationship between allies bound together by treaty.[5] Verse 27 concludes with the refrain "How the mighty have fallen!" followed by a reference to the weapons that have perished, never again to be used in the defense of Israel.

David's song of lament demonstrates his grief at the deaths of Saul and Jonathan, but it also demonstrates his loyalty to them and precludes any suggestion that he is disloyal to his king.

THE REIGN OF KING DAVID BEN JESSE IN JUDAH AND THE REIGN OF KING ISH-BOSHETH BEN SAUL IN ISRAEL – 2 SAMUEL 2:1–4:12

Second Samuel 2–4 recounts the reign of King David son of Jesse in Judah and King Ish-Bosheth son of Saul in Israel. The narrative is essentially an

---

[4]   T. Horner, *Jonathan Loved David: Homosexuality in Biblical Times* (Philadelphia: Westminster, 1978).

[5]   William Moran, "The Ancient Near Eastern Background of the Love of G-d in Deuteronomy," *CBQ* 25 (1963) 77–87.

account of the war between the two monarchs in which David, the
purported son-in-law of King Saul, serves as a vassal to the Philistines,
and Ish-Bosheth, although he is the only surviving son of Saul, appears to
be under the control of his father's army commander, Abner. Throughout
the narrative, David demonstrates qualities of leadership beyond those of
either Saul or Ish-Bosheth, and thereby demonstrates that he is best suited
to serve as the next King of Israel. The narrative comprises two major
components: the account of David's accession to the throne of Judah in
Hebron and his early actions as king in 2 Samuel 2:1–32, and the war
between the House of Saul and the House of David in 2 Samuel 3:1–4:12.
Second Samuel 3:1–4:12, in turn, comprises three sub-units: the initial
notice in 2 Samuel 3:1–5 of the continuation of the war, including
David's growing strength and Ish-Bosheth's growing weakness; the assassination of Abner in 2 Samuel 3:6–39; and the assassination of Ish-Bosheth
in 2 Samuel 4:1–12. The narrative makes special efforts to demonstrate that
David did not kill either Abner or Ish-Bosheth and that he remained loyal
to the House of Saul even as he was compelled to defend himself against
them. The narrative portrays David as a master strategist and leader who is
well qualified to serve as King of Israel.

David's Accession to the Throne of Judah in Hebron – 2 Samuel 2:1–32

2 **¹ After this David inquired of the LORD, "Shall I go up into any of the
cities of Judah?" The LORD said to him, "Go up." David said, "To
which shall I go up?" He said, "To Hebron."**

**² So David went up there, along with his two wives, Ahinoam of Jezreel
and Abigail the widow of Nabal of Carmel.**

**³ David brought up the men who were with him, every one with his
household, and they settled in the towns of Hebron.**

**⁴ Then the people of Judah came, and there they anointed David king
over the house of Judah.**

**When they told David, "It was the people of Jabesh-gilead who buried
Saul,"**

**⁵ David sent messengers to the people of Jabesh-gilead and said to them,
"May you be blessed by the LORD, because you showed this loyalty to
Saul your lord and buried him!**

**⁶ Now may the LORD show steadfast love and faithfulness to you! And I,
too, will reward you because you have done this thing.**

⁷ Therefore let your hands be strong and be valiant, for Saul your lord is dead, and the house of Judah has anointed me king over them."

⁸ But Abner son of Ner, commander of Saul's army, had taken Ishbaal son of Saul and brought him over to Mahanaim.

⁹ He made him king over Gilead, the Ashurites, Jezreel, Ephraim, Benjamin, and all Israel.

¹⁰ Ishbaal, Saul's son, was forty years old when he began to reign over Israel, and he reigned two years. But the house of Judah followed David.

¹¹ The time that David was king in Hebron over the house of Judah was seven years and six months.

¹² Abner son of Ner and the servants of Ishbaal son of Saul went out from Mahanaim to Gibeon.

¹³ Joab son of Zeruiah and the servants of David went out and met them at the pool of Gibeon. One group sat on one side of the pool, while the other sat on the other side of the pool.

¹⁴ Abner said to Joab, "Let the young men come forward and have a contest before us." Joab said, "Let them come forward."

¹⁵ So they came forward and were counted as they passed by, twelve for Benjamin and Ishbaal son of Saul and twelve of the servants of David.

¹⁶ Each grasped his opponent by the head and thrust his sword in his opponent's side, so they fell down together. Therefore that place was called Helkath-hazzurim, which is at Gibeon.

¹⁷ The battle was very fierce that day, and Abner and the men of Israel were beaten by the servants of David.

¹⁸ The three sons of Zeruiah were there, Joab, Abishai, and Asahel. Now Asahel was as swift of foot as a wild gazelle.

¹⁹ Asahel pursued Abner, turning neither to the right nor to the left as he followed him.

²⁰ Then Abner looked back and said, "Is it you, Asahel?" He answered, "Yes, it is."

²¹ Abner said to him, "Turn to your right or to your left, and seize one of the young men, and take his spoil." But Asahel would not turn away from following him.

²² Abner said again to Asahel, "Turn away from following me; why should I strike you to the ground? How then could I show my face to your brother Joab?"

²³ But he refused to turn away. So Abner struck him in the stomach with the butt of his spear, so that the spear came out at his back. He fell there and died where he lay. And all those who came to the place where Asahel had fallen and died stood still.

²⁴ But Joab and Abishai pursued Abner. As the sun was going down they came to the hill of Ammah, which lies before Giah on the way to the wilderness of Gibeon.

²⁵ The Benjaminites rallied around Abner and formed a single band; they took their stand on the top of a hill.

²⁶ Then Abner called to Joab, "Is the sword to keep devouring forever? Do you not know that the end will be bitter? How long will it be before you order your people to turn from the pursuit of their kinsmen?"

²⁷ Joab said, "As God lives, if you had not spoken, the people would have continued to pursue their kinsmen, not stopping until morning."

²⁸ Joab sounded the trumpet, and all the people stopped; they no longer pursued Israel or engaged in battle any further.

²⁹ Abner and his men traveled all that night through the Arabah; they crossed the Jordan, and, marching the whole forenoon, they came to Mahanaim.

³⁰ Joab returned from the pursuit of Abner, and when he had gathered all the people together, there were missing of David's servants nineteen men besides Asahel.

³¹ But the servants of David had killed of Benjamin three hundred sixty of Abner's men.

³² They took up Asahel and buried him in the tomb of his father, which was at Bethlehem. Joab and his men marched all night, and the day broke upon them at Hebron.

With the death of Saul and his three sons, a power vacuum opens in Israel. Ish-Bosheth ben Saul has not been previously mentioned, but the narrative introduces him in verse 8, although it makes it clear that Ish-Bosheth is in a very weak position and rules under the control of Abner. David is a vassal of the Philistines, who had just defeated Israel in a decisive battle that saw the deaths of Saul and Jonathan, Saul's heir apparent, as well as two of his other sons. The time has come for decisive action on the part of three principal figures who might emerge as the next leader of Israel, namely, Ish-Bosheth, Abner, and David. David will demonstrate that he is the best qualified to rule.

The narratives in 1 Samuel made it clear that David was building a strong base of support in Judah and that Saul was never able to bring him under control. Second Samuel 2 portrays David's initiatives to be appointed as King of Judah. He had already married Abigail, the widow of Nabal of Carmel, which gave him standing in the leading Calebite clan of Judah, and Ahinoam of Jezreel, who gave him standing in the Jezreel Valley, although the Jezreel may well indicate a region in Judah. His marriage to Ahinoam likewise enhanced his power in Judah.[6]

David's first move in 2 Samuel 2:1–4 was to inquire of YHWH whether he should go up to one of the cities or towns of Judah. As a Philistine vassal, such a move makes perfect sense, at least to the Philistines, who had just defeated Israel and would see David's move into Judah as a means to strengthen their control over Judah. But to David, such a move appears to be preparatory to extending his power in his own tribe of Judah and to place himself in a better position to take control of Israel. The inquiry would have been made through the use of the Urim and Thummim by the priest Abiathar, who was the only survivor of the massacre of the priests of Nob and a member of the priestly House of Eli (1 Sam 22:20–23; 23:6; 30:7–8). When YHWH answered David's inquiry in the affirmative, David followed up with a second inquiry as to which city he should go to, and YHWH answered, "Hebron." The choice of Hebron makes eminent sense as it is the leading city of Judah, which is where the Calebite clan is based (Josh 14:12; 15:13–14). Its alternative name, Kiriath Arba, "City of Four" (Gen 23:2; Josh 20:7), indicates that it is a city where alliances are made between the various power groups in pre-Judean Canaan, much as Shechem served in a similar role in the northern Israelite hill country. The very name, Hebron, based on the root *ḥbr*, "to join," indicates a place where alliances were made. Hebron also serves as the burial site for the ancestral family, beginning with Sarah and Abraham (Gen 23), and later including Isaac and Rebekah (Gen 35:27–39; 49:29–33) and Jacob and Leah (Gen 49:29–33; 50:1–14). Hebron therefore serves as the ideal power base for David in Judah. When he arrived in the city, the men of Judah anointed him as king.

David's first move as king appears in 2 Samuel 2:5–7, which builds upon the notice in 2 Samuel 2:4b, in which the men of Judah informed David that the men of Jabesh Gilead had buried Saul (1 Sam 31:11–13). David

---

[6] Jon D. Levenson and Baruch Halpern, "The Political Import of David's Marriages," *JBL* 99 (1980): 507–518.

then took the initiative to contact the men of Jabesh Gilead to bless them
for their burial of Saul and his sons and to announce that he had just been
named king in Judah. David's overture is a very strategic move. It shows
David's continued loyalty to Saul as King of Israel. Saul's deliverance of
Jabesh Gilead would have enabled him to control the Trans-Jordan as well
as the Jezreel Valley, thereby protecting the northern and eastern borders
of Israel. David's overture to Jabesh Gilead suggests to them that he would
be a suitable candidate, loyal to his former father-in-law, to serve as
their king.

There were two obstacles for David to become King of Israel. First,
David is still a Philistine vassal, the very power that defeated Israel and
killed Saul and his sons. This issue will be addressed in 2 Samuel 5 after
David is named as King of Israel. The second is that there is a fourth son of
Saul, Ish-Bosheth. This issue is addressed in 2 Samuel 2:8–32; 3; and 4.

Second Samuel 2:8–32 begins with the notice in 2 Samuel 2:8–11 that
Abner ben Ner, Saul's military commander, had taken Ish-Bosheth,
anointed him as King of Israel, and installed him in the city of
Mahanaim, located in the Trans-Jordanian regions of Israel. The identity
of Abner's father, Ner, is uncertain, although some suggest that he is Saul's
uncle (1 Sam 14:50; 1 Chr 8:33), or more likely Saul's grandfather since Ner
is identified as the father of Kish (1 Sam 9:1; 10:14–15). Abner appears to
be a senior member of the House of Saul, and Ish-Bosheth is a relatively
unknown younger son of Saul. Ish-Bosheth's unsuitability for leadership is
already suggested by his name, Ish-Bosheth, which means, "man of
shame," not quite the ideal name for a man who would be King of Israel,
but it appears to caricaturize him based on his given name, Esh-Baal, "Fire
of Baal" (1 Chr 8:33; 9:39). Those surprised that a son of Saul might carry a
Canaanite name should recall that the Judge Gideon was also known as
Jerubbaal, "May Baal be Magnified" (Judg 6:25–32), which renders the
name as "Let Baal Contend with Him," for tearing down the altar of Baal.
Furthermore, the name Israel, Hebrew, *yiśrā'ēl*, is a theophoric name that
means "El Rules," which combines the verb, *śrh*, "to rule," with the name,
El, the creator god of Canaanite culture, indicating Israel's origins as a
Canaanite nation (see Gen 32:23–32). Ish-Bosheth is not the power figure
in Israel, despite his birth; Abner is the power figure. The installation of
Ish-Bosheth in Mahanaim indicates weakness. Mahanaim is the site where
Jacob met Esau in Genesis 32. It is located in the Trans-Jordan in the
territory of Gad (Josh 13:26), near the confluence of the Wadi Jabbok and
the Jordan River, although its exact location is unknown. The narrative

indicates that Ish-Bosheth rules Gilead in the Trans-Jordan, Asher by the Mediterranean coast, the Jezreel Valley, Ephraim, and Benjamin, but the fact that Ish-Bosheth rules from Mahanaim means that the Philistines control the Israelite hill country.

The battle at Gibeon between the forces of David and the forces of Israel, led by Abner, appears in 2 Samuel 2:12–32. This is a decisive engagement that sees the defeat of Israel and opens the way for David to emerge as King of Israel. The reason for the battle is unclear, although it appears that Gibeon was known to be an ally of Israel under Joshua in Joshua 9–10, which would suggest that it remained an ally of Israel under Saul and Ish-Bosheth. But Abner's foray against Gibeon is an attack, and David's men are positioned to defend Gibeon against that attack. Such a scenario suggests that Gibeon had shifted its alliance with Israel to ally with Judah instead, a likely scenario following the defeat of Israel at Mt. Gilboa. Abner would advance against Gibeon in an attempt to force it back into its alliance with Israel, whereas David, a Philistine ally, would defend Gibeon to turn it into a Judean/Philistine ally.

Gibeon is identified with Tel el-Jib, located some five and a half miles north of Jerusalem.[7] Although the city had been abandoned during the latter Bronze Age, it was repopulated and rebuilt in the early Iron Age. The site of the battle is identified as a large pool by which David's army commander, Joab ben Zeruiah (David's sister, 1 Chr 2:16), positions his forces on one side of the pool, whereas Abner positions his forces on the other side. A pool has been discovered carved into bedrock, although it is located inside the Iron Age city wall on the east side of the city, where it is fed by a spring that lies outside of the wall.

A Closer Look at the Battle at Gibeon

Rather than engage in a full-scale battle, the combatants engage in a contest, signaled by the verb *wîśaḥăqû*, "and they shall play, engage in sport," in verse 14 (i.e., "let the boys arise, and they will play before us"). The narrative describes a scene in which twelve champions from each side come forward to fight on behalf of their armies, not unlike the battle between Achilles and Hector during the Greek siege of Troy as narrated in the Odyssey. Such a one-on-one context also appears in the Babylonian creation epic, the Enuma Elish, in which Marduk, the city god of

---

[7]   James B. Pritchard, "Gibeon," NEAEHL 2:511–514.

Babylon, and Tiamatu, the dragon goddess of salt water, meet to fight in single combat before their respective armies to decide the outcome of the battle.

The "contest" begins when twelve Judean champions advance to meet twelve Israelite – or Benjaminite – champions in single combat. Each warrior grabs the other's head with one arm and uses the other arm to stab at his opponent's torso, resulting in the deaths of all twenty-four men. A neo-Hittite orthostadt from Tell Halaf depicts such a combat between two warriors.[8] The site is named Helkath ha-Zurim, "the site of the flints/blades," to commemorate the event.

With the deaths of the champions, the contest is a draw, but a fierce battle ensued between the forces of Joab and Judah and the forces Abner and Israel. The Judeans defeated the Israelites or Benjaminites, who began to flee the scene with Judeans in hot pursuit. The narrative focuses on the three sons of David's sister Zeruiah (i.e., Joab, Abishai, and Asahel). Asahel, described as a swift runner, pursues Abner. As Abner flees, he shouts to Asahel to turn from him and take booty from other Israelites/Benjaminites who had fallen around the area, but Asahel continued with his pursuit. As he was about to overtake Abner, Abner stabbed at Asahel with his spear and killed him. Ancient warriors were trained to stab at enemies behind them; indeed, Asahel's momentum would have carried him into Abner's spear point, and ancient spears or javelins had points on both ends. Asahel's brothers, Joab and Abishai, continued to pursue Abner until sundown, when he reached the hill of Ammah by Giah on the way to Gibeon.

Abner and the surviving Benjaminites took positions atop the hill to defend themselves, allowing Abner to propose an end to the fighting to avoid excessive bloodshed. Joab accepted the truce but covered himself by announcing that the Judeans would have given up the chase the next morning. Abner and his surviving men marched back to Mahanaim by way of an unknown site known as Bithron, whereas Joab assembled his men and carried the body of his brother Asahel home for burial. Joab would not forget that Abner had killed his brother Asahel.

---

[8]   Walter Dietrich, *Samuel. 1 Samuel 27—2 Samuel 8* (BKAT 8/3; Göttingen: Vandenhoeck & Ruprect, 2019), 339; Fritz Stolz, *Das erste und zweite Buch Samuel* (ZBK; Zürich: Theologischer Verlag, 1981), 193. For full discussion of the model of individual combat presented here, see Dietrich, *Samuel*, 8/3, 336–339.

The War between the House of Saul and the House of David – 2 Samuel 3:1–4:12

Second Samuel 3:1–4:12 recounts the continuing war between the House of Saul and the House of David in three parts: the continuation of the war in 2 Samuel 3:1–5; the assassination of Abner in 2 Samuel 3:6–39; and the assassination of Ish-Bosheth in 2 Samuel 4:1–12.

The Continuation of the War between the House of Saul and the House of David – 2 Samuel 3:1–5

3 **¹ There was a long war between the house of Saul and the house of David; David grew stronger and stronger, while the house of Saul became weaker and weaker.**

² Sons were born to David at Hebron: his firstborn was Amnon, of Ahinoam of Jezreel;

³ his second was Chileab, of Abigail the widow of Nabal of Carmel; the third was Absalom son of Maacah, daughter of King Talmai of Geshur;

⁴ the fourth was Adonijah son of Haggith; the fifth was Shephatiah son of Abital;

⁵ and the sixth was Ithream, of David's wife Eglah. These were born to David in Hebron.

Second Samuel 3:1 addresses the issue of the war between Judah and Israel to point to the growing strength of David and the growing weakness of Ish-Bosheth. It therefore sets the conditions for the following two sub-units concerning the assassination of Abner in 2 Samuel 3:6–39 and the assassination of Ish-Bosheth in 2 Samuel 4:12, which bring the war to a close.

The listing of David's sons born in Hebron in 2 Samuel 3:2–5 contributes to the narrative agenda of the sub-unit. The list of David's wives and sons points to David's growing power. The designation of first-born sons applies to the mothers. Such sons would then be the candidates to succeed their father, depending on which matriarchal line in the House of David would be chosen to supply the next king of the dynasty. David's first wife, Michal bat Saul, is not mentioned here, presumably because she bore David no sons and because Saul had married her off to another man (1 Sam 25:44; 2 Sam 3:12–16). David's second wife, Ahinoam of Jezreel, is listed first with her first-born son, Amnon. Her name causes some confusion because Ahinoam was the name of Saul's wife and because the prophet Nathan would later state to David that YHWH had given him his master's wives, presumably those of Saul (2 Sam 12:8). But Ahinoam the wife of Saul is never identified as Ahinoam of Jezreel (1 Sam 14:50), whereas Ahinoam the wife of David is always identified as Ahinoam of Jezreel (1 Sam 25:43; 27:3; 30:5; 2 Sam 5:2:2; 3:2; 1 Chr 3:1). A further source of confusion is Ahinoam's identification with Jezreel (perhaps the Jezreel Valley, situated to the north of the northern Israelite hill country in the tribal territory of Issachar), but interpreters agree that Ahinoam of Jezreel is from a Judean city of the same name located not far from Carmel, where Abigail had resided (Josh 15:56).[9]

David's third wife, Abigail, the widow of Nabal the Carmelite, gave birth to Chileab. Chileab is problematic because he does not appear again in the Samuel narratives, whereas the other sons do. His name, Hebrew, *kil'āb*, appears to be a variant of Caleb, Hebrew, *kālēb*, which enigmatically means "dog," a not particularly complimentary name for a man in a culture that disparaged dogs. It would appear that *kil'āb*, which means, perhaps, "completion, accomplishment of the father," may be a more authentic understanding of the name of the founder of the chief clan in Judah. He is identified as Dalouia in the LXX text of 2 Reigns 3:3 and Daniel in 1 Chronicles 3:1.[10]

David's fourth wife, Maacah, daughter of King Telmai of Geshur, gave birth to Absalom, who will figure prominently as the son who leads a revolt against David in 2 Samuel 13–19. Geshur is an Aramaean kingdom located to the north and east of the Sea of Galilee.[11] Its name, Geshur, is Hebrew for "bridge," which indicates that it straddles the area from the Jordan River north of the Sea of Galilee to the Yarmouk River, which flows west into the Jordan to the south of the Sea of Galilee. David's alliance with Telmai enables him better to control northern Israel, especially the Israelite Trans-Jordan, and it gives him better defenses from Aram.

David's fifth wife is Haggith, the mother of Adonijah, who would attempt unsuccessfully to claim the throne (1 Kgs 1–2).[12] David's sixth wife is Abital, the mother of Shephatiah, and his seventh wife is Eglah, the mother of Ithream (cf. 1 Chr 3:3).

[9]   Janell A. Johnson, "Ahinoam," EBR 1:656–657; Bob Becking, "Jezreel," EBR 14:264–265.
[10] McCarter, *II Samuel*, 101–102.
[11] Walter C. Bouzard, "Geshur," EBR 10:138–139.
[12] Richard Jude Thompson, "Haggith," EBR 10:1151.

The list of David's wives and the first-born sons to each indicates that David is the father of a large family with ample first-born sons to succeed him on the throne. Ish-Bosheth has no one. Second Samuel 3:2–5 builds on the statement in 2 Samuel 3:1 that the House of David was getting stronger, whereas the House of Saul was growing weaker.

The Assassination of Abner – 2 Samuel 3:6–39

3 ⁶ While there was war between the house of Saul and the house of David, Abner was making himself strong in the house of Saul.

⁷ Now Saul had a concubine whose name was Rizpah daughter of Aiah. And Ishbaal said to Abner, "Why have you gone in to my father's concubine?"

⁸ The words of Ishbaal made Abner very angry; he said, "Am I a dog's head for Judah? Today I keep showing loyalty to the house of your father Saul, to his brothers, and to his friends and have not given you into the hand of David, yet you charge me now with a crime concerning this woman.

⁹ So may God do to Abner and so may he add to it! For just what the LORD has sworn to David, that will I accomplish for him:

¹⁰ to transfer the kingdom from the house of Saul and set up the throne of David over Israel and over Judah, from Dan to Beer-sheba."

¹¹ And Ishbaal could not answer Abner another word because he feared him.

¹² Abner sent messengers to David where he was, saying, "To whom does the land belong? Make your covenant with me, and I will give you my support to bring all Israel over to you."

¹³ He said, "Good; I will make a covenant with you. But one thing I require of you: you shall never appear in my presence unless you bring Saul's daughter Michal when you come to see me."

¹⁴ Then David sent messengers to Saul's son Ishbaal, saying, "Give me my wife Michal, to whom I became engaged at the price of one hundred foreskins of the Philistines."

¹⁵ Ishbaal sent and took her from her husband Paltiel the son of Laish.

¹⁶ But her husband went with her, weeping as he walked behind her all the way to Bahurim. Then Abner said to him, "Go back home!" So he went back.

¹⁷ Abner sent word to the elders of Israel, saying, "For some time past you have been seeking David as king over you.

¹⁸ Now then bring it about, for the L-RD has promised David: Through my servant David I will save my people Israel from the hand of the Philistines and from all their enemies."

¹⁹ Abner also spoke directly to the Benjaminites; then Abner went to tell David at Hebron all that Israel and the whole house of Benjamin were ready to do.

²⁰ When Abner came with twenty men to David at Hebron, David made a feast for Abner and the men who were with him.

²¹ Abner said to David, "Let me go and rally all Israel to my lord the king, in order that they may make a covenant with you and that you may reign over all that your heart desires." So David dismissed Abner, and he went away in peace.

²² Just then the servants of David arrived with Joab from a raid, bringing much spoil with them. But Abner was not with David at Hebron, for David had dismissed him, and he had gone away in peace.

²³ When Joab and all the army that was with him came, it was told to Joab, "Abner son of Ner came to the king, and he has dismissed him, and he has gone away in peace."

²⁴ Then Joab went to the king and said, "What have you done? Abner came to you; why did you dismiss him, so that he got away?

²⁵ You know that Abner son of Ner came to deceive you and to learn your comings and goings and to learn all that you are doing."

²⁶ When Joab came out from David's presence, he sent messengers after Abner, and they brought him back from the cistern of Sirah, but David did not know about it.

²⁷ When Abner returned to Hebron, Joab took him aside in the gateway to speak with him privately, and there he stabbed him in the stomach. So he died on account of the blood of Asahel, Joab's brother.

²⁸ Afterward, when David heard of it, he said, "I and my kingdom are forever guiltless before the LORD for the blood of Abner son of Ner.

²⁹ May the bloodguilt fall on the head of Joab and on all his father's house, and may the house of Joab never be without one who has a discharge, or who has a defiling skin disease, or who holds a spindle, or who falls by the sword, or who lacks food!"

³⁰ So Joab and his brother Abishai murdered Abner because he had killed their brother Asahel in the battle at Gibeon.

³¹ Then David said to Joab and to all the people who were with him, "Tear your clothes, put on sackcloth, and mourn over Abner." And King David followed the bier.

³² They buried Abner at Hebron. The king lifted up his voice and wept at the grave of Abner, and all the people wept.

³³ The king lamented for Abner, saying,

"Should Abner die as a fool dies?

³⁴ Your hands were not bound;

your feet were not fettered;

as one falls before the wicked

you have fallen."

And all the people wept over him again.

³⁵ Then all the people came to persuade David to eat something while it was still day, but David swore, saying, "So may God do to me and more, if I taste bread or anything else before the sun goes down!"

³⁶ All the people took notice of it, and it pleased them, just as everything the king did pleased all the people.

³⁷ So all the people and all Israel understood that day that the king had no part in the killing of Abner son of Ner.

³⁸ And the king said to his servants, "Do you not know that a prince and a great man has fallen this day in Israel?

³⁹ Today I am powerless, even though anointed king; these men, the sons of Zeruiah, are too violent for me. The LORD pay back the one who does wickedly in accordance with his wickedness!"

Second Samuel 3:6–39 portrays Abner as a man who recognizes that Ish-Bosheth is a failed leader as he attempts to enhance his own interests by several key, but failed, power moves. The first is his attempt to marry Rizpah daughter of Aiah, the concubine of Saul. The Samuel narratives make it clear that when a man marries the former wife or concubine of the previous ruler, that man is making a claim for the throne of the past husband. Abner is already sleeping with Rizpah, without any permission from Ish-Bosheth; such a move entails that Abner holds no respect for Ish-Bosheth as *pater familias* of the House of Saul, and that by claiming Rizpah as his own, Abner is making a claim on the Israelite throne. Ish-Bosheth's demand to know why Abner is sleeping with Rizpah communicates clear disapproval of Abner's act. Abner's response to Ish-Bosheth makes the tensions between the two men very clear. Abner, apparently an older male member of the House of Saul, has no patience with the younger, incompetent Ish-Bosheth. His response, "Am I a dog's head for Judah?" employs terminology to introduce his own claims to importance, but it also suggests some association with Judah, particularly since the Calebite line, into which David has married, is the ruling clan of Judah. Insofar as the name Caleb means "dog" in Hebrew, his response suggests that Ish-Bosheth sees him as a traitor to northern Israel. Abner asserts his own efforts on behalf of Israel with claims of loyal service to Saul; why should he not have Rizpah given all that he has done? But what has he done? Abner was the commanding general at Gibeon in which his forces suffered a major defeat against David. Abner lost the battle, not Ish-Bosheth, but Abner's grandiose claims suggest that he should not be held accountable for another major defeat of Israel at Gibeon following the catastrophic defeat by Philistia at Mt. Gilboa. Abner demonstrates his disloyalty and his disdain for Ish-Bosheth by openly stating that he will transfer the kingship of Saul to David. Ish-Bosheth's failure to respond to such an outrageous claim demonstrates that Ish-Bosheth is afraid of Abner.

The account of Abner's negotiation with David in 2 Samuel 3:12–19 demonstrates that he does indeed have the power to turn the Israelite kingdom over to David, but he does not have the sense to avoid a trap. Immediately following his angry exchange with Ish-Bosheth, Abner sends messengers to David proposing a covenant or treaty in which he will bring Israel over to David's side. Whereas Abner is rash, David is shrewd. He demands that Abner recover his first wife, Michal bat Saul, and return her to him before the negotiation can go any further. Some might argue that resuming his marriage to Michal would violate Israelite law in that Deuteronomy 24:1–4 forbids a man who divorces his wife the right to remarry her after she has married another man.[13] But David's statements to Abner make it clear that he did not divorce Michal. He paid the bride-price for her, namely, two hundred Philistine foreskins, double the amount that Saul demanded (1 Sam 18:17–29), but he makes no mention of having the bride-price returned to him as would be the case in a divorce. Of course, it is unlikely that he would want them back, but it would nevertheless be difficult to calculate the amount of money or goods that such a bride-price would fetch. The fact of the matter is that David did not divorce Michal; Saul took her and married her to another man, Paltiel son of Laish. Saul was in the wrong in this marriage. Why would David want her? David's marriage to Michal made him son-in-law of King Saul, and therefore a member of the royal House of Saul, eligible to claim the throne.

---

[13]   Cf. Anderson, *2 Samuel*, 58–59.

Abner then confers with the elders of Israel and the Benjaminites to validate his move. He reminds the elders of Israel concerning YHWH's promise to deliver Israel from the Philistines through the hands of David. First Samuel 9:16 indicates that YHWH had promised to anoint a man who would deliver Israel from the Philistines, but that narrative was about Saul – and Saul had failed in his task. Abner appears to stretch YHWH's promise to make it fit David. The elders of Israel and the Benjaminites agree. Apparently, both groups were dissatisfied with Ish-Bosheth and had already concluded that David was the best choice.

The assassination of Abner takes place in 2 Samuel 3:20–27 when Abner travels to Hebron to seal the proposed covenant or treaty with David. He brings with him a twenty-man escort for a feast with David at which Abner swore to bring Israel over to David. David subsequently sent Abner home unharmed in recognition of their new relationship.

A fundamental question emerges. If Abner, the commanding officer of the Israelite army, brings Israel over to David, what happens to Joab, the commanding officer of the Judean army? Abner had killed Asahel, Joab's brother. Joab's future would look very dim, and his reasons to block Abner are strong. Having seen Abner depart unharmed, Joab is compelled to ask why David would have released Abner when Abner was the commander of the Israelite army, David's enemy. Joab points out that Abner must have come to deceive David so that he could learn David's movements and use that knowledge to defeat him. Joab sent messengers after Abner, and Abner returned from the point he had reached by the Cistern of Sirah, a site identified with the *ṣirat el-ballā'i*, located some two miles north of Hebron.[14] When Abner returned, Joab took him aside in the gate of the city to speak with him privately, Hebrew, *baššelî*, lit., "in quietness," and stabbed him in the belly. Ironically, Joab's moved mimicked the combat of the twenty-four champions at Gibeon who grabbed each other by the head and stabbed their opponents in the gut (2 Sam 2:12–16).

Second Samuel 3:28–39 recounts David's very loud and public mourning for Abner and his efforts to ensure that Joab take the blame for Abner's death. Abner was a traitor to the House of Saul, and he was well played by David, but Abner was also foolish to place himself in the power of his enemy. Joab did David a favor, but David refuses to recognize what Joab has done in an effort to deflect any blame or criticism from

---

[14] Anderson, *2 Samuel*, 61.

himself. The curse leveled by David against Joab and his house calls for it never to lack any number of undesirables, such as men suffering discharges; men who work with weaving spindles like women; men who are killed by the sword; and men who lack food. David will continue to use Joab and benefit from his deeds for the rest of his life, but in the end David orders Solomon to kill Joab after his own death (1 Kgs 1–2). David orders Joab and his men to tear their garments, to wear sackcloth, and to engage in a public display of mourning. David himself walks behind Abner's bier (Hebrew, *miṭṭâ*, lit., "bed") as he is carried to his grave in Hebron. And David sings a dirge or Qinah for Abner, which charges that Abner was killed treacherously, thereby ensuring that Joab would take the blame for a heinous act. Why would David act like this? His motive was to win over the support of Israelites and Benjaminites so that they would accept him as their leader. Just as David mourned for Saul and Jonathan, so he mourns for Abner and wins Israel to his side.

The Assassination of Ish-Bosheth ben Saul – 2 Samuel 4:1–12

4 ¹ When Saul's son Ishbaal heard that Abner had died at Hebron, his courage failed, and all Israel was dismayed.

² Saul's son had two captains of raiding bands; the name of the one was Baanah, and the name of the other was Rechab. They were sons of Rimmon, a Benjaminite from Beeroth, for Beeroth is considered to belong to Benjamin.

³ (Now the people of Beeroth had fled to Gittaim and are there as resident aliens to this day.)

⁴ Saul's son Jonathan had a son who was crippled in his feet. He was five years old when the news about Saul and Jonathan came from Jezreel. His nurse picked him up and fled, and in her haste to flee it happened that he fell and became lame. His name was Mephibosheth.

⁵ Now the sons of Rimmon the Beerothite, Rechab and Baanah, set out, and about the heat of the day they came to the house of Ishbaal while he was taking his noonday rest.

⁶ They came inside the house as though to take wheat, and they struck him in the stomach; then Rechab and his brother Baanah escaped.

⁷ Now they had come into the house while he was lying on his couch in his bedchamber; they attacked him, killed him, and beheaded him. Then they took his head and traveled by way of the Arabah all night long.

[8] They brought the head of Ishbaal to David at Hebron and said to the king, "Here is the head of Ishbaal son of Saul, your enemy who sought your life; the LORD has avenged my lord the king this day on Saul and on his offspring."

[9] David answered Rechab and his brother Baanah, the sons of Rimmon the Beerothite, "As the LORD lives, who has redeemed my life out of every adversity,

[10] when the one who told me, 'See, Saul is dead,' thought he was bringing good news, I seized him and killed him at Ziklag – this was the reward I gave him for his news.

[11] How much more, then, when wicked men have killed a righteous man on his bed in his own house! And now shall I not require his blood at your hand and destroy you from the earth?"

[12] So David commanded the young men, and they killed them; they cut off their hands and feet and hung their bodies beside the pool at Hebron. But the head of Ishbaal they took and buried in the tomb of Abner at Hebron.

The account of the assassination of Ish-Bosheth ben Saul in 2 Samuel 4:1–12 closes out the account of the war between the House Saul and the House of David in 2 Samuel 3:1–4:12 in that Ish-Bosheth's death leaves the House of Saul without a clear successor to the throne other than David ben Jesse, the son-in-law of Saul. The narrative includes two major sub-units: 2 Samuel 4:1, which recounts the demoralization of Ish-Bosheth following the death of Abner, and 2 Samuel 4:2–12, which introduces the assassins and state of the House of Saul in 2 Samuel 4:2–4; the assassination per se in 2 Samuel 4:5–8; and David's reaction in 2 Samuel 4:9–12.

The first sub-unit in 2 Samuel 4:1 points clearly to Ish-Bosheth's demoralization. The verse does not even identify him by name; the identification of Ish-Bosheth as Memphibosthe in the LXX and as Mephibosheth in 4QSamuel[a] apparently confuses Ish-Bosheth with Mephibosheth, the son of Jonathan and the grandson of Saul in an effort to supply the missing name in the proto-MT.[15] The Peshitta reading of Ashbashul is a corruption of Esh-Baal ben Shaul. The absence of the name Ish-Bosheth in the MT and the corruption or contraction of the name in the Peshitta are attempts to avoid using the dishonorable name Ish-Bosheth, "Man of Shame," in an account of Esh-Baal's death. The notice that "his hands drooped," Hebrew,

[15]   See Eugene Ulrich, Jr. in Frank Moore Cross et al., *Qumran Cave 4. XII. 1–2 Samuel* (DJD 17; Oxford: Clarendon, 2005), 113, 116.

wayyirpû, is an idiomatic expression that means, "his courage failed," as translated by NRSVue or that "he became demoralized, dismayed, or powerless to act" due to his recognition that the death of Abner meant that he was likely to suffer the same fate. The alarm felt by all Israel indicated shock, surprise, and fear as the nation recognized its vulnerability due to the death of their military commander so soon after the defeat at Mt. Gilboa and the deaths of Saul and his sons.

Second Samuel 4:2–12 then demonstrates that Ish-Bosheth's fears were justified. The first segment of the passage in 2 Samuel 4:2–4 presents the background for Ish-Bosheth's assassination. The first element in this segment is the reference to the two captains of raiding bands, Baanah and Rechab, apparently lower-ranking officers who commanded small units that raided enemies on behalf of the crown. Both were sons of Rimmon the Beerothite. Beeroth, Hebrew, *bĕ'ērôt*, refers to a town known for its wells. Beeroth is identified either with modern el-Bireh/Ras et-Tahuneh, east of Ramallah and nine Roman miles north of Jerusalem, or a small site north of Gibeon/el-Jib, about four Roman miles from Jerusalem.[16] Beeroth lies in Benjaminite territory (Josh 18:25), and Joshua 9:17 identifies it as part of a coalition, led by Gibeon, that also included Chephriah and Kiriath Jearim.

The inclusion of Beeroth as a member of the Gibeonite coalition signals the motivation for the Rimmon brothers to assassinate Ish-Bosheth.[17] David's defense of Gibeon against Israelite forces was apparently prompted by a shift in the coalition's alliance with the House of Saul and Israel to David and Judah. Saul's defeat and death at Mt. Gilboa would have demonstrated Israel's inability to protect Gibeon and its allies, and it would have prompted Gibeon to seek an alliance with David and Judah, based especially on David's own alliance with Philistia, the power that had defeated Israel and now dominated the region. Abner's campaign against Gibeon was apparently a bid to force it back into its alliance with Israel, but David's intervention made it impossible for Israel to accomplish its goals. Indeed, later narratives, such as 2 Samuel 5–7, make it clear that David was able to ascend to the throne of Israel, presumably as son-in-law of Saul, in the absence of Saul's own sons, particularly since he was able to bring the Ark to Jerusalem from Kiriath Jearim, another member of the Gibeonite-

[16] Diana Edelman, "Beeroth," EBR 3:755–756.
[17] See esp. Joseph Blenkinsopp, *Gibeon and Israel: The Role of Gibeon and the Gibeonites in the Political and Religious History of Early Israel* (SOTSMS 2; Cambridge: Cambridge University Press, 1972).

based coalition. Second Samuel 21 indicates that David had an obligation to pay for his new relationship with the Gibeonites with the lives of Saul's descendants, and David immediately handed them over for execution. Second Samuel 4:4 indicates that Jonathan's son, Mephibosheth, also known as Merib-Baal, was too young to rule at five years of age.

To Baanah and Rechab, two Beerothite officers from the Gibeon-led coalition, Abner's death made it clear that northern Israel was finished under Ish-Bosheth, and they assumed that David would reward them for enabling David to ascend to the throne of Israel following Ish-Bosheth's death. They had already fled from Beeroth to Gittaim, a town of unknown location but apparently near to Beeroth and Gibeon (Neh 11:31–36),[18] probably to escape Philistine reprisals. Second Samuel 4:5–8 recounts the assassination of Ish-Bosheth by the Rimmon brothers in despicable terms. They entered Ish-Bosheth's house while the king was taking an afternoon siesta. The entrance was apparently unguarded, although there is a confusing statement about "taking wheat" in verse 6, which the LXX attempts to correct by stating that a porter who was cleaning wheat in the house had fallen asleep by the door. They entered his bedroom to kill him, and then they carried him in an all-night march to David to demonstrate David's presumed vengeance – and their own presumed initiative – against the House of Saul.

Second Samuel 4:9–12 recounts David's response to the brothers' overture in typical fashion by showing him to be loyal to the House of Saul and willing to judge anyone who dares to raise a hand against YHWH's anointed, no matter how much the death of a Saulide king or officer advances his own interests. In responding to Baanah and Rechab, David recalls his response to the Amalekite who brought him news of Saul's death and his own alleged role in dispatching the king to make the point loud and clear to anyone around, viz., if you kill YHWH's anointed, David will execute you for your crime. He does not refer to Ish-Bosheth as YHWH's anointed; instead, David refers to him as "a righteous man (Hebrew, *'iš-ṣaddîq*, "an innocent man") on his bed in his own house." David orders his men to execute the Rimmon brothers for their crime. Their bodies were hung by the pool in Hebron, where everyone went to draw water, with their hands and feet cut off to symbolize their guilt and shame.

---

[18] Pauline Viviano, "Gittaim," EBR 10:296.

6 Commentary Part IV: The Regnal Account of King David ben Jesse over Israel – 2 Samuel 5:1–24:25/1 Kings 2:11

Second Samuel 5:1–1 Kings 2:11 presents the regnal account of King David son of Jesse over Israel and Judah from his initial accession to the throne of Israel through his death. It is demarcated at the outset by the initial regnal account of David's reign over Israel and Judah in 2 Samuel 5–8; the account of David's care for Jonathan's son, Mephibosheth, in 2 Samuel 9; the account of David's adultery with Bath Sheba and the birth of Solomon in 2 Samuel 10–12; accounts of tension in the House of David in 2 Samuel 13–20; the account of David's handing over the sons of Saul to Gibeon for execution in 2 Samuel 21; the Psalm of David following YHWH's deliverance of him from his enemies and from Saul; the final words of David in 2 Samuel 23:1–7; the catalog of David's warriors in 2 Samuel 23:8–39; the account of YHWH's anger concerning David's census in 2 Samuel 24; and the account of the death of David and his designation of Solomon as his successor in 1 Kings 1:1–2:11.

Second Samuel 5–1 Kings 2:11 includes formal elements of the typical regnal account, such as the introductory regnal formula in 2 Samuel 5:4–5; the capture of Jerusalem and the recognition of David's rule by King Hiram of Tyre in 2 Samuel 5:6–12; the identification of the sons born to David in Jerusalem in 2 Samuel 5:13–16; narratives concerning additional major events of his reign, such as his defeat of the Philistines; his transfer of the Ark to Jerusalem; his refusal to father sons with Michal; and YHWH's eternal covenant, which recognized him as King of Israel in 2 Samuel 5:17–7:29; as well as the concluding regnal account of David's death and designation of Solomon as his successor in 1 Kings 1:1–2:11. Although the present form of 2 Samuel 5:1–1 Kings 2:11 may be read synchronically as the regnal account of David's reign, it is clear that the narratives comprise a redactional assemblage of elements that were written by various hands in various settings before they were edited to form the present text.

Altogether, 2 Samuel 5:1–1 Kings 2:11 includes elements of the Solomonic History and the Jehu Dynastic History, and it was read as part of the Hezekian, Josianic, and Exilic editions of the DtrH.[1]

THE INITIAL REGNAL ACCOUNT OF KING DAVID BEN JESSE OF ISRAEL AND JUDAH – 2 SAMUEL 5–8

Second Samuel 5–8 is the initial regnal account of King David ben Jesse of Israel and Judah.[2] The narrative comprises a number of elements: the account of David's anointing as King of Israel in 2 Samuel 5:1–3; the initial regnal formula of David's reign in 2 Samuel 5:4–5; the account of David's capture of Jerusalem in 2 Samuel 5:6–10; the recognition of David by King Hiram of Tyre in 2 Samuel 5:11–12; the catalog of David's sons born to him in Jerusalem in 2 Samuel 5:13–16; the account of David's defeat of the Philistines in 2 Samuel 5:17–25; the account of David's transfer of the Ark of the Covenant to Jerusalem in 2 Samuel 6:1–19; the account of David's refusal to father sons with Michal in 2 Samuel 6:20–23; the account of YHWH's eternal covenant of kingship with David and Israel in 2 Samuel 7; and the summation of the events of David's reign in 2 Samuel 8. The laudatory character of this text indicates that it was composed as part of the Solomonic History, insofar as David's reign and exploits provide the foundations for the dynastic House of David. There is no clear indication of wrongdoing by David, in contrast to the narratives in 2 Samuel 10–12; 13–19; 20; 21; and 24, which would indicate the interests of the Jehu Dynastic History and the Josianic edition of the DtrH.

The formal structure of 2 Samuel 5–8 includes the initial account of David's anointing as King of Israel in 2 Samuel 5:1–3, which introduces the regnal account of King David ben Jesse of Israel and Judah proper in 2 Samuel 5:4–8:18. Insofar as the initial regnal formula in 2 Samuel 5:4–5 is syntactically independent from the preceding material in 2 Samuel 5:1–3, it signals the beginning of the regnal account proper. The following sub-units are each syntactically joined by a *waw*-consecutive verbal formation to produce a narrative sequence concerning the major events of David's initial reign. These elements demonstrate David's qualification to serve as King of Israel, insofar as he succeeds where Saul has failed. David is a

---

[1] See the introduction to this volume.
[2] Contra. Walter Dietrich, *1 Samuel 27–2 Samuel 8* (BKAT 8/3; Göttingen: Vandenhoeck & Ruprecht, 2019), 509–516.

member of the House of Saul, but his leadership prompts YHWH to grant him an eternal covenant for the new House of David.

David's Anointing as King of Israel – 2 Samuel 5:1–3

5 **¹** **Then all the tribes of Israel came to David at Hebron and said, "Look, we are your bone and flesh.**

² For some time, while Saul was king over us, it was you who led out Israel and brought it in. The LORD said to you, 'It is you who shall be shepherd of my people Israel, you who shall be ruler over Israel.'"

³ So all the elders of Israel came to the king at Hebron, and King David made a covenant with them at Hebron before the LORD, and they anointed David king over Israel.

Second Samuel 5:1–3 presents a brief narrative introduction to the regnal account of King David ben Jesse of Israel and Judah, insofar as it recounts David's initial anointing at Hebron by the elders of Israel. Following the deaths of Saul, Jonathan, Abinadab, Malchishua, Ish-Bosheth, and even Abner, it would have been clear that David should serve as the next King of Israel by virtue of his status as the son-in-law of King Saul, the absence of viable direct descendants of Saul, and David's role as military commander of Israel during Saul's reign.

The Introductory Regnal Formula for David's Reign over Israel and Judah – 2 Samuel 5:4–5

5 **⁴** **David was thirty years old when he began to reign, and he reigned forty years.**

⁵ At Hebron he reigned over Judah seven years and six months, and at Jerusalem he reigned over all Israel and Judah thirty-three years.

The initial regnal formula for David's reign over Israel and Judah appears in 2 Samuel 5:4–5.[3] Such a formula normally appears as the introductory statement of the regnal accounts of the Kings of Israel and Judah in the Book of Kings. It is syntactically independent from the preceding material in 2 Samuel 5:1–3, but the following sub-units in 2 Samuel 5:6–10, 11–12,

---

3   Cf. Burke O. Long, *1 Kings, with an Introduction to Historical Literature* (FOTL 9; Grand Rapids, MI: Eerdmans, 1984), 158–165, 259; Marvin A. Sweeney, *1–2 Kings: A Commentary* (OTL; Louisville, KY: Westminster John Knox, 2007), 4–15.

13–25; 6:1–23; 7:1–29; and 8:1–18 are joined to 1 Samuel 5:4–5 by *waw*-consecutive verbal formations. Consequently, the regnal formula in 2 Samuel 5:4–5 introduces a sequence of episodes that recount the initial events of David's reign. The formula states David's age of thirty at the time of his accession to the throne, the overall duration of his reign at forty years, and the breakdown of seven and a half years as King of Judah alone in Hebron and an additional thirty-three years as King of Israel and Judah. Forty years is a typical period for an ideal reign (cf. Solomon, 1 Kgs 11:42; Othniel, Judg 3:7–11; Deborah, Judg 5:31; Gideon, Judg 8:28; Moses, Num 14:26–35; Deut 1:3; 34:7), even if the months do not quite add up.

The notice that David serves as King of both Israel and Judah is key to understanding the nature of David's reign. He did not rule over a fully united monarchy; rather, he ruled over a federation of the tribes of Israel that had been previously ruled by Saul and Ish-Bosheth, and the tribe of Judah that he ruled himself. Throughout the reigns of David and Solomon, Israel serves as a vassal to the House of David in Judah. Solomon's administration and taxation indicates that the northern tribes were divided into twelve districts that were to pay tribute to the monarchy for one month during the year (1 Kgs 4). Judah was never required to pay that tribute.[4]

David's Conquest of Jerusalem – 2 Samuel 5:6–10

5 [6] The king and his men marched to Jerusalem against the Jebusites, the inhabitants of the land, who said to David, "You will not come in here; even the blind and the lame will turn you back," thinking, "David cannot come in here."

[7] Nevertheless, David took the stronghold of Zion, which is now the city of David.

[8] David had said on that day, "Whoever would strike down the Jebusites, let him get up the water shaft to attack the lame and the blind, those whom David hates." Therefore it is said, "The blind and the lame shall not come into the house."

[9] David occupied the stronghold and named it the city of David. David built the city all around from the Millo inward.

[10] And David became greater and greater, for the LORD of hosts was with him.

---

4   Sweeney, *1 and 2 Kings*, 72–95.

The account of David's conquest of Jerusalem demonstrates once again David's capacity for leadership, insofar as he chooses a capital that will enable him to rule both portions of his kingdom following a very divisive war in which there would have been many cases, such as that of Abner and Asahel, in which Israelites and Judeans would have killed their counterparts and thereby left enduring enmity between the surviving family members. David's dilemma was that if he moved his capital to northern Israel, he would alienate his constituents in Judah, but if he remained in Judah, he would alienate his constituents in Israel.

A Closer Look at Jerusalem

Jerusalem was a Jebusite city, apparently one of the tribal or ethnic groups that constituted the Canaanite population of the land. The city had a long history prior to the emergence of Israel; it is mentioned prominently in the fourteenth century BCE Amarna letters as one of the Canaanite cities that were in communication with Pharaoh Amenhotep IV, also known as Akhenaten, who ruled Egypt in 1351–1334 BCE. The name Zion, which is well associated with Jerusalem, apparently indicates that the city was a mountain crossroads, insofar as the name appears to be derived from Hebrew, *ṣiyûn*, "signpost, monument" (2 Kgs 23:17; Jer 31:21; Ezek 39:15), which would indicate its role in guiding travelers through the Israelite and Judean hill country. Joshua 15:8 indicates that Jerusalem lay along the northern boundary of Judah, and Joshua 18:28 indicates that Jebus, also known as Jerusalem, was located in the territory of Benjamin. Jerusalem therefore occupied a strategic position between Judah to the south and Benjamin to the north, which meant that it lay at the boundary between southern Judah and northern Israel.

But Jerusalem was still a Canaanite/Jebusite city and not part of Israel or Judah, despite the claims of Joshua 10 (see Judg 1:21, which claims that Jebusites and Benjaminites lived together in Jerusalem). Jerusalem was a fortified city that could easily resist siege. The weak point of walled cities in antiquity, however, was their water systems. Fortified cities are generally built on defensible hilltops, but water is found in the lower-lying valleys outside of high city walls. People cannot survive a long siege without water, and so cisterns, wells, and tunnels must be cut through solid rock to reach the underground water below or the low-lying streams that lie beyond city walls. Canaanite Jerusalem was known for Warren's Shaft, a deep cistern that was cut through solid rock to reach below the walls of the city so that its inhabitants could gain access to underground aquifers and outlying streams. But such a system opens below the walls of the city, and an attacking enemy can use knowledge of such a system to send men up the cistern and into the city itself. Warren's Shaft had steps, partially cut into the rock and partially built of wooden scaffolding, so that people could descend into the deep cistern to fill buckets with water.

David's men took control of Jerusalem, but there is no record of his killing the defenders; apparently, Jebusites continued to live in the city with David's men just as they had lived with the Benjaminites (Judg 1:21). The text indicates that he fortified the city, although the basic Canaanite structure of the city's walls and buildings would have remained intact. The text mentions a structure called "the Millo," Hebrew, *hammillô'*, "the fill," apparently a beehive-shaped structure that gave support to structures built atop it during the pre-Israelite period.

David's choice of Jerusalem as his capital gave him an ideal site along the border of southern Judah and northern Israel to rule the two major portions of his federated kingdom. The text affirms that David's strength continued to grow and that YHWH of Hosts was with him.

Hiram's Recognition of David – 2 Samuel 5:11–12

5 **¹¹ King Hiram of Tyre sent messengers to David, along with cedar trees and carpenters and masons who built David a house.**

¹² David then perceived that the LORD had established him king over Israel and that he had exalted his kingdom for the sake of his people Israel.

Second Samuel 5:11–12 reports that King Hiram of Tyre sent messengers to David, apparently to seal a treaty between the two kings, and he sent materials, woodworkers, and stonemasons to build a palace for David. Hiram was not acting altruistically. As his relationship with Solomon shows, Hiram sought a trade relationship with Israel/Judah whereby Hiram could control the Mediterranean Sea trade, Israel/Judah could control the land routes through western Asia down to Egypt, and the two powers could combine to open sea trade with eastern Africa and the Arabian Peninsula by way of the Red Sea (1 Kgs 5:15–25; 9:26–28; 10:1–13). The text emphasizes that David's relationship with Hiram indicated that YHWH supported him as king.

The Birth of David's Sons in Jerusalem – 2 Samuel 5:13–16

5 [13] In Jerusalem, after he came from Hebron, David took more concubines and wives, and more sons and daughters were born to David.

[14] These are the names of those who were born to him in Jerusalem: Shammua, Shobab, Nathan, Solomon,

[15] Ibhar, Elishua, Nepheg, Japhia,

[16] Elishama, Eliada, and Eliphelet.

Second Samuel 5:13–16 focuses on David's increasing numbers of concubines, wives, daughters, and sons. Unlike 2 Samuel 3:2–5, no names are given for the women, indicating that these lists are not part of the same source. Eleven sons are named without reference to their mothers: Shammua, Shobab, Nathan, Solomon, Ibhar, Elishua, Nepheg, Japhia, Elishama, Eliada, and Eliphelet. A number of the theophoric names include the element Eli, an indication of the Canaanite character of the city insofar as El was recognized as the Canaanite god of creation but was at some point identified with YHWH, the G-d of Israel and Judah. It is unclear if David's son, Nathan, is to be identified with Nathan the prophet. The Solomon mentioned here is likely Bath Sheba's son, and the later narratives in 2 Samuel 10–12 about David's affair and marriage to Bath Sheba elaborate on how Solomon came to be born. Altogether, this segment demonstrates that David's house is growing, whereas the House of Saul is declining.

David's Defeat of the Philistines – 2 Samuel 5:17–25

5 [17] When the Philistines heard that David had been anointed king over Israel, all the Philistines went up in search of David, but David heard about it and went down to the stronghold.

[18] Now the Philistines had come and spread out in the valley of Rephaim.

[19] David inquired of the LORD, "Shall I go up against the Philistines? Will you give them into my hand?" The LORD said to David, "Go up, for I will certainly give the Philistines into your hand."

[20] So David came to Baal-perazim, and David defeated them there. He said, "The LORD has burst forth against my enemies before me like a bursting flood." Therefore that place is called Baal-perazim.

²¹ The Philistines abandoned their idols there, and David and his men carried them away.

²² Once again the Philistines came up and were spread out in the valley of Rephaim.

²³ When David inquired of the LORD, he said, "You shall not go up; go around to their rear and come upon them opposite the balsam trees.

²⁴ When you hear the sound of marching in the tops of the balsam trees, then be on the alert, for then the LORD has gone out before you to strike down the army of the Philistines."

²⁵ David did just as the LORD had commanded him, and he struck down the Philistines from Geba all the way to Gezer.

Despite the success indicated for David in 2 Samuel 5, David remained a Philistine vassal, and the Philistines would expect him to serve their interests. But as David grew stronger, the Philistines would have realized that he had become too powerful.

The narrative reports two Philistine attacks, which would have approached Jerusalem from the south in the Emeq Rephaim, the Valley of the Shades/Ghosts. This is an open farming and grazing area that stretches out to the south of the Hinnom Valley, the southern border of the city. The two attacks would have constituted two stages of a single campaign.

The first attack, in verses 17–21, would have been to test David's defenses. The narrative reports that David went down to his fortress, perhaps Adullam, located in the Judean Shephelah about twenty miles southwest of Jerusalem, where David had earlier based himself in a cave to gather men and defend Judah from the Philistines and from Saul (1 Sam 22:1). The site has been identified with Tell esh-Sheikh Madhkur, and there is speculation that it is identified with a water source called *'id ek-mâ'* that lies near some ancient ruins that have not yet been excavated.[5] David inquired of YHWH, who told him that he would defeat the Philistines. He then marched to Baal Perazim, identified with Mt. Perazim, although the location of this site is unknown.[6] The name means "Lord of Breakthroughs," and it is understood to celebrate David's break through the Philistines as water breaks through a dam. Once again, the narrative shows David succeeding where Saul had failed.

---

[5] Jeffries M. Hamilton, "Adullam," *ABD* 1:81; Jacques Briend, "Adullam," *EBR* 1:446–447.

[6] Yigal Levin, "Baal Perazim," *EBR* 3:225–226.

The Philistines attack a second time in 2 Samuel 5:22–25. This is the main attack and not a probe, and it comes from the west rather than the south. When David inquired of YHWH, he was advised to circle behind the Philistines and confront them by a stand of baca trees, perhaps to be identified as balsam trees, a type of tree that exudes aromatic balsam. When David hears the sound of marching in the tops of the trees, apparently an echo of Philistine movement in the top leaves of the tree, he is to attack because YHWH will go before him, much as the Assyrian gods went before their armies in battle.[7] David routed the Philistines all the way from Geba, five and half miles northeast of Jerusalem, to Gezer, a fortified city located some eighteen miles west-northwest of Jerusalem where the Ayalon Valley spills out into the coastal plain east of Ekron.[8] David freed himself of Philistine control and forced the Philistines to become his vassals (cf. 2 Sam 8:1). David achieves in two moves what Saul failed to achieve during his entire lifetime.

David's Transfer of the Ark to Jerusalem – 2 Samuel 6:1–19

6 [1] David again gathered all the chosen men of Israel, thirty thousand.

[2] David and all the people with him set out and went from Baale-judah to bring up from there the ark of God, which is called by the name of the LORD of hosts who is enthroned on the cherubim.

[3] They carried the ark of God on a new cart and brought it out of the house of Abinadab, which was on the hill. Uzzah and Ahio, the sons of Abinadab, were driving the new cart

[4] with the ark of God, and Ahio went in front of the ark.

[5] David and all the house of Israel were dancing before the LORD with all their might, with songs and lyres and harps and tambourines and castanets and cymbals.

[6] When they came to the threshing floor of Nacon, Uzzah reached out his hand to the ark of God and took hold of it, for the oxen lurched.

[7] The anger of the LORD was kindled against Uzzah, and God struck him there, and he died there beside the ark of God.

[7]   See Thomas W. Mann, *Divine Presence and Guidance in Israelite Traditions: The Typology of Exaltation* (Baltimore and London: Johns Hopkins University Press, 1977), esp. 213–230.

[8]   Steven M. Ortiz and Sam Wolff, "Gezer," *EBR* 10:178–181.

⁸ David was angry because the LORD had burst forth with an outburst upon Uzzah, so that place is called Perez-uzzah to this day.

⁹ David was afraid of the LORD that day; he said, "How can the ark of the LORD come into my care?"

¹⁰ So David was unwilling to take the ark of the LORD into his care in the city of David; instead, David took it to the house of Obed-edom the Gittite.

¹¹ The ark of the LORD remained in the house of Obed-edom the Gittite three months, and the LORD blessed Obed-edom and all his household.

¹² It was told King David, "The LORD has blessed the household of Obed-edom and all that belongs to him because of the ark of God." So David went and brought up the ark of God from the house of Obed-edom to the city of David with rejoicing,

¹³ and when those who bore the ark of the LORD had gone six paces, he sacrificed an ox and a fatted calf.

¹⁴ David danced before the LORD with all his might; David was girded with a linen ephod.

¹⁵ So David and all the house of Israel brought up the ark of the LORD with shouting and with the sound of the trumpet.

¹⁶ As the ark of the LORD came into the city of David, Michal daughter of Saul looked out of the window and saw King David leaping and dancing before the LORD, and she despised him in her heart.

¹⁷ They brought in the ark of the LORD and set it in its place, inside the tent that David had pitched for it, and David offered burnt offerings and offerings of well-being before the LORD.

¹⁸ When David had finished offering the burnt offerings and the offerings of well-being, he blessed the people in the name of the LORD of hosts ¹⁹ and distributed food among all the people, the whole multitude of Israel, both men and women, to each a cake of bread, a portion of meat, and a cake of raisins. Then all the people went back to their homes.

Second Samuel 6:1–19 presents the account of David's transfer of the Ark to Jerusalem. This is a key event in David's early kingship insofar as it is a public demonstration of his leadership in contrast to the failures of Saul. Whereas Saul was never able to defeat the Philistines decisively, David's victories over the Philistines turned the tables in favor of Israel. Israel would now be the suzerain master over Philistia, and the Ark could return to Israel in a demonstration of YHWH's divine kingship and David's role as King of Israel on YHWH's behalf.

David's victory over Israel at Gibeon in 2 Samuel 2 changed the balance of power in the region so that Gibeon abandoned its former relationship with Israel under Saul and began a new relationship with Judah under David.[9] The shift meant that David could rely on Gibeon and its clients, including Kiriath Jearim where the Ark was placed (1 Sam 7:1), for military and logistical support, first against Israel and later against Philistia and beyond. Once David became King of Israel and Judah, the relationship with Israel was reset, albeit with a newly emerging House of David in place of the declining House of Saul. David may have been a member of the House of Saul when he ascended the throne of Israel, but his refusal to father sons with Michal bat Saul in 2 Samuel 6:20–23 and his handing over the descendants of Saul to Gibeon in 2 Samuel 21 facilitated the rise of his own dynastic house independent of that of Saul.

A Closer Look at the Transfer of the Ark to Jerusalem

The procession to bring the Ark to Jerusalem is analogous to new year celebrations in Mesopotamia, such as the Akitu celebration in Babylon and other Mesopotamian cities.[10] Images of the gods of cities and nations allied with Babylon were paraded on carts through the streets of the city to the Entemenanki (i.e., the Temple of Marduk, the city god of Babylon) to celebrate the new year commemorating Marduk's creation of the world, the renewal of Marduk's kingship over creation, and the designation of the Babylonian king to rule as Marduk's regent.

The account begins with the notice that 30,000 men accompanied David to Baale-Judah, an alternative name for Kiriath Jearim (see Josh 15:9, which designates the site at Baalah, also known as Kiriath Jearim, "Town of Forests"). The name Baale-Judah means "Lords of Judah" and apparently represents a pre-Israelite understanding of the Canaanite gods of the land. The number of men is likely exaggerated, but it corresponds to the number of Israelite men reportedly killed when the Ark was captured by the Philistines at Aphek (1 Sam 4:10). The figure demonstrates Israel's recovery from the loss under David's leadership. The narrative likewise stresses the shift in the divine name associated with the Ark, that is, from the Ark of G-d to the Ark of YHWH of Hosts enthroned on the cherubim, another indication of a shift

[9] Joseph Blenkinsopp, *Gibeon and Israel: The Role of Gibeon and the Gibeonites in the Political and Religious History of Early Israel* (SOTSMS 2; Cambridge: Cambridge University Press, 1972).

[10] Jacob Klein, "Akitu," *ABD* 1:138–140; Beate Pongratz-Leisten, "Akitu," *EBR* 1:694–697.

from a Canaanite to an Israelite understanding of YHWH and the Ark of the Covenant. Exodus 25:10–22 describes the Ark as an acacia chest overlaid with gold, carried by poles, with two cherubs built on top. The cherubs, fearsome angelic creatures that combine human and animal features, typically guard the thrones of kings and the gates of ancient cities.[11] They function as guards for the Ark, conceived as the throne on which YHWH is seated above the cherubim, that is, they contribute to the portrayal of YHWH as King of Israel, Judah, and creation at large. When Solomon builds the Jerusalem Temple, 1 Kings 6:23–30 reports that he installs two additional cherubim in the Holy of Holies of the Temple in which the Ark is placed. Indeed, the three-room architectural design of Solomon's Temple, with a portico or Ulam, a Great Hall or Heichal, and a raised throne room, Holy of Holies, or Devir, is a typical Syro-Canaanite temple structure based on the design of a royal palace.[12] The purpose is to represent the deity of the nation as the divine King who authorizes the earthly king to rule on the god's behalf.

The Ark is then loaded on a new wheeled cart pulled by bovines (v. 6). The NRSVue translation of "oxen" is incorrect because oxen are castrated bulls,[13] whereas holy practice would have called for the use of animals that are unblemished, as in the holy offerings (see Lev 1:3). The procession begins at the house of Abinadab, located on the hill at Kiriath Jearim (1 Sam 7:1). Abinadab's sons, Uzzah and Ahio, accompany the Ark, with Uzzah walking alongside to ensure the Ark's stability and Ahio walking in front to guide the animals. The names of the two sons are problematic because 1 Samuel 7:1 names Eleazar as the son of Abinadab who had charge of the Ark, but he is not seen in this narrative. The name, Ahio, Hebrew, 'aḥyô, may indicate Uzzah's brother, Eleazar (Hebrew 'aḥyô repointed to 'aḥîw, means "his brother").[14] This makes sense because Ahio leads the procession. David and the House of Israel follow the Ark, dancing to music played on wind, stringed, and percussion instruments that would have been used in ancient Israel and the Near East.

A catastrophe occurs when the procession reaches the threshing floor of Nacon, an unknown location. When the bulls stumble or draw away in an attempt to break free of the harness (Hebrew, šāmēṭû, literally, "they drew away"; note that the animals are not castrated and are therefore more difficult to control), Uzzah touched the Ark with his hand to steady it. Because the Ark is holy, it is not fit for the Ark to be handled in such a way by a man who is not clearly a priest. YHWH

[11] Carol M. Meyers, "Cherubim," *ABD* 1:899–900.
[12] Baruch Halpern, *The First Historians: The Hebrew Bible and History* (San Francisco: Harper & Row, 1988), 46–54.
[13] I owe this insight to my graduate school days at Claremont and the late Professor William H. Brownlee, who was raised on a farm in Kansas.
[14] Cf. A. A. Anderson, *2 Samuel* (WBC 11; Grand Rapids, MI: Zondervan, 2000), 102–103.

strikes Uzzah dead for his error (Hebrew, *šal*, "error"). The site is therefore named Perez-Uzzah, "Outbreak of Uzzah," in memory of this incident. The location of the site is unknown, although McCarter speculates that it may refer to a breach in the wall of Jerusalem.[15] David was afraid to bring the Ark into Jerusalem and placed it instead at the house of Obed-Edom the Gittite, where it remained for three months until YHWH's blessing on Obed-Edom's house indicated that it was safe to bring the Ark into the city.

Once the procession resumed, it proceeded in sacred fashion with sacrifices of a bull and a fatling made for every six paces of the journey. David, dressed in an ephod like a priest, danced before the Ark as it was carried into the city. Second Samuel 8:18 identifies David's sons as priests. There are instances when northern Israelite kings act as priests, such as Jeroboam ben Nebat, who officiates at the altar at Beth El (1 Kgs 12:33–13:10). Insofar as northern Israel observed practices different from those of southern Judah, it may be that Israel expected the king to act as priest, whereas southern Judah did not.[16]

First Chronicles 16 presents a liturgical account of David's transfer of the Ark to Jerusalem in that it quotes the Psalms sung by the Levites as the Ark is brought into the city, including portions of Psalms 105:1–15, 23–33; 96:34–36; and 106:47–48.

Second Samuel 6:16 reports that Michal daughter of Saul, David's first wife, observed David dancing before YHWH and despised him in her heart. The portrayal of Michal in this verse employs a motif of a woman peering through a window, a classic narrative and art motif in ancient Israel to depict a woman who is somehow disappointed when she looks through the window of the harem where she resides (see Judg 5:28–30, which portrays the mother of Sisera futilely waiting for the return of her son).[17] The reference to Michal's reaction anticipates David's refusal to father children with her in 2 Samuel 6:20–23. The reason for Michal's dissatisfaction is that David is whirling about clad only in a linen ephod, which would expose his body before all the people, including the women (cf. Exod 20:23).

[15]   David L. Thompson, "Perez-Uzzah," *ABD* 5:226; P. Kyle McCarter, *2 Samuel* (AB 9; Garden City, NY: Doubleday, 1984), 161, 170.
[16]   Marvin A. Sweeney, "Israelite and Judean Religions," *The Cambridge History of Religions in the Ancient World. Volume I: From the Bronze Age to the Hellenistic Age*, ed. M. R. Salzman and M. A. Sweeney (Cambridge: Cambridge University Press, 2013), 151–150.
[17]   McCarter, *2 Samuel*, 172; Eleanor Ferris Beach, *The Jezebel Letters: Religion and Politics in Ninth-Century Israel* (Minneapolis: Fortress, 2005).

The narrative concludes in verses 17–19 with the celebration, including the *'ōlâ*, "whole burnt offering," offered only to YHWH (Lev 1) and the *šĕlāmîm*, "well-being offering," in which the people shared (Lev 3), and the food distributed to the people. David's display of generosity is another indication of his fitness to serve as king. Most importantly, David's transfer of the Ark publicly demonstrates his firm adherence to YHWH and his suitability to serve as king.

David's Refusal to Father Sons with Michal bat Saul – 2 Samuel 6:20–23

6 **²⁰ David returned to bless his household. But Michal the daughter of Saul came out to meet David and said, "How the king of Israel honored himself today, uncovering himself today before the eyes of his servants' maids, as any vulgar fellow might shamelessly uncover himself!"**

²¹ David said to Michal, "It was before the LORD, who chose me in place of your father and all his household, to appoint me as prince over Israel, the people of the LORD – I will dance before the LORD.

²² I will make myself yet more contemptible than this, and I will be humbled in my own eyes, but by the maids of whom you have spoken, by them I shall be held in honor."

²³ And Michal the daughter of Saul had no child to the day of her death.

David's refusal to father sons with Michal bat Saul in 2 Samuel 6:20–23 is a key element in his rise to power. Michal is his first wife and the daughter of Saul, which means that David becomes King of Israel as son-in-law of Saul and therefore a member of the House of Saul. Michal has good reason to be dissatisfied with David as he exposes himself before all Israel while dancing before YHWH dressed only in a linen ephod. She makes her dissatisfaction clear by sarcastically referring to how David "honored himself" before all the servant maidens and vulgar men in the city. But David responds in kind by stating that YHWH chose him over Michal's father, Saul, and his house to serve as prince (Hebrew, *nāgîd*, "designated ruler/leader") of Israel. He exclaims that he will make himself even more contemptible by honoring himself with all the maids of the city of whom she has spoken. This testosterone-fueled exclamation is more than an example of male indignation and self-exaltation. By refusing to sleep with Michal bat Saul, David ensures that she will never bear a son for the line of King Saul. Therefore, no son of Michal will ever be able to challenge his father for the throne (though 2 Sam 13–19 makes it clear that sons of David will challenge his throne, and 2 Sam 20 makes it clear that members of the House of Saul will do so as well). When combined with David's surrender of the sons of Saul to the Gibeonites in 2 Samuel 21, David ensures the end of the House of Saul and the beginning of the House of David. David might be portrayed as following Deuteronomic law insofar as a man who divorces his wife cannot remarry her after she has married another man (Deut 24:1–4).[18]

YHWH's Eternal Covenant of Kingship with David and Israel – 2 Samuel 7:1–29

7 [1] Now when the king was settled in his house and the LORD had given him rest from all his enemies around him,

[2] the king said to the prophet Nathan, "See now, I am living in a house of cedar, but the ark of God stays in a tent."

[3] Nathan said to the king, "Go, do all that you have in mind, for the LORD is with you."

[4] But that same night the word of the LORD came to Nathan,

[5] "Go and tell my servant David: Thus says the LORD: Are you the one to build me a house to live in?

[6] I have not lived in a house since the day I brought up the people of Israel from Egypt to this day, but I have been moving about in a tent and a tabernacle.

[7] Wherever I have moved about among all the people of Israel, did I ever speak a word with any of the tribal leaders of Israel, whom I commanded to shepherd my people Israel, saying, 'Why have you not built me a house of cedar?'

[8] Now therefore thus you shall say to my servant David: Thus says the LORD of hosts: I took you from the pasture, from following the sheep to be prince over my people Israel,

---

[18]   For legal background, see Zafrira Ben-Barak, "The Legal Background to the Restoration of Michal to David," in *Telling Queen Michal's Story: An Experiment in Comparative Interpretation*, JSOTSup 119, ed., D. J. A. Clines, and T. C. Eskenazi (Sheffield: Sheffield Academic Press, 1991), 74–90, who argues that in accordance with the laws of Eshnunna and Deuteronomy 24:1–4, Michal is forbidden to David, but he does not have relations with her.

⁹ and I have been with you wherever you went and have cut off all your enemies from before you, and I will make for you a great name, like the name of the great ones of the earth.

¹⁰ And I will appoint a place for my people Israel and will plant them, so that they may live in their own place and be disturbed no more, and evildoers shall afflict them no more, as formerly,

¹¹ from the time that I appointed judges over my people Israel, and I will give you rest from all your enemies. Moreover, the LORD declares to you that the LORD will make you a house.

¹² When your days are fulfilled and you lie down with your ancestors, I will raise up your offspring after you, who shall come forth from your body, and I will establish his kingdom.

¹³ He shall build a house for my name, and I will establish the throne of his kingdom forever.

¹⁴ I will be a father to him, and he shall be a son to me. When he commits iniquity, I will punish him with a rod such as mortals use, with blows inflicted by human beings.

¹⁵ But I will not take my steadfast love from him, as I took it from Saul, whom I put away from before you.

¹⁶ Your house and your kingdom shall be made sure forever before me; your throne shall be established forever."

¹⁷ In accordance with all these words and with all this vision, Nathan spoke to David.

¹⁸ Then King David went in and sat before the LORD and said, "Who am I, O Lord GOD, and what is my house, that you have brought me thus far?

¹⁹ And yet this was a small thing in your eyes, O Lord GOD; you have spoken also of your servant's house into the distant future. May this be instruction for the people, O Lord GOD!

²⁰ And what more can David say to you? For you know your servant, O Lord GOD!

²¹ Because of your promise and according to your own heart, you have wrought all this greatness so that your servant may know it.

²² Therefore you are great, O LORD God, for there is no one like you, and there is no God besides you, according to all that we have heard with our ears.

²³ Who is like your people, like Israel? Is there another nation on earth whose God went to redeem it as a people and to make a name for

himself, doing great and awesome things, driving out nations and their gods before your people, whom you redeemed for yourself from Egypt?

²⁴ And you established your people Israel for yourself to be your people forever, and you, O LORD, became their God.

²⁵ And now, O LORD God, as for the word that you have spoken concerning your servant and concerning his house, confirm it forever; do as you have promised.

²⁶ Thus your name will be magnified forever in the saying, 'The LORD of hosts is God over Israel,' and the house of your servant David will be established before you.

²⁷ For you, O LORD of hosts, the God of Israel, have made this revelation to your servant, saying, 'I will build you a house'; therefore your servant has found courage to pray this prayer to you.

²⁸ And now, O Lord GOD, you are God, and your words are true, and you have promised this good thing to your servant;

²⁹ now, therefore, may it please you to bless the house of your servant so that it may continue forever before you, for you, O Lord GOD, have spoken, and with your blessing shall the house of your servant be blessed forever."

YHWH's eternal promise of kingship to David and security for Israel in 2 Samuel 7 is a key element in the regnal account of King David ben Jesse of Israel and Judah in 2 Samuel 5–8.

The account is of great importance because it relates the origins of the longest-standing and most stable dynasty in Israelite and Judean history, and because it resolves the problems inherent in YHWH's selection of Saul as the first King of Israel. But there are problems. The term "covenant" is never used in the narrative, but 2 Samuel 23:5 identifies YHWH's relationship with David as an "eternal covenant," Hebrew, *bĕrît 'ôlām* (cf. Pss 89:20–37; 110:4). But YHWH's promise of an eternal Davidic House is not realized in the subsequent narrative in 2 Kings 24–25. Indeed, 1–2 Kings qualifies the eternal and unconditional Davidic promise of 2 Samuel 7 with statements that the Davidic promise in 1 Kings 2:1–4; 8:22–25; and 9:1–9 will be secure only if the royal descendants observe YHWH's commandments (cf. Ps 132:11–12).

The account of YHWH's eternal promise to David and Israel includes two major sub-units: Nathan's prophecy to David, in which YHWH promises him a secure house or dynasty, in 2 Samuel 7:1–16, and David's subsequent prayer to YHWH in 2 Samuel 7:17–29.

Second Samuel 7:1–16 presents the account of Nathan's vision from YHWH, in which YHWH promises that David will have a secure and eternal house (i.e., dynasty) forever and that Israel will have a secure and eternal place (i.e., land) forever as well.[19] The sub-unit is demarcated initially by the *waw*-consecutive statement in 2 Samuel 7:1, which introduces the narrative with a portrayal of David's dwelling in his house and YHWH's granting him peace from his enemies all around. The sub-unit concludes in verse 16 with YHWH's statement through Nathan the prophet that David's house and kingship will be secure and that his throne will be established forever. The following statement in verse 17 is syntactically independent from the preceding material, and it introduces the account of David's prayer in 2 Samuel 7:17–29 by noting that YHWH's promise is the reason why David prayed to thank YHWH.

The sub-unit begins in 2 Samuel 7:1–3 with a brief narrative account of David's initial consultation with the prophet Nathan concerning his intention to build a house (i.e., a temple) for YHWH now that he is settled safely in his own house (i.e., the palace built for him by King Hiram of Tyre; 2 Sam 5:11–12). According to 2 Samuel 5:14, David has a son named Nathan born to him in Jerusalem, but there is no suggestion that the prophet Nathan and David's son Nathan are one and the same man. David observes that he dwells in a house of cedar, apparently a reference to the palace that Hiram built for him as cedar was a prized commodity from the Lebanese mountain range, and that he now wants to build a house (i.e., temple) for YHWH. The interplay between the different understandings of the Hebrew word, *bayit*, "house," as "palace, temple, and dynasty" underlies and informs the entire account. Nathan agrees with David, which allows YHWH to state a very different understanding than that proposed by David.

A Closer Look at YHWH's Promise of an Eternal Dynasty for David

Second Samuel 7:4–16 presents an account of YHWH's night vision to Nathan in which YHWH proposes to build a house for David instead. The vision begins in verses 4–7 with YHWH's statements that a house or temple for YHWH is entirely unnecessary because YHWH has never had such a house, has never asked for one, and has been content to travel about with Israel from the time of their exodus from

---

[19] For discussion of Nathan, see Marvin A. Sweeney, "Nathan," *EBR* 20: 829–831.

Egypt to the present in a tent and a tabernacle, apparently references to the tent in which David housed the Ark in 2 Samuel 6:17 and the Tabernacle built for the Ark in Exodus 25–40. The narrative makes it clear that YHWH is the G-d of all creation and the redeemer of Israel; a temple of cedar might localize YHWH overmuch.

YHWH's statements concerning David in 2 Samuel 7:8–16 are formulated as instructions to Nathan, which employ the prophetic messenger formula, "Thus says YHWH of Hosts."[20] The language draws upon ancient Near Eastern treaty language by beginning with accounts of YHWH's past actions on behalf of David and Israel in verses 8–9 concerning YHWH's taking David from following flocks to becoming "prince," Hebrew, *nāgîd*, "designated ruler," of Israel and YHWH's actions to give David rest from his enemies.[21] They then turn to YHWH's promises to give David a great "name" or reputation and to establish a "place" (i.e., the land of Israel) in which the people will dwell without disturbance from enemies, as in the days of the Judges.

YHWH's statements then turn to promises of a house (i.e., a dynasty) for David. YHWH promises to establish David's offspring upon his throne, and he (i.e., Solomon) will build a house or temple for YHWH (see 1 Kgs 6–8). The statements that YHWH will be a father and that David's offspring will be a son echoes Psalm 2 and ancient Near Eastern suzerainty treaties in which the suzerain is the father and the vassal is the son.[22] YHWH will be understood as the true King of Israel (or Judah), and the Davidic monarch will be understood as the human regent who rules on YHWH's behalf. If the Davidic monarchs do wrong, YHWH promises to punish them, but YHWH reiterates the promise never to remove "steadfast love," Hebrew, *ḥesed*, "fidelity," from David's offspring as YHWH did with Saul.[23] YHWH's instructions to Nathan conclude with the promise that David's house (i.e., dynasty) and kingdom will be made sure (i.e., secure) and that David's throne shall be established forever (i.e., Hebrew, *'ad 'ôlām*). Although such a promise was made, it is theologically problematic as the later DtrH demonstrates that Jehoiachin and Zedekiah were the last kings of the House of David.

The account of David's prayer of thanksgiving to YHWH appears in 2 Samuel 7:17–29, where it is introduced by the syntactically independent statement in v. 17 concerning Nathan's communication of YHWH's words

---

[20] Marvin A. Sweeney, *Isaiah 1–39, with an Introduction to Prophetic Literature* (FOTL 16; Cambridge, UK, and Grand Rapids, MI: Eerdmans, 1996), 546.

[21] Philip J. Calderone, S.J., *Dynastic Oracle and Suzerainty Treaty* (Logos 1; Manila: Loyola House of Studies Ateno de Manila University, 1966); Moshe Weinfeld, "The Covenant of Grant in the Old Testament and the Ancient Near East," *JAOS* 90 (1970):184–203.

[22] Calderone, *Dynastic Oracle*, 53–57.

[23] Nelson Glueck, *Ḥesed in the Bible* (Cincinnati: Hebrew Union College, 1967).

to David. The notice that David sat before YHWH to present his prayer is problematic. Normally, only priests would be able to enter the presence of YHWH in the Temple and presumably the Tabernacle, but David's sons were priests (2 Sam 8:18), and as King of Israel, David appears to be qualified to take on priestly roles in keeping with northern Israelite practice (cf. 1 Kgs 8; 13, but note 2 Kgs 19; Isa 37).[24] Elements of thanksgiving appear in verses 21 as David deprecates himself before YHWH to offer thanksgiving for all that YHWH has done for him despite his confessed unworthiness to receive such beneficence. Elements of praise appear in verse 22–24 as David recounts YHWH's greatness and incomparability (cf. Exod 15, esp. v. 11) and all that YHWH has done on behalf of Israel. Elements of petition appear in verses 25–29, in which David asks YHWH to confirm and act on the divine word as promised.

Second Samuel 7 includes characteristic Deuteronomistic language,[25] but the conceptualization of YHWH's promise as eternal, the focus on David's offspring (i.e., Solomon, who will build the Temple for YHWH), and David's petition for confirmation, indicate that the base narrative was written as part of the Solomonic History.

The Summation of David's Reign – 2 Samuel 8:1–18

8 [1] **Some time afterward, David attacked the Philistines and subdued them; David took Metheg-ammah out of the hand of the Philistines.**

[2] **He also defeated the Moabites and, making them lie down on the ground, measured them off with a cord; he measured two lengths of cord for those who were to be put to death and one length for those who were to be spared. And the Moabites became servants to David and brought tribute.**

[3] **David also struck down the king of Zobah, Hadadezer son of Rehob, as he went to restore his monument at the River Euphrates.**

[4] **David took from him one thousand seven hundred horsemen and twenty thousand foot soldiers. David hamstrung all the chariot horses but left enough for a hundred chariots.**

[5] **When the Arameans of Damascus came to help King Hadadezer of Zobah, David killed twenty-two thousand men of the Arameans.**

---

[24] Sweeney, "Israelite and Judean Religions."
[25] D. J. McCarthy, "II Samuel 7 and the Structure of the Deuteronomistic History," *JBL* 84 (1965): 131–138; Dietrich, *1 Samuel 27–2 Samuel 8*, 636–649.

⁶ Then David put garrisons among the Arameans of Damascus, and the Arameans became servants to David and brought tribute. The LORD gave victory to David wherever he went.

⁷ David took the gold shields that were carried by the servants of Hadadezer and brought them to Jerusalem.

⁸ From Betah and from Berothai, towns of Hadadezer, King David took a great amount of bronze.

⁹ When King Toi of Hamath heard that David had defeated the whole army of Hadadezer,

¹⁰ Toi sent his son Joram to King David, to greet him and to congratulate him because he had fought against Hadadezer and defeated him. Now Hadadezer had often been at war with Toi. Joram brought with him articles of silver, gold, and bronze;

¹¹ these also King David dedicated to the LORD, together with the silver and gold that he dedicated from all the nations he subdued,

¹² from Edom, Moab, the Ammonites, the Philistines, Amalek, and from the spoil of the king of Zobah, Hadadezer son of Rehob.

¹³ David won a name for himself. When he returned, he killed eighteen thousand Edomites in the Valley of Salt.

¹⁴ He put garrisons in Edom; throughout all Edom he put garrisons, and all the Edomites became David's servants. And the LORD gave victory to David wherever he went.

¹⁵ So David reigned over all Israel, and David administered justice and equity to all his people.

¹⁶ Joab son of Zeruiah was over the army; Jehoshaphat son of Ahilud was recorder;

¹⁷ Zadok son of Ahitub and Ahimelech son of Abiathar were priests; Seraiah was secretary;

¹⁸ Benaiah son of Jehoiada was over the Cherethites and the Pelethites; and David's sons were priests.

The summation of David's reign in 2 Samuel 8 is stylized as a typical element of the regnal accounts of the Kings of Israel and Judah in the book of Kings. It focuses on David's conquests in verses 1–14 and David's administration in verses 14–18, but it lacks an account of David's death, burial, and succession. Although they are treated as historical accounts in many studies of David's life and reign,²⁶ there is relatively little

---

²⁶   E.g., Baruch Halpern, *David's Secret Demons: Messiah, Murderer, Traitor, King* (Grand Rapids, MI, and Cambridge, UK: Eerdmans, 2001), 107–226.

information to be gleaned from ancient Near Eastern sources outside the Bible. Interpreters must rely on the biblical material, particularly 2 Samuel 8, to gain an understanding of David's reign, but they must also be aware of the influence of propaganda, exaggeration, fictionalization, and admiration in this material.

The first element in the narrative is the summation of David's conquests in 2 Samuel 8:1–14, including David's subjugation of the Philistines in verse 1, the Moabites in verse 2, Hadadezer of Zobah in verses 3–8, Toi of Hamath in verses 9–12, and Edom in verses 13–14.

Second Samuel 5:17–25 has already recounted David's defeat of the Philistines in the Rephaim Valley (i.e., Emeq Rephaim), but 2 Samuel 8:1 takes the account a step further by noting David's subjugation of the Philistines and his taking of Metheg-Ammah. The reference of Metheg-Ammah is unclear. First Chronicles 18:1 understands the term to refer to "Gath and its daughters," based on an understanding of the term as "bridle of the mother (city)" (i.e., the central city of Gath and the surrounding villages that function as its dependencies). Others understand the term to refer to "a bridle of a cubit," or better, "bridle of Ammah," the site mentioned in 2 Samuel 2:24, to indicate the extent of Gath's control of the region.[27] The phrase likely alludes to Gath's control of the Hill of Ammah in 2 Samuel 2:24 and David's seizure of this territory in relation to his subjugation of Gath and the Philistines at large.

The notice of David's subjugation of the Moabites, particularly his execution of two-thirds of their number, has proved troubling to interpreters,[28] but David's actions would have been undertaken to eliminate an ongoing threat from an unrelenting enemy.

The account of David's subjugation of King Hadadezer ben/bar Rehob of Zobah and the Arameans raises many historical questions because so little is known about the region in the eleventh and tenth centuries BCE. Zobah, or Aram-Zobah, is located in the north Beqaʿ Valley of modern Lebanon to the east of the Anti-Lebanon Range and to the north of Damascus.[29] The city is known in cuneiform texts, but its exact location

---

[27] Frauke Uhlenberg, "Metheg-Ammah," *EBR* 18:1041–1042; McCarter, *2 Samuel*, 243, 247.

[28] E.g., Johanna W. H. van Wijk-Bos, *Reading Samuel: A Literary and Theological Commentary* (ROT; Macon, GA: Smyth and Helwys, 2011), 181–185.

[29] Wayne T. Pitard, "Zobah," *ABD* 6:1108; Wayne T. Pitard, *Ancient Damascus: A Historical Study of the Syrian City-State from Earliest Times until its Fall to the Assyrians in 732 B.C.E.* (Winona Lake, IN: Eisenbrauns, 1987) , 89–95; and esp. K. Lawson Younger, *A Political History of the Arameans: From Their Origins to the End of Their Polities* (ABS 13; Atlanta: Society of Biblical Literature, 2016), 192–204.

remains disputed. Some speculate that the account of David's subjugation of Zobah may be interrelated to the account of his campaign against Aram-Zobah and Beth Rehob in 2 Samuel 10:6–19. Second Samuel 8:3–12 indicates that David intercepted Hadadezer's forces while he was on his way to restore his "monument," Hebrew, *yad*, "hand, monument," at the Euphrates River, (i.e., he was restoring his claim to territory all the way north to the Euphrates). The narrative states that David captured 1,700 horsemen and 22,000 foot soldiers; hamstrung the chariot horses except for 100 that he kept for his own use; and defeated a relief force of 22,000 men sent from Damascus to aid Hadadezer. The narrative further states that David set prefects or garrisons in Aram and that the Arameans paid tribute to David. David took "gold shields," Hebrew, *šilṭê hazzāhāb*, better translated as "gold quivers," from Hadadezer's servants, apparently a royal guard, and that the cities of Betaḥ and Berothai supplied David with great quantities of bronze. Betaḥ might be identified with Tubiḫu in the Beqaʿ Valley,[30] and Berothai, known as Cun in 1 Chronicles 18:8 and known in Egyptian sources, may be identified with modern Bereithan in Lebanon.[31] There is no historical record of this campaign apart from the Bible (2 Sam 8:1–14 and 1 Chr 18:1–13; 2 Sam 10:6–19 and 1 Chr 18:6–19).

Second Samuel 8:9–12 asserts that David did have an Aramean ally, King Toi of Hamath, although the text claims that Toi allied with David after his victory over Hadadezer of Zobah and his allies in Damascus. Hamath is a well-known city in Aram, but Toi is otherwise unknown, not to mention his son, Joram, who shares a name with Israelite and Judean kings. When Toi sends his son, Joram, to greet David, Joram brings objects of gold, silver, and copper, which David dedicates to YHWH along with booty from Aram (NRSVue reads "Edom," due to the similarity of the letter *resh* in Aram and *daleth* in Edom, but this appears to be an error motivated by the following references to Edom in verses 12–14), Moab, Ammon, the Philistines, and the Amalekites, all of whom had been defeated by David either in 2 Samuel 8 or other narratives in Samuel. If such an alliance existed, it may well have preceded David's campaign against Hadadezer, but in the present context, it is a device to laud David and demonstrate his greatness.

---

[30] Jeremy M. Hutton, "Betah," *EBR* 3:947.
[31] Scott R. A. Starbuck, "Berothai," *EBR* 3:927.

Finally, 2 Samuel 8:13–14 recounts David's subjugation of Edom.[32] Other texts concerned with the subjugation of Edom include 1 Samuel 14:47, which portrays Saul's successful campaign against Edom; 1 Kings 11:15–16, which recalls David's successful campaign against Edom (cf. Ps 60:1–2); 1 Kings 22:48, which reports that Edom was ruled by a prefect rather than by a king; 2 Kings 3, which claims that an unnamed Edomite king joined King Jehoram of Israel and King Jehoshaphat of Judah in a campaign against King Mesha of Moab; 2 Kings 8:20, which states that Edom rebelled against King Joram of Israel and set up a king of their own; 2 Kings 14:7, which reports that King Amaziah of Judah killed 10,000 Edomites in the Valley of Salt and took Sela; and 2 Chronicles 28:16–18, which reports that Edomite and Philistine attacks against Judah prompted King Ahaz to appeal to Assyria for help. In later times, the Edomites allied with Assyria and Babylonia against Judah. Verse 14 makes it clear that the purpose of this passage is to impress the reader with David's power and support from YHWH.

Second Samuel 8:15–18 names the major figures in David's administration, which appears to be influenced by Egyptian administrative offices.[33] Joab son of Zeruiah (David's sister) was commander of the army. Jehoshaphat son of Ahilud was recorder, Hebrew, *mazkîr*, apparently keeper of records, although Fox identifies him as "herald"; Zadok son of Ahitub and Ahimelech son of Abiathar (or perhaps Abiathar son of Ahimelech in keeping with 2 Sam 20:25) were priests of the House of Eli. Seraiah (Sheva in 2 Sam 20:25) was the scribe, Hebrew, *sôpēr*. Benaiah son of Jehoiada was commander of the Cherethites, perhaps men from Crete, and the Pelethites, perhaps men from Philistia, who served as David's mercenary royal guard. The assertion that David's sons were priests has puzzled interpreters, but in northern Israel the first-born sons of mothers served as priests (see, e.g., Samuel son of Elkanah, an Ephraimite, who was first-born son to Elkanah's first wife, Hannah, in 1 Sam 1–3).[34] According

---

[32] See J. R. Bartlett, "Edom," *ABD* 2:287–295.

[33] Joachim Begrich, "Sōfēr und Mazkîr," *ZAW* 58 (1940–1941):1–29; reprinted in *Gesammelte Studien zum Alten Testament* (TB 21; Munich: Chr. Kaiser, 1964), 67–98; Nili Sachar Fox, *In the Service of the King: Officialdom in Israel and Judah* (Cincinnati: Hebrew Union College Press, 2000), esp. 96–121.

[34] Sweeney, "Israelite and Judean Religions," 151-173: Marvin A. Sweeney, "Samuel's Institutional Identity in the Deuteronomistic History," in *Constructs of Prophecy in the Former and Latter Prophets and Other Texts*, ed. L. L. Grabbe and M. Nissinen; Atlanta: Society of Biblical Literature Press, 2011), 165–174; Marvin A. Sweeney, "The Literary-Historical Dimensions of Intertextuality in Exodus–Numbers," in *Second Wave*

to Numbers 3:11–13, 40–43; and 8:13–19, first-born sons served as priests in Israel prior to YHWH's decision to sanctify the Levites.

DAVID'S EXERCISE OF KINGSHIP – 2 SAMUEL 9:1–24:25

Second Samuel 9–24 recounts David's exercise of kingship following the regnal account in 2 Samuel 5–8. Most interpreters follow Rost, who identified 2 Samuel 9–20; 1 Kings 1–2 as the Succession Narrative based on a diachronic assessment of its compositional history.[35] Others have modified Rost's hypothesis to identify the narrative as a Court History, due to uncertainty as to whether 1 Kings 1–2 properly belongs with the Samuel narrative.[36] In either case, 2 Samuel 21–24 were viewed as appendices to the basic Samuel narrative.

A synchronic reading of the narrative must be governed strictly by literary characteristics and not by reconstructed compositional histories, even if they are correct.[37] In this case, 2 Samuel 9–24 follows up on the regnal account in 2 Samuel 5–8 with a series of episodes that reflect and elaborate upon the preceding narratives by examining different aspects of David's reign defined by their formal features, thematic concerns, and their roles in the development of the plot. In synchronic form, the narrative presents ten discrete sub-units: the accounts of David and Mephibosheth in 2 Samuel 9; David's adultery with Bath Sheba in 2 Samuel 10–12; Amnon's rape of Tamar in 2 Samuel 13; Absalom's revolt in 2 Samuel 14–19; Sheba's revolt in 2 Samuel 20; David and the Gibeonites in 2 Samuel 21; the Song of David in 2 Samuel 22; David's oracle concerning the eternal covenant in 2 Samuel 23:1–7; David's heroes in 2 Samuel 23:8–39; and David's selection of the site for the Jerusalem Temple in 2 Samuel 24.

The diachronic dimensions of the narrative must also be considered. Rost's inclusion of 1 Kings 1–2 into the Succession Narrative is legitimate, although in the synchronic form of the narrative it serves as an

---

Intertextuality and the Hebrew Bible, ed. M. Grohmann and H. C. P. Kim; Atlanta: Society of Biblical Literature Press, 2019), 41–52.

[35] Leonhard Rost, *The Succession to the Throne of David* (Sheffield: Almond Press, 1982); Gillian Keys, *The Wages of Sin: A Reappraisal of the Succession Narrative* (JSOTSup 221; Sheffield: Sheffield Academic Press, 1996).

[36] For example, John Van Seters, *In Search of History: Historiography in the Ancient World and the Origins of Biblical History* (New Haven and London: Yale University Press, 1983), 277–291.

[37] Marvin A. Sweeney, *Tanak: A Theological and Critical Introduction to the Jewish Bible* (Minneapolis: Fortress, 2012), 207–233.

introduction to the reign of Solomon.[38] But Rost's understanding of the so-called Succession Narrative must be modified. Some elements (e.g., the account of David and Mephibosheth, which presents no inherent critique of David) must be viewed as the product of the Solomonic narrative, which lauds David on his rise to power, even though 2 Samuel 9 has been shifted to introduce concern with the succession to the Davidic throne. The accounts of David's adultery with Bath Sheba in 2 Samuel 10–12; Amnon's rape of Tamar in 2 Samuel 13; the revolt of Abshalom in 2 Samuel 14–19; and the revolt of Sheba in 2 Samuel 20, are all highly critical of David and the chaos that ensues from his adultery. They are best understood as part of the Jehu Dynastic History that was later read in the context of the Josianic edition of the DtrH.[39] The accounts of David and the Gibeonites in 2 Samuel 21; the Song of David in 2 Samuel 22; David's oracle concerning the eternal covenant in 2 Samuel 23:1–7; David's heroes in 2 Samuel 23:8–39; and David's selection of the site of the future Temple in 2 Samuel 24 all function as elements that illustrate David's reign in the Solomonic edition of the account of David's rise to power. These narratives would have been displaced by the insertion of the critical material concerning David in 2 Samuel 10–20 as part of the Jehu Dynastic History.

David and Mephibosheth – 2 Samuel 9:1–13

9 **¹ David asked, "Is there still anyone left of the house of Saul to whom I may show kindness for Jonathan's sake?"**

² Now there was a servant of the house of Saul whose name was Ziba, and he was summoned to David. The king said to him, "Are you Ziba?" And he said, "At your service!"

³ The king said, "Is there anyone remaining of the house of Saul to whom I may show the kindness of God?" Ziba said to the king, "There remains a son of Jonathan; he is crippled in his feet."

⁴ The king said to him, "Where is he?" Ziba said to the king, "He is in the house of Machir son of Ammiel, at Lo-debar."

---

[38] Sweeney, *1–2 Kings*, 26–30.

[39] Sweeney, *1 and 2 Kings*, 26–30; see also Antony F. Campbell, S.J., *Of Prophets and Kings: A Late Ninth Century Document (1 Samuel 1–2 Kings 10)* (CBQMS 17; Washington, DC: Catholic University Press, 1986); Antony F. Campbell, S.J., and Mark A. O'Brien, *Unfolding the Deuteronomistic History: Origins, Upgrades, Present Text* (Minneapolis: Fortress, 2000), 24–31.

⁵ Then King David sent and brought him from the house of Machir son of Ammiel, at Lo-debar.

⁶ Mephibosheth son of Jonathan son of Saul came to David and fell on his face and did obeisance. David said, "Mephibosheth!" He answered, "I am your servant."

⁷ David said to him, "Do not be afraid, for I will show you kindness for the sake of your father Jonathan; I will restore to you all the land of your grandfather Saul, and you yourself shall eat at my table always."

⁸ He did obeisance and said, "What is your servant, that you should look upon a dead dog such as I?"

⁹ Then the king summoned Saul's servant Ziba and said to him, "All that belonged to Saul and to all his house I have given to your master's grandson.

¹⁰ You and your sons and your servants shall till the land for him and shall bring in the produce, so that your master's grandson may have food to eat, but your master's grandson Mephibosheth shall always eat at my table." Now Ziba had fifteen sons and twenty servants.

¹¹ Then Ziba said to the king, "According to all that my lord the king commands his servant, so your servant will do." Mephibosheth ate at David's table, like one of the king's sons.

¹² Mephibosheth had a young son whose name was Mica. And all who lived in Ziba's house became Mephibosheth's servants.

¹³ Mephibosheth lived in Jerusalem, for he always ate at the king's table. Now he was lame in both his feet.

The account of David and Mephibosheth introduces the elaboration on David's reign in 2 Samuel 9–24 with a narrative that attempts to demonstrate David's fidelity to his covenant with Jonathan ben Saul in 1 Samuel 21 and his loyalty to the House of Saul throughout 1 Samuel 16–31. David is a member of the House of Saul by virtue of his marriage to Michal bat Saul, even though he opposes her brother Ish-Bosheth and ultimately takes control of the tribes of Israel following Ish-Bosheth's death. Although 2 Samuel 9 presents no inherent critique of David, its intertextual relationship with other texts in Samuel suggests that it is intended to explain and cover for various episodes in David's reign when he acts against the House of Saul, such as his battle against northern Israelite forces at Gibeon in 2 Samuel 2; his refusal to sire a son of the House of Saul with Michal bat Saul in 2 Samuel 6; and his handing over the remaining descendants of Saul to Gibeon for execution in 2 Samuel 21. All of these episodes demonstrate David's interest in advancing his own power and establishing his own dynastic house over against that of Saul (cf. 2 Sam 7). The mockery of David by Shimei, a member of the House of Saul, in 2 Samuel 16, indicates the dissatisfaction of the House of Saul with David's actions. Likewise, the revolt of Sheba in 2 Samuel 20 indicates the dissatisfaction of the northern tribes of Israel, Saul's former kingdom, with David. That dissatisfaction fuels the northern revolt against the House of David at the outset of the reign of King Rehoboam son of Solomon in 1 Kings 12.

Mephibosheth is the son of Jonathan, and David has promised to protect him. Mephibosheth, "from the mouth of shame," is obviously a polemical name, akin to the name Ish-Bosheth for the fourth son of Saul. First Chronicles 9:40 identifies him as Merib-Baal, "Baal contends," which indicates a potential Canaanite background for the House of Saul. Mephibosheth was introduced into the Samuel narrative in 2 Samuel 4:4, which reports that the five-year-old Mephibosheth was crippled in his feet when his nurse dropped him while fleeing from the court of Ish-Bosheth following news of the deaths of Saul and Jonathan at Jezreel. In keeping with his covenant with Jonathan, David inquires concerning the existence of any remaining members of the House of Saul now that David is firmly ensconced on the throne of Israel. Such a request demonstrates David's fidelity, Hebrew, ḥesed, to Jonathan, but it would also confirm his role as a member of the House of Saul who would serve as surrogate father to Jonathan's son, and therefore as the fitting member of the House of Saul to succeed his late father-in-law.

Ziba, a servant of the House of Saul, is brought before David, and he identifies Mephibosheth ben Jonathan as a surviving member of the Saulide dynasty. David's inquiries establish that Mephibosheth is crippled in the feet and living in the house of Machir son of Ammiel in the city of Lo-Debar. Lo-Debar, "no word," or perhaps better, "to him is a word," is a town in the Israelite Trans-Jordan (Li-Debir, Josh 13:26) that has been identified with a number of sites.[40] Machir son of Ammiel, apparently a member of the Machir clan in the Trans-Jordanian territory of Gad or Manasseh near Mahanaim and the Wadi Jabbok, was an ally of Saul.

Mephibosheth did appropriate obeisance to David as his king. David likewise responded appropriately with a pledge to show fidelity to Jonathan by taking care of his son. Mephibosheth would eat at the king's table,

---

[40]   Johannes Unsok Ro, "Lo-Debar," *EBR* 16:986–987; Diana V. Edelman, "Lo-Debar," *ABD* 4:345–346.

which meant that he would be supported by the crown and treated like a son of David, although David also pledged that Mephibosheth would retain all of his ancestral land. But eating at the king's table meant that Mephibosheth had to appear before David at mealtimes, which in turn meant that David could keep an eye on him and control him.

David told Ziba that he and his sons would work Mephibosheth's land to support the family of Mephibosheth as well as his own fifteen sons and twenty grandsons. Such a move ensured that Ziba would know that David had secured his support and that he would expect loyalty from Ziba and sons. The account ends with a notice that Mephibosheth had a son named Mica, which meant that the House of Saul was still intact.

Second Samuel 9 appears to have been written as part of the Solomonic History, which recounts David's rise, but it also functions as an appropriate introduction to the Jehu Dynastic History in 2 Samuel 10–20. Although designed to demonstrate David's fidelity to Jonathan and the House of Saul, 2 Samuel 9 shows a certain caution and concern with controlling the House of Saul by introducing the figure of Ziba, Saul's servant, who will serve as David's agent in overseeing the affairs of Mephibosheth. Later in 2 Samuel 19, David will question Mephibosheth's loyalty to the crown because he remained in Jerusalem during Abshalom's revolt. Although Mephibosheth appropriately explains his actions by noting that he is crippled in the feet and cannot flee with David, Mephibosheth will give up his claims to his father's property, including the crown of Israel, and David will award half of Mephibosheth's estate to Ziba, which will also cripple any efforts of the House of Saul to challenge Davidic rule.

David's Adultery with Bath Sheba – 2 Samuel 10–12

Many interpreters recognize that the account of David's adultery with Bath Sheba in 2 Samuel 10–12 is a self-standing unit within the larger narrative of 2 Samuel 9–24.[41] It appears to be a redactional assemblage in which the account of David's war with King Hanun of Ammon in 2 Samuel 10 presents the background for David's adultery with Bath Sheba and the consequences of his actions, including the murder of Bath Sheba's husband Uriah the Hittite and the birth of David's son, Solomon, in 2 Samuel

---

[41]   Cf. David Toshio Tsumura, *The Second Book of Samuel* (NICOT; Grand Rapids, MI: Eerdmans, 2019), 166–192; Karl Budde, *Die Bücher Samuel* (HCKAT VIII; Tübingen and Leipzig: J.C.B. Mohr [Paul Siebeck], 1902) 246–259.

11–12. Whereas the account of David's war with King Hanun of Ammon in 2 Samuel 10 presents no overt criticism of David, the account of his adultery with Bath Sheba is highly critical. As the analyses of 2 Samuel 10 and 11–12 demonstrate, 2 Samuel 10 appears to have been written as part of the laudatory account of the rise and reign of King David ben Jesse in the Solomonic History, whereas 2 Samuel 11–12 appears to have been written as part of the Jehu Dynastic History, which is so critical of the House of David.[42]

David's War with King Hanun of Ammon – 2 Samuel 10:1–19

10 [1] Some time afterward, the king of the Ammonites died, and his son Hanun succeeded him.

[2] David said, "I will deal loyally with Hanun son of Nahash, just as his father dealt loyally with me." So David sent envoys to console him concerning his father. When David's envoys came into the land of the Ammonites,

[3] the princes of the Ammonites said to their lord Hanun, "Do you really think that David is honoring your father just because he has sent messengers with condolences to you? Has not David sent his envoys to you to search the city, to spy it out, and to overthrow it?"

[4] So Hanun seized David's envoys, shaved off half the beard of each, cut off their garments in the middle at their waists, and sent them away.

[5] When David was told, he sent to meet them, for the men were greatly ashamed. The king said, "Remain at Jericho until your beards have grown and then return."

[6] When the Ammonites saw that they had become odious to David, the Ammonites sent and hired the Arameans of Beth-rehob and the Arameans of Zobah, twenty thousand foot soldiers, as well as the king of Maacah, one thousand men, and the men of Tob, twelve thousand men.

[7] When David heard of it, he sent Joab and all the army of the warriors.

[8] The Ammonites came out and drew up in battle array at the entrance of the gate, but the Arameans of Zobah and of Rehob and the men of Tob and Maacah were by themselves in the open country.

[9] When Joab saw that the battle was set against him both in front and in the rear, he chose some of the picked men of Israel and arrayed them against the Arameans;

---

[42]   Sweeney, *1 and 2 Kings*, 26–30.

¹⁰ the rest of the troops he put in the charge of his brother Abishai, and he arrayed them against the Ammonites.

¹¹ He said, "If the Arameans are too strong for me, then you shall help me, but if the Ammonites are too strong for you, then I will come and help you.

¹² Be strong, and let us be courageous for the sake of our people and for the cities of our God, and may the LORD do what seems good to him."

¹³ So Joab and the people who were with him moved forward into battle against the Arameans, and they fled before him.

¹⁴ When the Ammonites saw that the Arameans fled, they likewise fled before Abishai and entered the city. Then Joab returned from fighting against the Ammonites and came to Jerusalem.

¹⁵ But when the Arameans saw that they had been defeated by Israel, they gathered themselves together.

¹⁶ Hadadezer sent and brought out the Arameans who were beyond the River, and they came to Helam, with Shobach the commander of the army of Hadadezer at their head.

¹⁷ When it was told David, he gathered all Israel together and crossed the Jordan and came to Helam. The Arameans arrayed themselves against David and fought with him.

¹⁸ The Arameans fled before Israel, and David killed of the Arameans seven hundred chariot teams and forty thousand horsemen and wounded Shobach the commander of their army, so that he died there.

¹⁹ When all the kings who were servants of Hadadezer saw that they had been defeated by Israel, they made peace with Israel and became subject to them. So the Arameans were afraid to help the Ammonites any more.

The account of David's war with King Hanun of Ammon in 2 Samuel 10 comprises two major sub-units: Hanun's insolent response to David's embassy, sent to express condolences on the death of Hanun's father Nahash, in 2 Samuel 10:1–5, and the account of the defeat of the Ammonites and their Aramean allies by the Israelite forces sent in response to Hanun's insult.

Second Samuel 10:1–5 presents the cause of the war precipitated by Hanun's response to David's embassy. Hanun ben Nahash is the son of the Ammonite King Nahash, whom Saul had defeated in 1 Samuel 11. Hanun's actions demonstrated that he was just as reckless and lacking in intelligence as his father. Upon news of Nahash's death, David sent an embassy to console Hanun and represent Israel at the funeral, reasoning that he would show fidelity, Hebrew, *ḥesed*, with Hanun, who apparently was to continue as a vassal of Israel. Hanun's response was to insult David's embassy by shaving off one side of each of their beards and cutting off the lower half of their official garments to expose their buttocks before sending them on their way back to Jerusalem. Hanun's reasoning was that David sent them to observe their defenses so that Israel could "search out" the city. The Hebrew term, *lĕhapkāh*, actually means "to overturn it" or "overthrow it," as when G-d overthrew Sodom and Gomorrah (cf. Gen 19:21, 25, 29; Deut 29:22; Jer 20:16; Lam 4:6). Hanun's treatment of David's embassy was a declaration of war.

David advised the men to remain in Jericho, located along the west bank of the Jordan River north of the Dead Sea, to allow their beards to grow back and acquire new clothing before they returned to Jerusalem. David could then assemble his forces for an assault against Ammon.

Second Samuel 10:6–19 recounts the ensuing war. The sub-unit begins with the very surprising statement that the Ammonites "saw that they had become odious to David," as if they had expected some other outcome. They hired the Arameans of Beth Rehob, located in the southern portion of the Beqa' Valley in present-day Lebanon; the Arameans of Zobah (20,000 men), located in the northern portion of the Beqa' (cf. 2 Sam 8:3–8); the King of Maacah (1,000 men), an Aramean kingdom located in the Trans-Jordan to the south of Mt. Hermon and north of Rabbath Ammon;[43] and the men of Tob (12,000 men), an apparently Aramean city and region located in Gilead to the east of the Jordan River and the Sea of Galilee.[44]

Verses 6–14 recount the first battle, presumably at Rabbath Ammon, the Ammonite capital, identified with present-day Amman, Jordan. Rather than lead the Israelite army himself, David sent Joab to lead the army in an effort to quash Hanun's revolt and defeat the Aramean armies summoned to support him. Such a move demonstrates Joab's abilities as a military commander and David's reticence to take on such a task,[45] perhaps due to his advancing age or, more likely, the threat of insurrection

---

[43] D. G. Schley, "Maacah," *ABD* 4:430.

[44] Paul L. Redditt, "Tob," *ABD* 6:583.

[45] Cf. Sophia Katharina Bietenhard, *Das Königsgeneral. Die Heerführertraditionen in der vorstaatlichen und frühen staatlichen Zeit und die Joabgestalt in 2 Sam 2–220; 1 Kön 1–2* (OBO 163; Freiburg: Universitätsverlg; Göttingen: Vandenhoeck & Ruprecht, 1998), 147–167.

at home on the part of dissatisfied subjects in his own federated kingdom (see the revolts by Abshalom in 2 Sam 15–19 and Sheba in 2 Sam 20).

Joab faces a difficult situation. The Ammonite forces position themselves outside the city gate, whereas the combined Aramean forces position themselves out in the open. This arrangement means that if Joab attacks either force, he will expose himself to attack from the rear by the other force. He is therefore compelled to divide his army and take on both forces at once. His tactic is to choose from "the picked of Israel (Hebrew, *bĕḥûrê yiśrā'ēl*, "chosen of Israel," reading with the Qere; i.e., the more capable professional soldiers in David's army), to face the larger Aramean force, leaving the less capable conscripts, under the command of his brother Abishai, to face the Ammonites. Such an arrangement allows either force to support the other in case of need. As a result, Joab was able to defeat the Aramean forces, which prompted the Ammonites to flee into the fortifications of Rabbath Ammon.

Verses 15–19 recount the second battle at Helam. McCarter identifies Helam with the region east of the Sea of Galilee based on a reading of 1 Maccabees 5:26,[46] which explains David's need to cross the Jordan (v. 17). It would place the Aramean advance in the northern Trans-Jordan, which is the typical location through which Aram would attack Israel (e.g., 1 Kgs 22; 2 Kgs 10:32–34). David's forces defeated the Arameans, killing Shobach, the Aramean commander, 700 chariot men, and 40,000 horsemen. The numbers are exaggerated, but the narrative points to a second battle in which the Arameans made peace with Israel and became David's vassals. David's campaign against Aram-Zobah in northern Mesopotamia (2 Sam 8:3–8) would be a third campaign.[47]

The positive portrayal of David indicates the Solomonic History.

David's Adultery with Bath Sheba and the Consequences of His Actions – 2 Samuel 11:1–12:31

11 ¹ In the spring of the year, the time when kings go out to battle, David sent Joab with his officers and all Israel with him; they ravaged the Ammonites and besieged Rabbah. But David remained at Jerusalem.

---

[46] McCarter, *2 Samuel*, 273.
[47] Cf. Younger, *A Political History of the Arameans*, 199–200; Pitard, *Ancient Damascus*, 89–95.

² It happened, late one afternoon when David rose from his couch and was walking about on the roof of the king's house, that he saw from the roof a woman bathing; the woman was very beautiful.

³ David sent someone to inquire about the woman. It was reported, "This is Bathsheba daughter of Eliam, the wife of Uriah the Hittite."

⁴ So David sent messengers to get her, and she came to him, and he lay with her. (Now she was purifying herself after her period.) Then she returned to her house.

⁵ The woman conceived, and she sent and told David, "I am pregnant."

⁶ So David sent word to Joab, "Send me Uriah the Hittite." And Joab sent Uriah to David.

⁷ When Uriah came to him, David asked how Joab and the people fared and how the war was going.

⁸ Then David said to Uriah, "Go down to your house and wash your feet." Uriah went out of the king's house, and there followed him a present from the king.

⁹ But Uriah slept at the entrance of the king's house with all the servants of his lord and did not go down to his house.

¹⁰ When they told David, "Uriah did not go down to his house," David said to Uriah, "You have just come from a journey. Why did you not go down to your house?"

¹¹ Uriah said to David, "The ark and Israel and Judah remain in booths, and my lord Joab and the servants of my lord are camping in the open field; shall I then go to my house to eat and to drink and to lie with my wife? As you live and as your soul lives, I will not do such a thing."

¹² Then David said to Uriah, "Remain here today also, and tomorrow I will send you back." So Uriah remained in Jerusalem that day. On the next day,

¹³ David invited him to eat and drink in his presence and made him drunk, and in the evening he went out to lie on his couch with the servants of his lord, but he did not go down to his house.

¹⁴ In the morning David wrote a letter to Joab and sent it by the hand of Uriah.

¹⁵ In the letter he wrote, "Set Uriah in the forefront of the hardest fighting, and then draw back from him, so that he may be struck down and die."

¹⁶ As Joab kept watch over the city, he assigned Uriah to the place where he knew there were valiant warriors.

[17] The men of the city came out and fought with Joab, and some of the servants of David among the people fell. Uriah the Hittite was killed as well.

[18] Then Joab sent and told David all the news about the fighting,

[19] and he instructed the messenger, "When you have finished telling the king all the news about the fighting,

[20] if the king's anger rises and if he says to you, 'Why did you go so near the city to fight? Did you not know that they would shoot from the wall?

[21] Who killed Abimelech son of Jerubbaal? Did not a woman throw an upper millstone on him from the wall, so that he died at Thebez? Why did you go so near the wall?' then you shall say, 'Your servant Uriah the Hittite is dead, too.'"

[22] So the messenger went and came and told David all that Joab had sent him to tell.

[23] The messenger said to David, "The men gained an advantage over us and came out against us in the field, but we drove them back to the entrance of the gate.

[24] Then the archers shot at your servants from the wall; some of the king's servants are dead, and your servant Uriah the Hittite is dead also."

[25] David said to the messenger, "Thus you shall say to Joab, 'Do not let this matter trouble you, for the sword devours now one and now another; press your attack on the city and overthrow it.' And encourage him."

[26] When the wife of Uriah heard that her husband was dead, she made lamentation for him.

[27] When the mourning was over, David sent and brought her to his house, and she became his wife and bore him a son.

But the thing that David had done displeased the LORD,

12 [1] and the LORD sent Nathan to David. He came to him and said to him, "There were two men in a certain city, the one rich and the other poor.

[2] The rich man had very many flocks and herds,

[3] but the poor man had nothing but one little ewe lamb that he had bought. He brought it up, and it grew up with him and with his children; it used to eat of his meager fare and drink from his cup and lie in his bosom, and it was like a daughter to him.

⁴ Now there came a traveler to the rich man, and he was loath to take one of his own flock or herd to prepare for the wayfarer who had come to him, but he took the poor man's lamb and prepared that for the guest who had come to him."

⁵ Then David's anger was greatly kindled against the man. He said to Nathan, "As the LORD lives, the man who has done this deserves to die;

⁶ he shall restore the lamb fourfold because he did this thing and because he had no pity."

⁷ Nathan said to David, "You are the man! Thus says the LORD, the God of Israel: I anointed you king over Israel, and I rescued you from the hand of Saul;

⁸ I gave you your master's house and your master's wives into your bosom and gave you the house of Israel and of Judah, and if that had been too little, I would have added as much more.

⁹ Why have you despised the word of the LORD, to do what is evil in his sight? You have struck down Uriah the Hittite with the sword and have taken his wife to be your wife and have killed him with the sword of the Ammonites.

¹⁰ Now, therefore, the sword shall never depart from your house, for you have despised me and have taken the wife of Uriah the Hittite to be your wife.

¹¹ Thus says the LORD: I will raise up trouble against you from within your own house, and I will take your wives before your eyes and give them to your neighbor, and he shall lie with your wives in broad daylight.

¹² For you did it secretly, but I will do this thing before all Israel and in broad daylight."

¹³ David said to Nathan, "I have sinned against the LORD." Nathan said to David, "Now the LORD has put away your sin; you shall not die.

¹⁴ Nevertheless, because by this deed you have utterly scorned the LORD, the child born to you shall die."

¹⁵ Then Nathan went to his house.

The LORD struck the child whom Uriah's wife bore to David, and it became very ill.

¹⁶ David therefore pleaded with God for the child; David fasted and went in and lay all night on the ground.

¹⁷ The elders of his house stood beside him urging him to rise from the ground, but he would not, nor did he eat food with them.

¹⁸ On the seventh day the child died. And the servants of David were afraid to tell him that the child was dead, for they said, "While the child was still alive, we spoke to him, and he did not listen to us; how then can we tell him the child is dead? He may do himself some harm."

¹⁹ But when David saw that his servants were whispering together, he perceived that the child was dead, and David said to his servants, "Is the child dead?" They said, "He is dead."

²⁰ Then David rose from the ground, washed, anointed himself, and changed his clothes. He went into the house of the LORD and worshiped; he then went to his own house, and when he asked, they set food before him, and he ate.

²¹ Then his servants said to him, "What is this thing that you have done? You fasted and wept for the child while it was alive, but when the child died, you rose and ate food."

²² He said, "While the child was still alive, I fasted and wept, for I said, 'Who knows? The LORD may be gracious to me, and the child may live.'

²³ But now he is dead; why should I fast? Can I bring him back again? I shall go to him, but he will not return to me."

²⁴ Then David consoled his wife Bathsheba and went to her and lay with her, and she bore a son, and he named him Solomon. The LORD loved him

²⁵ and sent a message by the prophet Nathan, so he named him Jedidiah because of the LORD.

²⁶ Now Joab fought against Rabbah of the Ammonites and took the royal city.

²⁷ Joab sent messengers to David and said, "I have fought against Rabbah; moreover, I have taken the water city.

²⁸ Now, then, gather the rest of the people together, encamp against the city, and take it, lest I myself take the city and it is called by my name."

²⁹ So David gathered all the people together and went to Rabbah and fought against it and took it.

³⁰ He took the crown of Milcom from his head; the weight of it was a talent of gold, and in it was a precious stone, and it was placed on David's head. He also brought forth the spoil of the city, a very great amount.

³¹ He brought out the people who were in it and set them to work with saws and iron picks and iron axes or sent them to the brickworks. Thus he did to all the cities of the Ammonites. Then David and all the people returned to Jerusalem.

The account of David's adultery with Bath Sheba, the wife of Uriah the Hittite, and its consequences in 2 Samuel 11–12 comprises seven sub-units: an introductory statement in 2 Samuel 11:1 concerning the siege of Rabbath Ammon as the context for the narrative; the account of David's adultery with Bath Sheba in 2 Samuel 11:2–5; the account of David's role in the murder of her husband, Uriah the Hittite, in 2 Samuel 11:6–27a; the account of Nathan's confrontation with David in 2 Samuel 11:27b–12:14; the account of the death of David's first son with Bath Sheba in 2 Samuel 12:15–23; the account of the birth of David's second son with Bath Sheba, Solomon, in 2 Samuel 12:24–25; and the account of David's victory over the Ammonites in 2 Samuel 12:26–31.[48]

The introductory statement in 2 Samuel 11:1 provides context for the narrative in that it explains that the Israelite army, under the command of Joab, is besieging Rabbath Ammon while David remains behind in Jerusalem. The NRSVue does not adequately translate the statement, which should read, "At the turn of the year, the time when messengers go out, David sent Joab and his servants with him and all Israel; and they ravaged the Ammonites and they besieged Rabbath (Ammon), but David stayed in Jerusalem." "The turn of the year" would indicate the turn of the first month of the Jewish calendar, Nissan, which precedes Passover in March or April (springtime). The reference to "messenger," Hebrew, *mal'ăkîm*, likely appears due to the repeated references to sending messengers, albeit not always stated explicitly, in 2 Samuel 11:3, 4, 6, 14, 18, 22, 23, 25, 27; 12:27. Many Hebrew, Septuagint, and Peshiṭta manuscripts, either read or presuppose Hebrew, *mĕl'ākîm*, "kings,"[49] which must have been the correct reading.

The verse also points out an irony: David, who made his reputation as a great warrior, stays at home in Jerusalem while Joab leads the army in battle. There would be very good reasons to do so. Joab leads only a part of Israel's military strength, prompting him to request that David gather the rest of the army and come to take credit for the fall of Rabbath Ammon in 2 Samuel 12:26–31. David's kingdom was a federation of Judah, the northern tribes of Israel, the Philistines, and perhaps Moab and Edom. In such a federation, the threat of revolt is real, and someone needs to stay

---

[48] For discussion of 2 Samuel 11–12, see esp. Meir Sternberg, *The Poetics of Biblical Narrative: Ideological Literature and the Drama of Reading* (Bloomington, IN: Indiana University Press, 1987), 186–229.

[49] See Biblia Hebaraica Stuttgartensia note.

home to guard against revolt or attack. But David is aging.[50] Many aging
men seek to demonstrate that they are still the strong, virile man that they
were in younger age. Sitting in Jerusalem with little to do, David indulges
his manhood.

The account of David's adultery with Bath Sheba in 2 Samuel 11:2–5 is
stated in a very perfunctory manner. The narrative begins in 2 Samuel 11:2
with a statement David arose from his couch late one afternoon to walk
about on the roof of his house. Unfortunately, the remains of David's
house have never been identified, but it would likely have been placed on
the northern boundary of the City of David, where Solomon later built his
own palace complex to the south of the Temple (1 Kgs 7). Because the City
of David slopes down to the south of the Temple and palace region, such a
position would give a good view of the houses below.

Bath Sheba is identified as the daughter of Eliam and the wife of Uriah
the Hittite. Eliam is one of David's warriors and the son of David's
counselor, Ahithophel the Gilonite (2 Sam 24:34; note that Eliam is known
as Ammiel in 1 Chr 3:5). Giloh is located southwest of Hebron in the
southern Judean hill country.[51] Ahitophel remained behind to counsel
Absalom during the revolt and ended up committing suicide when
Absalom ignored his advice, ensuring David's victory (2 Sam 15:17;
17:23). Uriah the Hittite is another one of David's warriors (2 Sam
24:39). Although Uriah is identified as a Hittite, he has a YHWHistic
name, indicating his loyalty to David and YHWH. Bath Sheba would be
a member of the Davidic aristocracy.

Although some might suspect that Bath Sheba bathed atop her roof to
bait David, such a claim is unwarranted. The typical Israelite four-room
house is built with a long room against a city defensive wall, with two
rooms extending out from the broad room to form an open, unroofed
courtyard.[52] It might be one or two stories. The broad room is where the
family lives and sleeps, and two extended rooms are used for cattle,
cooking, and storage. There is no privacy for a woman to bathe, and so
the rooftop is the only place for a woman to have any privacy. But given
the downward slope of the City of David from the palace, nothing can hide

---

[50]   For example, Antony F. Campbell, S.J., *2 Samuel* (FOTL VIII; Grand Rapids, MI, and
       Cambridge, UK: Eerdmans, 2005), 97–110.
[51]   Ido Koch, "Giloh," *EBR* 10:282.
[52]   Cf. Ziony Zevit, *The Religions of Ancient Israel* (London and New York: Continuum,
       2001), 100–101.

her from the prying eyes of a middle-aged monarch. David summoned her to his palace, where he had intercourse with her. Deuteronomic law judges a man who commits adultery as subject to a death penalty together with the woman (Deut 22:22–27).

Second Samuel 11:6–27a recounts David's role in the murder of Uriah the Hittite. His action is despicable in that he had just committed adultery with Uriah's wife, and Uriah is portrayed throughout as a loyal servant of David who risks his life for the king. When David receives word that Bath Sheba is pregnant, he knows that this is a problem because Uriah has been away from home during the siege of Rabbath Ammon. David sent messengers to Joab instructing him to send Uriah the Hittite back to Jerusalem. When Uriah appeared before the king, David made perfunctory inquiries about the course of the siege. Upon hearing that all was well, David instructed Uriah to go home "to wash his feet," which indicates sleeping with his wife, to explain why Bath Sheba was pregnant. To facilitate the reunion, David sent "a present of the king," Hebrew, *maśś'at hammelek*, which literally refers to something of the king that must be carried. Most interpreters think it refers to a sumptuous meal from the royal kitchens.

Uriah does not go home as instructed; he spends the night at the entrance of the royal palace with other palace guards. When David questions Uriah, he explained that he could not go home to eat and drink and sleep with his wife when his comrades were risking their lives!

David then wrote a message to Joab to be carried by Uriah, who apparently does not read the message due to propriety or illiteracy. The message instructs Joab to place Uriah in the front lines where the fighting is fiercest and then to pull back his men so that Uriah will be killed. The ever-obedient Joab, who has a long record of eliminating David's problem people, obeys without question. He sent an attack where the best Ammonite warriors were located. When the Ammonites sallied out to defend their city, Uriah and others among David's men were killed.

When Joab sent his report back to David, he instructed the messenger on how to answer David, who would question Joab's actions. Joab's instructions were that if David were to become angry and question Joab's actions, the messenger should respond by telling David that Uriah the Hittite was among those killed. Upon hearing the messenger's report, David was assuaged from his anger and responded that people sometimes die in battle.

With the news that Uriah the Hittite was dead, 2 Samuel 11:26–27a reports that Bath Sheba mourned for her husband, after which David married her and she bore a son. With his marriage to Bath Sheba, David's problem of explaining her pregnancy is solved.

The account of the consequences of David's actions begins in 2 Samuel 11:27b–12:14 with an account of Nathan's confrontation with David. The account begins with a brief introductory statement in 2 Samuel 11:27b concerning YHWH's dissatisfaction with David's actions, and an account concerning Nathan's confrontation per se follows in 2 Samuel 12:1–14. Nathan the prophet has already appeared in 2 Samuel 7, in which he announced YHWH's promise of an eternal dynasty for the House of David coupled with eternal protection for Israel. In this case, the divine promise for David will be qualified. The passage does not rescind YHWH's promise to David, but it states that because of David's actions, the sword will never depart from the House of David and that YHWH will raise up trouble, Hebrew, *rā'â*, "evil," for David's house. In the immediate context, this means the death of David's first son born to Bath Sheba, but in the larger context of the Book of Samuel, it means catastrophe in the royal house, including the rape of David's daughter Tamar by his son Amnon and the murder of Amnon by Tamar's brother Abshalom, to be followed by Abshalom's revolt against David in 2 Samuel 13–19, the revolt of Sheba in 2 Samuel 20, the execution of the sons of the House of Saul in 2 Samuel 21, the plague against Israel due to David's census in 2 Samuel 24, and the deaths of so many of David's family and supporters when Solomon comes to the throne in 1 Kings 1–2. Within the larger context of Kings, it means revolt by the northern tribes of Israel; attack and subjugation by Aram, Assyria, and Babylonia; and ultimately, Babylonian exile and the end of the rule of the House of David.

Nathan's confrontation with David begins in 2 Samuel 12:1–4 when YHWH sends Nathan to David to recount to him a parable about a rich man and a poor man.[53] Second Samuel 12:5–14 then follows with David's outrage at the rich man for taking the poor man's lamb to feed his guest and Nathan's condemnation of David. The outraged David declares that the rich man deserves to die for what he has done, and that he should restore fourfold what he has taken from the poor man. Having sprung the trap, Nathan announces a prophetic prophecy of judgment against David, beginning with the declaration, "You are the man!"

---

53   Campbell, *2 Samuel*, 120–121.

The prophetic oracle of judgment follows in verses 7–12, beginning with the prophetic messenger formula that certified the following oracle by YHWH.[54] YHWH begins the oracle with a summation of all the blessings that YHWH has bestowed on David. The statement of the basis for punishment appears in verses 9–10, beginning with a rhetorical question, "Why have you despised the word of YHWH to do what is evil in his sight?" followed by accusations that David has murdered Uriah the Hittite and taken Uriah's wife as his own. The announcement of punishment then appears in verses 10–12. Although the announcement typically begins with the particle *lākēn*, "therefore," it does not appear here despite the NRSVue translation. Instead, it includes a simple declaration, introduced by *wĕ'attâ*, "and now," that the sword will not depart from the House of David due to his taking Uriah the Hittite's wife. A second announcement of punishment appears in verses 11–12, introduced by the prophetic messenger formula, that YHWH will raise trouble for David's house and that YHWH will take David's wives and give them to another man before the eyes of all Israel. This punishment is fulfilled in 2 Samuel 16:20–23 when Abshalom, on the advice of Ahitophel, enters David's harem and takes David's wives. Ironically, Ahitophel is the grandfather of Bath Sheba.

Nathan's confrontation with David concludes in 2 Samuel 12:13–14 when David admits his sins against YHWH. This enables Nathan to make a statement that YHWH forgives David's sins – which means that David will not be subject to a death penalty such as that stipulated by Deuteronomy 22:23–27. Nathan continues with a further announcement of punishment that David's son with Bath Sheba will die because he had scorned the word of YHWH.

The narrative then turns to the death of the son of David and Bath Sheba in 2 Samuel 12:15–23. After Nathan returned to his own house, YHWH struck the baby with illness. Throughout the Samuel narratives, David clearly loves his sons, but his love for them is so pervasive that he does not discipline them; indeed, David is a poor father who spoils his sons rotten, and this failure on David's part has its consequences when his sons bring chaos to his house throughout the rest of 2 Samuel and 1 Kings 1–2. David prays to YHWH on his son's behalf; he refuses food; he lies all night on the ground; and for a week he rejects the urging of the elders of his house to desist from these actions. But once the baby dies after seven days,

---

[54] For discussion of the prophetic judgment speech and the prophetic messenger formula, see Sweeney, *Isaiah 1–39*, 533–534, 546.

David rises, demands food, washes, changes clothes, and goes to the Temple of YHWH to worship before YHWH. It is not clear what structure might have served as the Temple of YHWH in Jerusalem, because Solomon had not yet built it.

David's actions raise concern among his household. When asked why he mourned while the baby was sick but resumed his normal activities after the baby had died, David responds that he hoped that YHWH might show favor to the baby – as YHWH had done for David from 1 Samuel 16 to the present – but after the baby died, there was nothing more that could be done to save the baby's life. This statement displays a very utilitarian side to David's character and his relationship with YHWH that serves the critique of David in the Jehu Dynastic History.

Second Samuel 12:24–25 then presents a brief narrative that portrays David's consoling Bath Sheba on the death of her son. As a result, their son, Solomon, is born. YHWH loved Solomon and sent a message to David through Nathan that the boy should be named Jedidiah, "beloved of YHWH." Jedidiah apparently was Solomon's personal name, whereas Solomon, which means, "his (YHWH's/El's) peace," would serve as his throne name.

Second Samuel 11–12 recounts Solomon's birth, but charges that the parents were involved in adultery and murder are not the kind of narrative that kings generally present about themselves. The highly critical and questionable account of Solomon's birth best serves the interests of the Jehu Dynastic History, which attempts to undermine the House of David, and the Josianic edition of the DtrH, which presents Josiah as the ideal monarch of the House of David.[55]

The final sub-unit of the narrative in 2 Samuel 12:26–31 returns the reader to the siege of Rabbath Ammon, which began the narrative in 2 Samuel 10. Joab sends word to David that he has conquered "the city of water" but sends a messenger to David to tell him that he should gather the rest of the army and come to complete the conquest of the city. Many capital cities in ancient Israel and the Near East are built with two compounds, one higher and the other lower, (e.g., Hazor, Lachish, and even Jerusalem).[56] The royal complex, which includes the

[55] Marvin A. Sweeney, *King Josiah of Judah: The Lost Messiah of Israel* (Oxford and New York: Oxford University Press, 2001), 93–109.

[56] Amnon Ben Tor, "Hazor," *NEAEHL* 2:594–606; David Usshishkin, "Lachish," *NEAEHL* 3:897–911; Yigal Shiloh, "Jerusalem," *NEAEHL* 2:701–712.

palace and temple, is generally built on high ground and has its own defensive walls, whereas the lower city is where most of the population lives within its own defensive walls that must be breached to reach the royal compound. The water systems of an ancient city are generally to be found in the lower city because water seeks out the lowest levels possible. Joab informs David that he needs to complete the conquest of Rabbath Ammon; otherwise, Joab will get the credit. But Joab is a loyal servant of David, and he makes sure that David's reputation and interests are always served at all costs.[57] David conquered the city and took the crown of "their king," Hebrew, *malkăm*," from upon his head. The NRSVue reads this statement with the Septuagint text of 1 Kings 11:5 and states that David took the crown of Milcom, the god of the Ammonites.[58] The weight of the gold, calculated at one square (Hebrew, *kikar*; i.e., one talent), would weigh some thirty kilograms (sixty-six pounds) or more.[59] Such a weight suggests that the crown is designed for an idol. David took the spoils of the city and set the people to work to rebuild the cities of Ammon.

Revolts against David ben Jesse – 2 Samuel 13:1–20:26

Second Samuel 13–20 presents the revolts against King David son of Jesse by Abshalom and Sheba son of Bichri. The account of Abshalom's revolt in 2 Samuel 13:1–19:44 comprises four major sub-units, beginning with the underlying causes of the revolt in David's failures of leadership in his own house as demonstrated in Amnon's rape of Tamar, Abshalom's murder of Amnon, and Abshalom's ongoing difficulties with David in 2 Samuel 13–14. This is followed by accounts of Abshalom's instigation of the revolt in 2 Samuel 15–16, Ahitophel's suicide as a result of his failure to convince Abshalom of the correct course of action to defeat David in 2 Samuel 17, and David's defeat of Abshalom and his return to Jerusalem in 2 Samuel 18–19. The account of Sheba's revolt in 2 Samuel 20 demonstrates that the issues with Israel are not yet settled.

---

57 Bietenhard, *Das Königsgeneral.*
58 Note that the Greek text of 2 Kingdoms 12:30 (= 2 Samuel 12:30) reads, *Milkol*, perhaps a butchered reference to Milcom.
59 Marvin A. Powell, "Weights and Measures," *ABD* 6:897–908, 905.

David's Failures of Leadership of His Own House – 2 Samuel
13:1–14:33

Second Samuel 13–14 recounts the causes of Abshalom's revolt as a
result of David's failure to demonstrate appropriate leadership in relation to Amnon's rape of his half-sister, Tamar, in 2 Samuel 13:1–22;
Abshalom's murder of Amnon in 2 Samuel 13:23–39; and the return of
Abshalom to David's court following his self-imposed exile to the court
of his grandfather, King Telmai or Geshur, in 2 Samuel 14:1–33. David
fails to act decisively to punish his sons Amnon and Abshalom when
they commit rape and murder, respectively. The result is Abshalom's
disillusionment with his father's leadership, which leads directly to
Abshalom's revolt.

The Rape of Tamar – 2 Samuel 13:1–22

13 ¹ Some time passed. David's son Absalom had a beautiful sister
whose name was Tamar, and David's son Amnon fell in love with
her.

² Amnon was so tormented that he made himself ill because of his sister
Tamar, for she was a virgin, and it seemed impossible to Amnon to do
anything to her.

³ But Amnon had a friend whose name was Jonadab, the son of David's
brother Shimeah, and Jonadab was a very crafty man.

⁴ He said to him, "O son of the king, why are you so haggard morning
after morning? Will you not tell me?" Amnon said to him, "I love
Tamar, my brother Absalom's sister."

⁵ Jonadab said to him, "Lie down on your bed and pretend to be ill, and
when your father comes to see you, say to him, 'Let my sister Tamar
come and give me something to eat and prepare the food in my sight,
so that I may see it and eat it from her hand.'"

⁶ So Amnon lay down and pretended to be ill, and when the king came to
see him, Amnon said to the king, "Please let my sister Tamar come and
make a couple of cakes in my sight, so that I may eat from her hand."

⁷ Then David sent home to Tamar, saying, "Go to your brother Amnon's
house and prepare food for him."

⁸ So Tamar went to her brother Amnon's house, where he was lying
down. She took dough, kneaded it, made cakes in his sight, and baked
the cakes.

⁹ Then she took the pan and set them before him, but he refused to eat. Amnon said, "Send out everyone from me." So everyone went out from him.

¹⁰ Then Amnon said to Tamar, "Bring the food into the chamber so that I may eat from your hand." So Tamar took the cakes she had made and brought them into the chamber to Amnon her brother.

¹¹ But when she brought them near him to eat, he took hold of her and said to her, "Come, lie with me, my sister."

¹² She answered him, "No, my brother, do not force me, for such a thing is not done in Israel; do not do anything so vile!

¹³ As for me, where could I carry my shame? And as for you, you would be as one of the scoundrels in Israel. Now therefore, I beg you, speak to the king, for he will not withhold me from you."

¹⁴ But he would not listen to her, and being stronger than she, he forced her and lay with her.

¹⁵ Then Amnon was seized with a very great loathing for her; indeed, his loathing was even greater than the lust he had felt for her. Amnon said to her, "Get out!"

¹⁶ But she said to him, "No, my brother, for this wrong in sending me away is greater than the other that you did to me." But he would not listen to her.

¹⁷ He called the young man who served him and said, "Put this woman out of my presence and bolt the door after her."

¹⁸ (Now she was wearing an ornamented robe with sleeves, for this is how the virgin daughters of the king were clothed in earlier times.) So his servant put her out and bolted the door after her.

¹⁹ But Tamar put ashes on her head and tore the long robe that she was wearing; she put her hand on her head and went away, crying aloud as she went.

²⁰ Her brother Absalom said to her, "Has Amnon your brother been with you? Be quiet for now, my sister; he is your brother; do not take this to heart." So Tamar remained, a desolate woman, in her brother Absalom's house.

²¹ When King David heard of all these things, he became very angry, but he would not punish his son Amnon because he loved him, for he was his firstborn.

²² But Absalom spoke to Amnon neither good nor bad, for Absalom hated Amnon because he had raped his sister Tamar.

The rape of David's daughter Tamar by his son Amnon demonstrates David's failure of leadership within his own family. Second Samuel 13:1–5 opens with an introduction to the major characters.[60] David's daughter Tamar is the beautiful, virgin sister of David's son Abshalom, who will become the main focus of attention in 2 Samuel 13–19. Abshalom is described in 2 Samuel 3:2–5 as David's third son, born to Maacah, the daughter of King Telmai of Geshur, an Aramean, whose kingdom is located along the northeastern shores of the Sea of Galilee.[61]

The narrator states that Amnon was so madly in love with Tamar that he made himself sick with his infatuation. Amnon is the son of David's wife Ahinoam of Jezreel. He is the first son of David named in 2 Samuel 3:2–5, which suggests that he is the apparent heir of David. The identity of his mother, Ahinoam of Jezreel, is disputed, primarily because she shares the same name as the wife of Saul, although the wife of Saul's full name is Ahinoam daughter of Ahimaaz (1 Sam 14:49, 50),[62] and she is never called Ahinoam of Jezreel. The prophet Nathan states in 2 Samuel 12:6 that YHWH gave David his master's wives, a presumed reference to Ahinoam daughter of Ahimaaz. Gibeah, Saul's capital, and the tribe of Benjamin were punished by the tribes of Israel in Judges 19–21 for their role in the rape of the Levite's concubine, who happened to hail from Beth Lehem, David's home town.[63] After the Benjaminites were defeated and the other tribes had sworn not to give their daughters to the Benjaminites in marriage, a procedure was established by which the men of Benjamin would wait in the vineyards of Shiloh to catch a maiden for marriage in an action that suggests rape. Nevertheless, it is not entirely clear that Ahinoam bat Ahimaaz and Ahinoam of Jezreel are one and the same woman. Amnon is portrayed as a very spoiled and self-entitled young man who lacks qualities of leadership.

[60] Cf. Shimon Bar-Efrat, *Narrative Art in the Bible* (JSOTSup 70; Sheffield: Sheffield Academic Press, 1992), 239–282, esp. 278–279, who argues that the plot of the narrative concerning Amnon and Tamar is built around seven conversations between two characters in the narrative.

[61] Walter C. Bouzard, "Geshur," *EBR* 10:138–139.

[62] See Jon D. Levenson and Baruch Halpern, "The Political Impact of David's Marriages," *JBL* 99 (1980): 507–518, who maintain that Ahinoam of Jezreel is Ahinoam bat Ahimaaz, the wife of Saul.

[63] Robert Polzin, *David and the Deuteronomist: A Literary Study of the Deuteronomic History. Part 3: 2 Samuel* (Bloomington and Indianapolis: Indiana University Press, 1993), 136–138; Marvin A. Sweeney, "Davidic Polemics in the Book of Judges," *VT* 47 (1997): 517–529.

A fourth, minor character is Jonadab son of Shimeah, the brother of David, known as Shammah in 1 Samuel 16:13. Jonadab is ironically described as "a very wise man," Hebrew, *'îš ḥākām mĕ'ōd*, translated as "a very crafty man" in the NRSVue. The nature of his "wisdom" is displayed when he advises Amnon how to rape his sister Tamar.

Second Samuel 13:6–22 recounts how Amnon acted on his cousin's advice. He took to bed and told his father, David, to send Amnon's sister Tamar to tend to him as Jonadab had advised, although he added that she should prepare some cakes that he might eat from her hand. The Hebrew term for "cakes" is *lĕbibôt*, which means literally "hearts." Modern readers might mistake such cakes as a form of Valentine's Day pastry, but the contemporary understanding of the shape of a heart is a relatively modern invention.[64] Tamar made the cakes as requested, but when she came to serve them to her brother, he sent everyone out of the room and asked that she feed them to him by hand. When she did so, he grabbed her by the hand and demanded that she sleep with him. Tamar first begs that he not act shamefully like one of the scoundrels, Hebrew, *nĕbālîm*, often translated as "fools." Her statement that if he were to ask David for permission, David would not deny her to him is controversial. Most interpreters maintain that such an obvious instance of incest would never be permitted (Lev 18; 20), but it is not clear that incest is the primary issue to a man who has no trouble committing adultery with the wife of one of his trusted soldiers. Rather, the issue may be how does one treat a woman who has been raped by a man. Deuteronomy 22:28–29 (cf. Exod 22:15–16) requires that a man who lies with an unengaged virgin is required to marry her, and he may never divorce her.

Having raped Tamar, Amnon's love for her now turns to contempt, which indicates his true nature. He now despises his sister as somehow beneath his self-envisioned high character. He demands that she leave, and Tamar responds that such an act is worse even than the rape, which suggests that the law in Deuteronomy 22:28–29 addresses the actual situation that she has in mind. Tamar is left to cry and lament by throwing dirt on her head and tearing her garment like one in mourning for the dead. Her garment, a *kĕtōnet happassîm*, variously translated as "a coat of many colors" or a "coat/robe with sleeves" (NRSVue) is described as the typical clothing of the king's daughters, but it is also worn by Joseph

---

[64]   Cf. McCarter, *2 Samuel*, 322.

(Gen 37:3), which suggests that it is a garment worn by children of high rank, whether female or male. When Abshalom finds her in the palace crying, he asks if Amnon was the one who did this. Abshalom's question suggests that he already knows the character of his half-brother and has deduced what has happened. He advises Tamar to remain silent over the matter – advice which is all too frequently given to women who have been raped since they are often unjustly accused of enticing the rapist. Abshalom supports his sister for the rest of her life, but his hatred for Amnon has been enflamed.

David hears about the matter, but he does absolutely nothing about it. Such inaction allows Abshalom's hatred to fester and ensures a sorry outcome.

Abshalom's Murder of Amnon – 2 Samuel 13:23–29

13 ²³ After two full years Abshalom had sheepshearers at Baal-hazor, which is near Ephraim, and Abshalom invited all the king's sons.

²⁴ Abshalom came to the king and said, "Your servant has sheepshearers; will the king and his servants please go with your servant?"

²⁵ But the king said to Abshalom, "No, my son, let us not all go, or else we will be burdensome to you." He pressed him, but he would not go but gave him his blessing.

²⁶ Then Abshalom said, "If not, please let my brother Amnon go with us." The king said to him, "Why should he go with you?"

²⁷ But Abshalom pressed him until he let Amnon and all the king's sons go with him. Abshalom made a feast like a king's feast.

²⁸ Then Abshalom commanded his servants, "Watch when Amnon's heart is merry with wine, and when I say to you, 'Strike Amnon,' then kill him. Do not be afraid; have I not myself commanded you? Be courageous and valiant."

²⁹ So the servants of Abshalom did to Amnon as Abshalom had commanded. Then all the king's sons rose, and each mounted his mule and fled.

Abshalom's murder of Amnon in 2 Samuel 13:23–29 takes place two years after the rape of Tamar. He proceeds in a manner far craftier than anything suggested by Jonadab's so-called wisdom. Abshalom begins by inviting David and "his sons" to come to his sheep-shearing festival to be held in Baal-Hazor, identified with the village of el-Khadhr, by Ephrathah, just to the west of Beth Lehem in the tribal territory of Judah.[65] Abshalom's invitation appears to be innocent, but it is likely that he already knew that David would decline. Once David declines, Abshalom suggests that Amnon might come to represent the crown.

Second Samuel 13:28–29 recounts Abshalom's instructions to his servants to wait until Amnon is drunk and then strike him dead without fear because he had ordered them to do so.

The narrative shifts to David and the royal palace in 2 Samuel 13:30–36. Word reached David that all of his sons had been killed, and he immediately tore his garment and lay on the ground in mourning, much as he had done for his first son with Bath Sheba. But Jonadab, the dubious wise man who was with David in the palace, knew better and told David that only Amnon was dead.

The account concludes in 2 Samuel 13:27–39 with a brief notice that Abshalom fled to his grandfather, King Telmai of Geshur, where he would remain for three years. David mourned for his son Abshalom, but he did nothing to address the fact that Abshalom had just committed murder. David's negligence in this matter will enable the situation to devolve further into Abshalom's plans to revolt against his own father. Deuteronomic law forbids murder in principle in Deuteronomy 5:17 (cf. Exod 20:13), and it calls for the execution of a murderer in Deuteronomy 19:11–13 (cf. Exod 21:14). Furthermore, Deuteronomic law calls for the execution of a rebellious son in Deuteronomy 21:18–21. David lacks basic qualities of leadership when it comes to his own sons.

Abshalom's Return to David's Court – 2 Samuel 14:1–33

14 **¹ Now Joab son of Zeruiah perceived that the king's mind was on Abshalom.**

² Joab sent to Tekoa and brought from there a wise woman. He said to her, "Pretend to be a mourner; put on mourning garments, and do not anoint yourself with oil, but behave like a woman who has been mourning many days for the dead.

³ Go to the king and speak to him as follows." And Joab put the words into her mouth.

---

[65]   Levin, "Baal Hazor," *EBR* 3:215–216.

⁴ When the woman of Tekoa came to the king, she fell on her face to the ground and did obeisance and said, "Help, O king!"

⁵ The king asked her, "What is your trouble?" She answered, "Alas, I am a widow; my husband is dead.

⁶ Your servant had two sons, and they fought with one another in the field; there was no one to part them, and one struck the other and killed him.

⁷ Now the whole family has risen against your servant. They say, 'Give up the man who struck his brother, so that we may kill him for the life of his brother whom he murdered, even if we destroy the heir as well.' Thus they would quench my one remaining ember and leave to my husband neither name nor remnant on the face of the earth."

⁸ Then the king said to the woman, "Go to your house, and I will give orders concerning you."

⁹ The woman of Tekoa said to the king, "On me be the guilt, my lord the king, and on my father's house; let the king and his throne be guiltless."

¹⁰ The king said, "If anyone says anything to you, bring him to me, and he shall never touch you again."

¹¹ Then she said, "Please, may the king keep the LORD your God in mind, so that the avenger of blood may kill no more and my son not be destroyed." He said, "As the LORD lives, not one hair of your son shall fall to the ground."

¹² Then the woman said, "Please let your servant speak a word to my lord the king." He said, "Speak."

¹³ The woman said, "Why then have you planned such a thing against the people of God? For in giving this decision the king convicts himself, inasmuch as the king does not bring his banished one home again.

¹⁴ We must all die; we are like water spilled on the ground, which cannot be gathered up. But God will not take away a life; he will devise plans so as not to keep an outcast banished forever from his presence.

¹⁵ Now I have come to say this to my lord the king because the people have made me afraid; your servant thought, 'I will speak to the king; it may be that the king will perform the request of his servant.

¹⁶ For the king will hear and deliver his servant from the hand of the man who would cut both me and my son off from the heritage of God.'

¹⁷ Your servant thought, 'The word of my lord the king will set me at rest,' for my lord the king is like the angel of God, discerning good and evil. The LORD your God be with you!"

¹⁸ Then the king answered the woman, "Do not withhold from me anything I ask you." The woman said, "Let my lord the king speak."

¹⁹ The king said, "Is the hand of Joab with you in all this?" The woman answered and said, "As surely as you live, my lord the king, one cannot turn right or left from anything that my lord the king has said. For it was your servant Joab who commanded me; it was he who put all these words into the mouth of your servant.

²⁰ In order to change the course of affairs your servant Joab did this. But my lord has wisdom like the wisdom of the angel of God to know all things that are on the earth."

²¹ Then the king said to Joab, "Very well, I grant this; go, bring back the young man Absalom."

²² Joab prostrated himself with his face to the ground and did obeisance and blessed the king, and Joab said, "Today your servant knows that I have found favor in your sight, my lord the king, in that the king has granted the request of his servant."

²³ So Joab set off, went to Geshur, and brought Absalom to Jerusalem.

²⁴ The king said, "Let him go to his own house; he is not to come into my presence." So Absalom went to his own house and did not come into the king's presence.

²⁵ Now in all Israel there was no one to be praised so much for his beauty as Absalom; from the sole of his foot to the crown of his head there was no blemish in him.

²⁶ When he cut the hair of his head (for at the end of every year he used to cut it; when it was heavy on him, he cut it), he weighed the hair of his head, two hundred shekels by the king's weight.

²⁷ There were born to Absalom three sons and one daughter whose name was Tamar; she was a beautiful woman.

²⁸ So Absalom lived two full years in Jerusalem without coming into the king's presence.

²⁹ Then Absalom sent for Joab to send him to the king, but Joab would not come to him. He sent a second time, but Joab would not come.

³⁰ Then he said to his servants, "Look, Joab's field is next to mine, and he has barley there; go and set it on fire." So Absalom's servants set the field on fire.

³¹ **Then Joab rose and went to Absalom at his house and said to him, "Why have your servants set my field on fire?"**

³² **Absalom answered Joab, "Look, I sent word to you. Come here that I may send you to the king with the question, 'Why have I come from Geshur? It would be better for me to be there still.' Now let me go into the king's presence; if there is guilt in me, let him kill me!"**

³³ **Then Joab went to the king and told him, and he summoned Absalom. So he came to the king and prostrated himself with his face to the ground before the king, and the king kissed Absalom.**

The Wise Woman of Tekoa is a key figure in 2 Samuel 14, but the true protagonist is Joab, who works behind the scenes to bring the Wise Woman from Tekoa to David's court and to instruct her on what to say.[66] Part of the problem in recognizing the full import of Joab's role is a proper understanding of 2 Samuel 13:39, which states that "David ceased to go out to Absalom because he was comforted concerning Amnon." Most interpreters read this statement as an indication of David's love for his sons. The reading is based on alternative readings to the MT in the Qumran and Greek manuscripts, but those readings are interpretative and meant to reconcile the grammatical difficulties of the proto-Masoretic text with an understanding of David's love for his sons, including Absalom.[67] Such an understanding explains why David did nothing about Abhalom's murder of Amnon. Other factors include his loud mourning over Abshalom's death at the hands of Joab in 2 Samuel 18 as well as his overall failure to discipline his sons even when they commit the most egregious of crimes.

---

[66]   For key studies on 2 Samuel 14, see April D. Westbrook, *"And He Will Take Your Daughters …" Woman Story and the Ethical Evaluation of Monarchy in the David Narrative* (LHBOTS 610; London and New York: Bloomsbury T and T Clark, 2015), 167–184; Larry L. Lyke, *King David with the Wise Woman of Tekoa: The Resonance of Tradition in Parabolic Narrative* (JSOTSup 255; Sheffield: Sheffield Academic Press, 1997).

[67]   Samuel R. Driver, *Notes on The Hebrew Text and The Topography of the Books of Samuel* (Oxford: Clarendon, 1960), 305, who maintains that the text is unreadable due to the combination of a feminine verb with a masculine subject. See LXX, "And the spirit of the king ceased to go out after Absalam"; 4QSamuel^a "[And the spir]it of the king ceased] to go[out after Absha]l[om]"; Frank Moore Cross et al., *Qumran Cave 4. XII. 1–2 Samuel* (DJD 17; Oxford: Clarendon, 2005), 148, 150; Josephus, *Antiquities* 7.181; Julius Wellhausen, *Der Text der Bücher Samuelis* (Göttingen: Vandenhoeck & Ruprecht, 1871), 190–191, 223; A. J. Rosenberg, *The Book of Samuel 2* (Judaica Books of the Bible; Brooklyn, NY: Judaica, 1986), 341.

A Closer Look at Joab's Role in Abshalom's Return to Court

The reading outlined in this section does not fully explain two major aspects of the narrative. One is the parable told by the Wise Woman of Tekoa, who is concerned that if her guilty son is put to death for the murder of her other son, she will have no one left in her family. The other is that David refuses to accept Abshalom in his court, which entails a measure of judgment in David's evaluation of his murderous son. Indeed, Abshalom sets Joab's fields on fire to get him to take action that would allow him to appear before David, even if it means that he would be executed for murder. Fokkelman and Polzin hold that David had planned to go out and seize Abshalom when he fled to the court of his grandfather and bring him back to Jerusalem to stand trial,[68] but he failed to do so after he accepted the death of Amnon due to Amnon's egregious crime.

Such a view prompts rethinking of Joab's role in the narrative. Joab does not act to comfort David for the absence of Abshalom; rather, he acts to restore Abshalom to David's court because of his belief that Abshalom acted justly. Such an understanding indicates a vigilante view of justice (i.e., Abshalom takes matters into his own hands and kills Amnon for his crime), but characters such as David and Joab show little concern for established procedure when undertaking their own actions, such as David's adultery with Bath Sheba, his role in the murder of Uriah, and Joab's role in the murders of Abner and Uriah.

David and Joab are ruthless in getting what they want. Abshalom is ruthless too, and Joab recognizes him as a kindred spirit. But Joab misjudges Abshalom in that he fails to realize the depth of Abshalom's anger, which will lead to revolt against David. Ultimately, Joab will be forced to kill Abshalom in 2 Samuel 18 when he realizes what a threat Abshalom poses to David – and to himself. But at this stage in the narrative, Joab has made a major miscalculation, and both he and David will pay dearly for his failure in judgment: Joab when David instructs Solomon to kill him in 1 Kings 1–2, and David when Abshalom revolts against him and forces him to flee from Jerusalem in 2 Samuel 15–19.

Second Samuel 14:1–33 comprises four major sub-units. The first relates Joab's efforts to set up the audience of the Wise Woman of Tekoa in 2 Samuel 14:1–3. The second recounts the audience of the Wise Woman of Tekoa with David in 2 Samuel 14:4–20. The third recounts David's dispatch of Joab to Geshur to return Abshalom to Jerusalem in 2 Samuel

---

[68]   J. P. Fokkelman, *Narrative Art and Poetry in the Books of Samuel. Volume 1: King David (II Sam. 9–20 & 1 Kings 1–2)* (Assen: Van Gorcum, 1981), 126–129; Polzin, *2 Samuel*, 133, 139–141.

14:21–24. The fourth focuses on Absalom and his efforts to appear before David in 2 Samuel 14:25–33.

Second Samuel 14:1–3 begins with a statement in verse 1 in which Joab recognizes David's preoccupation with Joab. Although 2 Samuel 13:39 indicates (in contrast to the NRSVue) that "David the king had ceased to go out to Absalom" (i.e., David had ceased his interest in bringing Absalom to justice), 2 Samuel 14:1 indicates that David remained preoccupied with Absalom. Joab recognized this problem and took action to resolve the matter by bringing a wise woman from Tekoa to appear before David so that she could play a role in returning Absalom to Jerusalem by speaking a parable about her own sons. The parable is not true; it was only meant to be a ploy, much like the one employed by Nathan in 2 Samuel 12:1–14 to accuse David of wrongdoing. Tekoa, the home of Amos the prophet (Amos 1:1), is a farming village identified with Khirbet Tequa, located some ten miles south of Jerusalem on the boundary between arable land and the Judean desert on the plateau overlooking the Dead Sea.[69] Joab instructs the woman to wear mourning clothes as well as advising what she should say to the king.

The audience of the Wise Woman of Tekoa follows in 2 Samuel 14:4–20. She tells David that she is a widow and that she had two sons who fought each other over some dispute, with the result that one son killed the other. When her clan confronted her to demand that she hand over the guilty son for execution, the woman protested that the death of the surviving son would leave her dead husband without an heir. When David instructed the woman to go home while he reflected on the matter, the woman reassured David that he would remain guiltless. When David advised her that no one would bother her further about the matter, the woman reiterated her plea that David protect her son, and David gave further reassurance.

This last exchange demonstrates that David was intent on protecting her son as she requested, but it also provides the basis on which she would reveal her true purpose to the king. She asks David why he does not apply the same criteria for judgment in his own family. David recognizes that Joab must have put her up to this encounter in a bid to return Absalom to Jerusalem. When David asks her about Joab's involvement, she confirms the king's suspicion.

Second Samuel 14:21–24 recounts David's instructions to Joab to go to Geshur to bring Absalom back to Jerusalem. When Joab returns

---

[69]   Lars Axelsson, "Tekoa," *ABD* 6:343–344.

Absalom to Jerusalem, David instructs him that Absalom should not
appear in court. David's refusal to give an audience to Absalom indicates
that he is not fully satisfied with his son.

Second Samuel 14:25–33 then focuses on Absalom. Verses 25–27 note
that Absalom is very good-looking, a quality that suggests charisma on
his part, much like Saul (cf. 1 Sam 9:2). But the example of Saul demonstrates that good looks do not entail competent leadership. The focus on
Absalom's ample hair (200 shekels would be about five pounds)[70] is
meant to enhance the prior statements about Absalom's good looks, but
it also prepares the reader for the account of Absalom's death in 2 Samuel
18 when his hair is caught in a tree, enabling Joab to kill him. The notice
that Absalom has three sons and a beautiful daughter named Tamar is
perplexing. Later, 2 Samuel 18:18 indicates that Absalom has no sons;
either they died in some unexplained manner or there is a contradiction in
the narrative that no one has adequately resolved. Perhaps it indicates that
the account of Absalom's revolt in 2 Samuel 15–19 has been worked into
a later redactional framework. As for his daughter, either Absalom named
his daughter after his sister, or he adopted his sister.

Finally, verses 28–33 demonstrate how Absalom takes action after two
years of waiting to resolve the matter with David. When Joab takes no
action to present Absalom to David in court, Absalom instructs his own
men to set Joab's field on fire to get Joab's attention. When Joab demands
an explanation, Absalom declares to Joab that he wants to appear before
the king even if it means that he will face execution. Joab arranges the
audience, and when Absalom appears before David, David signals his
acceptance of Joab by kissing him on the forehead. David thereby demonstrates his love for his son, and he clearly is unwilling to prosecute his son
for the crime of murder. But Absalom demonstrates his own uncom-
promising character and his willingness once again to engage in violence to
get what he wants. Both Joab and David fail to recognize the threat that
Absalom poses to the royal house.

Revolts against the House of David – 2 Samuel 15:1–20:26

Interpreters have long recognized that the account of the revolt of
Absalom against his father David in 2 Samuel 15–18 or 15–19 constitutes

---

[70]   Tsumura, *2 Samuel*, 227.

a lengthy, coherent literary unit, largely based on the singular thematic focus on the revolt and the key characters and events that constitute the narrative.[71] Following the initial sub-unit concerning Abshalom's garnering of support among the people of Israel in 2 Samuel 15:1–12, the subsequent sub-units include the account of David's flight from Jerusalem in 2 Samuel 15:13–16:14; the account of Abshalom's entry into Jerusalem, including his consultations with his advisors, in 2 Samuel 16:15–17:23; the account of David's victory over Abshalom, including Joab's killing of Abshalom, in 2 Samuel 17:24–19:9; and David's return to Jerusalem in 2 Samuel 19:10–44. Most interpreters consider Sheba's revolt in 2 Samuel 20:1–22 to be a discrete narrative, but the account concludes in 2 Samuel 20:23–26 with a list of David's officers to indicate who wields authority in the House of David.

Abshalom's Garnering of Support among the People of Israel and Judah – 2 Samuel 15:1–12

15 **[1] After this Absalom provided for himself a chariot and horses and fifty men to run ahead of him.**

[2] Absalom used to rise early and stand beside the road into the gate, and when anyone brought a suit before the king for judgment, Absalom would call out and say, "From what city are you?" When the person said, "Your servant is of such and such a tribe in Israel,"

[3] Absalom would say, "See, your claims are good and right, but there is no one deputed by the king to hear you."

[4] Absalom would also say, "If only I were judge in the land! Then all who had a suit or cause might come to me, and I would give them justice."

[5] Whenever people came near to do obeisance to him, he would put out his hand and take hold of them and kiss them.

[6] Thus Absalom did to every Israelite who came to the king for judgment, so Absalom stole the hearts of the people of Israel.

[7] At the end of four years Absalom said to the king, "Please let me go to Hebron and pay the vow that I have made to the LORD.

---

[71] Campbell, *2 Samuel*, 138–166; Budde, *Samuel*, 268–295; P. Paul Dhorme, *Les livres de Samuel* (EB; Paris: J. Gabalda, 1910), 380–401; Henry Preserved Smith, *The Books of Samuel* (ICC; Edinburgh: T and T Clark, 1899), 339–366.

[8] For your servant made a vow while I lived at Geshur in Aram: If the LORD will indeed bring me back to Jerusalem, then I will serve the LORD in Hebron."

[9] The king said to him, "Go in peace." So he got up and went to Hebron.

[10] But Absalom sent secret messengers throughout all the tribes of Israel, saying, "As soon as you hear the sound of the trumpet, then shout: Absalom has become king at Hebron!"

[11] Two hundred men from Jerusalem went with Absalom; they were invited guests, and they went in innocence, knowing nothing of the matter.

[12] While Absalom was offering the sacrifices, he sent for Ahithophel the Gilonite, David's counselor, from his city Giloh. The conspiracy grew in strength, and the people with Absalom kept increasing.

Second Samuel 15:1–12 recounts Absalom's efforts to garner support among the people of Israel in preparation for his planned revolt against David. The narrative opens with a temporal clause: "(And) after this, Absalom got himself . . ." (NRSVue). The narrative presents a model for leadership in that it demonstrates how a would-be ruler prepares for revolt by gathering the support necessary to overthrow the current monarch, although it also leaves some questions open. Interpreters have argued that with the death of Amnon and the presumed death of Chileab, Absalom is the oldest surviving son of David and the presumed heir to the throne; why should he instigate revolt when the throne will come to him anyway?[72] But such views overlook the fact that the history of the House of David demonstrates that the oldest surviving son is not always the heir to the throne. For example, David chooses Solomon over the older Adonijah in 1 Kings 1–2, and the people of the land choose Jehoahaz ben Josiah over the older Jehoiakim ben Josiah, only to see Pharaoh Necho of Egypt reverse their decision in 2 Kings 23:28–37. Absalom had already murdered Amnon, although he had cause, and his growing anger against his father was clear. There would be doubts about his capacity for leadership. His anger appears to be his primary motive in his revolt; he was unwilling to wait for his father to die or rely on the decision as to which of David's sons might rule in his place. Such a dilemma highlights David's failure to take appropriate action against Amnon or Abshalom for their crimes.

---

[72] Rosenberg, *2 Samuel*, 351–352.

Abshalom takes effective action to garner support among the people. He begins by acquiring a chariot, horses, and fifty men to run before him as his entourage to signal his importance (cf. Adonijah in 1 Kgs 1:5). Abshalom's practice of stationing himself by the gate of Jerusalem to proclaim that he would be a fair judge for the legal cases of the people serves as another effective means to gain support. Such a scenario suggests the potential for judicial corruption on Abshalom's part, but the Samuel narratives have already signaled judicial corruption by David, who failed to do anything when Amnon raped Tamar or when Abshalom murdered Amnon. David's own judicial corruption became evident when Nathan challenged him in court by charging him with adultery in the case of Bath Sheba and the murder of her husband, Uriah the Hittite, when David sat as judge of the people despite his own guilt in 2 Samuel 12:1–14. Deuteronomic law stipulates that the Levitical priests – not the king – should serve as the chief justices of the land in Deuteronomy 16:18–20; 17:8–13 (cf. Deut 17:14–20).

Abshalom's plans for revolt become clear in 2 Samuel 15:7–12. Although v. 7 states that Abshalom requested permission from the king to go to Hebron after forty years, such a time is obviously too long. Most scholars follow the Greek and Syriac versions in reading the time as four years (cf. NRSVue).

The reason for the choice of Hebron to declare the revolt is clear. Hebron is the capital of the tribe of Judah, where David first served as king for seven years. A declaration of Abshalom's kingship in Hebron would legitimize his rule like that of his father and enable him to claim further support among the people. The 200 men sent to fetch Ahitophel from Giloh to support the new king were apparently unaware of Abshalom's plans. But later episodes indicate that Ahitophel is a wise counselor who would give Abshalom sage advice. David would be forced to send Hushai to thwart that advice and thereby ensure Abshalom's defeat (2 Sam 16:15–17:23). Ahitophel, which means, "my brother is a fool," is obviously not his real name and represents a deliberate attempt to malign him, much like the use of Ish-Bosheth for Saul's son Esh-Baal. McCarter suggests that his name might actually be Ahiphelet,[73] which would mean, "my brother delivers." Giloh is in Judah, to the south of Hebron (see Josh 15:48–50).[74]

---

73   McCarter, *2 Samuel*, 357.
74   See McCarter, *2 Samuel*, 357.

David's Flight from Jerusalem – 2 Samuel 15:13–16:14

15 ¹³ A messenger came to David, saying, "The hearts of the Israelites have gone after Absalom."

¹⁴ Then David said to all his officials who were with him at Jerusalem, "Get up! Let us flee, or there will be no escape for us from Absalom. Hurry, or he will soon overtake us, and bring disaster down upon us, and attack the city with the edge of the sword."

¹⁵ The king's officials said to the king, "Your servants are ready to do whatever our lord the king decides."

¹⁶ So the king left, followed by all his household, except ten concubines whom he left behind to look after the house.

¹⁷ The king left, followed by all the people, and they stopped at the last house.

¹⁸ All his officials passed by him, and all the Cherethites, and all the Pelethites, and all the six hundred Gittites who had followed him from Gath passed on before the king.

¹⁹ Then the king said to Ittai the Gittite, "Why are you also coming with us? Go back, and stay with the king, for you are a foreigner and also an exile from your home.

²⁰ You came only yesterday, and shall I today make you wander about with us while I go wherever I can? Go back, and take your kinsfolk with you, and may the LORD show steadfast love and faithfulness to you."

²¹ But Ittai answered the king, "As the LORD lives and as my lord the king lives, wherever my lord the king may be, whether for death or for life, there also your servant will be."

²² David said to Ittai, "Go then, march on." So Ittai the Gittite marched on, with all his men and all the little ones who were with him.

²³ The whole country wept aloud as all the people passed by; the king crossed the Wadi Kidron, and all the people moved on toward the wilderness.

²⁴ Abiathar came up, and Zadok also, with all the Levites, carrying the ark of the covenant of God. They set down the ark of God until the people had all passed out of the city.

²⁵ Then the king said to Zadok, "Carry the ark of God back into the city. If I find favor in the eyes of the LORD, he will bring me back and let me see both it and the place where it stays.

²⁶ But if he says, 'I take no pleasure in you,' here I am, let him do to me what seems good to him."

²⁷ The king also said to the priest Zadok, "Look, go back to the city in peace, you and Abiathar, with your two sons, Ahimaaz your son and Jonathan son of Abiathar.

²⁸ See, I will wait at the fords of the wilderness until word comes from you to inform me."

²⁹ So Zadok and Abiathar carried the ark of God back to Jerusalem, and they remained there.

³⁰ But David went up the ascent of the Mount of Olives, weeping as he went, with his head covered and walking barefoot, and all the people who were with him covered their heads and went up, weeping as they went.

³¹ David was told that Ahithophel was among the conspirators with Absalom. And David said, "O LORD, I pray you, turn the counsel of Ahithophel into foolishness."

³² When David came to the summit, where God was worshiped, Hushai the Archite came to meet him with his coat torn and earth on his head.

³³ David said to him, "If you go on with me, you will be a burden to me.

³⁴ But if you return to the city and say to Absalom, 'I will be your servant, O king; as I have been your father's servant in time past, so now I will be your servant,' then you will defeat for me the counsel of Ahithophel.

³⁵ The priests Zadok and Abiathar will be with you there. So whatever you hear from the king's house, tell it to the priests Zadok and Abiathar.

³⁶ Their two sons are with them there, Zadok's son Ahimaaz and Abiathar's son Jonathan, and by them you shall report to me everything you hear."

³⁷ So Hushai, David's friend, came into the city just as Absalom was entering Jerusalem.

16 When David had passed a little beyond the summit, Ziba the servant of Mephibosheth met him with a couple of donkeys saddled, carrying two hundred loaves of bread, one hundred bunches of raisins, one hundred of summer fruits, and one skin of wine.

² The king said to Ziba, "Why have you brought these?" Ziba answered, "The donkeys are for the king's household to ride, the bread and summer fruit are for the young men to eat, and the wine is for those to drink who faint in the wilderness."

³ The king said, "And where is your master's son?" Ziba said to the king, "He remains in Jerusalem, for he said, 'Today the house of Israel will give me back my grandfather's kingdom.'"

⁴ Then the king said to Ziba, "All that belonged to Mephibosheth is now yours." Ziba said, "I do obeisance; let me find favor in your sight, my lord the king."

⁵ When King David came to Bahurim, a man of the family of the house of Saul came out whose name was Shimei son of Gera; he came out cursing.

⁶ He threw stones at David and at all the servants of King David; now all the people and all the warriors were on his right and on his left.

⁷ Shimei shouted while he cursed, "Out! Out! Murderer! Scoundrel!

⁸ The LORD has avenged on all of you the blood of the house of Saul, in whose place you have reigned, and the LORD has given the kingdom into the hand of your son Absalom. See, disaster has overtaken you, for you are a man of blood."

⁹ Then Abishai son of Zeruiah said to the king, "Why should this dead dog curse my lord the king? Let me go over and take off his head."

¹⁰ But the king said, "What have I to do with you, you sons of Zeruiah? If he is cursing because the LORD has said to him, 'Curse David,' who then shall say, 'Why have you done so?'"

¹¹ David said to Abishai and to all his servants, "My own son seeks my life; how much more now may this Benjaminite! Let him alone, and let him curse, for the LORD has bidden him.

¹² It may be that the LORD will look on my distress, and the LORD will repay me with good for this cursing of me today."

¹³ So David and his men went on the road while Shimei went along on the hillside opposite him and cursed as he went, throwing stones and flinging dust at him.

¹⁴ The king and all the people who were with him arrived weary at the Jordan, and there he refreshed himself.

The account of David's flight from Jerusalem has prompted interpreters to ask why David should leave.[75] Jerusalem is a fortified city, and it is easily defended if one protects the water supply. But Absalom would know Jerusalem well, particularly its weakness in the water system, which opens

---

[75] van Wijk-Bos, *Reading Samuel*, 217; Peter R. Ackroyd, *The Second Book of Samuel* (CBC; Cambridge: Cambridge University Press, 1977) 143.

to the Gihon spring below the city walls. Even if David were able to protect his water sources, he would still face the prospect of siege within his own city by his own subjects; such a scenario would be politically devastating. And even if he were to withstand a siege, the problems between Israel and Judah in his kingdom would remain unsolved, thereby ensuring that they would emerge once again until his rule was overthrown. David's military brilliance is based on his ability to maneuver and outflank his enemies at places where they least expect it. He is not a figure to withstand siege, and so he must cross the Jordan to seek support and choose the ground on which he will fight Absalom – and win.

David's entire household and his 600-man personal army accompany him on his flight from the city. He leaves only ten concubines to guard the royal house, which entails that he means to return.[76] They also give Absalom the means to claim kingship by lying with his father's women. As his men march out of the city, the Cherethites, a group of Aegean or Cretan origins who had been affiliated with the Philistines;[77] the Pelethites, a group of uncertain origin, believed to be Philistine;[78] and the Gittites lead the way. David stops Ittai the Gittite (i.e., a Philistine from Gath) to suggest that he return to Gath because he is a foreigner. The narrative stresses the loyalty of Ittai and his men to David; those who know David best remain loyal.

Verses 23–29 emphasize the weeping of David's people as they leave Jerusalem, but they also point to David's leadership qualities by focusing on his treatment of the Ark. The priests, Zadok and the Levites, together with Abiathar, carry the Ark to flee with David. But David instructs them to remain behind to suggest that the symbol of the presence of YHWH does not flee before Absalom. It also provides one of the means by which David will be informed of Absalom's plans. He instructs Zadok and Abiathar to return the Ark to the city and to employ their sons, Ahimaaz ben Zadok and Jonathan son of Abiathar, to serve as messengers who will report events in the city to David so that he might be informed of Absalom's plans.

The priests are not to be the only source of information and influence for David. Verses 30–37 continue to emphasize the weeping of the people as they flee in mourning barefoot and with heads covered by dirt. But

---

[76] Campbell, *2 Samuel*, 146.
[77] Carl Ehrlich, "Cherethites," *ABD* 1:898–899.
[78] Ehrlich, "Pelethites," *ABD* 5:219.

David is aware of Ahitophel's presence among the conspirators, prompting David to devise a way to thwart the advice of this wise counselor. He encounters Hushai the Archite, a member of a Benjaminite clan (see Josh 16:2), at the top of the Mount of Olives. David enlists Hushai to return to Jerusalem so that he might thwart the counsel of Ahitophel and report on the actions of Absalom and the state of the city by means of Ahimaaz ben Zadok and Jonathan ben Abiathar. This network will prove to be crucial to David.

David's next encounter takes place in 2 Samuel 16:1–4 when he meets Ziba, a servant of Mephibosheth ben Jonathan, shortly after crossing the summit of the Mount of Olives. Ziba brings David a team of two asses, 200 portions of bread, 100 raisin bunches, 100 bunches of summer fruit (perhaps figs), and a jar of wine. Ziba's provisions are similar to those of Abigail in 1 Samuel 25:18, although they are of lesser quantity. When David asks, "Where is your master?" Ziba libels Mephibosheth by claiming that he expects to be restored to the throne of his father. Only later will David learn that Mephibosheth is loyal but unable to flee with him due to the injury in his feet (2 Sam 19:25–31). This presents David with a problem that must be resolved immediately. David acts to his own immediate benefit by declaring that all of Mephibosheth's estate now belongs to Ziba, thereby ensuring Ziba's loyalty at a time when he needs allies most. Later, David will modify his decision to split the difference and award half the estate to Ziba, only to have Mephibosheth declare that Ziba can have it all now that the king is safe. Perhaps Ziba or Mephibosheth is lying, but David's later decision entails that he does not need to know; he rewards both and ensures their loyalty, even if it was falsely proclaimed.

Another encounter with a member of the House of Saul follows in 2 Samuel 16:5–14 near Bahurim, a Benjaminite village northeast of Jerusalem identified with Ras et-Tmim, where David encounters Shimei ben Gera.[79] Shimei, apparently a member of Saul's extended family, the Matrites, hurls stones at David and curses him for his crimes against the family of Saul.[80] These crimes would presumably include taking the throne of Saul and turning the sons of Saul over to the Gibeonites for execution (2 Sam 21). Although David could easily kill Shimei, to do so would be politically unwise as it would demonstrate David's willingness to kill his

---

[79]   Scott C. Jones, "Bahurim," *EBR* 3:345.
[80]   Cf. McCarter, *2 Samuel*, 373.

own subjects at a time of revolt. But David remembers, and at the end of his life he instructs Solomon to kill him (1 Kgs 2:8–9). When Abishai ben Zeruiah, the brother of Joab and commander of David's personal guard, asked why he let Shimei live, David gave a pietistic answer: "If my own son wants to kill me, how much more the Benjaminite whom YHWH instructed? Perhaps YHWH will show mercy to me for sparing his life." Such a position is meant for the ears of all around him to demonstrate David's compassion and piety rather than cruelty and ruthlessness. David's response signals that David is the true King of Israel and that he seeks to resolve this situation without unnecessarily harming his subjects.

Abshalom's Entry into Jerusalem and Consultation with His Advisors – 2 Samuel 16:15–17:23

16 **15** Now Absalom and all the Israelites came to Jerusalem; Ahithophel was with him.

16 When Hushai the Archite, David's friend, came to Absalom, Hushai said to Absalom, "Long live the king! Long live the king!"

17 Absalom said to Hushai, "Is this your loyalty to your friend? Why did you not go with your friend?"

18 Hushai said to Absalom, "No, but the one whom the LORD and this people and all the Israelites have chosen, his I will be, and with him I will remain.

19 Moreover, whom should I serve? Should it not be his son? Just as I have served your father, so I will serve you."

20 Then Absalom said to Ahithophel, "Give us your counsel; what shall we do?"

21 Ahithophel said to Absalom, "Go in to your father's concubines, the ones he has left to look after the house, and all Israel will hear that you have made yourself odious to your father, and the hands of all who are with you will be strengthened."

22 So they pitched a tent for Absalom upon the roof, and Absalom went in to his father's concubines in the sight of all Israel.

23 Now in those days the counsel that Ahithophel gave was as if one consulted the oracle of God, so all the counsel of Ahithophel was esteemed both by David and by Absalom.

17 **1** Moreover Ahithophel said to Absalom, "Let me choose twelve thousand men, and I will set out and pursue David tonight.

² I will come upon him while he is weary and discouraged and throw him into a panic, and all the people who are with him will flee. I will strike down only the king,

³ and I will bring all the people back to you as a bride comes home to her husband. You seek the life of only one man, and all the people will be at peace."

⁴ The advice pleased Absalom and all the elders of Israel.

⁵ Then Absalom said, "Call Hushai the Archite also, and let us hear too what he has to say."

⁶ When Hushai came to Absalom, Absalom said to him, "This is what Ahithophel has said; shall we do as he advises? If not, you tell us."

⁷ Then Hushai said to Absalom, "This time the counsel that Ahithophel has given is not good."

⁸ Hushai continued, "You know that your father and his men are warriors and that they are enraged, like a bear robbed of her cubs in the field. Besides, your father is expert in war; he will not spend the night with the troops.

⁹ Even now he has hidden himself in one of the pits or in some other place. And when some of our troops fall at the first attack, whoever hears it will say, 'There has been a slaughter among the troops who follow Absalom.'

¹⁰ Then even the valiant warrior whose heart is like the heart of a lion will utterly melt with fear, for all Israel knows that your father is a warrior and that those who are with him are valiant warriors.

¹¹ But my counsel is that all Israel be gathered to you, from Dan to Beer-sheba, like the sand by the sea for multitude, and that you go to battle in person.

¹² So we shall come upon him in whatever place he may be found, and we shall light on him as the dew falls on the ground, and he will not survive, nor will any of those with him.

¹³ If he withdraws into a city, then all Israel will bring ropes to that city, and we shall drag it into the valley until not even a pebble is to be found there."

¹⁴ Absalom and all the men of Israel said, "The counsel of Hushai the Archite is better than the counsel of Ahithophel." For the LORD had ordained to defeat the good counsel of Ahithophel, so that the LORD might bring ruin on Absalom.

¹⁵ Then Hushai said to the priests Zadok and Abiathar, "Thus and so did Ahithophel counsel Absalom and the elders of Israel, and thus and so I have counseled.

¹⁶ Therefore send quickly and tell David, 'Do not lodge tonight at the fords of the wilderness, but by all means cross over, lest the king and all the people who are with him be swallowed up.'"

¹⁷ Jonathan and Ahimaaz were waiting at En-rogel; a female slave used to go and tell them, and they would go and tell King David, for they could not risk being seen entering the city.

¹⁸ But a young man saw them and told Absalom, so both of them went away quickly and came to the house of a man at Bahurim who had a well in his courtyard, and they went down into it.

¹⁹ The man's wife took a covering, stretched it over the well's mouth, and spread out grain on it, and nothing was known of it.

²⁰ When Absalom's servants came to the woman at the house, they said, "Where are Ahimaaz and Jonathan?" The woman said to them, "They have crossed over the brook of water." And when they had searched and could not find them, they returned to Jerusalem.

²¹ After they had gone, the men came up out of the well and went and told King David. They said to David, "Go and cross the water quickly, for thus and so has Ahithophel counseled against you."

²² So David and all the people who were with him set out and crossed the Jordan; by daybreak not one was left who had not crossed the Jordan.

²³ When Ahithophel saw that his counsel was not followed, he saddled his donkey and went off home to his own city. He set his house in order and hanged himself; he died and was buried in the tomb of his father.

The account of Abshalom's entry into Jerusalem following David's flight focuses on Abshalom's consultation with his counselors, particularly the successful effort of David's plant, Hushai the Archite, to overturn the wise counsel of Ahitophel and set the stage for Abshalom's defeat. Ahitophel is the grandfather of Bath Sheba and ultimately the great grandfather of Solomon. Although his counsel is wise and would enable Abshalom to achieve victory over David, Ahitophel's willingness to counsel Abshalom would be based in the same outrage concerning David's actions – such as his adultery with Bath Sheba, his role in the murder of Uriah the Hittite, and his failure to act against Amnon following the rape of Tamar – that inflamed the hatred of Abshalom. Ahitophel is the consummate professional and will provide sound political advice even if it endangers the interests of his granddaughter and great grandson. In the end, he falls victim to David's political maneuvering and subterfuge, and he commits suicide when he recognizes what the outcome of Absalom's revolt must be.

The narrative begins in 2 Samuel 16:15–19 with Absalom's entry into Jerusalem and his audience with Hushai the Archite. Absalom is accompanied by Ahitophel, who likely understood its significance even if Absalom did not. Hushai is identified as the "friend" (Hebrew, *rē'a*), a royal official who keeps the king informed of events and issues in the kingdom.[81] Absalom appropriately questions Hushai's loyalty, but Hushai's responds that he is committed to service to the one that YHWH and the people of Israel have chosen as king.

Absalom turns to Ahitophel for counsel in 2 Samuel 16:20–23. Ahitophel advises the new king to enter David's harem and have intercourse with David's ten concubines. Such an act will make Absalom odious to David, and it will demonstrate that Absalom is the true King of Israel, particularly since taking the prior king's women is a bid for recognition as king in the Samuel narratives.[82] Ahitophel's advice is considered true like that of a word (NRSVue, "oracle") from G-d by both David and Absalom. But his advice suggests resentment against David. The tent is set up in the same location from which David observed Bath Sheba in 2 Samuel 10.

Ahitophel in 2 Samuel 17:1–4 advises Absalom to allow him to pick 12,000 men to pursue David immediately and strike while his men are weary before he has a chance to feed and organize them for battle. Ahitophel reasons that an early nighttime attack will throw David's men into a panic. This would allow him to kill David, the key figure in opposition to Absalom, and end the revolt there and then. Verse 3 is a very problematic reading; most interpreters, including the NRSVue, employ the LXX reading, "and I will bring back all the people to you, as a bride (Greek, *hē numphē*; Hebrew, *hakkallâ*, "the bride," in place of MT Hebrew, *hakkōl*, "all") comes home to her husband.[83] You seek the

---

[81] Fox, *In the Service of the King*, 121–128.

[82] Cf. Abner's demand for Rizpah, the concubine of Saul, in 2 Samuel 3:6–11; the statement by Nathan concerning YHWH's giving David his master' wives in 2 Samuel 12:8; and Adonijah's request for Abishag, the concubine of David, in 1 Kings 2:13–25.

[83] The problem goes back to medieval Rabbinic interpretation, see, for example, Rosenberg, *2 Samuel*, 367. For other early, critical discussion, see Otto Thenius, *Die Bücher Samuels* (Leipzig: Weidmann, 1842), 205; Wellhausen, *Samuelis*, 199; Driver, *Notes*, 320–321.

life of one man, and there will be peace for all the people." The expansive reading of the LXX represents an attempt to interpret the difficult Hebrew text, which reads, "and I will return all the people to you, when all return, the man whom you seek, then all the people will be at peace." The phrase, "the man whom you seek," appears to be a syntactically awkward early insertion into the text that focuses only on David in keeping with the larger literary context of the passage. The proto-Masoretic text is unclear, but the LXX does not represent an earlier reading of the Hebrew.

Abshalom then summons Hushai the Archite In 2 Samuel 17:5–6. He recounts Ahitophel's advice to Hushai and properly asks what Hushai thinks in order to get a full response from his advisors. Hushai's commission from David is to overturn the advice of Ahitophel, and he does so in 2 Samuel 17:5–14. He begins by noting that David and his men are experienced warriors who will not panic at the first sign of trouble, as Ahitophel presumes. He continues by observing that David will not sleep in camp with his men; rather, he will be hidden to prevent the surprise attack that Ahitophel envisions. And when some of Abshalom's men fall at the first attack, it is Abshalom's men who will be frightened, not David's men. Hushai then appeals to Abshalom's ego by advising that he first gather the army of all Israel, from Dan to Beer Sheba, and lead them as their king to crush David's men with superior numbers. Even if David takes refuge in a fortified city, Abshalom will have sufficient men to pull down the walls of the city and win the war. Abshalom and the men of Israel like Hushai's advice because it portrays Abshalom at the head of all Israel coming to defeat David.

Second Samuel 17:15–22 then recounts Hushai's efforts to inform David of what Abshalom intends to do. He is unable to bring the priests, Jonathan ben Abiathar and Ahimaaz ben Zadok, into the city to speak with them directly; if anyone sees them in the city, they will know that something is afoot and that the two men will inform David concerning Abshalom's plans. Hushai instead sends a servant girl to inform Jonathan and Ahimaaz concerning Abshalom's plans and Hushai's instructions concerning what David should do. Jonathan and Ahimaaz were at Ein-Rogel, "the spring of the runners," located outside the walls of the southern tip of Jerusalem where the Wadi Hinnom joins the Wadi Kidron, which then flows down the slopes of the Judean hills toward the Jordan Valley and the Dead Sea. Hushai instructs David to cross the Jordan immediately so that Abshalom's men cannot destroy him.

Jonathan and Ahimaaz are nevertheless spotted by a boy, who informs Abshalom. Realizing that search parties will be sent out to find them, Jonathan and Ahimaaz go immediately to the village of Bahurim, northeast of Jerusalem and the home of Shimei, a member of the House of Saul who cursed David as he left Jerusalem (2 Sam 16:5–14).[84] But they went to the house of an unnamed man who obviously supports David. The wife of the man hides the two priests in a well, which she covers with a cloth, spreading grain over the cloth to make it look like a surface used for sorting grain.[85] The ruse works. Once Abshalom's soldiers have returned to Jerusalem, Jonathan and Ahimaaz emerged from the well and went down the slopes to the Jordan. They instructed David to cross the fords immediately and reported Ahitophel's advice.

The final element of this unit appears in 2 Samuel 17:23, in which Ahitophel realizes that his advice has been ignored and that Abshalom's revolt will fail. He knows that when David returns to Jerusalem, his own treason will be punished. Ahitophel therefore returns to his home in Giloh, settles his affairs, and hangs himself. Although suicide is forbidden in Jewish tradition, the text indicates no condemnation. He thereby becomes a tragic figure who joins the other two suicides of the Hebrew Bible, Samson in Judges 16 and Saul in 1 Samuel 31.

David's Victory over Abshalom – 2 Samuel 17:24–19:9 (NRSVue, 19:8)

17 **²⁴ Then David came to Mahanaim, while Abshalom crossed the Jordan with all the men of Israel.**

²⁵ Now Absalom had set Amasa over the army in the place of Joab. Amasa was the son of a man named Ithra the Ishmaelite, who had married Abigal daughter of Nahash, sister of Zeruiah, Joab's mother.

²⁶ The Israelites and Absalom encamped in the land of Gilead.

²⁷ When David came to Mahanaim, Shobi son of Nahash from Rabbah of the Ammonites, and Machir son of Ammiel from Lo-debar, and Barzillai the Gileadite from Rogelim

²⁸ brought beds, basins, and earthen vessels, wheat, barley, meal, parched grain, beans and lentils,

---

84 Jones, "Bahurim," *EBR* 3:345.
85 Cf. Josh 2:6–7, where Rachab hides the Israelite spies.

²⁹ honey and curds, sheep, and cheese from the herd, for David and the people with him to eat, for they said, "The troops are hungry and weary and thirsty in the wilderness."

18 ¹ Then David mustered the men who were with him and set over them commanders of thousands and commanders of hundreds.

² And David sent forth the army: one third under the command of Joab; one third under the command of Abishai son of Zeruiah, Joab's brother; and one third under the command of Ittai the Gittite. The king said to the men, "I myself will also go out with you."

³ But the men said, "You shall not go out. For if we flee, they will not care about us. If half of us die, they will not care about us. But you are worth ten thousand of us; therefore it is better that you send us help from the city."

⁴ The king said to them, "Whatever seems best to you I will do." So the king stood at the side of the gate, while all the army marched out by hundreds and by thousands.

⁵ The king ordered Joab and Abishai and Ittai, saying, "Deal gently for my sake with the young man Absalom." And all the people heard when the king gave orders to all the commanders concerning Absalom.

⁶ So the army went out into the field against Israel, and the battle was fought in the forest of Ephraim.

⁷ The men of Israel were defeated there by the servants of David, and the slaughter there was great on that day, twenty thousand men.

⁸ The battle spread over the face of all the country, and the forest claimed more victims that day than the sword.

⁹ Absalom happened to meet the servants of David. Absalom was riding on his mule, and the mule went under the thick branches of a great oak. His head caught fast in the oak, and he was left hanging between heaven and earth, while the mule that was under him went on.

¹⁰ A man saw it and told Joab, "I saw Absalom hanging in an oak."

¹¹ Joab said to the man who told him, "What, you saw him! Why then did you not strike him there to the ground? I would have been glad to give you ten pieces of silver and a belt."

¹² But the man said to Joab, "Even if I felt in my hand the weight of a thousand pieces of silver, I would not raise my hand against the king's son, for in our hearing the king commanded you and Abishai and Ittai, saying, 'For my sake protect the young man Absalom!'

¹³ On the other hand, if I had dealt treacherously against his life (and there is nothing hidden from the king), then you yourself would have stood aloof."

¹⁴ Joab said, "I will not waste time like this with you." He took three spears in his hand and thrust them into the heart of Absalom while he was still alive in the oak.

¹⁵ And ten young men, Joab's armor-bearers, surrounded Absalom and struck him and killed him.

¹⁶ Then Joab sounded the trumpet, and the troops came back from pursuing Israel, for Joab restrained the troops.

¹⁷ They took Absalom, threw him into a great pit in the forest, and raised over him a very great heap of stones. Meanwhile all the Israelites fled to their homes.

¹⁸ Now Absalom in his lifetime had taken and set up for himself a pillar that is in the King's Valley, for he said, "I have no son to keep my name in remembrance." He called the pillar by his own name; it is called Absalom's Monument to this day.

¹⁹ Then Ahimaaz son of Zadok said, "Let me run and carry tidings to the king that the LORD has delivered him from the power of his enemies."

²⁰ Joab said to him, "You are not to carry tidings today; you may carry tidings another day, but today you shall not do so because the king's son is dead."

²¹ Then Joab said to a Cushite, "Go, tell the king what you have seen." The Cushite bowed before Joab and ran.

²² Then Ahimaaz son of Zadok said again to Joab, "Come what may, let me also run after the Cushite." And Joab said, "Why will you run, my son, seeing that you have no reward for the tidings?"

²³ "Come what may," he said, "I will run." So he said to him, "Run." Then Ahimaaz ran by the way of the Plain and outran the Cushite.

²⁴ Now David was sitting between the two gates. The sentinel went up to the roof of the gate by the wall, and when he looked up he saw a man running alone.

²⁵ The sentinel shouted and told the king. The king said, "If he is alone, there are tidings in his mouth." He kept coming and drew near.

²⁶ Then the sentinel saw another man running, and the sentinel called to the gatekeeper and said, "See, another man running alone!" The king said, "He also is bringing tidings."

²⁷ The sentinel said, "I think the first one runs like Ahimaaz son of Zadok." The king said, "He is a good man and comes with good tidings."

²⁸ Then Ahimaaz cried out to the king, "All is well!" He prostrated himself before the king with his face to the ground and said, "Blessed be the LORD your God, who has delivered up the men who raised their hand against my lord the king."

²⁹ The king said, "Is it well with the young man Absalom?" Ahimaaz answered, "I saw a great tumult when the king's servant Joab sent your servant, but I do not know what it was."

³⁰ The king said, "Turn aside, and stand here." So he turned aside and stood still.

³¹ Then the Cushite came, and the Cushite said, "Good tidings for my lord the king! For the LORD has vindicated you this day, delivering you from the power of all who rose up against you."

³² The king said to the Cushite, "Is it well with the young man Absalom?" The Cushite answered, "May the enemies of my lord the king and all who rise up to do you harm be like that young man."

³³ The king was deeply moved and went up to the chamber over the gate and wept, and as he went he said, "O my son Absalom, my son, my son Absalom! Would I had died instead of you, O Absalom, my son, my son!"

19 ¹ It was told Joab, "The king is weeping and mourning for Absalom."

² So the victory that day was turned into mourning for all the troops, for the troops heard that day, "The king is grieving for his son."

³ The troops stole into the city that day as soldiers steal in who are ashamed when they flee in battle.

⁴ The king covered his face, and the king cried with a loud voice, "O my son Absalom, O Absalom, my son, my son!"

⁵ Then Joab came into the house to the king and said, "Today you have covered with shame the faces of all your officers who have saved your life today, and the lives of your sons and your daughters, and the lives of your wives and your concubines,

⁶ for love of those who hate you and for hatred of those who love you. You have made it clear today that commanders and officers are nothing to you, for I perceive that, if Absalom were alive and all of us were dead today, then you would be pleased.

⁷ **So go out at once and speak kindly to your servants, for I swear by the
LORD, if you do not go, not a man will stay with you this night, and
this will be worse for you than any disaster that has come upon you
from your youth until now."**

⁸ **Then the king got up and took his seat in the gate. The troops were all
told, "See, the king is sitting in the gate," and all the troops came
before the king.**

Meanwhile, all the Israelites had fled to their homes.

David's victory over Abshalom in 2 Samuel 17:24–19:8 begins in 2 Samuel
17:24–29 with David's crossing the Jordan, a notice that Amasa ben Ithra
would lead the Israelite forces against David, and a notice that several of
David's loyal Trans-Jordanian allies, Shobi ben Nahash, Machir ben
Ammiel, and Barzillai the Gileadite, would support him at Mahanaim.

Mahanaim is a key Trans-Jordanian Israelite city in the tribal territory of
Gad (Josh 13:26; cf. 13:30) that served as Ish-Bosheth's capital during his
wars with David (2 Sam 2:8, 12, 29) and as an administrative center during
the reign of Solomon (1 Kgs 4:14).[86] It is also featured as the place where
Jacob divides his family into several camps to ensure the survival of at least
part of the family if Esau attacks (Gen 32–33). Most scholars identify the
site of Mahanaim with Tulu ad-Dhahab, which features two fortified Iron
Age sites that straddle the lower valley of the Wadi Jabbok, prompting the
name, Mahanaim, "two camps" in Hebrew.

Verse 25 identifies Amasa ben Ithra the Israelite as the man chosen by
Abshalom to command the Israelite army. There is some confusion concerning Ithra's identity. Second Chronicles 2:12–17 identifies him as an
Ishmaelite. Amasa's mother and Ithra's wife is identified as Abigal bat
Nahash, the Ammonite king, whom Saul defeated. But Abigal is also
identified as the sister of Zeruiah bat Jesse, Joab's mother and David's
sister. Second Samuel 17:25 identifies Abigal bat Nahash and Zeruiah as
sisters, and 1 Chronicles 2:16 identifies both women as sisters and daughters of Jesse. Perhaps David's mother was married to Nahash and bore
Abigal before she married Jesse, but this solution is speculative.

David's Trans-Jordanian vassals support him lavishly as their suzerain.
Shobi ben Nahash of Rabbath Ammon is the son of Nahash, whom Saul
had defeated. When David conquered Rabbath Ammon in 2 Samuel
10–12, Hanun ben Nahash was king, but with his defeat, David would

---

[86] Detlef Jericke, "Mahanaim," *EBR* 17:529–531.

have likely replaced him with a brother who would be more compliant.[87] Machir ben Ammiel of Lo-Debar, a Trans-Jordanian city of uncertain location,[88] had once given shelter to Mephibosheth ben Jonathan ben Saul (2 Sam 9:4–5) and readily turned him over to David. Machir appears to be an ally of David as there is no hint of tension between them. Barzillai of Rogelim, another Trans-Jordanian site of uncertain location,[89] is also a loyal ally of David. He declined David's invitation to join him in Jerusalem but suggested a substitute (2 Sam 19:32–40).

Second Samuel 18:1–8 recounts the battle per se. Although the victory is David's, he does not actually fight in the battle because of concern for his safety. David divides the army into three columns, and he appoints men in whom he has confidence to lead each, i.e, Joab, Joab's brother Abishai, son of Zeruiah (2 Sam 2:18), and Ittai the Gittite (2 Sam 15:19–23). It appears that David intends to strike the Israelite forces under Amasa in Gilead (2 Sam 7:25) from three different directions with his professional warriors to overwhelm Amasa's militia army.[90]

At the insistence of his men, David remained behind in Mahanaim. He gave orders to his commanders, Joab, Abishai, and Ittai, to "deal gently" (Hebrew, *lĕ'aṭ-lî,* "act gently for me") with Abshalom. Because David made this statement publicly, all the men heard it. David's statement will play a role in demoralizing his own men following Abshalom's death when David weeps for his son, despite the casualties suffered among his own soldiers (see 2 Sam 18:31–19:8). David's men easily defeated Abshalom's army in the Forest of Ephraim. There are questions about the name of the location as Ephraim is located in the hill country of Israel, west of the Jordan, south of Manasseh, and north of Benjamin and Judah.[91] The text claims that 20,000 Israelites died, but it is careful to note that the forest killed more than the battle, apparently in a bid to exonerate David's men from engaging in wholesale slaughter.

Second Samuel 18:9–18 then turns to Abshalom's death. The narrative portrays him riding on his mule alone, perhaps because he was deemed to

---

[87]   Stephen G. Dempster, "Shobi," *ABD* 5:1224–1225.

[88]   Ro, "Lo-Debar," *EBR* 16:986–987.

[89]   Georg Hentschel, "Barzillai," *EBR* 3:578–580.

[90]   Note the battle against Ai in Joshua 8, in which Joshua led a small contingent of attackers against the fortified city but fled before the defenders, which enabled a larger, hidden force to ambush and overwhelm the men of Ai when they came out to attack the fleeing Israelites. Perhaps David has a similar strategy here.

[91]   See McCarter, *2 Samuel,* 405.

be too valuable – or inexperienced – to take part in the battle. But the narrative highlights his vanity when it mentions his abundant hair (2 Sam 14:25–27). He passed under a large oak tree, which had a tangled mass of branches. The tree caught his hair in its branches and left him hanging, alone and vulnerable. When Joab was informed of Absalom's plight, he offered the man ten shekels and a belt, a piece of military equipment for carrying a weapon, to kill Absalom. But the man declined the offer because he was unwilling to kill the king, given David's public demand that Absalom be treated "gently." Such a motif had appeared before when David refused to kill Saul and executed those who had claimed to kill the king (1 Sam 24; 26; 2 Sam 1; 4). But Joab has no such qualms, as he understands the threat posed to David by Absalom; in other instances, Joab has no reservations about killing anyone who posed a threat to his own interests, for example, Abner (2 Sam 3) and Amasa (2 Sam 20). Consequently, Joab took three rods, Hebrew, šĕbāṭîm, "spears" (NRSVue),[92] thrust them into Absalom, and then commanded the ten men with him to finish Absalom. They buried Absalom in the forest and piled rocks over him to mark the grave while the Israelites fled to their homes. Verse 18 highlights Absalom's ego once again by noting that he had built a monument to himself, called "Yad Absalom, "Hand (Monument) of Absalom," because he allegedly had no son to remember his name, even though 2 Samuel 14:27 says that he had three sons and a daughter named Tamar. The location of the monument in the King's Valley, Hebrew, 'ēmeq hammelek, "Valley of the King," is identified with the Kidron Valley where it joins the Hinnom Valley, immediately south of biblical Jerusalem.[93]

Second Samuel 18:19–19:9 turns to the question of informing David about Absalom's death. The question of who informs David of Absalom's death is crucial because David had specifically ordered his commanders to treat Absalom "gently." Given past experience, Joab knows that if he is identified as the killer, he could die. Ahimaaz ben Zadok, the priest, volunteers to convey the bad news to David, but Joab objects, likely due to his recognition that David will kill the messenger and then come after him. He instead appoints a Cushite (i.e., an Ethiopian, and hence a foreigner) to carry the news to David – and suffer the consequences, if David decides to kill him. Nevertheless, Ahimaaz insists that he

---

[92]   See Driver, *Samuel*, 330.
[93]   See McCarter, *2 Samuel*, 408.

will run too, but he takes a route by way of the "Plain," Hebrew, *hakkikkār*, "the round, oval (plain)," the flat, oval-shaped plain of the Jordan River by which it eventually flows into the Dead Sea,[94] to beat the Cushite.

David was sitting between the two gates of the city. Ancient gates were constructed with multiple doors, so that an enemy would have to pass through more than one door, leaving them vulnerable to attack from the upper battlements of the gate structure as they attempted to break through the heavy wooden doors. A watchman posted on the battlements of the upper structure of the gate spotted a runner, apparently the Cushite, approaching the city. David observes that he must have news (of the battle) to report since he is running alone, but then the watchman spots another runner, whom he identifies as Ahimaaz. Ahimaaz reaches David first, and praises YHWH for giving David the victory against those who rise against him. When David asks about Absalom, Ahimaaz diplomatically responds that he saw a large tumult when he left, but he did not know what it was about. Ahimaaz therefore does not say that Absalom is dead, and David commands Ahimaaz to stand aside as the Cushite arrives. David asks the same questions of the Cushite, who states that YHWH has "vindicated," Hebrew, *šāpaṭ*, "judged," David favorably by giving him the victory. When David asks him about Absalom, he responds, "may the enemies of my lord the king and all who rise up to do you harm be like that young man."

David's reaction to the death of Absalom follows in 2 Samuel 9:1–9 (NRSVue 8:33–9:8). Verse 1 (NRSVue, 8:33) begins with the notice that David trembled (Hebrew, *wayyirgaz*; cf. NRSVue, "was deeply moved") upon hearing the news of Absalom's death, and he went up to the upper level of the city gate to weep, crying out, "My son, Absalom! My son! My son! Would that I had died instead of you, Absalom! My son! My son!" so that everyone could hear him. Joab immediately recognized the threat that such behavior posed to David's rule over Israel as he turned what should have been a victory celebration into a bout of mourning for the very man against whom David's men had fought and bled.

Joab spares no words in upbraiding David for his disgraceful behavior. He charges that David loves those who hate him and hates those who love him, that the lives of his men mean nothing to him, and that he would rather that Absalom had lived and that they had died. Joab then bluntly tells David to get up and speak kindly to his men. Otherwise, none will remain.

94   McCarter, *2 Samuel*, 409.

Joab speaks to David what David needs to hear. But David will never forgive him for killing his son; when he is about to die, David will instruct Solomon to kill Joab (1 Kgs 2:5–6).

The final notice appears in verse 9b (NRSVue, verse 8b), which states that the men of Israel had fled to their homes. Although some see this statement as the beginning of the account of David's return to Jerusalem, a Masoretic *setumah*, which defines the end of the paragraph, appears after verse 9 (NRSVue, verse 8) to indicate that this statement concludes verses 6–9 rather than opening the following section. The statement emphasizes that Israel had been defeated but had not remained behind to acknowledge David as their king. It thereby anticipates the account of the northern Israelite revolt led by Sheba son of Bichri in 2 Samuel 20.

David's Return to Jerusalem – 2 Samuel 19:10–44 (NRSVue, 19:9–43)

19 ⁹ All the people were disputing throughout all the tribes of Israel, saying, "The king delivered us from the hand of our enemies and saved us from the hand of the Philistines, and now he has fled out of the land because of Absalom.

¹⁰ But Absalom, whom we anointed over us, is dead in battle. Now therefore why do you say nothing about bringing the king back?"

¹¹ King David sent this message to the priests Zadok and Abiathar, "Say to the elders of Judah, 'Why should you be the last to bring the king back to his house? The talk of all Israel has come to the king.

¹² You are my kin; you are my bone and my flesh; why then should you be the last to bring back the king?'

¹³ And say to Amasa, 'Are you not my bone and my flesh? So may God do to me and more, if you are not the commander of my army from now on, in place of Joab.'"

¹⁴ Amasa swayed the hearts of all the people of Judah as one, and they sent word to the king, "Return, both you and all your servants."

¹⁵ So the king came back to the Jordan, and Judah came to Gilgal to meet the king and to bring him over the Jordan.

¹⁶ Shimei son of Gera, a Benjaminite from Bahurim, hurried to come down with the people of Judah to meet King David;

¹⁷ with him were a thousand people from Benjamin. And Ziba, the servant of the house of Saul, with his fifteen sons and his twenty servants, rushed down to the Jordan ahead of the king

¹⁸ while the crossing was taking place, to bring over the king's household and to do his pleasure.

Shimei son of Gera fell down before the king as he was about to cross the Jordan

¹⁹ and said to the king, "May my lord not hold me guilty or remember how your servant did wrong on the day my lord the king left Jerusalem; may the king not bear it in mind.

²⁰ For your servant knows that I have sinned; therefore, see, I have come this day, the first of all the house of Joseph to come down to meet my lord the king."

²¹ Abishai son of Zeruiah answered, "Shall not Shimei be put to death for this because he cursed the LORD's anointed?"

²² But David said, "What have I to do with you, you sons of Zeruiah, that you should today become an adversary to me? Shall anyone be put to death in Israel this day? For do I not know that I am this day king over Israel?"

²³ The king said to Shimei, "You shall not die." And the king gave him his oath.

²⁴ Mephibosheth grandson of Saul came down to meet the king; he had not taken care of his feet or trimmed his beard or washed his clothes from the day the king left until the day he came back in safety.

²⁵ When he came from Jerusalem to meet the king, the king said to him, "Why did you not go with me, Mephibosheth?"

²⁶ He answered, "My lord, O king, my servant deceived me, for your servant said to him, 'Saddle a donkey for me so that I may ride on it and go with the king.' For your servant is lame.

²⁷ He has slandered your servant to my lord the king. But my lord the king is like the angel of God; do therefore what seems good to you.

²⁸ For all my father's house were doomed to death before my lord the king, but you set your servant among those who eat at your table. What further right have I, then, to appeal to the king?"

²⁹ The king said to him, "Why speak any more of your affairs? I have decided: you and Ziba shall divide the land."

³⁰ Mephibosheth said to the king, "Let him take it all, since my lord the king has arrived home safely."

³¹ Now Barzillai the Gileadite had come down from Rogelim; he went on with the king to the Jordan to escort him over the Jordan.

³² Barzillai was a very aged man, eighty years old. He had provided the king with food while he stayed at Mahanaim, for he was a very wealthy man.

³³ The king said to Barzillai, "Come over with me, and I will provide for you in Jerusalem at my side."

³⁴ But Barzillai said to the king, "How many years have I still to live, that I should go up with the king to Jerusalem?

³⁵ Today I am eighty years old; can I discern what is pleasant and what is not? Can your servant taste what he eats or what he drinks? Can I still listen to the voice of singing men and singing women? Why then should your servant be an added burden to my lord the king?

³⁶ Your servant will go a little way over the Jordan with the king. Why should the king recompense me with such a reward?

³⁷ Please let your servant return, so that I may die in my own town, near the graves of my father and my mother. But here is your servant Chimham; let him go over with my lord the king and do for him whatever seems good to you."

³⁸ The king answered, "Chimham shall go over with me, and I will do for him whatever seems good to you, and all that you desire of me I will do for you."

³⁹ Then all the people crossed over the Jordan, and the king crossed over; the king kissed Barzillai and blessed him, and he returned to his own home.

⁴⁰ The king went on to Gilgal, and Chimham went on with him; all the people of Judah, and also half the people of Israel, brought the king on his way.

⁴¹ Then all the people of Israel came to the king and said to him, "Why have our kindred the people of Judah stolen you away and brought the king and his household over the Jordan and all David's men with him?"

⁴² All the people of Judah answered the people of Israel, "Because the king is near of kin to us. Why then are you angry over this matter? Have we eaten at all at the king's expense? Or has he given us any gift?"

⁴³ But the people of Israel answered the people of Judah, "We have ten shares in the king, and in David also we have more than you. Why then did you despise us? Were we not the first to speak of bringing back our king?" But the words of the people of Judah were fiercer than the words of the people of Israel.

David's return to Jerusalem in 2 Samuel 19:10–44 presents important lessons in leadership. The concluding notice of Israel's departure in 2 Samuel 19:9 (NRSVue, 19:8) indicates that dissatisfaction remains among the tribes of Israel. David must assemble his allies for a public show of support and grant positions of authority to some of those who opposed him in order to re-establish his authority as king.

The first sub-unit appears in 2 Samuel 19:10–15 (NRSVue, 19:9–14), in which David assembles his Judean supporters for his return to Jerusalem. The text begins with the tribes of Israel arguing over their relationship with David, noting that David had saved them from the Philistines, but they nevertheless anointed Absalom as their king. Upon hearing of these disputes, David summons the priests Zadok and Abiathar, who supported him during the revolt, to convince the elders of Judah to show their support for David by escorting him back to Jerusalem. His other move is to make Amasa ben Zeruiah, whom Absalom had appointed as commander of the army against David, as his new army commander in place of Joab. This move suggests that David punishes Joab for his role in the death of Absalom, but it also demonstrates David's need to rebuild his support among some elements of his own tribe of Judah, which also supported Absalom's efforts to dethrone David. As commander of the army under Absalom, Amasa's voice will be very influential in persuading the rebellious Judeans to accept David once again as their king. Furthermore, Amasa is a member of David's family as the son of David's half-sister, Abigal bat Zeruiah, and Ithra (2 Sam 17:25).

The second sub-unit, 2 Samuel 19:16–41 (NRSVue, 19:15–40), focuses on key non-Judean supporters, including Benjaminites such as Shimei ben Gera, who had earlier cursed David, and Ziba, the servant of Mephibosheth who had denounced his master (2 Sam 19:16–24, NRSVue, 19:15–23), Mephibosheth son of Saul (2 Sam 19:25–31, NRSVue, 19:24–30), and Barzillai the Gileadite, who supported David throughout the revolt (2 Sam 19:32–41, NRSVue, 19:31–40).

Second Samuel 19:16–24 (NRSVue, 19:15–23) focuses on Shimei and Ziba. Shimei, a member of the House of Saul, had thrown stones and cursed David as he and his supporters fled from Jerusalem to the Trans-Jordan in 2 Samuel 16:5–14. But now that David has defeated Absalom, Shimei rushes to be the first man of the House of Joseph (i.e., the key Israelite hill country tribes of Benjamin, Ephraim, and Manasseh) to return to David (see v. 21, NRSVue, v. 20). To underscore his support, he is accompanied by 1,000 men of Benjamin. David is a member of the House of Saul due to his marriage to Michal bat Saul, and the support of the Benjaminites will therefore be of utmost importance to the re-establishment of David's throne. David will not forget Shimei's actions as he will instruct Solomon to deal with Shimei in 1 Kings 2:8–9. David needs Shimei, and so he accepts Shimei's support and swears that he will not kill him, despite the insistence of Abishai ben Zeruiah that he do so. That task can be left to Solomon at a later time. Ziba, the servant of the House of Saul, also appears before David with his fifteen sons and twenty servants to escort David back to Jerusalem. Ziba had earlier denounced his master Mephibosheth by claiming that the grandson of Saul had hoped for David's downfall so that he might reclaim the throne (2 Sam 16:1–4).

Second Samuel 19:25–31 (NRSVue, 19:24–30) then turns to Mephibosheth ben Jonathan, whom David had earlier sworn to support (2 Sam 9). Mephibosheth comes to meet David at the Jordan. His unkempt state testifies to his self-neglect due to concern for the welfare of David. When David demands to know why Mephibosheth did not come to support him, Mephibosheth explains that his servant, Ziba, had deceived him. Mephibosheth's statement indicates that Ziba did not saddle an ass for Mephibosheth; instead, he loaded a pair of saddled asses with provisions for David and his men and lied to David about Mephibosheth's intentions (2 Sam 16:1–4). Mephibosheth asserts his loyalty to David with flattering language, claims that his family deserved death for what they had done, and acknowledged David's support by allowing him to eat at the king's table. David is faced with a conundrum: who to believe, Ziba or Mephibosheth? He responds in Solomonic fashion by dividing Mephibosheth's estate between Mephibosheth and Ziba (cf. 1 Kgs 3:16–28). Insofar as Mephibosheth is supported by the king, his declaration that Ziba can have the entire estate demonstrates his loyalty to David. But Mephibosheth's statement also entails that he gives up any claim to his grandfather's throne.

Second Samuel 19:32–41 (NRSVue, 19:31–40) turns to Barzillai the Gileadite, who had supported David and his men with provisions while they stayed at Mahanaim (2 Sam 17:27–29). Barzillai is from the region of Gilead, which lies to the east of the Kinnereth or Sea of Galilee and the Jordan River in territory that is assigned to the tribes of Manasseh and Gad. His name, Barzillai, means, in Aramaic, Son of Zillai, and it may be that he is Ammonite or even Aramean himself, much like Absalom's grandfather, King Talmai ben Ammihud of Geshur, an Aramean kingdom in the Trans-Jordan that was allied with David (2 Sam 13:37–39). Because

Barzillai's support is key to David's survival in Mahanaim, David invites Barzillai to accompany him back to Jerusalem so that he can live there with the support of the king. But Barzillai declines David's invitation, not because he is disloyal but because he is now old and unable to enjoy the pleasures of the royal court. He chooses to stay in his own city, Rogelim, to die near the graves of his parents. In his place, he offers Chimham, whom most interpreters assume is Barzillai's son or grandson. When David crosses the Jordan with his men at Gilgal like Joshua (Jos 3–4), David publicly kisses and blesses Barzillai as a sign of their close relationship as allies.

The final sub-unit appears in 2 Samuel 19:42–44 (NRSVue, 19:41–43), which makes explicit the tension in the relationship between Israel and Judah. The passage asserts that all of the men of Israel – not half as just mentioned in verse 41 (NRSVue, v. 40) – came to David to demand to know why the tribe of Judah "stole" the king away from them by escorting the king across the Jordan. The question entails some disingenuousness on Israel's part because they had fled the scene, although it is not entirely clear that David made sufficient gestures to the northern tribes. The reply of the men of Judah, viz., that they are the kinsmen of David and that they had received no food or gifts from the king, does not satisfy the Israelites. The Israelites claim that they are more powerful (i.e., ten tribes as opposed to only one for Judah) and that they were the first to propose that David come back (2 Sam 19:21; NRSVue, 19:20). Despite these claims, the men of Judah made stronger claims than the men of Israel. The result would be continuing tension between north and south (see 1 Kgs 12).

Sheba's Revolt – 2 Samuel 20:1–26

20 ¹ Now a scoundrel named Sheba son of Bichri, a Benjaminite, happened to be there. He sounded the trumpet and cried out,

"We have no portion in David,

no share in the son of Jesse!

Everyone to your tents, O Israel!"

² So all the people of Israel withdrew from David and followed Sheba son of Bichri, but the people of Judah followed their king steadfastly from the Jordan to Jerusalem.

³ David came to his house at Jerusalem, and the king took the ten concubines whom he had left to look after the house and put them in

a house under guard and provided for them but did not go in to them. So they were shut up until the day of their death, living as if in widowhood.

⁴ Then the king said to Amasa, "Call the men of Judah together to me within three days, and be here yourself."

⁵ So Amasa went to summon Judah, but he delayed beyond the set time that had been appointed him.

⁶ David said to Abishai, "Now Sheba son of Bichri will do us more harm than Absalom; take your lord's servants and pursue him, or he will find fortified cities for himself and escape from us."

⁷ Joab's men went out after him, along with the Cherethites, the Pelethites, and all the warriors; they went out from Jerusalem to pursue Sheba son of Bichri.

⁸ When they were at the large stone that is in Gibeon, Amasa came to meet them. Now Joab was wearing a soldier's garment, and over it was a belt with a sword in its sheath fastened at his waist; as he went forward, it fell out.

⁹ Joab said to Amasa, "Is it well with you, my brother?" And Joab took Amasa by the beard with his right hand to kiss him.

¹⁰ But Amasa did not notice the sword in Joab's hand; Joab struck him in the belly so that his entrails poured out on the ground, and he died. He did not strike a second blow.

Then Joab and his brother Abishai pursued Sheba son of Bichri.

¹¹ And one of Joab's men took his stand by Amasa and said, "Whoever favors Joab, and whoever is for David, let him follow Joab."

¹² Amasa lay wallowing in his blood on the highway, and the man saw that all the people were stopping. Since he saw that all who came by him were stopping, he carried Amasa from the highway into a field and threw a garment over him.

¹³ Once he was removed from the highway, all the people went on after Joab to pursue Sheba son of Bichri.

¹⁴ Sheba passed through all the tribes of Israel to Abel of Beth-maacah, and all the Bichrites assembled and followed him inside.

¹⁵ Joab's forces came and besieged him in Abel of Beth-maacah; they threw up a siege ramp against the city, and it stood against the rampart. Joab's forces were battering the wall to break it down.

¹⁶ Then a wise woman called from the city, "Listen! Listen! Tell Joab, 'Come here, I want to speak to you.'"

¹⁷ He came near her, and the woman said, "Are you Joab?" He answered, "I am." Then she said to him, "Listen to the words of your servant." He answered, "I am listening."

¹⁸ Then she said, "They used to say in the old days, 'Let them inquire at Abel,' and so they would settle a matter.

¹⁹ I am one of those who are peaceable and faithful in Israel; you seek to destroy a city that is a mother in Israel; why will you swallow up the heritage of the LORD?"

²⁰ Joab answered, "Far be it from me, far be it, that I should swallow up or destroy!

²¹ That is not the case! But a man of the hill country of Ephraim called Sheba son of Bichri has lifted up his hand against King David; give him up alone, and I will withdraw from the city." The woman said to Joab, "His head shall be thrown over the wall to you."

²² Then the woman went to all the people with her wise plan. And they cut off the head of Sheba son of Bichri and threw it out to Joab. So he blew the trumpet, and they dispersed from the city, and all went to their homes, while Joab returned to Jerusalem to the king.

²³ Now Joab was in command of all the army of Israel; Benaiah son of Jehoiada was in command of the Cherethites and the Pelethites;

²⁴ Adoram was in charge of the forced labor; Jehoshaphat son of Ahilud was the recorder;

²⁵ Sheva was secretary; Zadok and Abiathar were priests;

²⁶ and Ira the Jairite was also David's priest.

Sheba's revolt against the House of David in 2 Samuel 20 is a discrete episode within the larger literary framework of Samuel, but it is clearly tied to the preceding account of Abshalom's revolt in 2 Samuel 15–19. Abshalom's revolt ended with indications of considerable tension between the northern Israelite tribes that had once constituted Saul's kingdom and the southern tribe of Judah that had constituted David's original kingdom, even though both Israel and Judah joined in Abshalom's revolt. By the end of 2 Samuel 19, Judah had given their full support to David, whereas the northern tribes continued to believe that they had been neglected. There were also lingering tensions with the tribe of Benjamin, as demonstrated by the actions of Shimei ben Gera during David's flight from Jerusalem in 2 Samuel 16, although Shimei willingly submitted to David in 2 Samuel 19. The tensions with northern Israel would continue to simmer through the reign of Solomon as well, insofar as Solomon ruled the northern tribes as vassals, as indicated by his imposition of a state corvée, an obligation that was not imposed on his own tribe of Judah (1 Kgs 4–5).[95] Ultimately, Solomon's treatment of northern Israel proved to be the cause of their revolt against Solomon's son, Rehoboam, in 1 Kings 12. Sheba's battle cry in verse 1, "We have no portion in David, no share in the son of Jesse! Everyone to your tents, O Israel!" is nearly identical to the battle cry of the northern Israelite tribes when they revolted against Rehoboam in 1 Kings 12:16. Finally, there was the question of Amasa ben Ithra, David's great nephew due to his descent from Zeruiah, David's sister. Absalom had appointed Amasa as commander of the army in place of Joab (2 Sam 17:25). David left Amasa in command to attract the loyalty of the northern tribes, but Joab would resolve this matter in his customary fashion.

The notice in verses 2–3 focuses on David's concubines, taken by Absalom when David fled Jerusalem. Each of these women would have been given to David as part of an agreement with, for example, a city, a town, or a foreign kingdom that was allied with David, insofar as alliances would have been sealed with some form of marriage between the allies and the House of David. Their families would be concerned with their welfare. Because Absalom had lain with them, they were no longer available to David (cf. Lev 18:8; 20:11; Deut 24:1–4). But David ensures their future welfare, although they would be living widows (like Michal) since they would never again have relations with David and never bear children, who support women in old age.

Verses 4–22 turn to the campaign against Sheba son of Bichri. The first sub-unit, in verses 4–10a, takes up Amasa son of Ithra, whom David had appointed as commander of the army. He had also served as commander of the army under Absalom. David retained him because he was married to David's grandniece, Abigal daughter of Zeruiah, and because he was a useful asset who could bring the men of Israel back to David. But Joab had been replaced as army commander.

When David ordered Amasa to muster the men of Judah to pursue Sheba, he wanted the order carried out in three days. This is a difficult task in an age that lacked modern communication, although it could be accomplished by a combination of fire signals and runners. Joab was looking for an opportunity to get rid of Amasa, much as he had dispatched Abner and

---

[95] For discussion, see Sweeney, *1 and 2 Kings*, 82–95.

Abshalom. Amasa's delay in carrying out David's orders gave Joab the opening he needed.

Joab was still commander of David's royal guard (i.e., the Cherethites, the Pelethites, and the other warriors who marched with them). They, too, marched out to put down the revolt, and they assembled near the "large stone" at Gibeon, which might refer to the altar erected by Saul during his successful campaign against the Philistines at Gibeon (1 Sam 14:31–35). Joab approached Amasa, allegedly to greet him with a kiss of friendship. When Joab's sword "fell out" (i.e., protruded from under his garment), Joab could grasp it easily and kill Amasa.

Verses 10b–13 then depict the men of the army marching past Amasa as Joab and Abishai take charge of the operation to end the revolt. Joab left a trusted man to stand by Amasa's body as the men marched by, pausing to look at Amasa on the ground. Although the text states that Amasa is dead in verse 10a, verse 12 employs the verb, *mitgōlēl*, "wallowing (NRSVue, lit., 'causing himself to roll') in his blood," indicating that he did not die immediately. Once Amasa's motion ceased, Joab's man dragged him off the road and covered him with a garment as the men marched on after Joab and Abishai. Command of the army was settled.

Verses 14–15a then portray Sheba's flight to Abel Beth Maacah, identified with Tel Abel Beth Maacah, located in the territory of Naphtali or Dan some eight or nine miles west of the city of Dan.[96] The location indicates that Sheba was compelled to travel through the entire territory of the northern tribes of Israel to gain support.

Verses 15b–22 portray the negotiation with Joab initiated by the wise woman of Abel Beth Maacah.[97] She points out that the city has a reputation as a place of peace in which negotiation can take place, thereby eliminating the need for military action. Joab responds that this conflict can be settled by handing over one man, Sheba ben Bichri, who has revolted against David, much as Abshalom's revolt was settled with the life of Abshalom himself. Once Sheba's head was thrown to Joab over the wall of the city, the revolt was over.

Second Samuel 20:23–26 then presents a list of David's chief officers, much like 2 Samuel 8:15–18, albeit with some changes. Joab is again commander of the army. Benaiah ben Jehoiada is commander of the Cherethites and Perethites as before. Adoram is in charge of forced labor,

96   Michael T. David, "Abel-Beth-Maacah," *EBR* 1:67–68.
97   Westbrook, *And He Will Take Your Daughters*, 187–207.

Hebrew, *mas*, "tax, corvée," a new office that corresponds to Adoniram ben Abda in the list of Solomon's officers in 1 Kings 4:6. Forced labor refers to the obligation of the northern tribes of Israel as specified in 1 Kings 4, but the tribe of Judah was not obligated for such service. This obligation was apparently to control Israel, especially following the revolt. Jehoshaphat ben Ahilud is the recorder as before. Sheva is the scribe, apparently identified with Seraiah, a variant of the name, as before.[98] Zadok and Abiathar are the priests, much as Zadok ben Ahitub and Ahimelech ben Abiathar had served before. Ira the Jairite, apparently a non-Levite, serves as David's priest, whereas David's sons had previously served as priests.[99] As noted from the service of Samuel's and David's sons – all non-Levites – as priests in Samuel, Ira's service represents the service of first-born sons as priests prior to the designation of the Levites for such roles.[100] Given the behavior of David's sons Amnon and Abshalom, both first-born sons to their mothers, it is not surprising to find a new person appointed in their place.

Further Actions by King David ben Jesse of Israel and Judah – 2 Samuel 21:1–24:25

Most contemporary interpreters view 2 Samuel 21–24 as an appendix for the Book of Samuel, but such a view is based on the diachronic reading of the book as a collection of narratives that were composed in specific historical contexts with specific theological, political, historical, or literary intent, most notably, the so-called Succession Narrative in 2 Samuel 9–20. In such a view, 2 Samuel 21–24 can only serve as an appendix or appendices to the much larger and focused narrative concerning the succession to David's throne. But the rise of synchronic reading strategies, with their foci on literary plot development and characterization, call for a different strategy that examines the literary form and function of sub-units within a larger literary framework. Second Samuel 21–24 emerges not as a series of appendices to a larger, historically based composition but as a sequence of literary elements that contribute to a larger literary work.

---

[98] Anderson, *2 Samuel*, 245.
[99] McCarter, *2 Samuel*, 434, argues that Ira is from Gilead, which makes sense given David's need to control the area following Absalom's revolt.
[100] Sweeney, "Samuel's Institutional Identity"; Sweeney, The Literary-Historical Dimensions of Intertextuality in Exodus–Numbers."

A Closer Look at the So-Called Appendices in 2 Samuel 21–24

In earlier diachronic analysis of Samuel, interpreters followed Budde in viewing 2 Samuel 21–24 as a collection of six smaller, diachronically defined units, that were successively added to the book following the so-called Succession Narrative, that is, 2 Samuel 21:1–14; 24; 21:15–22; 23:8–39; 22; and 23:1–7.[101] But as later interpreters struggled in their attempts to define a convincing diachronic model for the presence of an appendix that interrupts the so-called Succession Narrative that concludes in 1 Kings 1–2, they raised questions concerning the Succession Narrative hypothesis and even diachronic analysis itself. Campbell, who is firmly rooted in diachronic form-critical research, began to speak about the literary characteristics of the Samuel narratives and argued that 2 Samuel 21–24 constitutes a third wave in the formation of the book following the stories of David's rise to power and the stories of David's middle years.[102]

The units in 2 Samuel 21–24 include varying generic elements: three accounts of David's actions, including the account of David's disposition of the sons of Saul in 2 Samuel 21:1–14, the account of David's battles against the Philistine giants in 2 Samuel 21:15–22, and the account of David's selection of the threshing floor or Araunah as the site for the future Temple in 2 Samuel 24; two psalmic compositions attributed to David, including David's thanksgiving psalm in 2 Samuel 22 and his last words in 2 Samuel 23:1–7; and one list of David's warriors in 2 Samuel 23:8–39. The generic character of these elements indicates that the three accounts of David's actions, each introduced by a *waw*-consecutive formation, constitute the basic narrative structural elements; the two psalmic compositions, each introduced by either a *waw*-consecutive or conjunctive *waw* formation, express, respectively, David's gratitude to YHWH for defending him and his confirmation of his eternal covenant with YHWH in the aftermath of his victories over the Philistines; and finally the list of David's warriors elaborates on David's warriors, who play such an important role in his battles.

The formal literary structure of the narratives would follow on the accounts of Abshalom's revolt in 2 Samuel 15–19 and Sheba's revolt in 2 Samuel 20 with the account of David's disposition of Saul's sons in 2 Samuel 21:1–14; the account of David's wars with the Philistine giants in 2 Samuel 21:15–23:39, including the account proper in 2 Samuel 21:15–22, followed by the two psalms in 2 Samuel 22 and 2 Samuel 23:1–7, and closed by the list of David's warriors in 2 Samuel 23:8–39; and finally, the account of David's selection of the threshing floor of Araunah in 2 Samuel 24:1–25.

---

[101] Budde, *Samuel*, 304.
[102] Campbell, *2 Samuel*, 184–210; Antony F. Campbell, S.J., "2 Samuel 21–24: The Enigma Factor," in *For and Against David. Story and History in the Books of Samuel*, ed., A. G. Auld and E. Eynikel, BETL 132 (Leuven: Petters, 2010), 347–358.

There are diachronic considerations as well. The first two accounts in 2 Samuel 21:1–14 and 2 Samuel 21:15–23:39 are retrospective and may have formed an earlier closure to the Book of Samuel. The account in 2 Samuel 24 is prospective in that it anticipates the building of Solomon's Temple in 1 Kings 6. Such a prospective view indicates an interest in linking the narratives of Samuel with those of Kings. All three portray David carrying out essential tasks during his reign, but each raises question about David. David's capacity to eliminate the House of Saul by turning his descendants over to the Gibeonites for execution in 2 Samuel 21:1–14 suggests murderous intent against the House of Saul; the role of Elhanan ben Jaare-oregim in the killing of Goliath in 2 Samuel 21:19 suggests that David took credit for the action of one of his men; and the selection of the threshing floor of Araunah as the site of the future Temple comes as a result of YHWH's dissatisfaction with David's census in 2 Samuel 24. Such questions about David are analogous to those raised about David in 2 Samuel 10–12; 13–14; 15–19; and 20, indicating that the narratives in 2 Samuel 21–24 were also written or edited by the Jehu Dynastic History, which critiques the House of David and the prior ruling houses of northern Israel to justify its own rule over Israel.

David's Disposition of the Sons of Saul – 2 Samuel 21:1–14

21 **1** Now there was a famine in the days of David for three years, year after year, and David inquired of the LORD. The LORD said, "There is bloodguilt on Saul and on his house because he put the Gibeonites to death."

2 So the king called the Gibeonites and spoke to them. (Now the Gibeonites were not of the people of Israel but of the remnant of the Amorites; although the people of Israel had sworn to spare them, Saul had tried to wipe them out in his zeal for the people of Israel and Judah.)

3 David said to the Gibeonites, "What shall I do for you? How shall I make expiation, that you may bless the heritage of the LORD?"

4 The Gibeonites said to him, "It is not a matter of silver or gold between us and Saul or his house; neither is it for us to put anyone to death in Israel." He said, "What do you say that I should do for you?"

5 They said to the king, "The man who consumed us and planned to destroy us so that we should have no place in all the territory of Israel,

6 let seven of his sons be handed over to us, and we will impale them before the LORD at Gibeon on the mountain of the LORD." The king said, "I will hand them over."

⁷ But the king spared Mephibosheth, the son of Saul's son Jonathan, because of the oath of the Lord that was between them, between David and Jonathan son of Saul.

⁸ The king took the two sons of Rizpah daughter of Aiah, whom she bore to Saul, Armoni and Mephibosheth; and the five sons of Merab daughter of Saul, whom she bore to Adriel son of Barzillai the Meholathite;

⁹ he gave them into the hands of the Gibeonites, and they impaled them on the mountain before the Lord. The seven of them perished together. They were put to death in the first days of harvest, at the beginning of barley harvest.

¹⁰ Then Rizpah the daughter of Aiah took sackcloth and spread it on a rock for herself, from the beginning of harvest until rain fell on them from the heavens; she did not allow the birds of the air to come on the bodies by day or the wild animals by night.

¹¹ When David was told what Rizpah daughter of Aiah, the concubine of Saul, had done,

¹² David went and took the bones of Saul and the bones of his son Jonathan from the people of Jabesh-gilead, who had stolen them from the public square of Beth-shan, where the Philistines had hung them up, on the day the Philistines killed Saul on Gilboa.

¹³ He brought up from there the bones of Saul and the bones of his son Jonathan, and they gathered the bones of those who had been impaled.

¹⁴ They buried the bones of Saul and of his son Jonathan in the land of Benjamin in Zela, in the tomb of his father Kish; they did all that the king commanded. After that, God heeded supplications for the land.

Second Samuel 21:1–14 recounts David's disposition of the sons of Saul to the Gibeonites, who pressed a blood claim against the House of Saul. The narrative comprises two major sub-units: David's response to the claim of the Gibeonites in 2 Samuel 21:1–9 and the proper burial of Saul, Jonathan, and the descendants of Saul executed by the Gibeonites in 2 Samuel 21:10–14.

David's response to the blood claim of the Gibeonites in 2 Samuel 21:1–9 begins with the notice of a three-year famine in the land in verse 1, which prompts an oracular inquiry by David. The response indicates that YHWH is dissatisfied because Gibeon has an unresolved blood claim against the House of Saul. Gibeon, identified with Tel el-Jib, some five

miles northwest of Jerusalem,[103] is the Canaanite city featured in Joshua
9–10 that made an alliance with Israel, enabling Joshua to defeat the
southern Canaanite kings and take possession of their territories. Earlier
narratives in 1 Samuel 21–30 recount David's efforts to defend himself and
Judah against Saul, but there is no account of Saul's direct assault against
Gibeon. However, 2 Samuel 2 offers a solution, although Saul was dead and
his son, Ish-Bosheth, ruled Israel. Ish-Bosheth's army, led by Abner,
attacked Gibeon, apparently in an effort to force it to submit to the
House of Saul. But David, a Philistine vassal, defended Gibeon. The
Gibeonite claim may be based on this attack.

When David inquires of the Gibeonites in verses 2–6 as to what will
settle their claim, the Gibeonites respond that they require the lives of
seven sons of the man who sought to destroy them despite their agreement
with Israel. The Gibeonites make it clear that they planned to execute the
seven sons (including grandsons) of Saul by impalement, a common form
of execution in the ancient Near Eastern world.[104] The timing of the
execution with the barley harvest (March-April), would have coincided
with Passover, which celebrates the beginning of the first fruits harvest.[105]
Barley matures earlier than wheat, and the execution of Saul's sons was
apparently meant to appeal to the deity for relief from the famine.

Second Samuel 21:7–9 indicates that David spared Mephibosheth, the
son of Jonathan and grandson of Saul, due to his oath to Jonathan (1 Sam
18:1–3; 20:17; 20:41–42). David instead turns over the sons of Saul by his
concubine Rizpah daughter of Aiah (i.e., Armoni and Mephibosheth;
2 Sam 3:7–11) and the five sons of Merab bat Saul,[106] fathered by her
husband, Adriel ben Barzillai the Meholathite. Barzillai the Gileadite is
David's ally (2 Sam 18:28–29; 19:32–39), and so Adriel's father, Barzillai
the Meholathite, is not the same man. Meholah is identified with Abel-

---

[103] Jeffrey Chadwick, "Gibeon, Gibeonites," *EBR* 10:217–219; James B. Pritchard, "Gibeon,"
       NEAEHL 2:511–514.
[104] The meaning of the Hiphil form of the Hebrew verb *yq'*, "to display with broken legs
       and arms," is disputed, although impalement is a common understanding of the term
       (*HALOT* 2:431). Impalement entails hanging a live person on a pole, often with the legs
       and arms pierced or broken, as in Roman crucifixion. For a visual depiction of Assyrian
       impalement by Sennacherib, see his relief of the siege of Lachish, *ANEP* 372–373,
       esp. 373, lower right, which depicts three men impaled on poles.
[105] Samantha Joo, "Barley (Hordeum Vulgare)," *EBR* 3:516–517.
[106] Second Samuel 21:8 identifies Michal as their mother, but this is impossible as Michal
       died childless (2 Samuel 6:23), and Merab was the wife of Adriel ben Barzillai the
       Meholathite (1 Samuel 18:19; see LXX Codex Coislinianus; Peshitta; Targum Jonathan,
       and the discussion in McCarter, *2 Samuel*, 439).

Meholah (Judg 7:22; 1 Kgs 4:12; 19:16), located on the Wadi Yabis, east of
the Jordan.[107] Upon hearing of Rizpah's attempts to protect the bodies of
her sons and grandnephews, David transferred the bones of Saul and
Jonathan from Jabesh Gilead together with the seven executed descendants
of Saul to the tomb of Saul's father, Kish, in Zela, an unknown site located
in Benjamin.[108] Once David carried out this burial, YHWH (G-d) ended
the famine.

David's Victories over the Philistine Giants – 2 Samuel 21:15–23:39

21 [15] The Philistines went to war again with Israel, and David went
down together with his servants. They fought against the
Philistines, and David grew weary.

[16] Ishbi-benob, one of the descendants of the giants, whose spear
weighed three hundred shekels of bronze and who was fitted out with
new weapons, said he would kill David.

[17] But Abishai son of Zeruiah came to his aid and attacked the Philistine
and killed him. Then David's men swore to him, "You shall not go out
with us to battle any longer, so that you do not quench the lamp of
Israel."

[18] After this a battle took place with the Philistines at Gob; then Sibbecai
the Hushathite killed Saph, who was one of the descendants of the
giants.

[19] Then there was another battle with the Philistines at Gob, and
Elhanan son of Jaare-oregim the Bethlehemite killed Goliath the
Gittite, the shaft of whose spear was like a weaver's beam.

[20] There was again war at Gath, where there was a man of great size who
had six fingers on each hand and six toes on each foot, twenty-four in
number; he, too, was descended from the giants.

[21] When he taunted Israel, Jonathan son of David's brother Shimei
killed him.

[22] These four were descended from the giants in Gath; they fell by the
hands of David and his servants.

22 [1] David spoke to the LORD the words of this song on the day when
the LORD delivered him from the hand of all his enemies and from
the hand of Saul.

[107] P. Kyle McCarter, 1 Samuel (AB 8; Garden City, NY: Doubleday, 1980), 306.
[108] Edelman, "Zela," ABD 6:1072.

² He said,

"The LORD is my rock, my fortress, and my deliverer,

³ my God, my rock in whom I take refuge,

  my shield and the horn of my salvation,

  my stronghold and my refuge,

  my savior; you save me from violence.

⁴ I call upon the LORD, who is worthy to be praised,

  and I am saved from my enemies.

⁵ For the waves of death encompassed me;

  the torrents of perdition assailed me;

⁶ the cords of Sheol entangled me;

  the snares of death confronted me.

⁷ In my distress I called upon the LORD;

  to my God I called.

From his temple he heard my voice,

  and my cry came to his ears.

⁸ Then the earth reeled and rocked;

  the foundations of the heavens trembled

  and reeled because he was angry.

⁹ Smoke went up from his nostrils

  and devouring fire from his mouth;

  glowing coals flamed forth from him.

¹⁰ He bowed the heavens and came down;

  thick darkness was under his feet.

¹¹ He rode on a cherub and flew;

  he was seen upon the wings of the wind.

¹² He made darkness around him a canopy,

  thick clouds, a gathering of water.

¹³ Out of the brightness before him

  coals of fire flamed forth.

¹⁴ The LORD thundered from heaven;

  the Most High uttered his voice.

¹⁵ He sent out arrows and scattered them,

  lightning and routed them.

¹⁶ Then the channels of the sea were seen;
   the foundations of the world were laid bare
at the rebuke of the Lord,
   at the blast of the breath of his nostrils.
¹⁷ He reached from on high; he took me;
   he drew me out of mighty waters.
¹⁸ He delivered me from my strong enemy,
   from those who hated me,
   for they were too mighty for me.
¹⁹ They came upon me in the day of my calamity,
   but the Lord was my stay.
²⁰ He brought me out into a broad place;
   he delivered me because he delighted in me.
²¹ The Lord rewarded me according to my righteousness;
   according to the cleanness of my hands he recompensed me.
²² For I have kept the ways of the Lord
   and have not wickedly departed from my God.
²³ For all his ordinances were before me,
   and from his statutes I did not turn aside.
²⁴ I was blameless before him,
   and I kept myself from guilt.
²⁵ Therefore the Lord has recompensed me according to my righteousness,
   according to my cleanness in his sight.
²⁶ With the loyal you show yourself loyal;
   with the blameless you show yourself blameless;
²⁷ with the pure you show yourself pure,
   and with the crooked you show yourself shrewd.
²⁸ You deliver a humble people,
   but your eyes are upon the haughty to bring them down.
²⁹ Indeed, you are my lamp, O Lord;
   the Lord lightens my darkness.
³⁰ By you I can outrun a troop,
   and by my God I can leap over a wall.

³¹ This God – his way is perfect;
   the promise of the LORD proves true;
   he is a shield for all who take refuge in him.
³² For who is God but the LORD?
   And who is a rock except our God?
³³ The God who has girded me with strength
   has opened wide my path.
³⁴ He made my feet like the feet of deer
   and set me secure on the heights.
³⁵ He trains my hands for war,
   so that my arms can bend a bow of bronze.
³⁶ You have given me the shield of your salvation,
   and your help has made me great.
³⁷ You have made me stride freely,
   and my feet do not slip;
³⁸ I pursued my enemies and destroyed them
   and did not turn back until they were consumed.
³⁹ I consumed them; I struck them down so that they did not rise;
   they fell under my feet.
⁴⁰ For you girded me with strength for the battle;
   you made my assailants sink under me.
⁴¹ You made my enemies turn their backs to me,
   those who hated me, and I destroyed them.
⁴² They looked, but there was no one to save them;
   they cried to the LORD, but he did not answer them.
⁴³ I beat them fine like the dust of the earth;
   I crushed them and stamped them down like the mire of the streets.
⁴⁴ You delivered me from strife with the peoples;
   you kept me as the head of the nations;
   people whom I had not known served me.
⁴⁵ Foreigners came cringing to me;
   as soon as they heard of me, they obeyed me.
⁴⁶ Foreigners lost heart
   and came trembling out of their strongholds.

⁴⁷ The LORD lives! Blessed be my rock,
   and exalted be my God, the rock of my salvation,
⁴⁸ the God who gave me vengeance
   and brought down peoples under me,
⁴⁹ who brought me out from my enemies;
   you exalted me above my adversaries;
   you delivered me from the violent.
⁵⁰ For this I will extol you, O LORD, among the nations
   and sing praises to your name.
⁵¹ He is a tower of salvation for his king
   and shows steadfast love to his anointed,
   to David and his descendants forever."
23 ¹ Now these are the last words of David:
The oracle of David, son of Jesse,
   the oracle of the man whom God exalted,
 the anointed of the God of Jacob,
   the favorite of the Strong One of Israel:
 ² The spirit of the LORD speaks through me;
   his word is upon my tongue.
 ³ The God of Israel has spoken;
   the Rock of Israel has said to me:
"One who rules over people justly,
   ruling in the fear of God,
 ⁴ is like the light of morning,
   like the sun rising on a cloudless morning,
   gleaming from the rain on the grassy land."
 ⁵ Is not my house like this with God?
   For he has made with me an everlasting covenant,
   ordered in all things and secure.
Will he not cause to prosper
   all my help and my desire?
 ⁶ But the godless are all like thorns that are thrown away,
   for they cannot be picked up with the hand;

⁷ to touch them one uses an iron bar

or the shaft of a spear.

And they are entirely consumed in fire on the spot.

⁸ These are the names of the warriors whom David had: Josheb-basshebeth a Tahchemonite; he was chief of the Three; he wielded his spear against eight hundred whom he killed at one time.

⁹ Next to him among the three warriors was Eleazar son of Dodo son of Ahohi. He was with David when they defied the Philistines who were gathered there for battle. The Israelites withdrew,

¹⁰ but he stood his ground. He struck down the Philistines until his arm grew weary, though his hand clung to the sword. The LORD brought about a great victory that day. Then the people came back to him – but only to strip the dead.

¹¹ Next to him was Shammah son of Agee the Hararite. The Philistines gathered together at Lehi, where there was a plot of ground full of lentils, and the army fled from the Philistines.

¹² But he took his stand in the middle of the plot, defended it, and killed the Philistines, and the LORD brought about a great victory.

¹³ Toward the beginning of harvest three of the thirty chiefs went down to join David at the cave of Adullam while a band of Philistines was encamped in the valley of Rephaim.

¹⁴ David was then in the stronghold, and the garrison of the Philistines was then at Bethlehem.

¹⁵ David said longingly, "Oh, that someone would give me water to drink from the well of Bethlehem that is by the gate!"

¹⁶ Then the three warriors broke through the camp of the Philistines, drew water from the well of Bethlehem that was by the gate, and brought it to David. But he would not drink of it; he poured it out to the LORD,

¹⁷ for he said, "The LORD forbid that I should do this. Can I drink the blood of the men who went at the risk of their lives?" Therefore he would not drink it. The three warriors did these things.

¹⁸ Now Abishai son of Zeruiah, the brother of Joab, was chief of the Thirty. With his spear he fought against three hundred men and killed them and won a name beside the Three.

¹⁹ He was the most renowned of the Thirty and became their commander, but he did not attain to the Three.

²⁰ Benaiah son of Jehoiada was a valiant warrior from Kabzeel, a doer of great deeds; he struck down two sons of Ariel of Moab. He also went down and killed a lion in a pit on a day when snow had fallen.

²¹ And he killed an Egyptian, a handsome man. The Egyptian had a spear in his hand, but Benaiah went against him with a staff, snatched the spear out of the Egyptian's hand, and killed him with his own spear.

²² Such were the things Benaiah son of Jehoiada did and won a name beside the three warriors.

²³ He was renowned among the Thirty, but he did not attain to the Three. And David put him in charge of his bodyguard.

²⁴ Among the Thirty were Asahel brother of Joab; Elhanan son of Dodo of Bethlehem;

²⁵ Shammah of Harod; Elika of Harod;

²⁶ Helez the Paltite; Ira son of Ikkesh of Tekoa;

²⁷ Abiezer of Anathoth; Mebunnai the Hushathite;

²⁸ Zalmon the Ahohite; Maharai of Netophah;

²⁹ Heleb son of Baanah of Netophah; Ittai son of Ribai of Gibeah of the Benjaminites;

³⁰ Benaiah of Pirathon; Hiddai of the wadis of Gaash;

³¹ Abi-albon the Arbathite; Azmaveth of Bahurim;

³² Eliahba of Shaalbon; the sons of Jashen: Jonathan

³³ son of Shammah the Hararite; Ahiam son of Sharar the Hararite;

³⁴ Eliphelet son of Ahasbai of Maacah; Eliam son of Ahithophel the Gilonite;

³⁵ Hezro of Carmel; Paarai the Arbite;

³⁶ Igal son of Nathan of Zobah; Bani the Gadite;

³⁷ Zelek the Ammonite; Naharai of Beeroth, the armor-bearer of Joab son of Zeruiah;

³⁸ Ira the Ithrite; Gareb the Ithrite;

³⁹ Uriah the Hittite – thirty-seven in all.

The first element of David's victories over the Philistine giants appears in 2 Samuel 23:15–22. Four encounters, each featuring a different warrior, appear in 2 Samuel 21:15–17; 21:18; 21:19; and 21:20–21, with a summation in 2 Samuel 21:22.

The first encounter focuses on David's efforts to defend himself against Ishbi-Benob, identified as one of the descendants of the Raphah (i.e., the Rephaim, the legendary giants of the past; see Gen 14:5; 15:20; Deut 2:10–11; 3:13; Josh 12:4; 13:12; 17:15). The Rephaim were understood to be descendants of Rapi'u, a giant ancestor, and the past generations of Rephaim, spirits of the dead ancestors who could come to the aid of Canaanites.[109] David is worn down by fighting this figure, prompting Abishai son of Zeruiah to kill the Philistine giant. As a result, the decision was made that David should no longer go out to battle, presumably due to advancing age. Earlier narratives note that the death of a leader of revolt (e.g., Absalom in 2 Samuel 15–19 or Sheba in 2 Samuel 20) would signal the defeat of their army. David had already been left behind while Joab led the army in battle against Rabbath Ammon in 2 Samuel 10. David's death would extinguish the lamp, Hebrew, $n\bar{e}r$, of Israel, a term that designates the dynasty of Israel.[110]

The second encounter appears in 2 Samuel 21:18, in which Sibbecai the Hushathite kills Saph, a Philistine Raphah (Giant) at Gob, an unknown location near the Philistine border.[111]

The third encounter, again at Gob, appears in 2 Samuel 21:19, in which Elhanan son of Jaare-oregim from Bethlehem killed Goliath the Gittite. This reference is controversial due to the claim that David killed Goliath in 1 Samuel 17. Solutions include claims that David's birth name was Elhanan or that David took credit for a victory won by one of his own warriors.

The fourth encounter, this time at Gath, appears in 2 Samuel 21:20–21, in which Jonathan son of Shimei, identified with David's brother Shammah (1 Sam 16:9; cf. 2 Sam 13:3), kills a Philistine Raphah with six fingers on each hand and six toes on each foot.

Finally, 2 Samuel 21:22 summarizes the four encounters.

The second element of David's encounters with the Philistine giants appears in 2 Samuel 22:1–51, which presents David's Song of Thanksgiving for YHWH's Deliverance from His Enemies and from Saul. Many interpreters treat this psalm as an independent unit, in part because it is generically distinct as a psalm and in part because it largely replicates

---

[109] Tsumura, 2 Samuel, 298; H. Rouillard, "Rephaim," DDD² 692–700.
[110] D. Kellerman, "$n\bar{e}r$," TDOT 10:14–24, esp. 18.
[111] Koch, "Gob," EBR 10:382.

Psalm 18, with only minor differences.[112] The introduction in verse 1 and the speech formula in verse 2aα, "and he said," tie the psalm into the narrative framework of 2 Samuel 22:15–23:39. The introduction notes YHWH's deliverance from David's enemies and from Saul, but the narrative context indicates that David thanks YHWH specifically for deliverance from the Philistine giants mentioned throughout 2 Samuel 21:15–22, particularly from Ishbi-Benob, who nearly killed him. The narrative introduction in verse 1 largely replicates the introduction in Psalm 18:1, which might suggest that Psalm 18 constitutes the original form of this text. The unique narrative character of this introduction would better suggest that 2 Samuel 22 originally stood in another narrative location within 2 Samuel, following David's victories in 2 Samuel 8. Insofar as 2 Samuel 8 concludes the pro-Davidic account of David's rise, 2 Samuel 22 would originate in relation to David's rise to kingship in 1 Samuel 1:1–2 Samuel 8. Only later was this narrative expanded by the addition of a narrative critical of David in 2 Samuel 9–21, which would originate in the Jehu Dynastic History. Second Samuel 22 would have been placed in the first book of Psalms, that is, Psalms 1–41, after the expansion of Samuel by the Jehu Dynastic History.

Analyses of the structure of 2 Samuel 22 and Psalm 18 vary widely, due in part to the location of the former in a narrative context and the latter in a psalmic context.[113] Nevertheless, the narrative context is determined by the introduction in vv. 1–2aα, including the narrative introduction proper and the speech formula, which introduces the psalm as a speech of David. The psalm proper then appears in vv. 2aβ–51. Although interpreters have attempted to separate the generic psalm of thanksgiving from the hymn of praise for deliverance, a synchronic analysis of the strophic structure focuses on the primary subject in each strophe, noting both syntax and that each strophe concludes on a motif that anticipates the next strophe.

The psalm combines the genres of thanksgiving song and song of praise to produce a full account of the psalmist's – David (v. 1) or David and his

---

[112] For example, J. P. Fokkelman, *Narrative Art and Poetry in the Books of Samuel. Volume 2: The Crossing Fates (1 Sam. 13–31 & II Sam. 1)* (Assen/Maastricht: Van Gorcum, 1986), 333–355; André Caquot and Philippe de Robert, *Les Livres de Samuel* (CAT 6; Geneva: Labor et Fides, 1994), 596–597.

[113] See the markedly different analyses of the structure of 2 Samuel 22 and Psalm 18 in Campbell, *2 Samuel*, 194–198, and Gerstenberger, *Psalms, Part 1, with an Introduction to Cultic Poetry* (FOTL 14; Grand Rapids, MI: Eerdmans, 1988), 96–100.

anointed descendants (v. 51) – gratitude to YHWH for enabling him to defeat the enemies that seek to kill him.[114]

Following the introduction in verse 1 and the introduction to the psalmist's/David's speech in verse 2aα, the psalm of Thanksgiving for Deliverance appears in verses 2aβ–51.

The invocations in verses 2aβ–21 comprise three basic hymnic elements. The initial invocation in verses 2aβ–3 presents a general introductory invocation of YHWH as the psalmist's/David's rock and deliverer.

The second invocation, in verses 4–6, takes the invocation a step further with two basic elements. The first is an invocation proper in verse 4, which signals the result of YHWH's actions on behalf of the psalmist/David, namely, deliverance from enemies. The second, in verses 5–6, introduced by causative *kî*, "for, because," specifies the enemies metaphorically by representing them as "waves of death," "torrents of perdition (Belial, one who is worthless, evil; cf. 1 Sam 10:27)," "the cords of Sheol (the under-world)," and "the snares of death."

The third invocation in verses 7–21 provides a full account of the results of YHWH's support. Verse 7 introduces this segment with an invocation of YHWH proper and an initial characterization of the results of YHWH's support, that is, YHWH hears the psalmist/David from the Temple, Hebrew, *hêkāl*, "palace," a term that describes the Great Hall of the Jerusalem Temple where the ten Menorahs or candelabras and the ten incense burners are located (1 Kgs 6).[115] A detailed portrayal of YHWH's response to deliver the psalmist/David then follows in verses 8–20. The portrayal appears in the form of a theophany in which creation (i.e., the earth and the foundations of the heavens) shakes and trembles as in an earthquake. Smoke, representing the imagery of the incense smoke, and fire, representing the imagery of the Menorahs in the Temple, serve as metaphors for YHWH's anger as YHWH comes down from the heavens in thick darkness, mounted on a Cherub, one of the four composite winged human and animal figures that guard the Ark of the Covenant in the Holy of Holies of the Temple. Employing the imagery of storm and cloud, YHWH looses bolts of lightning like arrows against the enemies. The sea beneath roars to represent the enemies as forces of chaos as YHWH

---

[114] Gerstenberger, *Psalms, Part 1*, 14–19, 99–100.

[115] Sweeney, *1 and 2 Kings*, 104–116; cf. Marvin A. Sweeney, *Jewish Mysticism from Ancient Times through Today* (Grand Rapids, MI: Eerdmans, 2020), 108–112.

delivers the psalmist/David. The segment ends with recognition that YHWH delights in the psalmist/David.

The second segment of the psalm in 2 Samuel 22:21–28 presents the reasons for YHWH's deliverance of the psalmist/David, specifically, because the psalmist/David is righteous and pure. The psalm emphasizes that the psalmist/David is righteous and pure because he observes YHWH's ordinances, Hebrew, *mišpāṭîm*, "laws," and ordinances, Hebrew, *ḥuqqōtîm*, "statutes," the same terminology that introduces the Deuteronomic law code in Deuteronomy 12:1. Interpreters argue that this is a later Deuteronomic section that joins the thanksgiving psalm in verses 2aβ–20 with the song of praise or thanksgiving for YHWH's deliverance in verses 29–31.[116] But such a view misses the point that the thanksgiving song and the song of praise are indeed intertwined so that both of them combine to make the final point of the psalm (v. 51), that YHWH's steadfast love, *ḥesed*, "fidelity," will last forever, a motif clearly tied to the rise of David, especially the promise of eternal kingship (2 Sam 7; cf. 2 Sam 22:26).

The third segment of the psalm in 2 Samuel 22:29–37 offers a song of praise for YHWH as the psalmist's/David's "lamp," sustainer, supporter, and protector. The imagery of YHWH as protector employs the term, *māgēn*, "shield," which in later times produces the term Magen David, "shield of David," which designates the six-pointed Star of David.

The fourth segment of the psalm, in 2 Samuel 22:38–46, portrays the psalmist's/David's victories over his enemies as the result of YHWH's support. This segment makes the crucial point that YHWH acts through human agents in the living world of creation.

The fifth and final segment of the psalm, in 2 Samuel 22:47–51, presents the psalmist's/David's renewed praise of YHWH. The praise proper appears in verses 47–49 with assertions that YHWH lives and that YHWH delivers the psalmist/David. The following verses 50–51 present the psalmist's/David's singing praises (i.e., thanksgiving) to YHWH for divine support. It reiterates the eternal Davidic promise in 2 Samuel 7 that YHWH shows steadfast love, Hebrew, *ḥesed*, "fidelity," to David and his anointed descendants "forever."[117] Such an assertion indicates that this psalm originally played a concluding role together with 2 Samuel 23:1–7 following the conclusion of the rise of David in 2 Samuel 8.

---

[116] For example, Anderson, *2 Samuel*, 262.
[117] Glueck, *Ḥesed in the Bible*.

The third element is David's Last Words in 2 Samuel 23:1–7. Although many interpreters treat this as an independent unit due to its superscription in verse 1a and its psalm-like character, it is joined syntactically to the larger unit concerning David's encounters with the Philistines in 2 Samuel 21:15–23:39. The superscription in verse 1a reads in Hebrew, *wĕ'ēlleh dibrê dāwid hā'aḥărōnîm*, "now these are the last words of David" (NRSVue), which should read, "and these are the last words of David," to indicate their syntactical relationship with the preceding material. The passage celebrates YHWH's *bĕrît 'ôlām*, "eternal covenant," with David (see verse 5; cf. 2 Sam 7:1–16), which stands as the basis for YHWH's fidelity to David and enables him to defeat enemies that threaten Israel.

Second Samuel 23:1–7 is formulated as a prophetic oracle from YHWH spoken by David. The oracle begins with the difficult Hebrew statement, *nĕ'um dāwid ben yišay ûnĕ'um hageber huqam 'al mĕšîaḥ 'ĕlōhê ya'ăqōb ûnĕ'îm zimrôt yiśrā'ēl*, which is properly translated, "the oracle of David ben Jesse and the oracle of the man who was established over the anointed one of the G-d of Jacob and (over) those uttering (lit., 'moving [the lips]') the songs of Israel." The problematic particle *'al*, "over," indicates that David is established "over the anointed one of the G-d of Jacob," a reference to the anointed priest of YHWH, "and (over) those uttering[118] the songs of Israel." The statement refers not simply to David as the anointed King of Israel, but to David as the man who is placed over the liturgical staff, including the anointed priest of the G-d of Jacob and those liturgical singers who "move (their lips)" to sing the songs of Israel.[119]

The twofold use of the Hebrew term *nĕ'um*, "oracle, utterance," indicates a prophetic oracle, and it appears in the introductions to the oracles of the Aramean oracular prophet or *baru* priest, Balaam ben Beor. Balaam was hired by the Moabite King Balak ben Zippor to curse Israel as they were encamped in Moab by the east bank of the Jordan River prior to their entry into the land of Canaan (see Num 22–24, esp. Num 24:3b, 15b).

Following the introduction in 2 Samuel 23:1b, the oracle per se follows in verses 2–7. Verses 2–3 identify YHWH as the G-d of Israel who speaks through David, indicating that David here acts as a prophet of YHWH.

---

[118] The Hebrew term *nā'îm*, "(those) moving," from the root, *nw'*, is employed here to depict the moving lips of those who sing, pray, or chant the songs of liturgical worship. Cf. 1 Samuel 1:13, where the verb, *nā'ôt*, is employed to portray the movement of Hannah's lips as she prays to YHWH for a son at the Shiloh sanctuary.

[119] See 1 Chronicles 6:1–33, which elaborates on David's role in appointing the Levites who would serve as the Temple singers.

Verse 4 compares YHWH with the shining of the morning sun, which indicates YHWH's role as creator and points to the daily role of sunrise as a symbol of the stability and eternity of creation. Verse 5 then presents David's statement that YHWH will likewise see to the stability and eternity of his house (i.e., his royal dynasty, promised to him in 2 Samuel 7:1–16), which is identified as YHWH's "eternal covenant" with David that ensures his success. Verses 6–7 then elaborate on YHWH's role in ensuring David's success in defeating Israel's enemies, "the wicked," who will be thrown aside like thorns by one who bears iron and the shaft of a spear to ensure that they are burned "on the spot." Such language employs the concept of YHWH's eternal covenant to ensure his success in defeating Israel's enemies, and thereby ensuring the eternal existence of his dynastic house and his people, Israel and Judah.

The fourth and final segment of David's encounters with the Philistines appears in 2 Samuel 23:8–39, which lists the names of David's warriors and their home towns. These men enabled David to defend Israel against its enemies and ensure the continuity of his dynastic house and his nation. The passage is also introduced with a superscription in verse 8a, "these are the names of David's warriors" (cf. NRSVue). The home towns noted in the list indicate that the men came mainly from Judah and Benjamin, although a few come from other locations, many of which are unknown.[120] First 1 Chronicles 11 and 27 represents the Chronicler's efforts to correct Samuel.

The list does not include Joab, who served as general commander of the army and would therefore have been one of David's highest-ranking officers (see 2 Sam 20:23). Verses 8b–23 name five of David's secondary ranks of military commanders, including a group of three men who appear to be the commanders of the three major divisions in David's army (see 2 Sam 18:1–2). The first three men named are Joseheb-Hashebbeth of Tahchemon or Hachmon (v. 8b), an unidentified site[121]; Eleazar son of Dodo ben Ahohi, a Benjaminite gentilic name,[122] whose home town is presumably Beth Lehem as indicated for his son in v. 24 (vv. 9–10); and Shammah son of Agee, a Hararite, which appears to be a gentilic name of

---

[120] Benjamin Mazar, "The Military Élite of King David," *The Early Biblical Period: Historical Essays* (Jerusalem: Israel Exploration Society, 1986), 83–103.

[121] Thompson, "Tahchemonite," *ABD* 6:308.

[122] Schley, "Ahohi," *ABD* 1:124.

uncertain location (vv. 11–12).[123] A brief aside in verses 13–17 relates an incident in which David expressed his desire for a drink from a well in his home city of Beth Lehem and how his three commanders risked their lives to get it. When they brought it, David refused to drink it and offered it instead as a libation to YHWH because his desire was not worth the cost of a man's life. The story demonstrates the loyalty and bravery of David's men. A fourth man, Abishai son of Zeruiah, the brother of Joab, who won a name among the three commanders but did not become one of them, is also named and honored for his exploits (vv. 18–19). He is perhaps from Beth Lehem in Judah since his mother, Zeruiah, is David's sister. Verses 20–23 recount the exploits of a fifth man, Benaiah son of Jehoiada of Kabzeel, identified with Tell Garrah, located approximately halfway between Beer Sheba and Arad in southern Judah. Benaiah was the commander of David's personal bodyguard.[124]

Verses 24–39 present a list of warriors who were among the Thirty, which may indicate lesser units within the three major army divisions noted above. They include Asahel, the brother of Joab, presumably from Judah (v. 24); Elhanan son of Dodo of Beth Lehem, whose father is listed above (v. 24); Shammah of Harod, perhaps identified with Khirbet Haredan, a few miles southeast of Jerusalem (v. 25)[125]; Elika, also of Harod (v. 25); Helez the Paltite, perhaps a gentilic town identified with Beth Pelet near Beer Sheba (Josh 15:27)[126]; Ira son of Ikkesh of Tekoa, a major Judean town and home of Amos (Amos 1:1), identified with Khirbet Tequa, located approximately ten miles south of Jerusalem (v. 26)[127]; Abiezer of Anathoth, a Benjaminite town and home of Abiathar and Jeremiah (Jer 1:1–3), identified likely with Ra el-Kharrueh, less than two miles off the main road between Jerusalem and Shechem (v. 27)[128]; Mebunnai the Hushathtite, apparently a reference to a Judean town located some 3.7 miles west of Beth Lehem on the way to Jerusalem (v. 27)[129]; Zalmon the Ahotite, apparently a gentilic name for a Benjaminite clan, although the son of Dodo figures named above in verses 9–10 and 24 may be associated with Beth Lehem (v. 28); Maharai of Netophah, identified

---

[123] Dempster, "Hararite," *ABD* 3:59.
[124] Tom Wayne Winnett, "Kabzeel," *ABD* 4:1.
[125] Melvin Hunt, "Harod," *ABD* 3:62.
[126] Thompson, "Paltite, The," *ABD* 5:138.
[127] Axelsson, "Tekoa," *ABD* 6:343–344.
[128] John L. Peterson, "Anathoth," *ABD* 1:227–228.
[129] Dale C. Liid, "Hushah," *ABD* 3:338.

with Khirbet Bedd Falul, about three and a half miles southeast of Beth Lehem (v. 28)[130]; Heleb son of Baanah, also of Netophah (v. 29); Ittai son of Ribai of Gibeah in Benjamin (v. 29); Benaiah of Pirathon, an Ephraimite town identified with Farata, six miles southwest of Shechem (v. 30)[131]; Hiddai of Nahale (Torrents of)-Gaash, an Ephraimite site located south of Timnath-Serah or Timnath-Heres (v. 30)[132]; Albi-Albon the Arbathite, which may be associated with the Arabah (Jordan Valley) or Beth Arabah, a village on the border of Benjamin and Judah (v. 31; see Joshua 15:6, 61; 18:22)[133]; Azmaveth the Barhumite, identified with Bahurim, a Benjaminite village located on the road from Jerusalem to the Jordan Valley north of the Mount of Olives (v. 31)[134]; Eliahba of Shaalbon, identified with Shaalbim, a Danite town identified with Selbit, roughly three miles northwest of Aijalon (v. 32)[135]; the sons of Jashen (son of) Jonathan, an apparently corrupt reading (vv. 32–33); Shammah the Hararite (v. 33; see vv. 11–12 above); Ahiam son of Sharar the Hararite (v. 33); Eliphelet son of Ahasbai son of the Maachahite, a reference to Maachah, home of Abshalom's maternal grandfather, Telmai, an Aramean kingdom in the northern Trans-Jordan, east of the Jordan Valley and north of the Yarmuk basin (v. 34)[136]; Eliam son of Ahitophel the Gilonite and apparently a father or uncle of Bath Sheba (v. 34); Hezrai of Carmel, the home of Abigail and her first husband, Nabal, a Judean town located approximately eight miles southeast of Hebron (v. 35)[137]; Paarai the Arbite, a reference to a site in the Judean hill country (Josh 15:52; v. 35); Igal son of Nathan of Zobah, an Aramean kingdom located in the north Beqa' Valley of modern Lebanon (v. 36)[138]; Bani the Gadite, a reference to the tribal territory of Gad in the Trans-Jordan (v. 36); Zelek the Ammonite, a reference to the Ammonite kingdom in the Trans-Jordan (v. 36); Naharai the Beerothite, the arms bearer of Joab from Beeroth, a Hivvite city of disputed location and allied with Gibeon in the tribal territory of Benjamin (Josh 9:17; 18:25; v. 37)[139]; Ira the Ithrite, a Calebite clan located near

[130] Randall W. Younker, "Netophah," *ABD* 4:1986.
[131] Robert W. Smith, "Pirathon," *ABD* 5:373.
[132] Elmer H. Dyck, "Gaash," 2:861.
[133] Schley, "Arbathithite," *ABD* 1:353–354.
[134] Schley, "Bahurim," *ABD* 1:568.
[135] Wesley J. Toews, "Shaalbim," *ABD* 5:1147.
[136] Schley, "Maachah," *ABD* 4:430.
[137] LaMoine F. DeVries, "Carmel," *ABD* 1:873.
[138] Pitard, "Zobah," *ABD* 6:1108.
[139] David A. Dorsey, "Beeroth," *ABD* 1:646–647.

Kiriath Jearim (Josh 9:17; v. 38)[140]; Gareb the Ithrite (v. 38); and Uriah the Hittite, first husband of Bath Sheba (v. 39). The closing statement counts thirty-seven in all, apparently to account for all the warriors named in verses 8–39.

David's Selection of the Threshing Floor of Araunah as the Site for YHWH's Altar – 2 Samuel 24:1–25

24 **¹ Again the anger of the LORD was kindled against Israel, and he incited David against them, saying, "Go, count the people of Israel and Judah."**

² So the king said to Joab and the commanders of the army who were with him, "Go through all the tribes of Israel, from Dan to Beer-sheba, and take a census of the people, so that I may know how many there are."

³ But Joab said to the king, "May the LORD your God increase the number of the people a hundredfold while the eyes of my lord the king can still see it! But why does my lord the king want to do this?"

⁴ But the king's word prevailed against Joab and the commanders of the army. So Joab and the commanders of the army went out from the presence of the king to take a census of the people of Israel.

⁵ They crossed the Jordan and began from Aroer and from the city that is in the middle of the valley, toward Gad and on to Jazer.

⁶ Then they came to Gilead and to Kadesh in the land of the Hittites, and they came to Dan, and from Dan they went around to Sidon

⁷ and came to the fortress of Tyre and to all the cities of the Hivites and Canaanites, and they went out to the Negeb of Judah at Beer-sheba.

⁸ So when they had gone through all the land, they came back to Jerusalem at the end of nine months and twenty days.

⁹ Joab reported to the king the number of those who had been recorded: in Israel there were eight hundred thousand soldiers able to draw the sword, and those of Judah were five hundred thousand.

¹⁰ But afterward, David was stricken to the heart because he had numbered the people. David said to the LORD, "I have sinned greatly in what I have done. But now, O LORD, I pray you, take away the guilt of your servant, for I have done very foolishly."

---

[140] Dempster, "Ithrite," *ABD* 3:582–583.

¹¹ When David rose in the morning, the word of the LORD came to the prophet Gad, David's seer, saying,

¹² "Go and say to David: Thus says the LORD: Three things I offer you; choose one of them, and I will do it to you."

¹³ So Gad came to David and told him; he asked him, "Shall seven years of famine come to you on your land? Or will you flee three months before your foes while they pursue you? Or shall there be three days' pestilence in your land? Now consider and decide what answer I shall return to the one who sent me."

¹⁴ Then David said to Gad, "I am in great distress; let us fall into the hand of the LORD, for his mercy is great, but let me not fall into human hands."

¹⁵ So the LORD sent a pestilence on Israel from that morning until the appointed time, and seventy thousand of the people died, from Dan to Beer-sheba.

¹⁶ But when the angel stretched out his hand toward Jerusalem to destroy it, the LORD relented concerning the evil and said to the angel who was bringing destruction among the people, "It is enough; now stay your hand." The angel of the LORD was standing by the threshing floor of Araunah the Jebusite. David looked up and saw the angel of the LORD standing between earth and heaven and in his hand a drawn sword stretched out over Jerusalem. Then David and the elders, clothed in sackcloth, fell on their faces.

¹⁷ When David saw the angel who was destroying the people, he said to the LORD, "I alone have sinned, and I, the shepherd, have done evil, but these sheep, what have they done? Let your hand, I pray, be against me and against my father's house."

¹⁸ That day Gad came to David and said to him, "Go up and erect an altar to the LORD on the threshing floor of Araunah the Jebusite."

¹⁹ Following Gad's instructions, David went up, as the LORD had commanded.

²⁰ When Araunah looked down, he saw the king and his servants coming toward him, and Araunah went out and prostrated himself before the king with his face to the ground.

²¹ Araunah said, "Why has my lord the king come to his servant?" David said, "To buy the threshing floor from you in order to build an altar to the LORD, so that the plague may be averted from the people."

²² Then Araunah said to David, "Let my lord the king take and offer up what seems good to him; here are the oxen for the burnt offering and the threshing sledges and the yokes of the oxen for the wood.

²³ All this, O king, Araunah gives to the king." And Araunah said to the king, "May the LORD your God respond favorably to you."

²⁴ But the king said to Araunah, "No, but I will buy them from you for a price; I will not offer burnt offerings to the LORD my God that cost me nothing." So David bought the threshing floor and the oxen for fifty shekels of silver.

²⁵ David built there an altar to the LORD and offered burnt offerings and offerings of well-being. So the LORD answered his supplication for the land, and the plague was averted from Israel.

The third major action of David appears in 2 Samuel 24:1–25, which recounts David's choice of the threshing floor of Araunah as the site for an altar for YHWH, eventually Solomon's Temple.

The narrative comprises five major sub-units, including the account of YHWH's anger against Israel and incitement of David against Israel in 2 Samuel 24:1–4; the account of the census of Israel and Judah in 2 Samuel 24:5–9; the account of David's regret over the census and YHWH's punishment of David and Israel in the form of a plague in 2 Samuel 24:10–17; the account of David's purchase of the threshing floor of Araunah in 2 Samuel 24:18–24; and the account of David's erection of an altar to YHWH on the site in 2 Samuel 24:25.

The first sub-unit, in 2 Samuel 24:1–4, sets the narrative plot of the passage into motion, beginning with YHWH's anger against Israel and incitement of David to take a census of the nation in v. 1. The narrative does not give a reason for YHWH's anger, which prompted the Chronicler to assert that Satan and not YHWH was the actual instigator of the action in 1 Chronicles 21. Another attempt to explain YHWH's anger points to the prior mention of Uriah the Hittite, whom David set up for murder, in 2 Samuel 23:39, although this explanation does not indicate why all Israel should suffer. A better explanation is to consider the synchronic literary context of the passage to point to Israel's (and Judah's) revolt against David following David's mishandling of his own household and the kingdom in 2 Samuel 10–20. A diachronic understanding of the passage, however, would suggest that 2 Samuel 21–24 originally followed 2 Samuel 8 or 9, when David became king over all Israel and Judah. The census would then make sense for establishing the tax basis for the combined kingdom of Israel and Judah as well as the conscription of men of military age for defending and expanding the kingdom. Such a concern was signaled at the outset of the narratives concerning the selection of a king in 1 Samuel 8, when Samuel warned the people that a king would tax their property and income and draft their sons and daughters to serve in his army and his palace. Second Samuel 24 indicates the reasons for dissatisfaction with David upon which Absalom capitalized to incite his own revolt.

The second sub-unit, in 2 Samuel 24:5–9, recounts Joab's obedience to David's command over the course of nine months and twenty days. The census was a major undertaking, which included the territory of Israel and Judah from Dan to Beer Sheba west of the Jordan as noted in verse 2, but it also included all the territory of the Trans-Jordan, where David took refuge during Absalom's revolt. Earlier narratives, such as Joshua 22, indicate that the Trans-Jordan was a problematic area that might consider itself independent of the rest of Israel.

The route of Joab and his army commanders (see v. 4) resembles a *palu* campaign as practiced by the Neo-Assyrian Kings, who would gather the army every spring following the initial plantings and harvest of first crops to tour the empire and gather tribute from the subjects of the Assyrian crown.[141] They start from Jerusalem, cross the Jordan, and encamp at Aroer, identified with Khirbet 'Ara'ir, which lies along the north bank of the Wadi Arnon in the Trans-Jordan at the southern boundary of the Israelite tribes of Reuben and Gad, with Moab to the south (Num 32:34; Deut 3:12; Josh 3:16; Judg 11:26; 1 Chr 5:8).[142] From Arnon, they go north to Jazer, the location of which is disputed. It may be identified with Khirbet Jazzir at the head of the Wadi Shu'eib, which marks the boundary between the Israelite tribe of Gad and the Ammonites to the east (Num 21:24).[143] They continue further north into Gilead, through the half-tribe of Manasseh to Tahtim-Hodshi, an unknown site, which is identified with Kadesh in Naphtali according to the Septuagint, although this is viewed as a guess. McCarter identifies the site as the region south of Mount Hermon, although this, too, remains problematic.[144] Dan-Jaan, likely identified with Dan, the northernmost city of Israel (cf. LXX) is next,[145] followed by Sidon and Tyre in Phoenicia.[146] The cities and towns of the Hivvites and the Canaanites refer to northern Israel and southern Judah. The final stop is

---

[141] Haim Tadmor, "The Campaigns of Sargon II of Assur: A Chronological-Historical Study," *JCS* 12 (1958): 22–40, 77–100.

[142] Levin, "Aroer," *EBR* 2:803–807, esp. 804–805.

[143] Juha Pakkala, "Jazer," *EBR* 13:794; Peterson, "Jazer," *ABD* 3:650–651.

[144] McCarter, *2 Samuel*, 504–505.

[145] Avraham Biran, "Dan," *ABD* 2:12–17.

[146] Phillip C. Schmitz, "Sidon," *ABD* 6:17–18; H. J. Katzenstein and Douglas R. Edwards, "Tyre," *ABD* 6:686–692.

Beer-Sheba,[147] the southernmost city of Judah, followed by a return to Jerusalem. The census totals include 800,000 men ready to draw the sword in Israel and 500,000 men ready to draw the sword in Judah. Israel is more powerful than Judah, although Israel is divided into some ten tribes, which suggests disunity.

The third major sub-unit is 2 Samuel 24:10–17, in which David expresses regret at having carried out the census and YHWH gives him the choice of punishment to accept for his act.

Speaking through the prophet Gad (1 Sam 22:5), YHWH gives David three choices to assuage his guilt: a seven-year famine, a three-month period in flight before his enemies, or three days of pestilence. David diplomatically responds that the decision should be left to YHWH, but he specifies that he should not fall into the hands of enemies. YHWH chooses the third option (i.e., to send a three-day pestilence). This choice resembles the plagues of the Exodus narratives, particularly the death of the first-born, insofar as the angel of death (vv. 16, 17), Hebrew, *hammašḥît*, "the destroyer" (cf. Exod 12:23), does the killing. YHWH relents before turning the angel loose against Jerusalem. When David sees the angel at the threshing floor of Araunah, he, too, relents, and exclaims that the people should not suffer, because he alone is guilty.

The fourth sub-unit in 2 Samuel 24:18–24 recounts David's purchase of the threshing floor of Araunah as the place to build an altar. A threshing floor is an ideal site to build an altar or a temple because threshing floors are normally set atop a hill where the wind can help to separate the wheat from the chaff when the grain is crushed on the threshing floor. A threshing floor is a necessary installation for a temple, where grain is brought to present as offerings. Most interpreters agree that the name Araunah is a Hittite or Hurrian name in keeping with his designation as a pre-Israelite Jebusite, although 1 Chronicles 21 names him Ornan to ensure that he has a Semitic name.[148] When David offers to buy the threshing floor, Araunah diplomatically offers to give it to the king, a move designed to win the favor of the monarch and ensure his survival and prosperity. But David insists on paying for the threshing floor himself, reasoning that he cannot present offerings to YHWH if he has not actually

---

[147] Ze'ev Herzog, "Beersheba," *NEAEHL* 1:161–173; Herzog, "Beersheba," *NEAEHL* 5:1594–1598.

[148] McCarter, *2 Samuel*, 512.

purchased the site. Fifty shekels is the amount specified for the annual Temple tax for a man of the age of majority (Lev 27:3).

The fifth and final sub-unit is David's construction of an altar to YHWH on the site of Araunah's threshing floor in 2 Samuel 24:25. This may be the site of the tent that housed the Ark during David's reign (2 Sam 6:17; cf. 2 Sam 7:6) and later, Solomon's Temple.

Author Index

Subject Index

For EU product safety concerns, contact us at Calle de José Abascal, 56–1°,
28003 Madrid, Spain or eugpsr@cambridge.org.

www.ingramcontent.com/pod-product-compliance
Ingram Content Group UK Ltd.
Pitfield, Milton Keynes, MK11 3LW, UK
UKHW020401140625
459647UK00020B/2586